SOCIAL
REGISTER
2019

SOCIALIST REGISTER 2019

A WORLD TURNED UPSIDE DOWN?

Edited by LEO PANITCH and GREG ALBO

THE MERLIN PRESS
MONTHLY REVIEW PRESS
FERNWOOD PUBLISHING

First published in 2018
by The Merlin Press Ltd.
Central Books Building
Freshwater Road
London
RM8 1RX

www.merlinpress.co.uk

© The Merlin Press, 2018

British Library Cataloguing in Publication Data is available from the British
Library

ISSN. 0081-0606

Published in the UK by The Merlin Press
ISBN. 978-0-85036-735-5 Paperback
ISBN. 978-0-85036-736-2 Hardback

Published in the USA by Monthly Review Press
ISBN. 978-1-58367-750-6 Paperback

Published in Canada by Fernwood Publishing
ISBN. 978-1-77363-143-1 Paperback

Printed and bound in the UK on behalf of Stanton Book Services

CONTENTS

CONTRIBUTORS

Aijaz Ahmad is the Chancellor's Professor at the Department of Comparative Literature, University of California, Irvine.

Elmar Altvater was professor of Political Science at the Otto-Suhr-Institut of the Free University of Berlin and editor of the journal, Prokla.

Nicole Aschoff holds a PhD in sociology from the Johns Hopkins University. She is author of *The New Prophets of Capital* and on the editorial boards of the *Socialist Register* and *Jacobin*.

Marco Boffo holds a PhD in economics from SOAS, University of London. He has taught the political economy of development at SOAS and worked as a research fellow at the Leeds University Business School.

Patrick Bond is professor of Political Economy at the Wits School of Governance, University of the Witwatersrand, South Africa.

Alan Cafruny is Henry Platt Bristol Professor of International Affairs at Hamilton College in New York state.

Ben Fine is professor of Economics at SOAS, University of London.

Ana Garcia is professor of International Relations at the Federal Rural University of Rio de Janeiro.

Jayati Ghosh is professor of Economics at the Centre for Economic Studies and Planning, Jawaharlal Nehru University, New Delhi.

Sam Gindin is the former research director of the Canadian Auto Workers Union and an adjunct professor at York University, Toronto.

Adam Hanieh is a senior lecturer in Development Studies at the University of London's School of Oriental and African Studies.

Doug Henwood publishes the *Left Business Observer* newsletter and hosts 'Behind the News' on KPFA radio. His most recent book is *My Turn: Hillary Clinton Targets the Presidency*.

Ray Kiely is professor of Politics at Queen Mary University of London.

Colin Leys is co-chair of the Centre for Health and the Public Interest in the UK, and honorary research professor at Goldsmiths, University of London.

Lin Chun is associate professor in Comparative Politics, London School of Economics.

Birgit Mahnkopf is professor of European Social Policy at the Berlin School of Economics and Law.

Umut Özsu is assistant professor at the Department of Law and Legal Studies, Carleton University, Ottawa.

Leo Panitch is Senior Scholar and Emeritus Professor of Political Science, York University, Toronto.

Alfredo Saad-Filho is a professor in Development Studies at SOAS, University of London.

Sean Kenji Starrs is assistant professor of International Relations at the City University of Hong Kong.

David Whyte is professor of Socio-Legal Studies at the University of Liverpool.

PREFACE

Since the Great Financial Crisis swept across the world in 2008, there have been few certainties regarding the trajectory of global capitalism, let alone the politics taking hold in individual states. A decade on, all that may be said to be clear is that the contradictions of neoliberalism have deepened, especially as these have been intertwined with the class inequalities exposed by the crisis and the ever-growing contradictions of global migration and ecological degradation. And this has opened more and more political space for far right forces challenging not so much neoliberalism itself as conventional liberal democratic norms, as well as key pillars of the global capitalist order which had been built up over past the half century.

There was already considerable disorientation abroad in the face of Brexit's aggravation of the ongoing crisis of the European Union, wherein anti-globalist right-wing political movements and policy advisors openly proclaim their attraction to the authoritarian bravado of Vladimir Putin's 'strong state'. But even this has now given way to palpable confusion regarding what sense to make of this world in a political conjuncture marked by Donald Trump's 'Make America Great Again' presidency of the United States, on the one hand, and, on the other, Xi Jinping's ambitious agenda to consolidate his position as 'core leader' at the top of the Chinese state. Trump's explicit disdain for the modes of leadership the US exhibited in the making of global capitalism since the Second World War – including providing the scaffolding for the institutions underpinning integrated global production and trade, financial flows, development support, international regulatory coordination, and geo-military alliances – is daily on full display. Such is today's topsy-turvy world that it is Xi who has offered himself up as the defender of globalization and world capitalism in the face of Trump's trade protectionism and broader distancing from heretofore US-led global institutions. When it is the tensions with allies that now garner the daily headlines, it is hard to envision the US mobilizing anything like the political capacities and administrative dexterity that enabled it to coordinate a global response to the economic collapse a decade ago – including from China. If there are good reasons to remain cautious about declarations of a new multipolar world order, the growing contradictions at the centre of the inter-state system still suggest that a major redrawing of the map of global capitalism is underway.

A number of intersecting questions beg for deliberate assessment in tracing the changing relationships among states as well as relevant capitalist and progressive forces in this conjuncture. Is an unwinding of globalization in train, or will it continue, but only with an overall shift in the centre of power and accumulation alongside the disintegration of certain regional blocs, and severe limitations on the mobility of labour? What implications might this have for recalibrating state institutions in ways that undermine not only geostrategic cooperation but even coordination between states in containing economic – and in particular financial – crises? To what extent would this involve a confrontation with multinational corporations as well as financial capitalists and, in turn, a further restructuring of state apparatuses? What would be the implications of any and all of this in terms of social as well as environmental reproduction? Have the lingering effects of the first great economic crisis of the 21st century produced a legitimation crisis for the institutions of neoliberalism even while neoliberal practices continue to form state policy? Are we witnessing the emergence of a new form of 'exceptional state' as an authoritarian mutation of liberal democracy, entailing the closure of democratic political space? How far will internal bourgeoisies go in support of a right-wing nationalist break with neoliberal globalization?

Such complex questions cannot be addressed via general abstractions; they need to be located with respect to specific countries and regions, and with particular sensitivity to their class, racial, gender, and environmental dimensions, the main commonality being the continued growth of the hard right in government and out. Over the past decade, the *Socialist Register* has tracked many of the developments that have led to the current political conjuncture. Indeed, in the Preface to the 2011 volume on *The Crisis This Time*, we noted, with equal measure of disgust and frustration, that it was 'the ruling classes, not the labour movements, that have seized the crisis as an opportunity', and that 'the response of capitalist states has been to shore up, however they can, the very model that brought the economy to ruin'. Yet we saw this as no harbinger of political stability, especially insofar as it was bound to reinforce the political trends over recent decades whereby 'it is the Right that has gone from strength to strength'. If that seemed too sombre at the time of Occupy, the importance of acknowledging the depth of the political challenge was reinforced by the 2016 Register on *The Politics of the Right*, which demonstrated how the forces of reaction were on the ascendancy, albeit varying by place and in specific ideological and organizational forms.

This increasingly raises the stark question of whether we should once again be thinking of the options facing the world in terms of 'socialism versus barbarism redux'. What are the strategic implications, including the drawbacks, of posing the issue this way? Does it divert attention from the need to build new popular fronts in the short term against powerful reactionary forces? Or, given the level of disorganization of the working classes, *and* with left political forces as disorganized as they have ever been, is it necessary instead to concentrate on developing longer-term socialist goals and strategic capacities? In a world overturning old certainties, soberly assessing the prospects for a way forward for the left requires setting out new left agendas for confronting the corporate powers of capital, and identifying new hopeful organizational dynamics that could lead to state transformations. In other words, to say that it is the right that now appears to be overturning the world order is by no means to suggest that the promising stirrings on the international left over the last decade have been superseded by events and are now closed. Anything but – as many of the essays in this volume indicate.

Entitling this, our 55th volume, *A World Turned Upside Down?* is in fact a way of posing a challenge to the international left to redouble its efforts. This title of course recalls Christopher Hill's classic 1972 study which sought to find a beacon of light amidst 'the tough world of early capitalism' in the radical ideas that surfaced among the popular classes during the uprisings of the English Revolution of the mid-17th century. Hill himself drew his title from a ballad of the time, '*The World Is Turning Upside Down*', which remained well enough known through the following century and more that it was 'played, appropriately enough, when Cornwallis surrendered to the American revolutionaries at Yorktown 1781'. The original 'broadside ballad' went back to the 1640s when so many 'masterless men' were rendered mobile as never before by the fluctuations of the early capitalist cloth market, spawning the 'nameless radicals who yearned for the upside down world', and causing 'considerable panic in ruling circles'. Groups known as the Diggers, Levellers and Ranters advanced notions sometimes remarkably similar to those heard from the recent Occupy movement protests, asserting there were 'no grounds in Scripture why one man should have £1000 per annum, another not £1'. As Hill's invaluable book tells us, the defeats the 'radicals of the English revolution' suffered in the face of ruling-class reaction and restoration led Gerald Winstanley to conclude his last pamphlet with words all too relevant to the present political conjuncture: 'Truth appears in light, falsehood rules in power; To see these to be is cause of grief each hour.'

Even while preparing this volume dissecting the tough world of late capitalism in our own sinister times, we have been developing plans for forthcoming volumes that will explore emergent socialist ambitions, strategies and organizations, beginning with two which will address not only the dystopian ways we are now living but also visions of how we might alternately live in the 21st century. As is the case with the volume before you now, these have been planned with the very active help of the Register's editorial collective over the past number of years. A few members are leaving the collective amidst the renewal it is undergoing this year, and we thank them here for their various contributions, while welcoming on board eight new members whose contributions we will very much be counting on in the years to come.

Alongside all those who contributed essays to the current volume, we are especially grateful to Alfredo Saad-Filho and Ray Kiely for their great help in conceiving this volume and for making arrangements for the highly successful Register workshop in London in November 2017 where outlines of the essays were first presented. We also wish to underline our thanks for their work on this volume to Steve Maher and Alan Zuege, our two inventive and industrious Assistant Editors, who bring their own intellectual and political insights into conceiving each volume and improving all of the essays in substance as well as style. Our gratitude also extends to Adrian Howe and Tony Zurbrugg of Merlin Press whose steady hands and continued support make possible an annual Register volume with such high production standards. Last but by no means least, we once again acknowledge with great admiration the remarkable skills of Louis Mackay for his brilliant cover design, and thank him for the fascinating note he has prepared on its inspiration by the 17th and 18th century woodcuts of 'The World Turned Upside Down'.

We are very sad that one of the most valued members of our collective for the past two decades, Elmar Altvater, passed away this spring after a long illness. At the same time, we are very proud that his final essay appears in this volume. His passing this year tragically coincides with the deaths of James O'Connor, Joel Kovel, and Julian Tudor Hart, whose involvement with and contributions to the Register at various points we greatly valued. Amidst an array of intellectual and practical accomplishments, their common determination to advance the health of people and of nature in the face of capitalist degradation especially stands out. We can be sure their work will still provide invaluable guidance in the development of an ecological Marxism and the international movement for eco-socialism.

GA
LP
July 2018

TRUMPING THE EMPIRE

LEO PANITCH AND SAM GINDIN

The widespread political expression of hyper-nationalist sentiment against globalization has its roots in one of the most paradoxical aspects of the making of global capitalism. Since this did not bypass states, but rather depended on states facilitating and codifying a globalizing capitalism as well as cooperating in its management internationally, state legitimation still depended on justifying all this as an expression of the 'national interest'. This not only sustained national identity but also provided ground for those expressing nationalist ideology in anti-globalization terms. For a good many states, this now appears to have mutated into a political crisis, with profound implications not only for the most advanced transnational projects like the European Union, but also the traditional mainstream political parties which sponsored neoliberal globalization within each state. This political outcome of the first great capitalist crisis of the twenty-first century was especially heightened, following on the outcome of the Brexit referendum and the electoral successes of hyper-nationalist anti-immigration parties in Europe, with Donald Trump's election to the presidency of the American empire.

The practice of justifying globalization through appeals to the national interest could be clearly seen in the American case not despite but *precisely because of* the central role of its state in the making of global capitalism. Even as many of the empire's cosmopolitan functionaries billed the US as the 'indispensable nation', this coincided with an enduring strain of patriotism which extolled American power while at the same time fuelling resentment against the burdens and responsibilities of superintending global capitalism. This repeatedly emerged as a contradiction inside the state itself, whether as expressed in the form of Congressional hostility to funding international financial institutions or to the Treasury 'raising the debt ceiling' as required to sustain the dollar as the global reserve currency, and even to the Federal Reserve's concealment of lending to foreign banks to contain international financial crises. The roots of this contradiction were always material as well as ideological insofar as neoliberal globalization entailed significant effects in terms of domestic economic restructuring, downward pressure on wages and benefits, and job insecurity – alongside international labour flows and migration.

Trump's 'Make America Great Again' logo echoes Reagan's rhetoric in the wake of the crisis of the 1970s, at a time when there was also much talk of American decline. The package of militarist bravado, tax cuts, and protectionist measures of the early 1980s was accompanied by the ringing of alarm bells about what the rapid economic rise of Japan, aided by special privileges allegedly tolerated for far too long by previous administrations, suggested about American capitalism's loss of competitiveness. Yet this turned out to be the political prolegomena to the much further advances of US-led globalization of capitalism through the final decades of the twentieth century, and well into the twenty-first.

As the continuing reverberations of the financial crisis and great recession of 2008-09 aggravated long-accumulated frustrations with global and regional shifts in manufacturing production, this provided the conditions for Trump's 'Make America Great Again' to have such resonance. What distinguishes the Trump administration is that rather than circumventing particularistic protectionist claims articulated in Congress, it is itself making such claims on behalf of – usually not even at the behest of – certain American industries. Its expressed determination is to claw back concessions previous administrations made in order to draw other countries into the American-led global neoliberal order, and to make others bear the burden of the contradictions which that order has systematically generated. Of course, the greater the effects this has on the behaviour of the American state, both at home and abroad, the more can we expect that this will itself have effects on the balance of social forces in other states. Alongside the material effects, this may take the form of emulation as well as revulsion.

Ironically, in presenting Trumpism as both symptom and expression of American global decline, a wide spectrum of the left ends up almost mirroring Trumpist dogma. Insofar as there is, in fact, a political crisis of global capitalism today it is not because of the US empire's economic decline. It is because the US firmly remains at the centre of world capitalism that the political contradictions of globalization have taken the stark form they have inside the American state. The question that is posed in this context is whether the American state still has the capacity to manage global capitalism. This in turn entails new contradictions for every other capitalist state, and not only because of the pressures to accommodate to US demands, and the internal tensions this generates. It is also because of the implications for all states if the American state cannot play the leading facilitating, superintending, and crisis-containment roles it heretofore has.

No other state in the world could have behaved as the Trump administration did in its first years in office without having had to suffer the wrath of the 'international community'. The exception is embedded in the rule, since the 'international community' is a euphemism for a constellation of institutions and norms centred on the informal American empire. Of course, the world is still far from having been turned upside down. The competitive forces driving capital around the world in search of ever more accumulation are very much still at work, and this certainly includes American capital as much or more than ever. Even while Trump's fulminations often seem to draw on the rhetoric of an earlier age of imperialism, this itself does not alter the fact that the capitalist world today is very different from what it was at the turn of the twentieth century.

To a very significant extent, it was what the American state did in the interim which made this difference: how capitalism actually developed on a world scale depended very much on what (at least certain) states did. But what states do and when – not least in the responsibility they take (or not) for promoting, orchestrating and overseeing capital accumulation – reflects the balance of social forces within their national space, entailing complex relations between societal and state actors. It was a specific concatenation of these forces and relations, emerging out of both the domestic and international contradictions of neoliberal globalization, that seeded the many discontents which the patriotic scoundrels of the new right have fanned. They combined well-worn offers of tax cuts, deregulations, social programme defunding, and union busting with hyper-nationalist anti-globalization rhetoric. What brought a scoundrel like Trump to the White House was the crosscutting nature of these messages amidst the strong currents of socio-economic turmoil and class resentments going every which way. Nativism, sexism, homophobia, racism, and xenophobia were interwoven with the celebration of private property and wealth in such a way as to paint the Make American Great Again logo in its own many bold colours.

In this way, the American empire's role in the making of global capitalism has come to be challenged from within rather than, as had been so widely expected, from without. As we argued in *The Making of Global Capitalism*, 'the significance of the fact that the political fault-lines of global capitalism run within states rather than between them is … replete with implications for the American empire's capacity to sustain global capitalism in the 21st century'.[1] We will attempt here to trace out these implications as they have unfolded since the crisis of 2008, up to and including the Trump administration's first years in office.

THE FIRST CRISIS OF THE TWENTY-FIRST CENTURY

It was not only the depth of the crisis that erupted in the US in 2008 but also how it reverberated around the globe along a protracted path to recovery which justified its characterization as the fourth great global crisis of capitalism. The first such crisis during the last quarter of the nineteenth century had in large part coincided with capitalism's vast global expansion but also seeded the inter-imperial rivalries that ended in the First World War. The second, beginning with the US financial collapse in 1929 and running through the Great Depression of the 1930s, once and for all wrote finis to the international gold standard amidst high tariffs and extensive capital controls. By contrast, even as the third great crisis, effectively running from 1968 until 1982, severely disturbed the Bretton Woods institutional framework established under the aegis of the United States after the Second World War, it did not interrupt the US-led making of global capitalism but rather led to it being extended much further.

As the financial crisis triggered in US mortgage securities led to the overall economic collapse of 2008-09, a Democratic president came to office committed to the American state maintaining an active role in sustaining globalization as it strove to contain the crisis. The Obama administration was immediately involved not only in bailing out the Wall Street banks, but in doing so with an eye to preventing the collapse of banks abroad; not only in undertaking the largest fiscal stimulus in US peacetime history, but in coordinating the timing of it with the other G20 states; not only in massively ramping up global monetary expansion as fiscal austerity quickly followed in many states, but also in steadfastly reinforcing the Bush administration's success in late 2008 in securing the continuing commitment of those states to free trade and untrammelled capital movements.

This proved very important given that the return to global economic growth after 2010 was extremely moderate, and marked by great unevenness within the major regional zones as well as between them. The onset by then of the euro crisis soon brought with it severe austerity and depression-like conditions in southern Europe, and this was followed by the collapse of commodity prices in 2014 which so badly shook the developing world. Whereas from 2004 to 2007 world growth had increased by an annual average of just over 5 per cent, average annual growth from 2010 to 2013 did not even reach 4 per cent, with a good many countries still in recession. It was only by 2017 that there was a return to anything resembling synchronized global economic growth.

Certain characteristics of the aftermath of the crisis in the US have been striking. The remarkable disparity between the rapid return to historically high profits and the muted expansion of investment, although by no means confined to the US alone, is especially notable. Directly related to this, the long period of uninterrupted economic expansion since 2010 − so far the second longest such period in US history − was marked by its relatively low rate of growth. And while the unemployment rate trended steadily downwards, from 10 per cent at the peak of the crash to under 4 per cent at mid-2018, wage growth remained stuck at extremely low levels.[2] Both the revival of the housing market and the overall level of consumption were again sustained by credit expansion, involving a return to massive personal indebtedness.

Longer term structural developments − rooted in the defeat of labour, the growing importance of financial capital and moves by corporations to correct imbalances in their finances − seemed to be at play here. The much-noted disparity between corporate profits and investments after the crisis was in fact not all that new. By the turn of the millennium, the financial gap between capital spending and internal funds for global corporations, which had averaged 1.2 per cent of GDP over the two previous decades (reflecting their traditional role as borrowers), had already disappeared, not least due to their lower wage costs at a global level. These corporations themselves became savers, to the extent of averaging 1.7 per cent of GDP from 2001 to 2004.[3] While moderate investment continued, this came nowhere near matching their very high profits, and a 'corporate saving glut' emerged which far surpassed the saving glut due to state financial rebalancing after the Asian 1997-8 financial crisis which Ben Bernanke had emphasized.[4]

The impact of household finances, especially in the US, also factors into the longer-term structural developments behind high profits and low investment. The maintenance of household consumption through increased indebtedness and an inflated housing market that was the product of the stagnation of wages since the crisis of the 1970s[5] famously proved to be a major cause of the 2008 crisis. After it, working-class households confronting unemployment and lower wages, let alone the loss of their own homes, attempted to restore their savings by restraining their consumer spending. This reinforced the savings glut after the crisis ended in 2010, as corporations refrained from raising investment to higher levels in spite of the return to high profits and the cheap credit readily available to them.

Given the persistence of muted investment in the private sector, growth depended on the state picking up the slack. Obama's massive 2009-10 fiscal stimulus, coordinated with other states, played a crucial role in preventing another Great Depression. But this had to be sustained to restore rates of growth to the levels of the 1990s. The reluctance to act more decisively in this regard was driven by the ballooning size of the deficit and a context in which restoring the confidence of financial institutions was of primary concern. As a result of the tax impact of the crisis, alongside the costs of bailing out the banks as well as the economic stimulus, the fiscal deficit reached 10 per cent of GDP by 2010. This far surpassed any other deficit since the Second World War (even during the 1930s fiscal deficits never reached much higher than 5 per cent).[6] The majority secured in Congress by the Republicans in 2010 sealed the return to the fiscal orthodoxy of austerity. This weakened the Obama administration's credibility when it came to urging, as it did, that Germany should not apply even more draconian austerity on Europe in the context of the euro crisis that erupted in 2010 just as the US was slowly pulling out of the Great Recession triggered by the 2008 financial crisis.

The effect of the tepid recovery on manufacturing jobs was that whereas 2.5 million had been lost from 2008 to 2010, only 1 million such jobs were regained from 2011 to 2016, leaving the US economy with 1.5 million fewer manufacturing jobs than just before the crisis. But even preceding the crisis 3 million manufacturing jobs had been lost from 2001 to 2007. Indeed, since the end of the previous crisis in 1982, although the real output of manufacturing grew, corporations systematically reduced the size of the manufacturing workforce. The introduction of new technology and the reorganization of work were as important factors in this as corporations relocating or expanding their international supply chains. This especially accelerated with China's rapid integration into global capitalism after its admission to the WTO in 2001. The loss of manufacturing jobs, which redounded to Obama's electoral benefit in 2008, would carry even greater weight in bringing Trump to the presidency.

The restructuring that came in the wake of the 1970s crisis had included the shift of manufacturing jobs to rural areas in the Midwest, which by the 1990s raised their economic prospects. However, many of these plants closed both before and after the 2008 crisis, leaving these communities in a state of permanent recession. Right in the midst of the 2016 election campaign, plant closures in counties which traditionally voted for the Democratic Party proved a key factor in enlisting them behind Trump's Make America Great Again logo.[7] Indeed, he could make much of the fact that, despite Obama's bailout of GM and Chrysler, the increased share of the North American industry locating in Mexico – in train since the mid-1990s under NAFTA – had by 2016 yielded a $70bn US trade deficit in the auto sector, which more than accounted for the entire $65bn deficit with Mexico. Speaking in terms of the economic 'carnage' evidenced by 'rusted out factories scattered like tombstones across the landscape of our nation',[8] Trump expressed a popular anxiety about American decline based on frustrations with the false promises of free trade for American workers. Even such an active player in the American-led making of global capitalism as the McKinsey consultancy could now be found acknowledging that 'the post-Cold War narrative of progress fuelled by competitive markets, globalization, and innovation has lost some luster ... These contradictions are showing up in politics'.[9]

Figure 1. US Manufacturing Employment and Real Output, 1979-2017

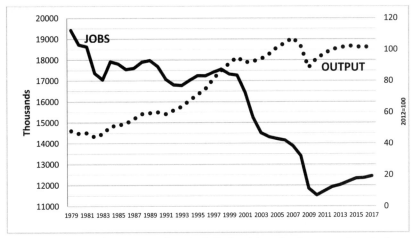

Source: 'All employees, manufacturing'; 'Industrial production, manufacturing',
Federal Reserve Economic Data (FRED).

NEITHER DEGLOBALIZATION NOR DECLINE

Far from peaking with the crisis, the continuing processes and pressures of capitalist globalization were expressed in intensified competition among global corporations. Moreover, one of the foremost intents of the American approach to the crisis was preserving the internationalization of capital, and it also succeeded in this. Widespread predictions that the crisis would result in 'deglobalization', or at least 'peak globalization', proved quite wrong. As the table below shows, by 2016 international trade had increased very significantly beyond the level it had reached before the crisis began. The total employment abroad of multinational corporations actually increased by two thirds, from under 50 million before the crisis to over 82 million in 2016. The global stock of foreign direct investment (FDI) also increased substantially over this ten-year period.[10] And although there was a decline in FDI in 2017, this was offset by an explosion of cross-border takeovers and mergers in early 2018. The 2018 UNCTAD report notes that 'sales of foreign affiliates are growing at twice the rate of assets and employees, in a continuation of the asset-light international production trend'.[11]

Notably, despite the rise in hyper-nationalist sentiments, there was no letup in the competition among states to attract foreign investments via material incentives and accommodating legal changes. Indeed, 58 states adopted 84 policy measures which 'promoted or facilitated' foreign investment in 2016, the highest number since 2006. And, as UNCTAD's most recent report notes, 'new national investment policy measures continue to be geared mostly towards investment liberalization and promotion' – so much so that, in 2017 alone, no less than 65 countries adopted 93 such measures, with those facilitating liberalization accounting for over 80 per cent of investment policy changes.[12]

Chart 1. Global Economic Trends, 2006-2016

	2006	2016	CHANGE
TRADE, MERCHANDISE	$2.9 trillion	$4.8 trillion	66%
TRADE, COMMERCIAL SERVICES	$8 trillion	$11 trillion	38%
FDI, INWARD STOCK (% OF GDP)	27.1%	35%	
EMPLOYMENT, FOREIGN AFFILIATES	49.5 million (avg. 2005–07)	82.1 million	66%

Sources: see note 10

Nor, by any objective measure, can the dominance of US corporations in global capitalism be said to have waned, despite all the predictions of 'decoupling' as soon as the crisis began. If the crisis decade confirmed the continuing weakness of American labour, it also confirmed the relative strength of American capital, both at home and abroad. For US capitalists, this was emphatically *not* a profitability crisis, as the following graphs show. Even for non-financial corporations, the 2008 economic collapse was preceded by high pre-tax profits measured by the rate of return on capital invested. By 2012 corporate profits had already returned to their prerecession highs by this measure, near or above their previous highs over the three decades before the crisis, while after-tax profits actually reached the highest level in half a century by 2013-14, and were sustained at that level even before Trump's massive corporate tax cuts. As a share of GDP, moreover, both pre- and after-tax corporate profits have also increased since 2010 to their highest since the mid-1960s.

Corporate Profits, Rate of Return, 1960–2016

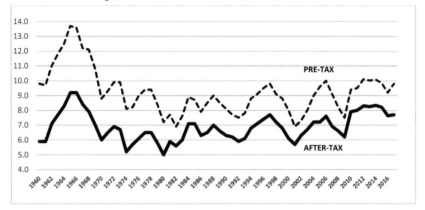

Corporate Profits, Share of GDP, 1960–2016

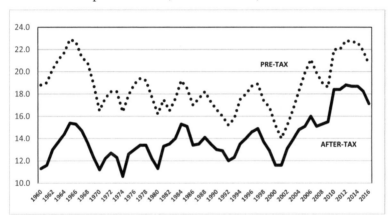

Source: Sarah Osborne and Bonnie A. Retus, 'Returns for domestic nonfinancial business, 2017', Bureau of Economic Analysis, December 2017.

To be sure, this sustained period of high profits has not been matched by parallel increases in the rate of investment, while both labour and capital productivity growth have remained historically low. But this is not unique to the US. As the IMF has emphasized, 'The drop in total factor productivity growth following the global financial crisis has been widespread and persistent across advanced, emerging, and low-income countries'.[13] Not surprisingly, US stock market valuations – encouraged by persistently low interest rates as well the high profits – have exploded to record levels. It is by virtue of these kinds of measures that Citi Bank could exult in 2018 that:

... if anyone had predicted that synchronous worldwide growth would be accelerating in the ninth year of a global recovery after the second worst economic downturn of the past 100 years, we would have been impressed. Had they further predicted that this acceleration would occur after the UK voted to leave the European Union and after the US elected a volatile, inexperienced real estate billionaire as its president, we might have thought them daft. And yet here we are.[14]

Of course, by a different set of measures, it is clear to see what has so tarnished the American Dream:

> The first signs of decline are physical. Citizens don't grow as tall. They don't live as long. They start killing each other in large numbers. Sounds like the post-mortem for a society that disappeared long ago … This time, however, the diagnosis is being provided in real time. And the society in decline is the most powerful country in the world. According to the most recent global health surveys, the United States is witnessing a decline in life expectancy for the first time in nearly a quarter century. America is also the first high-income country to see its adults, on average, no longer growing taller. U.S. decline has been ongoing for some time … with particularly mediocre scores in environmental quality, nutrition and basic medical care, and access to basic knowledge … After what Donald Trump does to the United States, Americans won't be able to stand tall and proud. That's because we'll either be short, sick, or dead.[15]

If this speaks to a palpable sense of domestic social decay in the United States, it does not itself gainsay, as the author makes clear, the US remaining 'the most powerful country in the world'. Whether it will remain so may turn less on what Trump adds to Americans' miseries at home than on what effect Trumpism will have on the centrality of the United States in global capitalism. In this sense, the discourse whereby US decline, whether worried or welcomed, is all but taken for granted usually turns out to be misleading and even self-contradictory – as in a recent *New York Times* feature essay on 'Adapting to American Decline' which ended with: 'The United States is the most important country in the world and will remain so for many years.'[16]

Indeed, the centrality of the US economy to global capitalism continues to be evidenced by its remaining by far the largest destination for both the world's exports and investment. The US imports one-third more goods and services than does China, which ranks second on this score, and twice as much as Germany, which ranks third. It is also the recipient of the most foreign direct investment by a significant margin (an average inflow of

$400 billion annually from 2015-17, three times that of China, which ranks second). American corporations account for more investment abroad (an annual average of $300 billion from 2015-17) than those of the next two countries, China and Japan, taken together.[17] While national trade data tend to confirm why Trump's strident complaints resonate with the sense that many workers have of US decline, once the sales of the subsidiaries of all multinational corporations are taken into account, this measure of 'aggregate trade balance' shows a strong US surplus with the rest of the world and even a small surplus with China.[18] Insofar as both trade data and the foreign investments of US MNCs reflect a global shift in the location of production in certain manufacturing sectors, what is especially significant is the dominance of US corporations in the most dynamic and influential high tech sectors, spanning computers, telecommunications, aerospace, pharmaceuticals, and health sciences as well as key business services such as accounting, advertising, consultancy, engineering, and computer programming, as well as legal and finance services.[19]

The role of the US dollar, far from being challenged, has been further consolidated as the world currency, thereby sustaining the US economy's unique access to global savings. As documented in the BIS triennial report, the dollar 'has remained the dominant vehicle currency, being on one side of 88 per cent of all trades'; the shares accounted for by the euro and yen actually fell; and even with the renminbi's increasing share it only accounted for 4 per cent of total trades.[20] Moreover, the dollar's overwhelming position as the global reserve currency has been reinforced. Already by far the largest in the world, the Treasury market further expanded significantly in recent years, to $14 trillion in total securities outstanding in 2017, trading at over $500 billion per day. China is now the number one purchaser of US Treasury securities; it actually increased its holdings over the year ending March 2018 by almost 10 per cent.[21] The dollar's continued role as the pivotal anchor of world money and foreign exchange reserves thereby sustains the centrality of the US in global capitalism.

THE POLITICAL CRISIS OF EMPIRE

Just as synchronized global growth seemed to finally mark the end to the first great economic crisis of the twenty-first century, the election of Donald Trump heralded a political crisis for global capitalism. As the events of 2018 already demonstrate, this political crisis will severely test the capacities of its governing structures, not least those rooted in the American state itself, even while it remains utterly clear that no other state is capable of taking over its leading role. While G7 meetings do not themselves constitute the key decision-making forums of global capitalism, the current chaos surrounding their future efficacy can't be written off as a marginal episode. In a lead article written just before a piqued Trump tweeted his infamous reversal of the June 2018 Quebec G7 communique he had just signed, *The Economist* tried to capture the difference between the current US administration and earlier ones. The article, 'Present at the Destruction', was a pointed reference to Dean Acheson's *Present at the Creation,* in which Acheson describes his years in the State Department during the crucial wartime and early post-war years when the foundations for the American informal empire and its role in the making of a global capitalism were effectively laid.[22] Without explicitly mentioning Acheson, *The Economist* thus sharply posed the question of whether that role was being abandoned. Refusing to make definitive assertions about this uncharted territory, it conceded, on the one hand, that Trumps' bullheadedness might even deliver short term results that effectively furthered American interests; on the other, it asked whether his capricious behaviour couldn't help but have negative long-term consequences for the global order.

Was Trump really 'trumping' the American empire? There have always been loud voices in the US against carrying the burdens of its informal empire, often taking the form of protectionism as a recurring feature of the political landscape. This already was the case in the 1940s when the Treasury undertook its massive popular mobilization campaign to secure Congressional approval for the Bretton Woods Agreement, and when the State Department did the same for the Marshall Plan. Even after the informal empire was already well-established, successive Republican administrations would echo the infamous remark – 'It's our dollar but your problem' – of Nixon's Treasury Secretary, John Connally, at a meeting of European finance ministers shortly after the unilateral suspension of the dollar's link to gold and the imposition of import surcharges. It is now often forgotten (although Trump used this in his own election campaign) that it was Ronald Reagan, long regarded as an ideological champion of free trade, who vowed as President to 'not stand by and watch American businesses fail because of unfair trading practices abroad ... and watch American workers lose their jobs because other nations do not play by the rules'. According to his own Treasury Secretary James Baker, Reagan 'granted more import relief to U.S. industry than any of his predecessors in more than half a century'.[23]

Belying both Connally's and Baker's remarks was the increasing attention the American state in fact gave to international economic coordination around free trade under the revamped dollar standard through the 1970s and 1980s. In particular, the creation of the G7 by the mid-1970s involved building up the infrastructures to facilitate closer ties between the US Treasury officials and their counterparts. With the annual meetings of finance ministers on the one hand, and heads of state on the other, the G7 became the leading venue for the promotion of shared beliefs and the endorsement of greater economic integration among the leading capitalist states. This smoothed the way for the new US dollar standard to be overseen through the ever closer ties between the US Federal Reserve and other central banks at the same time as the G7 became a key locus for free trade 'discourse construction'.[24]

This crucially involved coordinating with other states the adoption of legal frameworks for market-making and guaranteeing property rights to sustain the international mobility of capital and integrated production and trade, as well as disciplining states in their application of these 'rules of law'. This was facilitated by the 1974 Trade Act's expediting appeals for 'adjustment assistance' for workers and firms affected by increased imports, which was designed to show 'the willingness of the American government to take on itself the cost of trade liberalization rather than imposing it on others'. It was of course also designed to render 'the political influence of protectionists less determinant of the final outcome ... [as to] whether a specific industry was eligible for protection'.[25] Alongside the creation of the Office of the US Trade Representative, this facilitated the American successes over the following decades in the negotiations of bilateral as well as multilateral free trade agreements. In the end, the Reagan administration's protectionist measures, selective and temporary as they proved to be, served as crucial levers to further open markets at home and abroad, and to facilitate the flow of capital into as well as out of the US.

This laid the basis not only for the ever more integrated networked production with Canada and Mexico under NAFTA, but for its extension and deepening around the world under the WTO framework established in 1996. This was extended to China after 2001, and further supplemented by more and more bilateral trade treaties. This came to structure the path of capitalist globalization right up to the Trump administration. Far from being a smooth ride, however, it was always a tension-filled and bumpy one, not only because veiled and unveiled protectionist threats persisted under the 'rules-based order', but also because of the disruptive effects of dozens of financial crises even before the great one in 2008. The containment of these crises increasingly preoccupied the US Treasury, and in the wake of the Asian financial crisis motivated it to establish the infrastructure for the new G20 of finance ministers. When the next Republican administration came to office voicing complaints about the burdens of empire, John O'Neill, George W. Bush's first Treasury Secretary, derided his Democratic predecessors for acting as 'chief of the fire department'. Yet what was significant was how far the Treasury under the Bush administration went to keep the infrastructure of global economic coordination going. By the fall of 2008, this was extended to bringing the G20 heads of state together for their first summit.

Trying to stave off the potentially devastating effects the crisis now threatened to have for all those countries that had become so integrated into global capitalism, the 'Commitment to an Open Global Economy' in the final communiqué from the G20's November 2008 Summit in Washington, D.C. was especially significant: 'We underscore the critical importance of rejecting protectionism and not turning inward ... we will refrain from raising new barriers to investment or to trade in goods and services.'[26] Together with the success of the internationally coordinated fiscal stimulus announced at the second G20 Summit in London in April 2009 in preventing a replay of the Great Depression, this allowed the G20 leaders to declare at their subsequent Summit in Toronto in June 2010: 'While the global economic crisis led to the sharpest decline of trade in more than seventy years, G20 countries chose to keep markets open to the opportunities that trade and investment offer. It was the right choice.'[27]

The seismic shock that the Trump administration has delivered to the global capitalist order must be measured against the backdrop of the meticulous construction of that order by previous US administrations in ways that, while certainly imperious, nevertheless strove to be consensual. The shock was captured at the G7 Summit in Quebec in June 2018 by the photo of Trump sitting smirking with his arms folded as Angela Merkel stood beseeching him surrounded by other grim-faced leaders and officials. One of those officials reported to the *Toronto Star* that the German chancellor told Trump 'it was unacceptable that after two generations of alliance where they had worked to integrate their economies Trump would sandbag his G7 allies with steel and aluminum tariffs "without talking to anybody"'.[28] Merkel's wounded reference at this meeting on Canadian soil to 'two generations of economic integration' brought to mind that by the late 1960s and early 1970s this process was already being labelled as 'Canadianization' by keen European observers. Notably, Trump withdrew his approval from the joint communiqué amidst a barrage of hostile tweets against Justin Trudeau for having had the temerity to say at the closing press conference that, while Canada would go very far in trade negotiations, it resented being 'pushed around'.

But this denouement, after all the haggling by American officials over language expressing the G7's traditional commitment to 'the rules-based global system', had already been signalled over the previous year within the infrastructures of the G7 and the G20 which the US Treasury had so painstakingly built up over so many decades through its preparatory work in pre-drafting consensual communiqués before these meetings. The tone was set when Trump's newly appointed Treasury Secretary, Steve Mnuchin, baldly refused to sign on to a communiqué endorsing 'free trade' at the G20 finance ministers meeting in Germany in March 2017. A year later, following the US announcement of solar panel and washing machine tariffs in January 2018, Mnuchin told the G20 finance minister's meeting in Argentina that 'the expectation [that] America totally subordinates its national interests in order for the free trade system to work, is just one we don't accept'.[29] This presaged Trump's imminent announcement of steel and aluminum tariffs, leading to an acrimonious G7 finance ministers meeting a week before the Quebec Summit, where the other ministers undertook an unprecedented rebuke to the US Treasury Secretary, demanding that he should 'communicate their unanimous concern and disappointment … [that] collaboration and cooperation has been put at risk by American trade actions'.[30]

IMPERIAL STATE CAPACITIES

Whereas earlier administrations had found themselves acting defensively to contain recurring protectionist demands from Congress, Trump has not only led the attack on free trade but at the same time overseen the erosion of institutional capacities essential to managing the global capitalist economy. To some extent, the persistent inability of the Treasury under the Obama administration to influence German policy during the euro crisis already spoke to diminishing imperial capacities, as did its clumsy failure to prevent other states from joining the Chinese-led initiative for the Asian Infrastructure Investment Bank. But this now looks like small change compared to the Trump administration's deliberate undermining of institutional capacities through underfunding, unfilled senior positions, appointments of people hostile to regulation, as well as general understaffing and cuts to training.[31] That Trump so quickly and so contemptuously slashed the budget of the Department of State, so fundamental as it has been to the past leadership role of the US, is certainly telling. As for the Treasury, not only was staffing cut at the Office of the Comptroller of the Currency (responsible for national bank supervision), what may be more important is that funding of the interagency bodies established after the 2008 crisis to oversee financial stability programmes has been 'quietly choked off'. Thus, the staff of the Financial Stability Oversight Council, housed in the Treasury, was cut by 50 per cent, and the staff at the Office of Financial Research, responsible for 'high-quality financial data, standards, and analysis' was cut by 38 per cent.[32]

As this suggests, just as the recent G7 and G20 meetings indicate a diminution of the Treasury's purpose and capacities in terms of international state coordination, so has this been the case in terms of the role the Treasury plays in coordinating the multitude of domestic state agencies engaged in financial codification and regulation. This raises serious questions about the Treasury's crucial role as 'firefighter-in-chief', if not in terms of preventing crises, then at least in containing them both domestically and internationally. Indeed, the Treasury itself led the deregulatory thrust of the Trump administration, including the 2018 Congressional amendments (with support from many Democrats as well as Republicans) which rolled back the 2010 Dodd-Frank banking regulations. As early as June 2017, a series of Treasury reports issued under Mnuchin's name had already targeted 'improperly tailored capital, liquidity and leverage requirements as well as the tremendous increase in activities-based regulation ... [which] have undermined the ability of banks to deliver attractively priced credit in sufficient quantity to meet the needs of the economy'.[33]

This of course has much to do with explaining 'Why Corporate America Loves Donald Trump', as *The Economist* put it: 'Bosses reckon that the value of tax cuts, deregulation and potential trade concessions from China outweighs the hazy costs of weaker institutions and trade wars.'[34] But as Trump raised the ante on tariffs through the spring of 2018, opposition to this was increasingly sounded by the National Association of Manufacturers and even by the US Chamber of Commerce – traditionally the least supportive of free trade and globalization among the major capitalist class associations – and this was accompanied by their dissent to Trump's upping the hyper-nationalist ante on the immigration front by separating children from parents seeking asylum at border crossings. This is not to say that the capitalist class is unified on this front. Nor should it be imagined that, even if it were, it could necessarily control what Trump does. The very nature of Trumpism, with its claims to represent the interests of the great unwashed, leaves American capitalists holding their breath as much as it does states from China to Canada.

The complex process whereby for well over three decades the Office of the US Trade Representative – through its more than 30 advisory committees bringing together over 700 business officials from every industrial and agricultural sector – worked at translating firm-specific interests into 'coherent trade policy positions' appears a thing of the past under the Trump administration.[35] This leaves even many of the most important US corporations exposed by the suddenness and jerkiness of the Trump administration's trade manoeuvres. This was highlighted by Harley Davidson's own sudden announcement that it would have to increase production abroad to avoid European counter-tariffs, and the wrath it incurred from Trump in threatening the maker of the iconic American motorcycle: 'The Aura will be gone', he tweeted, 'and they will be taxed like never before.'[36]

At the same time, however, the Trump administration is itself increasingly exposed to the very cut-throat business behaviour so trumpeted by almost all its principal actors. The trade-hawk Commerce Secretary, Wilbur Ross – who made his money and fame as an asset-stripping takeover artist in the auto and steel sectors at the height of the restructuring of US manufacturing – had the unmitigated gall to blame speculators for 'profiteering' as steel prices began to rise in the wake of the introduction of tariffs in June 2018. 'What has been happening is a very unsatisfactory thing', Ross said, pointing to 'intermediaries' stockpiling steel and withholding it from the market. 'It is clearly a result of anti-social behaviour in the industry.'[37]

It is notable in this respect that in mid-June 2018, just as Trump's noisy trade offensive was finally registering on the world's stock markets (and especially on the market valuations of US corporations like Boeing and Caterpillar whose production lines are so dependent on steel and aluminum inputs), the new Chair of the Federal Reserve, Jerome Powell, told a meeting of European Central Bankers, 'for the first time we are hearing about decisions to postpone investment, postpone hiring, postpone making decisions. That is a new thing.'[38] That this important reminder of the structural constraints on Trump's protectionist trajectory should have come from the Federal Reserve is significant. Powell's appointment by Trump to take over from Janet Yellen as chair of the Fed at the beginning of 2018 represented much greater continuity than had Mnuchin's appointment at the Treasury. Both before his appointment and since, Powell was careful to 'dispel notions' that he would take a more 'hawkish approach' than had Yellen in relation to post-crisis monetary policy in terms of only cautiously and slowly raising interest rates and unwinding quantitative easing. [39]

As an experienced Fed insider, Powell could draw on a long learning curve with regard to habitual anti-social behaviour on Wall Street. Speaking shortly before his nomination as Fed chair to the heads of the private financial firms engaged in marketing Treasury securities bonds, who were meeting as members of the Treasury Markets Practices Group (TMPG) at the Federal Reserve Bank of New York, he told them:

I first encountered Treasury markets in a serious way 25 years ago, when I served as Under Secretary of the Treasury for Finance under President George H. W. Bush. These markets made national headlines when we learned that a Salomon Brothers' trader had repeatedly circumvented Treasury auction rules to corner the market for the on-the-run two-year Treasury. As it became clear that Salomon's senior management had known about the issue for several months without alerting regulators, the scandal threatened to bring down one of the largest financial firms of that time. Over one memorable August weekend, we first prohibited the firm from dealing in government securities on behalf of customers, and then reduced that sanction as top Salomon management left the firm and Warren Buffett, then a large Salomon shareholder, agreed to assume the chairmanship of the board of directors. This event takes up a chapter in Buffett's biography ... I reread that chapter every couple of years. It still gives me nightmares.[40]

For Powell this was 'a good illustration of why we need the TMPG' and why 'after the dust settled, we had to grapple with the wider implications of the scandal for the market itself and particularly the role of regulatory oversight'. The TPMG was then created under the auspices of the Federal Reserve Bank of New York, as a way to both reproduce the central role of private capitalist actors in the financial sector and to aid in the state's central role in the management of it. As to why the central bank has had to engage in organizing the capitalist class to the end of containing the effects of shyster practices on top of the volatility endemic to capitalist finance, Powell explained, in words echoing every Fed Chair:

Outside this room, you are competitors, and that vigorous competition serves your firms, your customers, and ultimately the U.S. taxpayer. But when members of the TMPG attend meetings, they bring their long experience and deep expertise to bear to safeguard the functioning and overall health of these markets. As I have heard a number of people say, TMPG members check their partisan interests at the door. The TMPG is the place where market participants recognize and address their responsibilities to each other.

Perhaps the greatest irony of central bank independence, explicitly designed by states and capital working together to protect the making of global capitalism from the progressive tendencies of democratic pressures on elected governments, is that it may yet come to be seen as saving global capitalism from the chaos of the Trump presidency. The greatest test of this will be the Fed's behaviour in face of the gathering financial storms abroad, from Argentina to Italy to Turkey to Indonesia, and their likely contagion effects. The impact which a rising American dollar and even marginally higher interest rates inevitably have on international debt payments is already showing up here. This will be further compounded by the Fed's tapering of its balance sheet as part of ending quantitative easing as well as the draining of dollars from global markets as the Trump tax cuts increase US government debt issuance and encourage American corporations to repatriate their profits.

The marked differences in institutional purposes and competencies, even under the Trump regime, should serve as a reminder that it is always a mistake to analyze the state as monolithic rather than carefully delimiting and examining its component institutions. The widespread expectations, and even explicit demands, that the Federal Reserve must act as the world central bank are indicative of how sensitive global capitalism remains to what the key institutions of the informal American empire will be inclined to do – and will have the capacity to do – amidst the disruptions emanating from the Trump White House.[41]

CONCLUSION

Trumpism is palpably tarnishing the informal US empire's ideological hegemony amidst the political crisis that hyper-nationalism has brought to global capitalism. Of course, it is possible to imagine that by the start of the next decade, this will all appear as a bad American nightmare and that hegemony will be restored under a new Democratic president. This, at least initially, appeared to be the case with Obama in the wake of the utter mess left by the Bush administration's foreign policies and military invasions. But just as the Obama administration's own severe limitations in coping with this mess proved, so should we expect that the accumulated frustrations and persistent contradictions associated with capitalist globalization which produced Trump will not go away. Nor, given the ever-greater challenges that managing the global capitalist order will certainly entail, will it be easy to restore the informal empire's ideological hegemony.

Despite the ambitions of the proselytizers of American-led globalization, it could hardly ever have been seriously expected that the rest of the world could be integrated within the informal American empire along the lines of Germany or Japan, let alone Canada. The enormous challenges entailed in integrating Russia and China within the US informal empire relate to many factors, including of course their critical designation as the leading adversaries in US military strategy. Lying behind this is that the US did not play the kind of internal role in the reconstitution of those states as it did with Germany and Japan after 1945, with all the implications that has had in terms of sustaining Russia and China's traditional world power self-images, even as these have been reconstituted as capitalist states integrated in many ways with global capitalism.

That said, the all too common misinterpretation of the world today in terms of China (let alone Russia) as an alternative hegemon challenging the United States, effectively mimicking the old theory of inter-imperial rivalry at the beginning of the twentieth century, ignores what the making of global capitalism has entailed by way of interpenetrations in production and finance with profound structural effects. Indeed, the very centrality of the US in the global economy may mean that Trump has more room than is usually recognized in terms of shifting the economic burdens of empire by opening up some markets abroad and closing others at home, not least through even more state protections of American capitalists' property rights abroad. Notably, Xi Jinping told a gathering in China of executives of multinational corporations at the height of Trump's June 2018 trade offensive:

The great door of China's opening will not close, it will only get bigger and more open ... China will continue to greatly ease market access, create a more attractive investment environment, strengthen the protection of intellectual property rights, voluntarily expand imports, and create a more relaxed and orderly environment for domestic and foreign entrepreneurs to invest in and start businesses.[42]

This remarkably direct appeal to foreign corporations in the midst of the Trump administration's aggressive economic measures spoke to the confident new status of China in the world. But Xi did so while conceding to long-standing demands from US governments, before and since they acceded to China's admission to the WTO.[43] Yet for the Chinese state to play the role in the twenty-first century that Xi outlines would necessitate it developing much greater institutional capacities and taking on responsibilities that would go far beyond its role in the G20 after the crisis of 2008-9 in the management of global capitalism.

Even apart from China, the continuing unevenness that has inevitably accompanied the rapid export-oriented industrial, agricultural, and financial integration of the former 'third world' countries in capitalist globalization does not gainsay the deep structural significance of the extensive *and* intensive capitalist development that has taken place generally in those countries. Those who seek to refurbish the mid-twentieth century reformulation of the theory of imperialism in terms of the postcolonial reproduction of underdevelopment through unequal exchange fail to register sufficiently the significance of this.[44] In many cases, the lack of internal coherence among social, economic, and state structures – reflecting the contradictions which combined and uneven integration in the making of global capitalism entail amidst export-oriented production and multinational corporate penetration – has further complicated the problems involved in coordinating and superintending global capitalism. This is not least because political crises in these states can also foster nationalist forces. As Gerard Greenfield so presciently observed in his 2005 *Socialist Register* essay on South East Asia, 'certain kinds of anti-globalization nationalism' were already very much on the scene, usually taking the form of political alliances with local bourgeoisies. Yet as sections of domestic capitalists are 'themselves able to internationalize … [they] emulate the logic of global capital', including by expecting 'the US imperial state to pursue its role in managing global capitalism'.[45]

Whether Trump's bullying of other states leads to a series of trade wars, or even whether he succeeds in getting them to accede to his demands, the hyper-nationalism to which neoliberal globalization has led inside the US itself has had the effect of producing a government which is openly disdainful of the American empire's role in managing global capitalism. This appears to be undermining the capacity of at least some of its state institutions to play that role, and makes it very murky what those institutions will now take 'the logic of global capitalism' to be. Insofar as it is not supported by the American empire, this itself considerably disturbs the notion that such a logic must necessarily play itself out across the world.

Those pundits and practitioners of globalization who saw it as inevitable and unstoppable – an economic and technologically driven process without an author – are suddenly forced to come face-to-face with their illusions, or at least their evasions. Since the middle of the twentieth century, the American informal empire has been the primary author of capitalist globalization. This entailed the internationalization of the American state, in the sense of taking responsibility for the extension and reproduction of global capitalism even while it of course remained the state of a very distinct social formation. It is hardly surprising that when that responsibility is explicitly shirked by an American government, the capitalist world should be thrown into confusion. In the end, it may not be at all unlikely that, given the centrality of the US in the global economy, Trump the protectionist will have furthered capitalist globalization, alongside having set a new pace for corporate tax cuts and deregulation at home for other states to emulate abroad. The grave danger is that in thereby exacerbating further the inequalities, insecurities, and resentments which already have provided so much ground for hyper-nationalist reactionaries to play on, they will move on to follow their inclinations to close down democratic political space.

The dark sense of foreboding on the left today internationally, in spite of Trump's apparent undermining of American ideological hegemony, reflects an acute awareness of these severe political dangers that come with hyper-nationalist reaction. These dangers are not at all likely to be diminished by the kinds of modifications in trade agreements, or unilateral responses to Trump's protectionism, that would salvage a few plants while affording even greater scope for exploitation. It is important that the response to Trumpism should not lead to support for an allegedly 'kinder' version of free trade amidst a reproduction of neoliberal globalization. It has been that orientation on the part of liberal and social democratic forces over the past quarter century, reflecting a depressing combination of political naivety and strategic timidity, that in fact opened the way for the Farages, Le Pens, and Trumps to deploy xenophobic appeals to express popular anxieties.

The immediate task of the left is to reframe the debate, all the while engaging in ongoing collective efforts to keep open as much democratic political space as possible amidst the current reaction. Reframing the debate means going beyond the kind of earlier opposition to free trade agreements that extolled the status quo ante, let alone falling back into an abject defense of such agreements because of the new hyper-nationalist offensive against them. But reframing the debate also means going beyond the culture of protest, disdainful of electoral politics and state transformation, commonly expressed during the years of the 'anti-globalization' movement. The lesson we must learn now is that the underlying trajectory of capitalism's determined expansion and penetration into all aspects of people's lives, everywhere, finally needs to be confronted by a renewed socialist internationalism.

Yet if the patriotism of scoundrels like Trump teaches us anything, it is surely that it is delusional to imagine that realizing socialist internationalism is possible without prior fundamental change in nation states. This is not merely a matter of changing policies; it has to entail the democratic transformation of discrete institutions of the state and the recasting of relations among them as well as with society. And in this respect, especially in light of the need for progressive immigration policies and the protection of minorities, a socialist internationalism which has substance must be one that builds on, rather than denigrates or wishes away, overlapping national and class social identities. Even in a global capitalist world, socialist internationalism today can only be conceived as securing greater room for manoeuvre for progressive class struggles taking place at the level of nation states.

NOTES

1   Leo Panitch and Sam Gindin, *The Making of Global Capitalism: The Political Economy of American Empire*, London: Verso, 2012, p. 21.

2   The low unemployment rate, while very significant, didn't capture the number of workers who had left the labour market and so weren't included in those statistics. This is better captured by the employment-population ratio (the proportion of the population over 16 with jobs) and it had only increased by 1 percentage point (from 59.3 to 60.3 from 2009 to 2018); this ratio stood lower than it was in any year between 1986 and 2008. US Bureau of Labor Statistics, 'The Employment Situation', available at www.bls.gov/charts/employment-situation/employment-population-ratio.htm.

3   'The corporate savings glut' *The Economist,* 7 July 2005.

4   Jan Loeys, 'Corporations are driving the saving glut', JP Morgan Research, 24 June 2005. See also: Peter Chen, Loukas Karabarbou, Brent Neiman, 'The Global Rise of Corporate Saving', Research Division, Federal Reserve Bank of Minneapolis, Working Paper 736, Revised March 2017.

5   The increase in real wages at the end of the 1990s proved to be temporary, with real wages by 2007 lower than they were in 2001. See: Federal Reserve Bank of St Louis Economic Data, 'Employed fulltime: median usual weekly earnings: wage and salary workers', at www.fred.stlouisfed.org.

6   "US National Debt and Deficit History', at www.usgovernmentspending.com/debt_deficit_history.

7   Mike Davis, 'The Great God Trump & the White Working Class', *Catalyst,* 1(1), Spring 2017, Tables 4 and 5, pp. 163-6.

8   Donald J. Trump, 'Inauguration Speech', 20 January 2017, at www.whitehouse.gov.

9   Ezra Greenberg et al., 'The Global Forces Inspiring a New Narrative of Progress', *McKinsey Quarterly*, April 2017.

10   WTO, 'World Trade Statistical Review', Geneva: WTO, 2017; UNCTAD, World Investment Report 2017; UNCTAD press release, 'WIR-Global Foreign Direct Investment Flows Fell Sharply in 2017, United Nation Reports', 6 June 2018; Eurostat, European Commission Database; McKinsey Global Institute, 'Playing to Win, The New Global Competition for Profits', London: McKinsey and Company, September 2015; Greenberg et al., 'The Global Forces Inspiring a New Narrative of Progress', *McKinsey Quarterly*, 2017.

11   At one extreme, the US digital economy does not have to 'go abroad' (in terms of major physical investments) because of the extent to which it already *is* abroad.

12   UNCTAD, 'World Investment Report 2018', Geneva: UNCTAD, 2018, p. 99.

13   Gustav Adler, et al., 'Gone With the Headwinds: Global Productivity', IMF Staff Discussion Notes, No.17/04, April 3, 2017.

14   'Accelerating Global Growth: Profits and Pitfalls', Outlook 2018, New York: CITI Bank, October 2018, p. 1, available at www.privatebank.citibank.com.

15   John Feffer, 'America Is in Warp-Speed Decline – It's Way Bigger Than Trump', March 3, 2017 *AlterNet*, available at www.alternet.org.

16   Christopher A. Preble, 'Adapting to American Decline', *New York Times*, 22 April 2018.

17   WTO, 'World Trade Statistical Review 2017', Geneva: WTO, 2017, Tables A6, A8, pp. 102, 104. UNCTAD, 'World Investment Report', 2018, Annex Table 1, pp. 184-5.

18   This calculation was undertaken in a Deutche Bank report to counter Trump's complaints, its real significance lies in highlighting the relative global success of US MNCs. See: 'The $1.4 Trillion U.S. "Surplus" That Trump's Not Talking About', *Bloomberg News*, 11 June 2018.

19   Useful sources here are the statistics compiled by the National Science Foundation as its Science and Engineering Indicators at nsf.gov/statistics/2018/nsb20181/data/tables; and the listing of top corporations by sector in Forbes, 'Forbes 'Global 2000', 2018, available at www.forbes.com.

20   Bank of International Settlements, 'Triennial Central Bank Survey': Foreign Exchange Turnover in April 2016, Basel: BIS, September 2016, available at www.bis.org.

21   U.S. Department of the Treasury, 'Major Foreign Holders of Treasury Securities', March 2018, at ticdata.treasury.gov.

22   'Present at the Destruction', *The Economist,* 9 June 2018.

23   This took the form, apart from the notorious quotas for imports of Japanese motorcycles and automobiles, of import restrictions on sugar, lumber, machine tools and steel from Japan in the early 1980s and the 100 per cent tariff in 1987 on televisions and computers (the latter to address the alleged underpricing, or 'dumping', of Japanese semiconductors). See: Louis Jacobson, 'Donald Trump Cites Ronald Reagan as a Protectionist Hero. Was He?' *PolitiFact*, 1 July 2016, available at: www.politifact.com; Steve Hanke, 'I've Seen The Horror Of Trump's Tariffs Before, With Reagan's Terrible Trade Policies', *Forbes*, 2 March 2018.

24   See Andrew Baker, *The Group of Seven: Finance Ministries, Central Bank and Global Financial Governance*, London: Routledge, 2006, pp. 109-10.

25   Nitsan Chorev, *Remaking US Trade Policy*, Ithaca: Cornell University Press, 2007, pp. 87-8, 92.

26   G20 Leaders Statement, 'Declaration on Financial Markets and the World Economy', 15 November 2008, p. 4.

27   G20 'Toronto Summit Declaration', 27 June 2010, p. 7.

28   Tonda Maccharles, 'Behind the Scenes at the G7 Summit', *Toronto Star*, 11 June 2018.

29   'US Treasury's Mnuchin at G20 Emphasizes Free Trade, Reciprocal Terms: Official', *Reuters Business News*, 19 March 2018.

30   'Chair's Summary: G7 Finance Ministers and Central Bank Governors' Meeting', Whistler, British Columbia, 2 June 2018, available at: www.g8.utoronto.ca.

31   Eric Yoder, 'Understaffing, Lack of Training at Agencies Hampering Agency Services to Public, Personnel Agency Says', *Washington Post,* 8 February 2018.

32   Gregg Gelzinis, 'The Trump Administration Is Quietly Slashing Financial Stability Funding', *American Progress*, 7 December 2017. The reports by Office of Financial Research are at www.financial research.gov.

33   U.S. Department of the Treasury, *A Financial System That Creates Economic Opportunities*: *Banks and Credit Unions*, Report to President Donald J, Trump, Executive Order 13772 on Core Principles for Regulating the United States Financial System, 12 June 2017.

34   'Why Corporate America Loves Donald Trump', *The Economist*, 24 May 2018.

35   Jamey Essex, 'Getting What You Pay For: Authoritarian Statism and the Geographies of US Trade liberalization Strategies', *Studies in Political Economy*, 80, Autumn 2007, pp. 84-6.

36   Shawn Donnan, Jim Brunsden, and Camilla Hodgson, 'Motorcycle Maker Will Be "Taxed Like Never Before"', *Financial Times*, 27 June 2018.

37   Shawn Donnan, "Ross reveals steel price probe,' *Financial Times*, 21 June 2018.

38   Balazs Koranyi, and Francesco Canepa, 'Top Central Bankers See Growing Gloom in Global Trade War', *Reuters Business News*, 20 June 2018.

39   See the grateful editorial in the *Financial Times* 'Central Banks Correctly Go Their Separate Ways: Monetary Policy Should Continue to Stand Ready for Downward Shocks', 16 June 2018.

40   Governor Jerome H. Powell, 'Treasury Markets and the TMPG', Federal Reserve Bank of New York, New York, 5 October 2017, available at www.federalreserve.gov.

41   See the recent urgings of the Governor of the Reserve Bank of India, Urgit Patel, 'Emerging Markets Face a Dollar Global Whammy', *Financial Times,* 4 June 2018; and the earlier observations by Daniel Moss, 'What U.S. Decline? The World Still Watches the Fed', *Bloomberg*, 19 September 2017.

42   Lucy Hornby, 'XI Courts Foreign Executives Over Tariffs', *Financial Times,* 22 June 2018.

43   Lucy Hornby, 'China Loosens Investment Curbs as Trade War Looms', *Financial Times,* 30 June 2018.

44   See John Smith, *Imperialism in the Twenty-First Century: Globalization, Super-Exploitation, and Capitalism's Final Crisis,* New York, Monthly Review Press, 2016; and Prahbat Patnaik and Utsa Patnaik, *A Theory of Imperialism*, New York: Columbia University Press, 2017.

45   Gerard Greenfield, 'Bandung Redux: Anti-Globalization Nationalisms in Southeast Asia', in Leo Panitch and Colin Leys, eds, *Socialist Register 2005: The Empire Reloaded*, London: Merlin Press, 2004, pp. 180-81.

EXTREME CAPITALISM
AND 'THE NATIONAL QUESTION'

AIJAZ AHMAD

'Nationalism' has emerged in many of the contemporary discourses on the left, as much as in the corporate media, as the name for a whole range of modern malignities. In most such narratives, though not in all, these growing 'nationalisms' are said to be intrinsically opposed to neoliberalism and globalization, a state of affairs entirely negative from the standpoint of the corporate media. The left, however, is also in a quandary: One does want this neoliberal order to perish – but not at the hands of the nationalist monster! In some other narratives, these 'nationalisms' are construed to be not neoliberalism's opponents but its rebellious offspring. Let us propose, then, that there may well be something wrong in the perception itself, hence in the way the question then gets posed.

For a starter, the word neoliberalism is used so carelessly these days that everything that is done in the interest of capital gets called neoliberal. There is hardly any demarcation between what is specifically neoliberal and what has been quite familiar from older histories of laissez-faire economics dating back to classical liberalism as well as strands within neoclassical economics itself – not to speak of some libertarianisms that command great financial clout in our own time and have a platform far more vicious than the neoliberalism we know from the Reagan-Thatcher days.[1] Moreover, as we shall argue at some length below, there does not seem to be a structurally necessary correlation between neoliberal thought and policy prescriptions which arose in a specific conjuncture, and the long-term historical process of the globalization of capital. In most contemporary discourses, the term globalization gets reserved for the multifaceted new form of that larger historical process, but as if it was an entirely novel phenomenon, *sui generis* as it were. We shall use the term as a periodizing concept but without the sense of a necessary structural relation with neoliberalism. There is undoubtedly a temporal coincidence: the time of neoliberal dominance in a host of capitalist countries coincides with the time of greatest intensification of the globalizing processes; that the capitalist core was pressing the whole world to go neoliberal also meant that the evolving forms of globalization would bear an overwhelmingly neoliberal imprint. Even so, the analytic difference must always be kept in view since it is perfectly possible to accept the one without the other. The Chinese government, we would argue, has embraced globalization most enthusiastically but adopted neoliberal prescriptions only very selectively. In Europe, a whole range of leftist currents, from Corbyn and Melenchon to Syriza and Podemos, would display different degrees of hostility to the neoliberal package of policies but would not be notably opposed to globalization per se.

There is a similar sort of problem with the promiscuous use of the word 'nationalism' across many currents on the left. Nor does attaching the word 'right-wing' to 'nationalism' (to get 'right-wing nationalism') solve the problem. Indeed, the word 'nationalism' has fallen into such disrepute in so many leftist circles that it is just presumed to be right-wing in any case. This is surpassingly strange for one who grew up among Marxists who used the term nationalism simply to mean anti-colonialism or anti-imperialism, and for whom the transition from colonial subjection to national citizenship was a historic turning point. For something like a quarter century, I have held a working hypothesis that there really is no such a thing as nationalism, per se, with an identifiable, trans-historical essence, over and above particular historical practices and projects. At the deepest, most abstract level, nationalism is today the reflection, in thought, of the fact that nation-*state* either already exists in the world of material relations or is sought to be obtained in the future, as in the case of the Palestinians for example. Transnational capital and the multinational corporation, neoliberalism and globalization, all operate in a world of nation-states, which as a *form* is not, contrary to all rumour, at all on its deathbed. Nation is thus among the absolutely basic conditions of political existence for humanity in general. As a reflection of the material, nationalism too has a materiality of its own which requires of us that we distinguish among its various possible manifestations very carefully. For, in every one of its many possible forms of manifestation, nationalism always appears as a second-degree ideology which derives its meaning from the power bloc that takes hold of it and presses it into its own service. Nationalisms are serviceable for all sorts of purposes: as a revivalist ideology that purports to link a desired future with an imagined past that never was; as ideology of resistance to colonial rule; as the ideology of a fictive unity in which the exploiter and the exploited, irreconcilable in practice, can be made to appear as equal members of a national community;

a racist majoritarianism for which all others within the national boundary are really not truly national, or as a project for creating not just legal but also substantive equalities within the nation and its nation-state. We could think of nation, and of nationalism as its corollary, as a terrain that various kinds of political forces and class coalitions seek to define and occupy. No single definition of nationhood emerges from these competing projects, and there is no logical reason why nationalism, even right-wing nationalism, would be necessarily aligned with or opposed to neoliberal forms of globalization. We do have irrefutable evidence, however, which goes to show that neoliberalism has always been an agenda of the right. As such, it would be hard to imagine the right abandoning its most profound class commitments at the altar of some new-fangled nationalism.

THE INCOHERENCE OF 'RIGHT-WING NATIONALISMS'

The range of political phenomena which gets covered under the category of right-wing nationalism is so wide as to not cohere; a designation that ranges all the way from the Brexit campaign to Hindutva rule in India, not to speak of Marine Le Pen or the Golden Dawn, would seem to mean not very much. This difficulty is compounded when, contrary to available evidence, it is often assumed that these right-wing nationalisms are opposed to neoliberalism. Some detailed commentary on the evidence should prove the point. As I have detailed these matters at some length in a previous essay in the *Socialist Register*, I need not dwell much on the nexus between the Indian far right, the cream of the capitalist class, the US imperial designs, and the sturdy neoliberal structures that have gone from strength to strength one year to the next, under governments of the liberal right and the far right alike.[2] Some other cases may be taken up at some moderate length.

The xenophobic anti-immigrant hysteria in British politics is decades old and used to be focused on immigration from the former colonies. This hysteria remained a very small minority trend in the early post-war years when the dissolution of the Empire was in progress and the first great wave of non-white immigrants arrived in a Britain that was legally still open to almost unrestricted travel from the former colonies that were now getting assimilated into a Commonwealth. Attlee's Labour Government had coincided with years of post-war reconstruction, an expanding economy, full employment, labour shortages, and the making of a social state out of the state regulatory systems that had arisen during the then-recent years of the war economy. That explains why the racist backlash remained very restricted; an expanding economy, jobs for all, expectations of inclusive social justice, a strong left, and an organized working class backing the social state trumped the racist bigotry. Subsequently, though, as that moment passed and the boom years began petering away, that deep-rooted racist resentment also kept growing until it became a flood, alongside that 'Little Englander nationalism' which has been so much a part of English identity since days of the Empire's high noon. By the time Thatcher was elected and proceeded to usher in a neoliberal dispensation, immigration was already an explosive issue in British politics and all sections of the British elite, Tory or Labourite, had to abide by it.

The novelty in the recent expansion of this hysteria, in a deeply fractured society with oceans of misery for the workers and the unemployed, is that it is now directed as much against the new arrivals from Europe's own periphery and, to a lesser degree, against refugees generated by Anglo-American wars in the Middle East as against that earlier pattern of colonial immigration. These new arrivals, mostly from Eastern Europe, arrived in the UK not in consequence of globalization but as a result of the post-communist expansion of the EU. The unemployed fear competition over jobs that are hard to find in any case, the immiserated generally fear that the ever-narrowing range of social services will now have new claimants. These fears lead predictably to a certain ingathering of the tribe which, in turn, gets denounced as narrow-minded nationalism that is ranged against the EU's enlightened cosmopolitanism; too great a denunciation of this 'nationalism' tends to mask the EU's depredations. It is also well to recall that there has always been, from the beginning, a very strong anti-EU sentiment in England, going all the way up to a large section of the Tory elite. Even the decision not to join the eurozone came surely out of cold financial calculation but was presented to the British public as the triumph of commitment to the UK's own distinctive self.

The sense of a unique British national identity has old and deep roots, mostly in the colonial past and particularly precious to Englanders, but it is also perfectly at home with neoliberalism and globalization, all the more so because British capital was after all the first to get thoroughly globalized thanks to the breadth of empire. The so-called 'nationalism' of the Brexit campaign cannot be separated from this much larger and older framework of Englishness. Conversely, the Brexit campaign brought together a conjunctural aggregation of diverse forces arising out of numerous fissures in English society which simply do not add up to a nationalism.[3] I might add that since Scotland and Wales are subordinate units of England's Ukania, the Brexit campaign found far less traction there.

The xenophobic extremities of the French National Front go back to the colonial days, the defeats in Indochina and then in Algeria. Sarkozy, hardly a nationalist of that stripe, was vitriolic in rhetoric and brutal in action against the North African immigrant underclass, first as Minister of the Interior (in a government headed by Mitterrand) and then as president. Today's fascists of Ukraine or Greece, nationalist in their own peculiar ways, come out of much older histories, including the fascist ones, and the respective crises that have provided new kinds of opportunities for them were hardly the result of globalization. The question of the refugees and asylum seekers in Greece, by contrast, is a much more recent phenomenon and connected not so much to globalization as to the ravages of ongoing wars in large parts of the Middle East and Africa. Historical specificities of this kind regulate the so-called 'nationalisms' across Europe, from Denmark to Poland, Hungary, Austria, and the rest.

The same is true of Hindutva nationalism in India or Erdogan's offensive to redefine Turkish national particularity in Islamist terms. Both embrace neoliberal globalization with open arms. Modi, a fervent neoliberalizer and iconic leader of Hindutva nationalism, is as closely aligned with the US and its vast project from the Middle East to the South China Sea as his predecessors and opponents. No less open to neoliberal globalization than Modi, Erdogan pursued full EU membership as diligently as *his* predecessors and opponents for some years, trying to obtain full access to EU markets and greater European investments in Turkey. The EU leaders continued to resist a faster process toward full accession, for a variety of reasons. Meanwhile, Erdogan started defining for himself a host of other priorities: systematic purges of the Turkish Armed forces, quickened pace of Islamization within Turkish society and polity, resumption of war against the Kurds inside and beyond the country, a larger role for Turkey across the Middle East and even in North Africa, as well as expanding Turkish nationalism into the post-Soviet, Turkic-speaking, resource-rich republics in Central Asia. The sharp focus on EU membership receded. However, for all his various forms of brinksmanship, he will remain a loyal member of NATO and a loyal, all-weather ally of the US. The Hindutva and AKP varieties of nationalism are defined in strictly domestic terms, rooted in conflicts and visions that date back to the 1920s. Both subscribe to a communal majoritarianism, a religio-cultural identity, anti-secular social conservatism and imperial nostalgia – the realities of the Ottoman Empire in Turkey's case and, in the Indian instance, a very odd mixture of fact and fantasy about glories of a Hindu Golden Age in the remote past. Meanwhile, the economic violence of neoliberal policies go unabated: free economy in a xenophobic, backward-looking, strong state, so to speak.

Perhaps the most interesting case in this regard is that of China. Nationalism has been a punctual feature in Chinese politics since at least the Revolution of 1911, if not the Taipei Uprising or even before. If the Goumindang was officially described as the Nationalist Party of China, the Communist party won much of its prestige and popular mass base by fighting a war of national liberation against the Japanese. A credible argument can be made that Mao himself was probably more of a nationalist than a communist and it was only the bitter experience of the Korean War that convinced him that a prolonged nationalist struggle against US imperialism required a total break with capitalism. Xi Jinping, the current Chinese leader, invokes Mao's 'New Democracy' of the 1940s (alliance of four classes including the national bourgeoisie) as an inspiration for what the official ideology calls 'Socialism with Chinese Characteristics'. Yet no country has embraced globalization with more aplomb and sweeping vigour than China. Indeed, Chairman Xi claims that it is China which will lead the world into the 'Golden Age' of globalization. The striking fact, however, is that, for all its enthusiasm for globalization, China has embraced neoliberalism only partially, picking up only certain policies out of the whole package and rejecting others, while safeguarding the leading role of the state and its control of the main financial institutional architecture; even the neoliberal policies that have been adopted can be modified, restricted, or even reversed if need be, in light of practical results.

This side of the Chinese experience raises an interesting question. Is it possible to separate globalization from neoliberalism, conceptually and perhaps practically as well? Or are the two, globalization and neoliberalism, so closely intertwined as to be virtually identical, the one not possible without the other? The question is not easy to answer and we don't have the space for a theoretical exposition, so we shall have to make do with a maxim: a state that is weak, or has weakened itself, in relation to capital, domestic and transnational, would find it very difficult, virtually impossible, to make that separation; a strong state, on the other hand, that has preserved its relative but very real autonomy is likely to be able to preserve precisely that autonomous space for policy formulation that can, with a strong enough material base, choose to participate fully in structures of global economy but compromise with only those aspects of neoliberalism that are imperative for participating in those structures and go on to mould those imperatives to its own purposes.

In the case of China, of course, the crucial fact is that it is not the Chinese bourgeoisie, as we now know it, that has created the Chinese state, even as we now know it; rather, it is the Chinese state that has constructed the economic structure which has made the rise of that bourgeoisie possible, 'hothouse-fashion' (in the memorable phrase of Karl Marx in his chapter on primitive accumulation). Will this current relation between class and state remain, or will it get reversed? When, and with what results? In any case, it would be hard to emulate the Chinese state, except in countries like Vietnam, because it is a historically unique compromise between its Maoist past and its ultra-Dengist present – what Gramsci might have called a product of the Revolution-Restoration dynamic.

US IMPERIAL SOVEREIGNTY AND
THE POST-DEMOCRATIC STATE

Anti-statism is central to the discursive space that postmodernist left – subalternists in the Indian case – shares with neoliberal theory. In practice, however, neoliberalism has never sought a weak state. It arrived in Chile with the big bang of a military dictatorship based on political terror and sweeping restructuring of the economy through technocratic fiat; in this case neoliberalism simply abolished the liberal-democratic polity that the socialist government of Unidad Popular had so painstakingly preserved. In the Anglo-American zone of advanced capital, the Reagan and Thatcher regimes were anything but the minimalist ones of Hayekian theory; they began by breaking the back of organized labour, strengthening a militarised patriotic hysteria (Falklands War, the Star Wars against the 'Evil Empire' as Reagan called it), adopting policies that were far from neutral but highly aggressive in extending privileges of property and capital, engineering massive transfers of wealth upward and dismantling long-standing social compacts, with massive state apparatuses which required the bulk of the revenues for their own reproduction. Neoliberalism is so combative a partisan on behalf of capital and against labour that it needs a permanently strong state to mobilize all its apparatuses, from the repressive to the ideological ones, to maintain the neoliberal order. That neoliberalism weakens the state is an ideological fiction. What globalized neoliberalism wants is a state that is weak in relation to capital and ruthlessly strong in relation to labour. The starting point for understanding the contemporary state is not globalization but, as always, the capital-labour relation.

Political order in this world of globalized neoliberalism appears to be undergoing an extraordinary transformation. On the one hand, we witness the emergence of what I have called 'Imperial Sovereignty' that is exercised routinely and globally, often refracted through proxy international or local agencies but radiating always from an imperial centre. At the national level, a new generalized norm seems to be emerging in more and more places in the form of something like a post-democratic state which takes it elements both from the familiar forms of the liberal state as well as from what Poulantzas had called the 'exceptional' forms, viz., fascism and dictatorship.[4] The term 'post-democratic' is far less precise in that the presumption of a prior democratic structure is neither historically accurate in a great many cases, China or Iran for example, nor structurally necessary in trying to comprehend this emergent new form.

What needs emphasis, however, is that the widespread contagion of this form in postcolonial societies, in all its local variants, contradicts the postulate of liberal theory that liberal capitalism necessarily gives rise to liberal democracy.[5] It is undoubtedly true that democratic demand is perennial and sometimes breaks through like a flood in all contemporary societies. However, in most cases, the popular classes seem to understand their own democratic demand primarily in terms of social and economic justice while it is the elite reformers, themselves brought up on liberal precepts and 'Democracy Promotion' offensives, who graft their own understanding of liberal democracy on to those popular demands. Refusal to address the demand for restructuring societies and economies to meet the needs of the democratic classes then leads to the inefficacy of whatever concessions are made in the domain of political rights, and the state reverts more or less swiftly to the mixture of the liberal and the 'exceptional' which I have provisionally called post-democratic. In many cases, notably Turkey and India, 'post-democractic' is accurate in the precise sense that this new constitutionalized authoritarianism has risen well after highly secularised forms of liberal democracy had been obtained. In most cases, the brisk advance of capitalist structures in much of the formerly colonized zones seems to have bypassed or reversed political liberalism. That this post-democratic form will only grow stronger as the class contradictions nurtured by neoliberalism become deeper seems very likely. Nor is this a matter of the non-western world. Europe already has this form in Hungary, Poland, Ukraine, Austria, and beyond. Now the US itself seems to be going down that same incline.

If neoliberalism needs a strong, highly repressive – post-democratic – state to do its will in every national domain, globalization is beset by the contradiction that the capital that is dominant world-wide has been thoroughly transnationalized, yet it lacks a state of its own and has to operate in a world of nation-states whose own realms it does not control directly but exceeds in all instances. *This is the gap that the US state, as the chief guardian of the globalized imperialist system, seeks to fill.* This global function bestows upon it a dual character whereby it must act as the state whose paramount function is the protection and advancement of the interests of US-based national capital, and, simultaneously, as the state of transnational capital as a whole, militarily, economically, politically, ideologically. This duality has the permanent potential of producing an irresolvable conflict between the national and the transnational within the US state. This is the objective ground on which it has increasingly claimed the whole world as an eminent domain for the exercise of its own imperial sovereignty which supersedes not only laws of other nations but international law as well.

As an expression of this imperial sovereignty, US officials routinely refer to the Westphalian settlement, Geneva conventions, etc. as outmoded relics in this age of globalization and novel modes of warfare.[6] Historically, the doctrine of sovereignty was developed in increasingly complex forms over time but always in relation to the nation-state. Indeed, the presumption was that nation-states had the inviolable right to sovereign power in their own territorial domain. As such, imperial sovereignty has been pronounced and practised in the concrete practical world without the systematic development of a doctrine. Some form of imperial sovereignty was doubtless inherent in the colonial system as such, but it is structurally different in our time since this is the conception of sovereign jurisdiction of one pre-eminent nation-state, the US, over other formally sovereign nation-states. Most pertinent for an understanding of this imperial sovereignty are the debates among the German jurists of the inter-war period, especially those who were attracted to the legal justifications of the Nazi abrogation of the liberal order at home, the State of Exception, and imperialist expansion abroad.[7] Schmitt of course continued to think of these matters well after the Nazi state had been eliminated and some of the provocative thinking on the question of sovereign domain comes precisely in his later writings on global space.

This is not the place to delve into all that. Suffice here to say that US claims of imperial sovereignty became more frequent after the collapse of the communist state system, i.e., in the period of globalization in the proper sense, and particularly after a global war against terror was announced (an 'endless task' according to President Bush Jr). This sovereignty is mostly exercised beyond American shores. Its domestic supplement should not be underestimated, however, in the form of the prodigious extension of the national security state within the US in the twenty-first century: as witnessed, for instance, in the creation of the Department of Homeland Security, in creeping militarization of the police forces, in increasing deployment of this military police and of paramilitary forces to 'secure the borders', and the accumulating plethora of legislation and judicial interpretation. All this ground was prepared during the Bush and Obama presidencies. But there is backstory to this that goes back much further.

FORWARD MARCH OF THE RIGHT:
GOLDWATER TO TRUMP

A few months after the US invasion of Iraq, I wrote an essay, 'The Imperialism of Our Time',[8] the title of which was chosen as an homage to Kalecki's seminal essay, 'Fascism of Our Time',[9] which addressed Barry Goldwater's bid for US Presidency in 1964. Recalling Kalecki's essay seemed pertinent because the kind of forces Kalecki had so feared some decades ago were beginning to take hold of state power in the United States during the Bush Presidency. Ideological premises as well as policy projections for the Bush regime were getting formulated already by a cabal-like combination of Wall Street luminaries, Christian fundamentalists, Zionists, neoconservatives, and militarists; Bush Jr himself was a 'born-again' Christian. It seemed likely even then that economic power and political culture in the US would keep moving further to the right, with the possibility of even more extremist regimes rising there in the not too distant future, and that imperialist aggressions would become more widespread and even more brutal.[10] Those premonitions were bleak, but what was then feared has now come to pass in the shape of the Trump presidency. Far from being an altogether novel phenomenon, and even though Trump is on some issues distinctly to the right of Nixon and Reagan, his ascent to presidential power represents a point of culmination for an escalating offensive of the far right in the United States that first got politically consolidated with the presidential campaign of 1964 in which Goldwater won close to 40 per cent of the vote. As he famously said in his acceptance speech on securing the nomination at the Republican Convention: 'Extremism in the pursuit of liberty is no vice.'

What were the underlying forces pushing that 'extremism' forward? Kalecki's analysis was prescient. In a surprising first proposition, he compared 'Goldwaterites' with the German neo-Nazis and the short-lived French OAS (quite literally 'Secret Military Organization'). It is sobering to recall that some of the founders of what we now know as the French National Front were veterans of the OAS, and it is the latent neo-Nazi tendency in German culture and politics that has now blossomed into AfD (Alternative for Germany) that recently won 92 seats in the Bundestag, becoming the main opposition party against the fragile ruling coalition. Kalecki was undoubtedly clairvoyant but what all this goes to show is that the far right in the Euro-American zones that has become so menacing today has been gestating and gathering strength over virtually the whole of the post-war period. Echoes of the pre-war 1930s, as it were, except that the main adversary of the far right in that period, communism, is nowhere in sight.

Kalecki then emphasized that racism and chauvinism, with the targeting of African-Americans in the US and North African immigrants in France as examples, served as detonating ingredients in the political rhetoric of such groupings. The stress he put on this stands in refreshing contrast with today's fairly common tendency to use the figure of 'nationalism' to occlude the deep-seated racisms of the various far right groupings in the Euro-American zones. Even in the US today, polite circles prefer not to speak consistently of white racism and prefer euphemisms like 'white nationalism' or 'white supremacy'. Kalecki further emphasized that the devising of anti-communism as a popular ideology had already prepared a fertile ground for right-wing and fascist elements to grow, and that although 'government intervention has become an integral part of "reformed" capitalism' such elements 'attack not only government "intervention" but even social insurance'.

The political groundwork for Goldwater's campaign had indeed been laid much earlier with the unleashing of the post-war anti-communist crusade in which Senator McCarthy's televised spectacles were only the tip of a vast iceberg. But much had changed in America, explosively, between the public discrediting of McCarthy in 1954 and Goldwater's presidential bid ten years later: desegregation of schools and the banishing of official prayers and mandatory Bible reading in public schools by the Warren Court; the 382 day boycott of Alabama buses led by Martin Luther King; the emergence of such as Malcolm X and Students Nonviolent Coordination Committee (SNCC) to the left of King; the election of the first Catholic President of the United States, John F. Kennedy, a Harvard-educated scion of a patrician Boston-Irish family; and much else besides. The whole spectrum of forces opposed to all that were to coalesce around Goldwater. Significantly, he won his nomination against Nelson Rockefeller, the very symbol both of liberalism and of the power elite of the Eastern seaboard within the Republican Party. Rockefeller was again roundly defeated by Nixon in the bid for Republican nomination four years later, in 1968. The liberal current as well as the power of Old Money in the Republican Party began then to decline terminally, never to recover, even though Rockefeller was to later serve as Ford's vice president.[11]

It is well to recall, also, that it is only the distorted nature of the American electoral college which created a lasting impression that Goldwater had been badly trounced. Although less than 10 per cent of the electoral votes and mere 6 states out of 50 went to him, he actually won 38.47 per cent of the vote. This was a shockingly high percentage considering that his adversary, Lyndon Johnson, was riding a sympathy wave after the assassination of Kennedy whose legacy he now represented, quite aside from the Civil Rights Act of 1964 Johnson had shepherded through Congress himself, and a whole array of anti-poverty programmes he was proposing. In other words, the 1964 election was a direct political contest, with structures of race and class very much at issue, between a familiar kind of New Deal capitalism – welfare liberalism so to speak – and a very bigoted form of conservatism which shrewd minds were already suspecting of a fascist temper. (War was not such a big issue since Goldwaterites were perfectly pleased with Johnson's liberal imperialism and the Vietnam War was only just gathering real scale and momentum.) To a certain extent, this battle was also fought within the Democratic Party itself. Johnson's principal opponent for the Democratic nomination was George Wallace, the segregationist four-term Governor of Alabama, and a large part of his racist support went on to vote for Goldwater in the presidential race.

Goldwater's bid came in the midst of a full-employment boom during what many have called the Golden Age of Capitalism, for which the party of the New Deal and reform capitalism of the Kennedy-Johnson-Humphrey variety could take virtually all the credit. That a far right still in its organizational infancy could capture well above a third of the popular vote was impressive indeed.

In a remarkable closing paragraph to his 1964 essay, Kalecki wrote:

'It seems fairly certain that after the murder of John Kennedy the government would have been able to deal a mortal blow to the rightwing extremists. But the way of conducting the inquiry as presented in the Warren Commission report, shows the contrary tendency to evade implicating anyone but Oswald – who in the meantime had been successfully eliminated. It is in this state of lawlessness that the origins of Goldwater's candidacy may be found. In turn, this tendency was not firmly opposed inside the Republican Party, as it was directly controlled by Big Business. ... Goldwaterism is wanted by the ruling class as a pressure group against an excessive relaxation of international tensions and in order to restrain the Negro Movement. Goldwater ... will be saved by those to whom he lost.'

Unlike Goldwater, who lost the election, Trump has captured power and what 'the ruling class' fears is not 'excessive relaxation of international tensions' but that he might not focus adequately on the military aspect of those tensions and create, instead, unnecessary ones in the economic sphere, even with allies. For the rest, it is quite remarkable that already in 1964 Kalecki perceived a shared political interest in maintaining the status quo and something of a class alliance between Democrats and Republicans that is underwritten by 'Big Business': Democrats commanded the sympathy of the whole nation but did not try to smash the far right either after that assassination or after those of Dr. King and Robert Kennedy that followed – and they effectively authorized the state-sponsored repression of Black Panthers, we might add. The Republican Party, meanwhile, failed to oppose Goldwater because it was beholden to the same plutocracy that was supporting his candidacy.

THE 2008 CRISIS AND
THE OBAMA TO TRUMP TRANSITION

Barack Obama, having been the first Black president of the Harvard Law Review and anointed by Ted Kennedy as the keeper of his brother John's legacy, got elected as the first Black President of the United States in the midst of what has been called in these pages 'the first Great Depression of the 21st century'.[12] Immediately after receiving the nomination he flew into Washington to start working closely with the Bush Administration on a rescue package for the profligate financial institutions that were in trouble. Obama won the elections about a month after TARP (Troubled Assets Relief Program) went into effect, to enable the rescue package of some $700 billion. He initially promised that $50 billion of those would be earmarked for the victimised homeowners; as of November 2012 about $4 billion of those had been spent. In other words, all the homeowners at the receiving end of the crisis collectively received less than one per cent of what Wall Street received. Democracy of the one per cent was fully at display.

Obama had fought the elections with a promise to end the Bush-era wars, rebuild America's infrastructure, and expand employment across the board. That implied readiness for either radical cuts in the war economy or openly embracing enhanced deficit spending in the short run – or both. Yet neither in the economic policy nor in war policy was he significantly different from the preceding Bush Administration. He was spuriously awarded the Nobel Peace Prize soon after coming into office, in recognition of the mere campaign promise that he would end the Bush-era wars and work for a world free of nuclear weapons. In the event, he added wars in Libya, Syria, and Yemen to Bush's wars in Afghanistan and Iraq while putting in place planned expenditure of a trillion dollars for upgrading America's nuclear arsenal. During the eight years of his Presidency, corporate and investor taxes were cut by more than $6 trillion and U.S. corporate profits more than doubled, with 97 per cent of all gross domestic product (GDP) income gains going to the top 1 per cent, the managing committee of America's dysfunctional liberal democracy.

An opportunity for overhaul of a system had presented itself to a president who commanded great authority at the moment, only to be turned down. He and his cohort had no such inclinations. That was the first act of policy: save finance, leave the victims essentially to their own devices. Moreover, as has been widely noted, nothing at all was done for expansion of employment or of the productive economy more broadly. Priorities remained the same. If Blair had borrowed from Thatcher extensively,[13] Obama often expressed great admiration for Reagan while declaring 'there are no blue states or red states, only the United States'. In other words, he wished to be a bipartisan President.

As the Crisis exploded, there was an extraordinarily swift and complete coordination among various states of the Western world as well as the governments of China and Japan for creation of vast amounts of money and funnelling them into the financial systems of the various countries, which were now little more than overlapping local networks of a globally integrated organism. None deviated from the shared norms; all acted essentially in the footsteps of the Federal Reserve. Little quarrels were just set aside. There was no wave of protectionism, no attempt to gain a competitive edge. If Obama's commitment to deregulation and refusal to intervene for significant expansion of employment and economic security of the populace stood in such sharp contrast to the glory years of the New Deal, the coordinated and uniform responses by the various major states of the world in this case stood in equally sharp contrast with the situation in the aftermath of the 1929 Crash when coordination was minimum, points of friction numerous, rise of protectionism quite widespread, and each nation-state basically devised its own ways of coping. This is an epochal contrast. The 1929 Crash occurred in an era when, for all the cross-border trade and investment, and for all the famous 'export of capital', bourgeoisies and capital formations were essentially national; the locus for the protection of national capital in times of crisis was in the final instance the nation-state itself. Now, almost a century later, in this epoch of globally integrated finance capital, the locus of authority that offers protection for the whole is nowhere and everywhere; the US Federal Reserves normally serves as the prime mover and the final arbiter but only in so far as finance ministries and central banks of the other key countries coordinate with it, which they were structurally compelled to do.

China and India were the two countries that emerged relatively less devastated or scathed than most other countries that got hit by the 2007-08 crisis. In both cases, the degree of state control over the financial sector was arguably the decisive factor. In China, where most of the banking sector was still state-owned, those controls were more extensive and the devastation was measurably less. In India, where state ownership of banks is less than in China, the economic impact of the global crisis was proportionately more. Quite predictably, despite the demonstrable fact that state ownership in the banking sector protected their interests during the crisis, bourgeoisies in India as well as China are clamouring for more deregulation of finance, as is transnational capital, with increasing success. Interestingly, moreover, while this evidence of the positive effect of state control of banking during the crisis was widely discussed in both China and India during the crisis, it was little noted in Western countries, even in the writings of the Marxist left. And, thanks to the stranglehold of neoliberal thinking, such talk as arose during the crisis in these countries of bank nationalization – or re-nationalization – died down fairly quickly.

As the crisis began to unfold, many came to argue that it signified the beginning of the end of the neoliberal era. There was in fact no basis for such an interpretation, unless one believed in some capitalist rationality which could see that the execution of neoliberal policies had brought about the crisis and should now be abandoned or at least restrained through countermeasures. It is undoubtedly true that a crisis opens up a wide space for action, from the left as well as the right. There was an opportunity, but where was the agent of change? The left was fragmented and unmoored, the working classes supine and beaten into submission. Neoliberalism had been highly profitable for the capitalist class which had no reason to abandon it unless forced to. Indeed, once the anxieties about Obama's true intentions had subsided, Wall Street capital proceeded to use the crisis and the state's response to it as an opportunity, denying reprieve to the victims, and posting some of the highest profit rates since such records began to be kept. The hope that the neoliberal era was beginning to end turned out to be a chimera.

As for the Obama–Trump transition, it needs to be said right away that Hillary Clinton received 2.9 million more of the popular vote than Trump but it was the distorting effects of the electoral college which awarded Trump the presidency on the grounds that he had won a majority of the delegates in that highly restricted college. Instead of blaming the electoral college for having stolen the presidency the popular vote had given her, and calling for sweeping reform of the US electoral system, she assisted in the creation of a perception among the populace that the Russians were somehow to be blamed. We can also ignore the canard that racist backlash against the fact of a Black president somehow played a significant role in 2018 election, or that an entity called 'the white working class' had shifted en masse to Trump and his 'white supremacy'. Trump won 53 per cent of the white women's vote, the same margin as Obama had won in a contest with Romney, a white male and former Governor of Massachusetts. Hillary Clinton lost six states that Obama had won twice: Florida, Pennsylvania, Michigan, Iowa, Wisconsin, Ohio – states that included some of the most devastated centres of US manufacturing and the 'white working class'. Quite plausibly, Obama's blackness had made no difference, but during the eight years of his administration, with which Hillary Clinton was centrally involved, it had done nothing to make possible a recovery from that de-industrialization and for the workers who had lost their jobs. Many of them probably did vote for Trump, not in favour of his racism or his misogyny but out of resentment and wanting to believe in his promises of job creation. Would this vote have gone to Sanders if he were the Democratic candidate? Racism was undoubtedly an issue in 2018 as it always is in the US elections and it is very likely that Trump has hateful attitudes to Black people in general or that anti-Black racism is rampant in his core constituency. That, however, was not an overt motivating force in his campaign. Rather, the issue that he seized upon was the same as the one turning Europe upside down: immigrants, Muslims in particular – and, in the American case, the Mexicans as well!

What is absolutely clear is that the American far right is very much more formidable today than it was in 1964, with the Nixon and Reagan presidencies behind it, with a vast empire of think-tanks and propaganda organs at its command, with the Christian right and the Evangelical-Zionist alliance along with their mega-churches and lobbies working for it, and the Republican Party itself having been restructured into a menacing force by the neocons and the not-so-neocon warriors, the Tea Party crowd, the Ryans and the Gingriches, the Adelsons and the Koch Brothers, the Ayn Rand enthusiasts within Trump's own crowd (including himself and the House Speaker Paul Ryan). We are no longer speaking of a configuration that arose for or against neoliberalism or one that can be termed 'nationalist' in some simple way, but of something very much older but now very much deeper and wider. For an analogue, one would have to revert to nineteenth century European irrationalisms, the European far right of the inter-war years or, in a contemporary reference, the long-term project of the Hindutva far right in India.

Imperialism has always been a bipartisan issue in American politics, and that remains. What no longer has any purchase on the Democratic Party is the New Deal reform capitalism that was still its basic domestic ethos under Kennedy, Johnson, Hubert Humphrey, and the rest. What the Democratic Party that emerged out of the eight years of Obama's narcissistic rule now resembles most is what the Republican Party became under President Ford:

clueless, rudderless, colourless. When a New Deal Democrat of precisely that earlier sort rose in 2008 from outside its ranks to seek its presidential nomination, after a distinguished career in the Senate as an independent, and then went on to electrify vast numbers inside its electoral base and beyond, the party did not know what to do with him. The Democratic National Committee (DNC) did what it could to sabotage his campaign and gave the whole of the party machinery and much of its finance to the already well-financed campaign of Hillary Clinton. She eventually received 6 million votes less than Obama. One now wonders: had the DNC remained impartial between the two candidates, giving equal support to both, and accepting Sanders if he were to emerge victorious in the primaries, would the six million who drifted away – to Trump or abstention or whatever – come to Sanders? The margin of victory in the popular vote might have been even far greater than what the Hillary campaign did accomplish, thus overcoming the obstacles posed by the electoral college. A concrete challenge to neoliberalism, as well as to the Far Right, might have then materialized.

NEOLIBERALISM AND POST-COMMUNIST POLITICS IN THE OCEAN OF CHEAP COMMODITIES

This has been the story in other countries as well. Neoliberalism has been the joint project of the centre-right and the centre-left alike, not just the Reagans and the Thatchers as is often claimed. TINA ('There is No Alternative') became the mantra of New Labour under Blair and beyond, the Democrats under the Clintons and Obama, the German and French socialists, and so on. Sanders was contained not by the far right but by the Democrats. Corbyn, an old and familiar face on the Labour left, was attacked as vigorously by the still powerful Blairite machinery within Labour as by the Tories. When Melenchon, formerly a veteran member of the Socialist party, broke with it, organized a Presidential campaign in opposition to neoliberalism and the neo-fascist right, started gaining the same kind of popular support as Sanders in the US, the Socialist Party, running far behind him, refused an alliance of the left and threw its support behind Macron, the very personification of the neoliberal elite which manages French corporate capital. As we draft this article, roughly the same is happening in Spain: the Socialists have formed a fragile government but turned down the offer from Podemos to join in a unity government of the Left that would have commanded an overwhelming majority. The corporate media and the centre-left have a word for all such challenges: 'ultra-left' – which means irresponsible, a passing fashion or a fringe, a dangerous element that does nothing but bring bad name to the responsible left, etc. This lack of acknowledgement of all the very substantial challenges the left has mounted against neoliberalism is then combined with an alarmist campaign in that same media which says that the 'nationalist', xenophobic right is the main force fighting to disrupt neoliberal globalization as well as cosmopolitan entities such as the EU.

The 1929 Crash shook the entire system, including the entire liberal political order, starting in the Euro-American centres and reaching into diverse regions of the world. The 2008 Crisis served only to stabilize and deepen the system. The factors that are currently generating a whole host of instabilities are largely external to that crisis. For instance, refugees that are entering Europe as a result of the Euro-American wars in the Middle East are shaking up the European political order, as fuel for a whole range of organized European racisms, far more than anything that is traceable to the economics of 2008. Rather, it is the long-term stagnation of the European economies and a fragile job market which turn every refugee or immigrant into an immediate threat to one's own livelihood, a sense of threat that decades of anti-immigrant campaigns by racist Europeans have now made permanent, with roots in the colonial past on the one hand, centuries of European anti-semitism on the other. Compared to these social upheavals and racist hysterias, practices and institutions of neoliberalism have remained remarkably stable, contrasted to the enormous contraction of space for unbridled or even just liberal capitalism in the aftermath of 1929.

A fundamental factor ensuring stability for this globalized neoliberalism was, and still is, that the productive capacity and supply chains of industrial consumer goods, located now mostly outside the capitalist West, which undergirds global supply and demand, remained stable. The name of the game is China, supplemented of course by other concentrations of cheap labour, all the way from Bangladesh to Mexico. This fundamental stability is reflected in the fact that among all the major economies China was impacted the least and recovered the fastest, even though, as elsewhere, only with injections of enormous money supply into the system, which was easier for China precisely because of the great surpluses accumulated primarily by export of those consumer goods.

The broader historical fact is that while colonialism had divided the world between an industrialized core in the Euro-American zones and a vast agricultural hinterland in Asia and Africa (minus little oases like Japan), dissolution of colonial empires introduced a new division between advanced industrial zones and the backward ones. In the backward zones of capital, industrial centres were sporadic but, cumulatively, the supplies of cheap labour for urban and/or industrial employment was impressive and growing. Meanwhile, new technological innovations made it possible for the TNC's to contemplate building new industrial plant and even shifting some of the existing plant to those zones of cheap labour. Then, at the height of neoliberalism's ascendency in the West, and just as it was beginning to spread in some countries of backward capital, came the implosion of the communist system. Contrary to many perceptions, implosion began not in the Soviet Union but in China with the declaration of 'Socialism with Chinese Characteristics' in December 1978, when neoliberalism was just beginning to pick up steam elsewhere. However, even in China the decisive moment for across-the-board dissolution arrived with Deng's famous Southern Tour in 1992, the year after USSR was dissolved.

Capitalism, and neoliberalism with it, went global. For the first time in history, capitalism became not just dominant in the world but a mode of production that penetrated even the remotest corner of global production. The globally available pool of cheap labour doubled, in which labour coming from former socialist countries, such as China, was healthier, much better educated and used to modern work disciplines than, say, in India. The high-wage Western working class became too expensive and faced the possibility of declining wage rates and stable employment opportunities. If the history of most of the twentieth century was crucially marked by the presence of communism, the history of the past three decades has been crucially marked by the absence of it. It is customary in Western Marxism to greatly underrate the contribution of that implosion to the stability of neoliberal capitalism and the devastating political effect it had outside the transatlantic Euro-America. The fact of cheap Chinese labour is generally treated as just a fact, as if it was ordained by God or some principles of Hayekian economics, not a direct result of the fall of communism, which is generally regarded as an unproblematic political advance: just a 'Revenge of History' as the title of the celebratory book by Alex Callinicos puts it.[14]

I will return presently to the economic consequences which underwrite the stability of globalized neoliberalism, after some brief reflections on the political consequences which have greatly undermined the possibilities of effective opposition. For, regardless of the kind of states they were for their own people, the transformation of China and the Soviet Union into secondary zones of capital meant that global restraints on imperialist prerogatives were greatly reduced and paved the way, in the United States, for a set of beliefs that can be characterized as the doctrine of a globalized imperial sovereignty that is in itself a permanent State of Exception. For great many oppositional movements and nation-states in Tricontinental zones, the COMECON countries had offered an alternative pole of support. When this author asked the Indian prime minister who had introduced neoliberalism into the country what happened to his pinkish convictions, his answer was simple: 'the Soviet Union died on me.'

The fate of the weaker socialist countries (Yugoslavia, Cuba, Vietnam, the beleaguered Nicaragua of the original Sandinistas) was sealed by that implosion, in different ways and to varying degrees. The same applied to the national liberation movements, as witnessed in the disarray within the PLO as well as the alliance of the ANC and the South African Communist Party (SACP). Some of the degeneration in both the PLO and the ANC had older roots. However, the Oslo Accords and the first formation of Mandela's government came in the immediate aftermath of that implosion. Thus, the Oslo process was formally initiated in December 1992 and concluded with the signing of what has come to be known as Oslo II in September 1995. The final negotiations between the Apartheid regime and the ANC started in 1990 when a leftward consolidation was still possible and concluded in 1994 when it got foreclosed. This was the span of time that witnessed the dissolution of the Soviet system, the onset of 'Shock Therapy', social and political decomposition throughout the COMECON territories – the very countries on which those movements had relied for political support and the weapons that had made their armed struggles viable. It is doubtful that the PLO and the ANC did not register how very much the power balance had shifted. That lesson was learned across the Tricontinent. The will to fight imperialism did not dissipate but got weakened; there was a dimming of colours all across the horizon.

Thanks precisely to this enhanced political stability in the onward march of globalized neoliberalism, more and more of the Marxist left began looking at *Crisis* – this one or that – as the possible next great force that would interrupt that onward march. Meanwhile, as neoliberal devastation began undermining employment opportunities and living standards for the working classes all across Europe, it was accompanied by the death and/or decline of what Hobsbawm has felicitously called 'the Enlightenment Left' (communism and left social democracy). In particular, as extant social democracy itself became part of the neoliberal establishment, great opportunities opened up for the far right to present itself as the champion of the native working classes against the incoming immigrant hordes as well as the Brussels bureaucracy (while only vaguely and demagogically opposed to the crux of neoliberal policies as such). As all the countries in the Afro-Asian zones were faced with a race to the bottom while competing for more and more exports at the lowest possible prices, what had remained of the *dirigiste* states collapsed, the global wage rate continued on a downward spiral, problems got deeper in all sectors of production other than the export sector, many kinds of social decomposition set in, including the intensification of ethnic conflicts (with West-funded NGOs taking the side of ethnicity against the national). In this context, the release of transcontinental maladies, including jihadi Islam, reflected the rise of political forces which sought to occupy the space that was previously held by secular, left-oriented anti-imperialism.[15]

In the economic domain, the key role of cheap commodities produced by Chinese labour in helping keep the social peace first in the US and now increasingly in Western Europe, by ensuring that the working classes can maintain something resembling the standard of living they are accustomed to, is a staple in analyses of globalized capitalism. The opening up of China for foreign corporate investment as a vast field for Western capital, not just the famous TNCs like Apple or Walmart, in production and distribution networks, but also countless lesser known firms that profit from involvement in production and supply chains in which China plays the central role. China is of course simply the largest economy occupying such a position. Other countries, such as India and Taiwan (the latter partly through its investments in China) play a critical role in production and provisioning of IT products that would be far more expensive if they were to be produced in the Euro-American zones. All in all, the implosion of communism brought down the global wage rate dramatically and this effect is likely to last into the foreseeable future.

Meanwhile, the collapse of the COMECON countries led not only to German unification but also opened up a huge new zone for Western capital in general and German capital in particular, benefiting all classes in the EU in all kinds of ways, giving, for example, even the middle-middle of those classes the opportunity to pick up magnificent properties for a song. When I asked a friend during a visit to a part of Budapest that had been home to the bourgeoisie in pre-communist days who now owned those properties, the pat reply was: 'German dentists.'

BY WAY OF A CONCLUSION

The far right is making great strides and this is bound to increase in the Trump times, as the left's challenge to neoliberalism as well as the neoliberal character of globalization – overlapping but somewhat distinct issues – gets provisionally contained. And, as the demagogic, nativist, racist right in the Western countries fashions a rhetoric that lumps economic refugees as well as the war refugees together with globalization, the pitch of a fundamentally fascist hysteria is going only to rise. Trump will continue to stoke the flames of American imperial nationalism as he single-mindedly pursues a second presidential term. Imperial nationalism is a permanent fixture of American political life, since what George Washington called 'an infant empire' and what Jefferson called 'an empire of liberty' was first founded. This will endure, albeit in the quite specific form of Trump times.

The Nazis had three sides to their nationalism, in almost equal measure, an imperial nationalism focused on conquering the world (directed primarily against the leading colonizing powers plus the USSR as the chief obstacles to world conquest), an economic nationalism (to safeguard and rebuild the German economy so as to finance that conquering mission but also to win over the German masses by bringing them prosperity), and a racist nationalism (of 'Blood and Soil' – directed primarily against Jews). Trump and his tribe are also likely to use highly publicized small doses of economic nationalism for propaganda effect, without disturbing the neoliberal order of globalization to any significant degree. But they will concentrate especially on greatly augmenting the highly inflammable 'Blood and Soil' nationalism. The same is to be expected as to the likely general behaviour of the European far right groupings, with local variants. In the process, the post-democratic state might shed some of its liberalism, and increase some of its 'exceptionalism'. It is very unlikely, though, that the basic institutional architecture of liberal constitutionalism would be, for the foreseeable future, in any grave danger. The far right can realize all its political objectives within liberal constitutionalism, since the working classes have been beaten into submission and are currently quiescent.[16] On the other hand, it also seems quite clear that the centre-left into which traditional social democrats had dissolved the radical visions of their ancestors has also lost credibility and, in many cases, even institutional viability, while traditional conservatism has been ceding more and more of its terrain to the far right. Objectively, the left could gain ground quite rapidly.

But that is another story and requires a different reflection.

NOTES

1   In Jane Mayer's *Dark Money: The Hidden History of the Billionaires Behind the Rise of the Radical Right* (New York: Doubleday, 2016), the dominant presence is that of the Koch Brothers, the legendary rightwing libertarians. Collectively, the configuration of billionaire families whose fundings and projects she traces have been intent since the early 1970s on organizing a far more comprehensive class offensive than neoliberalism per se.

2   Aijaz Ahmad, 'India: Liberal Democracy and the Extreme Right', in Leo Panitch and Greg Albo, eds, *Socialist Register 2016: The Politics of the Right*, London: Merlin Press, 2015.

3   See the highly nuanced analysis by Susan Watkins in 'Casting Off' in *New Left Review*, 100(July/August), 2016; also useful is Tom Hazeldine, 'British Divisions', *New Left Review*, 105(May/June), 2017.

4   Nicos Poulantzas, *Fascism and Dictatorship*, London: NLB, 1974.

5   For a somewhat extended reflection on the difficult relations between liberalism and democracy, especially in the backdrop of colonialism and imperialism, see my 'Twelve Jottings on the Liberalization of Democracy', in Akeel Bilgrami, ed., *Marx, Gandhi and Modernity: Essays Presented to Javeed Alam*, New Delhi: Tulika Books, 2014.

6   Some lengthier but still preliminary comments on these twin concepts, imperial sovereignty and the post-democratic state, can be found in my 'The Fallouts of 1989', in C.P.Chandrasekhar and Jayati Ghosh, eds, *Interpreting the World to Change It: Essays for Prabhat Patnaik*, New Delhi: Tulika Books, 2017. Full explication awaits publication of my 'The Return of the Repressed: Figurations of the National', 2017 Wellek Library Lectures, University of California at Irvine, May 31-June 2, 2017.

7   For Schmitt, the state of exception was a permanent attribute of sovereignty as such. Agamben adds that provision for a state of exception is in any case universally available in all liberal constitutions. Acting beyond the existing law is thus an attribute not necessarily of the fascist or the 'exceptional' state but of *all* capitalist states. See Carl Schmitt, *Political Theology: Four Chapters on the Concept of Sovereignty*, Chicago: University of Chicago Press, 1985 [German original 1922]; and Giorgio Agamben, *State of Exception*, Chicago: University of Chicago Press, 2005.

8   Aijaz Ahmad, 'The Imperialism of Our Time', in Leo Panitch and Colin Leys, eds, *Socialist Register 2004: The New Imperial Challenge*, London: Merlin Press, 2003; reprinted in Aijaz Ahmad, *Iraq, Afghanistan and the Imperialism of Our Time*, New Delhi: LeftWord Books, 2004.

9   Michael Kalecki, 'The Fascism of Our Time', in his *The Last Phase in the Transformation of Capitalism*, New York: Monthly Review Press, 1972.

10   I have borrowed some of the phrasing here and in a couple of other places in the present text from an earlier essay of mine, 'The Fallouts of 1989'.

11   Kalecki had written of the power of the 'young' and 'dynamic' sectors of capital, 'oil interests' and 'armament industries' in particular, as backing the Goldwaterite forces ('The Fascism of Our Time', p.102). That he would refer to armament industries as 'young' reminds one of Eisenhower's famous 'Farewell Speech' of January 1961 in which he warned against the newly-risen, dangerous phenomenon of the 'military-industrial complex', in a phrase he coined for this then-novel phenomenon.

12   Anwar Shaikh, 'The First Great Depression of the 21st Century', in Leo Panitch, Greg Albo, and Vivek Chibber, eds, *The Crisis This Time: Socialist Register 2011*, London: Merlin Press, 2010.

13   In his landmark essay of 1990, 'All That Melts Into Air is Solid', *Race and Class*, 31(3), 1989, A. Sivanandan had described New Labour as 'Thatcherism in drag' even before it took power.

14   Alex Callinicos, *The Revenge of History: Marxism and the East European Revolutions*, Cambridge: Polity Press, 1991.

15   For a fuller examination of this phenomenon, see Aijaz Ahmad, 'Islam, Islamism and the West' in Leo Panitch and Colin Leys, eds, *Socialist Register 2008: Global Flashpoints*, London: Merlin Press, 2007; and Aziz al-Azmeh, *Islams and Modernities*, London: Verso, 2009, particularly chapter 10 in this expanded 3rd edition. For all the anti-imperialist pretensions among some jehadi tendencies, there is copious literature documenting collusion between the US and political Islam throughout the Cold War period, culminating in the creation of a fully-fledged Jehadi International to fight against the

communist government of Afghanistan and its Soviet allies. Robert Dreyfuss offers a reliable account of that collusion in *Devil's Game: How the United States Helped Unleash Political Islam*, New York: Dell Publishing, 2005.

16 Unless the Corbyns and the Sanderses have surprises in store for us. The worst in history is reversible.

THE CONTRADICTIONS OF GLOBAL MIGRATION

ADAM HANIEH

In the wake of Donald Trump's 2016 election victory, commentators have frequently pointed to the new administration's erratic style of governance, constant policy reversals, and apparent lack of strategic vision. In spite of this seeming chaos, however, there is one consistent anchor to both Trump's political messaging and practice: the claim that weak borders and lax immigration laws constitute an existential threat to the fabric of US society. Unlike the zigzagging seen in other policy areas, Trump's heavily racialized discourse has steadfastly vilified migrants as the root cause of numerous ills – poverty, crime, terrorism, low wages, and unemployment. Emblematic of social decay in general, the image of the migrant has come to symbolize danger and criminality in Trump's steady stream of twitter tirades: these are people who would never 'go back to their huts', 'the animals that we've been protecting for so long', and by whom 'our country is being stolen'. While it is essential not to forget the *actual* anti-migrant record of the Obama administration – indeed, the annual rates of migrant deportation and arrests in the three years of Obama's first term were more than double that of Trump's first year[1] – the willingness of Trump to openly articulate such repugnant tropes marks a rhetorical break with preceding years. Such language has not only helped normalize racist and white supremacist movements across the US, it has been central to Trump's carefully cultivated image of maverick-outsider, detached from the accepted niceties of conventional bourgeois politics.

In all of this, Trump's rise has aligned seamlessly with the startling renewal of right-wing populism and nativist forces throughout the rest of the world. These movements deploy a wide range of symbolic referents, with varying material roots that have found fertile ground in the decades-long crisis of social democracy; but what is most striking about the current conjuncture is how the question of migration has been rendered so central to all political speech. Debates over national security, economic growth, crime, the erosion of public services, and even ecological sustainability are inevitably framed as issues of migration; while struggles over the meaning, causes, and implications of migration shape the constellation of political power and forms of popular mobilization at every level. The movement of people across (and within) borders has been entwined with the development of capitalism since its origins – but there has rarely been a period in modern history where political discourse has been so pervasively saturated by the figure of the migrant.

Why is this so? What is it about the present moment that has propelled the issue of migration to the centre of political debate, and how should we respond to the emergence of Trumpism and other anti-migrant movements across the globe? For many, the answers to these questions are largely found at an ideological level, with the rise of a newly branded right representing a resurgence of protectionism, a narrow parochial outlook, and a national chauvinism epitomized in slogans such as 'Make America Great Again'. One liberal response to this has been to reassert a universalism based on human rights and international norms, emphasising respect for the dignity of refugees and other kinds of migrants, the provision of humanitarian assistance, and the meeting of government obligations under international law. In place of the foreign 'threat', a welcoming attitude to migrants is said to offer considerable benefits to host countries – bringing skills, entrepreneurial dynamism, demographic growth, and increased consumer demand.

Such positive framings of migration can be found across the political spectrum – from business leaders arguing that migrants are vital for firms to meet their skilled labour needs, to politicians depicting migrants as a necessary source of population growth in the face of slowing birth rates, and NGOs in the US and UK asking us to imagine what a 'day without immigrants' would look like. Yet while providing a counterweight to overt racist stereotyping, such arguments in defence of migration frequently reinforce the implicit categories of 'deserving' and 'non-deserving' migrants, with a balance sheet ultimately measured in relation to an ill-defined national good. The bogey of the 'good' migrant versus the 'bad' emerges, and the policy challenge becomes one of managing, identifying, and filtering the movement of people across borders in accordance with the needs of the national economy.

Running through all these perspectives is a conception of migration as a contingent epiphenomenon of the world economy; one that arises from a variety of factors 'somewhere else' and ends up at 'our' borders demanding a policy response. In this essay, I propose that this framing is not only false, but that it also leads to a set of political problems for those concerned with building campaigns to support migrant struggles today. In place of such perspectives, I argue that we need to situate migration as an internal feature of how capitalism actually functions at the global scale – a movement of people that is relentlessly generated by the movement of capital, and which, in turn, is constitutive of the concrete forms of capitalism itself. Only from this global perspective can we understand the recent rise of racism and xenophobia, and the profound changes in how borders operate and are managed throughout much of the world. Most importantly, such a perspective allows us to sketch what an effective solidarity with migrants might look like.

In making this argument, I focus on three interconnected features of migration in the current period. First, I examine how migration arises from the inherent dynamics of capitalism: a totalising system of accumulation that continually generates multiple forms of dispossession. Within this process, the movement of people across borders becomes an essential factor in how class formation – of both labour *and* capital – actually occur. Such an approach runs counter to standard neoclassical and institutionalist explanations of the drivers of migration, which typically focus on individual choice and so-called 'push'/'pull' factors. For Marxists, as I explore further below, foregrounding migration in capitalism (and vice-versa) carries a range of significant implications for how we think concretely about categories such as class in the global economy.

I then turn to look at the instrumental role of borders in these dynamics, analysing the ways in which borders act to demarcate various forms of difference within national and global labour markets (including the value of labour power, and the construction of categories such as race and illegality). Through this differentiation, borders act as filters, mediating the concrete ways that classes come into being. There have been major transformations in how borders and migration policy operate across the world over recent times, including: (1) the securitization of borders; (2) the growing weight of private capital in migration and border management; and (3) so-called extra-territorialization, where responsibility for border controls is increasingly offloaded to third countries. These changes have occurred as part of the mantra of 'managed migration' that continues to dominate policy-making circles across the world, and I outline and examine some of their consequences below.

Finally, migration is also essential to how periods of crisis unfold and are perceived – a theme that is explored in the final section of this essay. Precisely because of the centrality of migration to capital accumulation, a very large proportion of the world's population has been integrated into global financial circuits through the sending and receiving of remittances. At moments of economic downturn, this relationship permits the (partial) spatial displacement of crisis through the corridors of migration and remittance flows. Moreover, migration itself is frequently portrayed in terms of 'crisis' – most notably in the case of the millions of people now displaced across the Middle East and around the Mediterranean Sea. In this latter case, I show how the framing of migration *as* crisis is being utilized as a means to further deepen neoliberal market-led development models throughout much of the affected region.

MIGRATION, DISPOSSESSION, AND CLASS

As with much conventional social science, standard explanations of migration typically take as their starting point a conception of society made up of rational, atomized individuals motivated by the desire to maximize self-interest. When faced by worsening conditions of income and employment at home, individuals make a self-interested choice to move to another location in search of better wages.[2] This process is often described through the terminology of 'push-pull' factors: migrants are pushed from a particular location, while simultaneously pulled by the lure of better conditions elsewhere. Within such accounts, the policy challenge becomes one of properly 'managing' migration to produce a positive sum outcome – matching labour-surpluses with labour-demand in an orderly fashion, and channelling migrant remittances in such a way that they can be an 'aid to development'.

In the academic literature, a range of probabilistic rational choice schemas have been developed to model such flows, encompassing factors such as the asymmetries of information on labour markets and wage rates, costs of journey, the chance of unemployment, and an assortment of other variables.[3] Beyond these mathematical complexities, however, the basic notion of 'push' and 'pull' has become part of the common-sense way of understanding contemporary cross-border migration. As the International Organization of Migration (IOM) puts it in their 2018 annual report on global migration:

> Factors underpinning migration are numerous, relating to economic prosperity, inequality, demography, violence and conflict, and environmental change. While the overwhelming majority of people migrate internationally for reasons related to work, family and study, many people leave their homes and countries for other compelling reasons, such as conflict, persecution and disaster.[4]

Such accounts have an alluring simplicity, and capture the obvious reality that – for a range of possible reasons – people move from where they are in order to seek better conditions of life elsewhere. But what usually goes unspoken in these kinds of 'push-pull' framings is their implicit view of the world market as a simple agglomeration of divided national territories whose developmental trajectories are externally related to one another.[5] Despite the clear sympathies that organizations like IOM and a range of other international institutions may demonstrate with the plight of migrants and refugees, the reasons behind displacement are almost always explained as purely contingent factors whose causes are to be found simply at the point of origin, unrelated to the policies that richer countries may pursue overseas, or the systemic patterns of unevenness that capitalism incessantly breeds.

In contrast, if we insist that the forms of power and accumulation within global capitalism act to generate and exacerbate the social conditions that push people to migrate, while *simultaneously* contributing to the wealth of core zones such as the US and EU, then it makes little sense to think about migration from the vantage point of territorialized silos of individualized choice. The conditions underlying migration are produced by the very nature of capital accumulation and the hierarchies that sustain it, including features such as imperialist war, economic and ecological crises, and the deep-seated neoliberal restructuring of recent decades. The latter factor is almost always ignored in popular discussions of migration, as it directly implicates Western states and international financial institutions in producing displacement and dispossession.[6] Seen from such a perspective, the uneven and combined development that typifies contemporary capitalism means that the 'pull' is causally linked to the 'push' (and vice-versa) in a mutually reinforcing process. In this sense, as David Bacon has compellingly argued in relation to Mexican migration to the US, it is capitalism's undermining of 'the right to stay home' that has actually made the 'right to move' such a perilous imperative.[7]

Framing migration through the dynamics of capital accumulation at the global scale highlights a further critical insight into what happens to people when they move: through the very dispossession that generates movements of people across (and within) borders, migration comes to powerfully shape processes of class formation in specific national contexts. Of course this connection between capitalism and migrant labour is not new – as Cedric Robinson reminds us in relation to Europe: 'there has never been a moment … that migratory and/or immigrant labor was not a significant aspect of European economies'.[8] Indeed, the origins of the modern world system were underpinned by the forced transfer of millions of enslaved people from the African continent – and such movements continued through the indentured labour programmes of the nineteenth and twentieth centuries, mass migrations to the settler-colonies, and the European 'guest worker' schemes established in the wake of World War II.[9] However, alongside the deep restructuring of the global economy over the last four decades, there have been numerous major shifts in the key patterns of international migration. These include an increased predominance of South-South migration flows, the growing feminization of migrant labour, and the proliferation of temporary labour migration schemes that connect labour markets in the North and South.[10]

At the most fundamental level, these emerging migration patterns are strongly associated with transformations in the nature of capitalist accumulation. For instance, the fact that a very high proportion of migrants now move along South-South corridors – often clustering in special economic zones located on borders, and producing goods within regional production chains – is partly indicative of the regionalization of capitalist production circuits, and the emergence of new poles of accumulation in places such as East Asia.[11] The role that women migrants play in 'global care chains' is closely connected to the erosion of welfare provisions in North America and the EU, with social reproduction tasks externalized through drawing on the labour of women from poorer countries who, in turn, must then find ways to meet their own care needs.[12] In Canada, the astonishing rise of temporary migrant work programs in agriculture, service, and domestic work have been integral to the implementation of austerity and the re-regulation of Canadian labour markets.[13] Many more examples could be given, but the essential point is that the key characteristics of contemporary migration – the principal corridors along which people move, the kinds of work they perform, the ways in which these flows are gendered, racialized, and spatially clustered – can tell us a great deal about the underlying dynamics of capitalist accumulation and economic restructuring.

Migration and the concept of the working class

One of the conclusions arising from this fundamental role of migrant labour in many sectors of the world economy is that we need to expand our conceptualization of class away from container-like views of national scale, breaking with the often-unconscious assumptions that limit class to those who hold citizenship. Class is not simply an abstract category describing a certain relationship to the reproduction of capital and surplus value within national spaces; at a concrete level, it comes into being through the interlinking of geographical spaces and is continually forged through the flows (and displacement) of human beings across borders. In this manner, migration can be seen *as* a process of class formation, a means by 'which capitalist states create, mobilize, equip and reorganize the workforce, and the population as a whole'.[14] The fact that we tend to lose sight of this reality points to a persistent methodological nationalism within much of the political economy literature, a view that tends to frame categories such as 'working class' through the lens of national identity, citizenship, and state borders.[15]

Foregrounding our conception of the working class *in* migration (and vice-versa) raises several implications for how we understand cross-border movements of people. First, it forces much greater attention onto the ways in which migration flows are gendered and racialized in specific and often unique ways. In this respect, as is elaborated further below, borders play a critical role in sifting and categorising populations along particular lines, setting up 'discourses of race and racialized hierarchies … [and acting] as mechanisms of social, political, and economic control'.[16] For women migrant workers in particular, the types of transnational circuits that have emerged around sectors such as care and domestic work have had profound impacts on household structures across the globe. Women migrants have also been a major – and, in some cases, predominant – source of factory and agriculture labour throughout much of the South, with countries such as China, Thailand, and Mexico, drawing upon gendered forms of violence and exploitation to accentuate the 'disposable' nature of female, migrant workforces.[17] Placing migration at the centre of contemporary processes of class formation demands an irrevocable break with the old stereotypes of what labour is supposed to look like and where it occurs; thinking through these categories of class, race, and gender as internal-relations and not as separate or dichotomized aspects of social existence is essential to comprehending the nature of migration today.[18]

Second, approaching migration in all its diverse forms as a basic feature of class formation implies moving beyond the sharp dichotomization between forced and 'economic migration' that is typically found in mainstream debates. Such typologies tend to overlook the systemic compulsion to sell one's labour power that sits at the heart of capitalist accumulation and which encompasses *all* migrants – including those displaced by war, conflict, or other disasters. Although the proximate reasons for why people move varies in multiple ways – the question of how people inevitably become *classed* in the process of their dispossession is crucial to unpack. Refugees are workers too – often precarious, unemployed, or pushed to the shadows of underground economies – but nonetheless, they form a vital part of how working classes are constituted (and exploited) in many places around the world (including the Middle East, Europe, and Africa). The left needs to much more closely examine the ways in which refugees are integrated into the making of capitalist economies, not treat them simply as passive objects of humanitarian support and aid.

Finally, such a global perspective on class and migration extends not only to people on the move, but also to the potential pools of migrant labour that can be drawn upon by capital when needed, and whose presence enters into the calculation of the value of labour power.[19] Marx insisted we think of the reserve army of labour as *part of* the working class; just because these workers happen to exist outside the borders of where they may be seeking work, makes them no less essential to the constitution of the category of class. Perhaps nowhere is this more clearly illustrated than the Gulf Arab states, the most important zone of South-South migration today, where temporary migrant workers make up more than half of the total labour force and many more millions of people from South Asia, the Middle East, and Africa constitute an additional reserve army of labour that can be contracted as needed. The presence of these surplus populations – mediated by border controls and differential citizenship rights – means that the value of labour power (understood in a Marxian sense) is not simply determined within the borders of the Gulf states, but depends to a great degree on the costs of reproducing labour power found in surrounding regions.

In short, migration is both generated *by* processes of global accumulation and simultaneously constitutive *of* the concrete forms of class and capital that exist throughout a highly internationalized world market. Precisely because migrants are from 'over there' – and can thus be constructed as 'categories of workers with different sets of rights tied to their immigration status'[20] – they form a significant part of the precarious and highly exploitable layers of the international working class. Whether it be the Burmese migrant workers found in economic zones at the Thai border,[21] Zimbabwean women migrants in South Africa,[22] or the undocumented refugees labouring in the agricultural fields of Southern Europe – migrants constitute a mobile army of international labour that originates in the displacement generated by capitalism's unevenness, and whose peripatetic wanderings feed capitalist accumulation across the world.

Migration and capitalist class formation

Paralleling migration's central role in the making of international labour markets is its growing significance in how capitalist classes are also constituted. This aspect of contemporary migration is often overlooked, but is essential to capturing the complex intersections of migration and class formation. Although absolute numbers may be very small relative to total migration flows, there is a clear strategic orientation by many ruling-class families across the globe to seek second passports or multiple residency rights outside of their home countries. These new forms of 'strategic'[23] or 'flexible'[24] citizenship provide a means for wealthy individuals to overcome restrictions on movement, exploit national differences in tax regulations, and secure their fortunes safely outside of their domestic jurisdictions (including wealth earned illicitly). Reflecting this shift, 'dual nationality' is now an accepted and standard category of status – indeed, by 2010 around four-fifths of countries in Europe and the Americas permitted the holding of multiple citizenships, a figure that had grown from less than one-third in 1990.[25]

A revealing indication of how this form of 'capitalist migration' has become not only normalized but also actively encouraged is the widespread proliferation of Citizenship by Investment Programmes (CIP), which allow the direct purchase of residency rights and a fast-track to citizenship for those able to afford it. Virtually all of the major capitalist states have introduced such routes to citizenship over the last decade, with minimum prices ranging from around US$500,000 in various European countries and the US, to between £2-10 million in the UK. CIPs and similar 'golden visa' schemes are frequently aimed at elites whose origins lie outside of North America and Europe – indeed, wealth advisory firms involved in facilitating the purchase of citizenship estimate that the vast majority of buyers now come from China, Russia, India, and the Middle East. China, in particular, stands out; according to research conducted by Associated Press, wealthy Chinese have taken more than 70 per cent of investor visas offered by the US, Australia, and Portugal over the last decade, and are the top recipients of such visas in Canada, the United Kingdom, New Zealand, Spain, Hungary and Malta.[26]

Through such programmes, the granting of citizenship and residency rights has itself become commodified, deployed by states in an attempt to attract pools of surplus capital from around the world. Often these capital flows are specifically directed into investments in real estate and the built environment – helping buttress the more general phenomenon of inflationary real estate bubbles in major global cities – or are earmarked for government bonds and special investment funds. For the UK, where a golden visa programme was introduced in 2008, the total amount of investment earned through the scheme is estimated to have reached at least £3.18 billion by 2015, with more than 60 per cent of successful applicants coming from China and Russia.[27] In the US, over $18 billion worth of investment entered the country through its equivalent EB-5 visa programme between 2008 and 2017, with much of this going into real estate and hotel development.[28] The tiny Caribbean country of St. Kitts and Nevis – where a passport costs a mere $250,000 and offers visa-free access to over 139 states, including the UK and all European Union countries – saw income from its CIP provide a staggering 14 per cent of GDP in 2014.[29] Since the Eurozone crisis of 2012, numerous EU countries – including Portugal, Spain, Malta, Greece, and Cyprus – have also launched CIPs or similar visa schemes in an attempt to attract funds into flailing economies. In these European cases, the guarantee of mobility within the Schengen area acts to further augment the price of citizenship.[30]

Paraphrasing the *Communist Manifesto*, Harpaz and Mateos have noted how these tendencies towards commodification point to the 'tearing-away of the sentimental veil' that traditionally marked notions of citizenship.[31] Although freedom of movement and the ability to settle in places such as the North America and Europe have always been relatively dependent upon access to wealth and resources, the naked cash nexus underpinning these contemporary programmes – and the ease with which citizenship can be obtained for those with the necessary funds – shows how migration is increasingly implicated in capitalist class formation at a global scale. The composition of capitalist classes has come to straddle multiple geographical spaces and citizenships, a fact that disrupts any simple notions of a 'national bourgeoisie' framed through a singular or distinct national identity.

Most importantly, the cross-border movement of capitalists and other wealthier elites (such as well-educated professionals, managers, and so forth) needs to be situated alongside the forms of migration discussed in the preceding section. Through integrating into the accumulation circuits of Western states as *citizens*, these individuals also become part of the class structure of migrant communities themselves. By virtue of their wealth and access to political power, this can often establish intra-community dynamics marked by exploitative patronage networks and a widening differentiation of socio-economic interests that cuts against a supposed shared national identity. Moreover, the migration of these elites can also deepen and institutionalize class distinctions in their countries of origin – enhanced mobility and opportunities for education, employment, and wealth accumulation act to further amplify social gaps back home.

At the same time, this particular kind of migration is closely bound up with the highly unstable contradictions that mark the present moment. Despite its financial lure, the ease of movement of non-Western capitalist elites often does not sit comfortably with the racist and xenophobic discourse unleashed by Trump and European leaders – a discourse that is profoundly accentuated at times of social and economic crisis. The fact that wealthy Chinese and Russians have been such eager customers of fast-track routes to Western citizenship stands in contrast with the escalating tensions around trade and geopolitics that have marked the most recent period. It is impossible to forecast the future course of these tensions, but the opposing tendencies of integration and fragmentation that always mark capitalist class formation – and which are now partially constituted at the level of the world market through the phenomenon of capitalist migration – will undoubtedly shape the course of world politics in significant and unpredictable ways over the coming years.

BORDERS, RACE, AND ILLEGALITY

Clearly emerging from the foregoing discussion is the manifold significance of borders in differentially mediating flows of people, the value of labour power, and the subjective identities (of both migrants and non-migrants) that arise around these processes.[32] As I emphasized, it is important not to consider borders as pre-given, static containers, or the simple outcome of historical contingencies. Rather, state borders are produced as part of the necessary territorialization of social relations within a world market divided between competing capitals.[33] Paolo Novak has observed that it is through the production of such territorialized spaces that 'various social forces heterogeneously configure themselves'.[34] Borders thus underpin and help to create difference within the social, providing 'socio-spatial criteria for defining and identifying a "here" and a "there", (some of) "us" and "them", and what/who is and is not'.[35] Indeed, as Nicholas De Genova reminds us, without borders the category of migration would simply not exist – we would speak only of mobility.[36]

The concrete implications of this can be seen in the processes of racialization that shape the making of migrant working classes. The ideological tropes of criminality, desperation, violence, and cultural 'pollution', that animate the xenophobic discourses of the Trump administration and a slew of right-wing forces are functionally dependent upon the presence of borders. Precisely because the border acts to demarcate spatial difference – the 'over there', the 'foreign', or 'other' – they are a necessary element to how migrants are racially constructed. A corollary of this is that attempts to 'illegally' cross borders are construed as transgressions against the national body – an ever-looming threat to the supposed ordered purity of national identity. The infamous poster used by UKIP during the UK Brexit referendum – a long line of refugees pictured as marching upon Europe, emblazoned with the slogan 'Breaking Point' – powerfully illustrates how this sense of threat is racially configured through the image of border transgression.

In the current conjuncture, all of this helps explain the singular obsession of mainstream politicians with the tightening of border controls and the increased use of racial categories for determining the entry of people into states. For the US, this has included the Trump administration's 'Muslim ban' and the promise to wall-out Central American migrants. The fact that the latter has also included a pledge to make Mexico pay for the wall is not simply a financial question, but also points to how the responsibility of border transgression has been ideologically configured as the 'fault' of Mexico and other Central American countries.[37] In Europe, we see the callous treatment of migrants trying to cross the Mediterranean, shoot-to-kill policies at the Greek-Turkey border, and the encampment of refugees in Greek islands.[38] Perhaps the world leader in this respect is Australia, where race-based entry policies have long been a central feature of immigration control, and the country's Minister for Immigration and Border Protection has recently called for the fast-tracking of special visas for white South African farmers, arguing that they face 'persecution' and 'horrific circumstances' in South Africa and thus deserve the protection of a 'civilized country'.[39]

While all of these examples certainly illustrate the rise of racist speech and practices against migrants – and overlap considerably with the sanitization of neo-fascist and right-wing forces within normal bourgeois political discourse – we should not lose sight of how these border processes act to produce and deepen precarity, and thereby drive down the cost of labour power. A key element to this is the generation of illegality.[40] By definition, borders allow some people in and block others from entering. Those who enter in an undocumented fashion are thus immediately cast into the most precarious of positions – unable to access the normal (although increasingly curtailed) advantages of citizenship, and facing an ever-present threat from the state.[41] This illegality is not an accidental by-product of how borders work but embedded in their very nature. It is also a critical element to how labour markets form in certain sectors. Capitalist globalization of food production, for example, has meant that agricultural sectors in places like Southern Europe and the United States now depend significantly upon such undocumented labour in the face of increased international competition and the downward pressure on production costs. Indeed, many sectors that have been unable to internationalize due to their inherent spatial fixity – such as construction, services, domestic and care work – have come to rely heavily upon undocumented and/or other forms of migrant labour in an attempt to reduce costs. In this sense, the primary effect of border controls is *not* the exclusion of undocumented workers, but rather the actual *creation* of illegality itself.[42]

'Managing' migration

Of course, as discussed above, not all migrants are created equal and neither are the experiences of borders. Once again, this is closely connected to the nature of contemporary capitalism – where transnational corporations operate across a variety of different national spaces and often cluster their 'command and control' functions in hubs aimed at specific regional markets. Such an internationalized world market has shaped the form of border control and migration policy for managerial and high-skilled labour, where freedom of movement has become a prerequisite for doing business. In this regard, various visa arrangements found across the world – such as the EU's Blue Card scheme, which facilitates easy movement into the EU, the ability to obtain citizenship, and the rights to resettle family – reflects a different side of how global labour markets are organized today.

All of this goes to illustrate how borders function as filters, rather than as impenetrable barriers – and from this perspective, oft-cited descriptions of current border policies (e.g. 'Fortress Europe') can be misleading, as they overlook the ways that borders act fundamentally as generators and markers of difference and inequality, not as absolute blocks to mobility.[43] In this context, there are a number of recent developments in border management and migration policy that are critical to unpack in greater detail. In all cases, these trends are closely connected to processes of neoliberal restructuring and the changing nature of state power – they thus provide further illustration of how the management of migration flows is coupled with contemporary forms of capital accumulation.

The first of these trends has been described as the 'securitization of migration'.[44] In line with the discussion above, this term refers to the ways in which migrants, asylum seekers, and refugees are increasingly mobilized and presented as a security threat. This discourse is articulated throughout the public sphere by politicians, the media, and political movements; and opens the way for the entry of a whole new range of bureaucratic practices at – and crucially inside – national borders. Such techniques involve heightened surveillance of borders and migrant populations, the erection of physical barriers such as walls and electric fences, the pervasive use of tracking technologies involving biometric data, the use of armed border patrols and drones, the profiling of populations and pre-emptive 'risk' assessments, and the widespread use of complex, internationally-linked databases that sift and sort people into various categories. Most significantly – and not at all surprising to any student of the late twentieth century – these new technologies of control have helped catalyze a reworking of bureaucratic power within states, positioning military and security forces at the center of opaque and unaccountable border and migration regimes. In this sense, securitization works to reinforce the more generalized authoritarian characteristics of contemporary neoliberal states. It thus needs to be viewed as a process not directed solely at migrants or encountered at the border crossing, but one that inevitably extends to the growing surveillance, monitoring, and cataloguing of all who live within the borders of the securitized state.

A little-noted feature of the securitization discourse is the way in which a rights-based language is increasingly employed as a means of supporting tightened border controls. The clearest example of this is the growing prominence of anti-trafficking and anti-slavery messaging within popular discussion and media coverage of migration. A number of scholars have provided powerful critiques of the ideological frames used by these campaigns – including Julie O'Connell Davidson's superb work on the concept of 'modern slavery' and the rhetoric of the 'new abolitionists', which she situates in a formidable and explicit critique of capitalism. Not only does Davidson show how the notion of modern slavery is cast as an aberrant violation to the supposed spirit of individual 'free choice' in normal wage labour, thereby removing any sense of compulsion from the labour-capital relation,[45] but she also demonstrates how 'the claim that "trafficking is nothing short of modern slavery" has been frequently and vigorously asserted' and how, because of this, 'any and all measures … can be presented as measures to protect the human rights of its victims'.[46] In this manner, the securitization of borders and the 'cracking down on "illegal immigration" becomes part of a fight to secure fundamental human rights, as opposed to implying a violation of those rights'.[47] Such language has become a ubiquitous feature of the ways in which migration is spoken about in mainstream political discourse. Ivanka Trump, for example, has made the issue of trafficking a signature element to her position as White House advisor, calling it a 'top priority for the Trump administration'. Similarly, during the Mediterranean migration 'emergency' of 2015, European leaders repeatedly conflated smugglers with trafficking, and thereby justified the heavy militarization of European borders in the name of defending the rightless against organized crime.

Closely related to securitization is a second shift in the nature of border regimes: the growing role of private capital and non-governmental bodies in managing migrant populations.[48] In this sense, the so-called migration crises of recent years have been accompanied by the opening of new market opportunities, which see private firms benefit from lucrative state contracts for operating detention and deportation centres, building the physical and technical infrastructure of securitized borders, and even direct involvement in the interdiction of migrant populations attempting to cross borders. This trend is exemplified in Trump's recent pronouncements on the building of 'the wall' on the Mexican-US border. Some estimates for the cost of this wall reach up to $14 billion, not including maintenance, the cost of border patrols, or the purchase of land from Texas property owners.[49] If previous work on US border infrastructure is any indication, prominent multinational companies, such as the US aerospace firm Boeing, and Israel's largest private defence contractor, Elbit Systems, will be likely beneficiaries of such funds. Further evidence of the profitable opportunities in migrant management can be seen in Europe, where the value of the border security market has been estimated at €15 billion in 2015, and is predicted to grow to 29 billion euros annually by 2022.[50] Many of the world's largest service delivery firms – such as G4S, Serco, Bouygues, and Veolia – are heavily enmeshed with the border security business through contracts for operating and maintaining migrant detention centres.[51] In this sense, migration management fits seamlessly with the general features of neoliberal restructuring – the outsourcing of state functions to powerful networks of private actors.

But the implications of this privatization of migration management must be understood beyond simply the expanding sphere of market relations. By displacing direct control away from state entities, private bodies (including NGOs and individual citizens) are drafted into the day-to-day responsibility for monitoring and controlling migrant populations.[52] Not only does this shift increase the vulnerability of migrants to violence, abuse, and poor detention conditions, it has also acted to diffuse and internalize the logic of securitization throughout the wider citizen population – private citizens become, in effect, an arm of state policy. Such trends are encountered throughout all Western states, including requirements for private landlords to check the migration status of tenants, university or staff who are compelled to monitor attendance and travel of international students. They also have important precursors in the ways citizen/non-citizen relations have been constructed in other non-Western states; scholars working on the Gulf Arab states, for example, have long noted how the control of migrant workers has been an important feature of binding citizen populations – both materially and ideologically – to state and ruling-class interests.[53]

A third and final trend in border and migration management has been the externalization or extra-territorialization of borders.[54] By this, borders and the control of migrant movement is pushed back onto the countries of origin and transit, rather than the countries of destination. This policy relies first and foremost on an approach that promises financial aid, trade and other commercial agreements, and visa liberalization policies (for select groups) to those countries willing to assist in controlling the movement of their populations. Such outsourcing of migration control to third countries is not a new phenomenon. Since 2001, Australia has led the way globally through the detention of refugees and asylum-seekers in detention centres on 'prison islands' outside of Australian territory. But since the so-called refugee crisis that unfolded in 2015, the European Union has been at the forefront of implementing these measures of extraterritorial control. To this end, the EU has signed a number of agreements since 2016 with countries in the Middle East and Africa, aiming to engage these non-European states in the control over migrant movement.

Such policies have effectively seen the wide scale enlistment of security and military forces across Africa and the Middle East into the policing of European borders. The close cooperation of these forces with the EU acts to exacerbate the root causes of migration, strengthening military regimes and authoritarian states and adding international legitimacy to those governments willing to act as *gendarmes* for European migration control. And because migrant journeys tend to involve crossing multiple countries on the way to Europe, externalization policies have pushed migrants into ever more dangerous routes. Some researchers have noted, for example, that more West African migrants have died attempting to cross the Saharan desert than the Mediterranean.[55] Moreover, the political justifications for these policies have relied heavily upon the rhetoric of 'protecting' migrants, with intelligence agencies such as the European Police Agency (Europol) drawn in to help countries 'tackle migrant smuggling and those who profit from it … [and] to take specific action against traffickers' networks'.[56] In this manner, the externalization of borders has worked to reinforce the framing of migrant mobility as a question of organized crime, which can only be halted through further securitization.

MIGRATION AND CRISIS[57]

Throughout this essay, I have emphasized that migration needs to be seen as a constitutive feature of global accumulation and integral to the ways in which classes form within and across national borders. A key consequence of this is that circuits of variable capital have also been extended geographically, with large bodies of the world's population dependent for their day-to-day reproduction upon remittance flows from family members working overseas. This is a trend that has been deeply accentuated through the years of neoliberal globalization; back in 1999, only eleven countries worldwide had remittances greater than 10 per cent of GDP; by 2016, this figure had risen to thirty countries.[58] In 2016, just over 30 per cent of all 179 countries for which data was available recorded remittance levels greater than 5 per cent of GDP – a proportion that has doubled since 2000. [59] Astonishingly, around one billion people – one out of seven people globally – are directly involved in remittance flows as either senders or recipients.[60] These remittance flows do not solely involve migrants working in core zones such as North America and the EU; according to the International Fund for Agricultural Development (IFAD), 'emerging markets' now account for '40 percent of global remittance in-and outflows', and just five of these countries – Kuwait, Qatar, Russia, Saudi Arabia, and the United Arab Emirates – are the source of one-fifth of all remittances sent home globally.[61]

These cross-border flows of money far exceed levels of foreign direct investment and official bilateral aid for many countries in the South, indicating that migration (and its associated remittance flows) is a major route through which much of the world's population is integrated into global capitalism. This fact compels us to place all the various trends mapped above – growing levels of xenophobia and racism, the securitization of borders, the overall precarity of migrant labour, and so forth – in their global context. The marginalization and exclusion of migrant workforces do not simply affect migrants directly in their countries of destination; such measures also constitute an attack on their families back home. They are part of capital's *global* offensive against workers, forming an intrinsic element to how imperialism actually functions in a concrete sense.

The full ramifications of these flows and linkages are most clearly illustrated during economic crises. At such times, migration and remittance corridors can act as transmission belts for economic downturn, allowing wealthier states to spatially displace the impact of crisis onto poorer zones of the world market. A clear example of this can be found in the case of Saudi Arabia, the world's second largest source of remittances (after the US). Following the oil price decline that set in mid-2014, Saudi Arabia began a programme of austerity and cutbacks to government expenditure on major infrastructure and construction projects. While these measures have significantly affected the Kingdom's economic growth, their major implications need to be viewed through migration and remittance flows. As Saudi firms shut down construction projects or placed them on hold, hundreds of thousands of migrant workers lost their jobs. Government-backed deportation campaigns began simultaneously, with millions of migrant workers rounded up and expelled. Between November 2014 and March 2015, the government reported that workers were being sent home at the astonishing rate of 2000 people per day;[62] by end-2015, the Interior Ministry claimed that more than 1.2 million workers had been removed from the country since the beginning of 2014.[63] Many of these workers – typically from South Asia,

Yemen, Ethiopia, and Somalia – were beaten and abused while in detention and awaiting deportation.[64] A further deportation campaign, dubbed 'A Nation without Violators', was announced on 19 March 2017, which sought to secure the removal of an additional one million migrant workers from Saudi Arabia (out of a total migrant population of 9-12 million, this figure represents around 10 per cent of the official non-citizen workforce). By the end of July 2017, over 600,000 workers had left the country as part of this new campaign according to media reports.[65]

One result of such redundancies and deportation campaigns was a startling drop in remittance flows from Saudi Arabia between 2015 and 2017, with absolute levels falling by over 13 per cent during the first quarter of 2017 compared to the same period in 2015.[66] This ongoing plunge in remittances – one that is replicated throughout other neighbouring Gulf states also grappling with the oil price decline – indicates that a class structure built around non-citizen labour has allowed Saudi Arabia to effectively displace a large part of the impact of economic downturn onto neighbouring countries through the channel of migration and remittances.[67] If this continues for any sustained period of time it could have critical outcomes for labour-sending countries. Across South Asia, for example, remittance inflows are greater than 5 per cent of GDP in Pakistan, Bangladesh, Sri Lanka, and Nepal (according to 2016 figures), and the vast majority of overseas workers from these countries – approaching 90 per cent in some cases – are located in the Gulf.[68] In this sense – and echoing the ways that we must move beyond methodologically nationalist perspectives on class formation – any analysis of the impact of crisis cannot be confined within the borders of the national scale.

Saudi Arabia and other Gulf states may appear as outliers in the global economy due to the preponderant weight of migrant flows in their labour forces and the specific ways in which boundaries between citizens and non-citizens are regulated and institutionalized, but these patterns should be viewed as a matter of degree rather than one of qualitative difference. In many ways, the Gulf can be seen as one of the models (alongside Australia) of how capitalism attempts to manage migration for the benefits of capital accumulation – differentiated rights accorded to people on the basis of citizenship and national origin; 'outsourcing' migration management to private citizens and firms; linking temporary work visas to status; blocking paths to citizenship and long-term residency except for wealthy foreign elites; and a vast apparatus of surveillance and securitization governing the control of migrant populations. To a considerable extent, the trends in migration policy that we now encounter in places such as the EU and North America are prefigured in the Gulf – including the ways in which economic crises tend to reverberate through the corridors established by migration flows.

Migration 'as' crisis

Of course, the relationship between migration and crisis extends beyond simply moments of economic downturn, with the movement of people across borders increasingly described in itself as an instantiation of social collapse and breakdown. This was perhaps no better illustrated than during 2015, as images of mass displacement from the Middle East and Africa played out on the Mediterranean Sea and the borders and streets of Western Europe. At this time, numerous commentators noted that the language of crisis played a powerful discursive role in further consolidating the militarization of borders and legitimating the politics of the right; the prevailing terms often drawing upon metaphors of water – 'flood', 'tide', 'wave', and 'tip of the iceberg'[69] – to position Europe as under siege from an unstoppable flow of people. The crisis was, in effect, reframed as one *of Europe* – to be met with tightened security, the externalization of borders, increased use of migrant detention, and further restrictions on the rights to asylum – rather than a crisis experienced by those who had been directly displaced.

What has gone largely unnoticed in these discussions, however, are the ways in which the language of crisis and the policies put in place to deal with refugees have played out in the Middle East itself, where catastrophic wars in Syria and elsewhere have led to the displacement of millions of people across the borders of neighbouring states (in addition to internal displacement on an unprecedented scale). In the case of Lebanon, for example, it is estimated that the population has increased by a remarkable 25 per cent since the onset of the war in Syria; Jordan has also seen a very large increase in numbers of Syrian refugees, now estimated at more than 650 thousand registered refugees and probably closer to one million in total. These two countries now host the highest proportion of refugees of any place in the world. Such mass levels of displacement show that if we are to justifiably speak about a 'refugee crisis', it is one largely experienced in the Middle East and not in Europe.

Such displacement has placed enormous pressures on both refugees themselves as well as their host communities, and international support has come in the form of billions of dollars in aid and the entry of a large number of humanitarian organizations into the region. Most revealing about this moment, however – poorly understood by most observers, who frame this largely through a humanitarian lens – is the way in which the displacement of refugees in the Middle East has been seized upon to further deepen and extend the sphere of the market. Ever vigilant to the openings presented by social breakdown, international financial institutions and Western states are using mass displacement to push forward a series of economic transformations that have previously been blocked or appeared difficult to implement. Echoing the notion of 'crisis as opportunity' that scholars have explored at other historical junctures,[70] the unprecedented displacement now occurring in the Middle East is being used to refashion economic policies and reconstitute the ties of debt and dependency that have characterized the region for many decades.

Striking confirmation of this came at the 'Supporting Syria & the Region Conference', a meeting convened in London in early February 2016 that was billed as a turning point in international donor support for Syrian refugees. Indeed, according to then-UK Prime Minister David Cameron, the conference saw a record in the amount of humanitarian funds ever raised in a one-day appeal. Beyond the headlines, however, the meeting's most substantial achievement was the recasting of Syrian refugees as justification for privatization and market liberalization in host countries. This was explicitly expressed in the conference's primary objective: 'turning the Syrian refugee crisis into a development opportunity',[71] through financial aid for programmes that 'expand investment, promote exports and public-private partnerships'.[72] As such, the vast majority of pledges came in the form of non-concessionary loans by international financial institutions – chiefly the World Bank, European Investment Bank, the European Bank for Reconstruction and Development (EBRD), and the Saudi-based Islamic Development Bank – that were linked to the acceptance of structural adjustment measures. The total amount of loans promised at the conference reached US$41 billion (of which only $1.7 billion worth were earmarked as concessionary), compared to US$5.9 billion in bilateral humanitarian support.[73] In this manner, the deepening of neoliberal structural adjustment throughout the Middle East – a region that has long experienced the disastrous consequences of such measures[74] – was championed as a humanitarian solution to the 'refugee crisis'.

Jordan, as one of the principal host countries of Syrian refugees, has witnessed this twinning of refugee crisis and neoliberal reform most directly. Addressing the 2016 EBRD Annual Meeting and Business Forum, a Jordanian government representative confirmed that the 'Supporting Syria' conference committed Jordan to improving its 'business and investment environment' and to 'tak[e] forward a detailed plan on measures and structural reforms needed in this regard ... [including] incentives that can be offered to domestic and international investors'.[75] Along these lines, the needs of Syrian refugees have become a major driving factor behind privatization in Jordan; including recent PPPs in energy, wastewater, and education. According to Mouayed Makhlouf, the Middle East head of the International Finance Corporation (the private sector arm of the World Bank), his institution's 'championing of PPPs for the past seven or eight years' is a direct response to the influx of Syrian refugees. 'If you look at places like Jordan, Lebanon, and to a certain extent Iraq, in some places populations have increased by 30 percent or more, so demand on public services has increased manifold … The need is greater than ever for the private sector to step up to fill the gaps the public sector has not been able to fill.'[76] In a related sense, the Jordanian government has worked closely with the European Union to establish special economic zones that draw upon low-wage Syrian refugee labour in return for preferential trade access to European markets.[77] This EU-Jordan Compact is an integral feature of the European Union's wider goal of deepening market liberalization and free trade in countries throughout the Middle East; indeed, its text explicitly confirms that the Compact is part of enhancing the EU's efforts 'to improve [Jordan's] business climate and to implement structural reforms to enhance productivity and labour market condition'.[78]

Several commentators have rightly noted that these policies are closely connected to the securitization of migration and the attempt to push the responsibility for 'warehousing' surplus populations onto countries distant from Western borders.[79] But such policies go far beyond the goal of simply filtering entry into Western states: they also point to how the management of the 'migrant and refugee crisis' in the Middle East is wielded as a means of recasting neoliberal measures as humanitarian solutions. This is increasingly true at an international level, with humanitarian intervention around refugees acting as leverage for wider economic change and helping to further consolidate the power of dominant states and international financial institutions. The tragic urgency of the present becomes a clarion call for accelerated reform, while the outcomes of previous rounds of restructuring are absolved of any responsibility for contemporary conditions. Once again, we can see the indissoluble bond between forms of capitalist development and the movement of people across borders – constitutive elements to how crises are experienced, projected, and resolved.

CONCLUSION

The philosopher Thomas Nail has recently presented an excoriating critique of the taken-for-granted assumptions about stasis, citizenship, and the fixity of borders that underlie many of our conceptions of the modern (and ancient) world. In place of these assumptions, Nail has called for a methodological re-centring of political theory on what he calls 'kinopolitics' – the study of people on the move. Utilizing this focus on movement, Nail argues that migration represents a form of 'social expulsion' with roots in specific and ongoing historical conditions, and which to varying degrees involves a loss in territorial, political, juridical, or economic status. Seen from this perspective, 'contemporary migration is not a secondary phenomenon that simply occurs between states. Rather, [it] is the primary condition by which something like societies and states is established in the first place ... expulsion of the migrant is a condition for social expansion and reproduction: it is constitutive.'[80]

Such an approach affirms many of the arguments of this essay. Placing migration at the centre of capitalism's wider logics and its crisis tendencies allows us to see the movement of people across borders as fundamentally a process of class formation – one situated in a deeply-integrated world market, in which the key migrant-destination countries are directly implicated in generating the patterns of dispossession and unevenness that drive people from their homes in the first place. Seen from this vantage point, flows of people across borders are simultaneously an outcome of – and constitutive element to – capitalism's concrete forms of existence. Such an approach helps to unpack the dichotomous ideological forms that run through standard typologies of migration – most notably classifications such as forced/economic/trafficked/slave – while also demonstrating how the principal patterns of migration reinforce and reflect the shifting nature of capitalist accumulation at the global scale. Borders play a fundamental role in all of this, mediating the value of labour power and differentiating populations through categories of race, status, and access to rights.

It is beyond the scope of this essay to fully explore the ramifications of this for left political strategy, labour, and other social movements, but some concluding remarks are in order. First, for activists in the West, it is necessary to fully reject the widely prevalent liberal politics that frames the defence of migrants and migration on the basis of economic 'worth', societal 'contribution', or legal status. Implicit to such approaches is a separation of the 'push' and the 'pull' – a refusal to admit the complicity of Western states in sustaining and exacerbating the conditions that cause dispossession across the globe.[81] Instead, effective struggles against anti-migrant racism must be based upon a politics that continually foregrounds opposition to the forces driving forms of capitalist development across the world; an internationalism that links conditions at home to those existing overseas. Precisely because of the ways in which capitalism works to generate the circumstances that compel people to move in the first place – and depends so fundamentally on the results of such dispossession as a means of governing the conditions of labour *in general* – struggles against imperialism and the global neoliberal offensive are elemental to defending and extending all workers' rights. Such an approach helps counter the implicit social chauvinism that judges migration from the citizen-centric perspective of the 'national good', and recaptures the meaning of international solidarity as an organic and necessary component of a left politics qualitatively different from simple charity or benevolence.

Of course the particular forms this might take differ from country to country and depend heavily on the state of the labour movement, the concrete ways that migrant labour has been incorporated into capitalist accumulation within specific national contexts, and the levels of self-organization and combativeness of migrant workers themselves.[82] In many cases, migrant workers organize largely outside the confines of bureaucratized and top-down labour unions, and can challenge these organizations claims to represent the interests of all workers and thereby help to revitalize independent forms of worker organization. A particularly important model is found in the migrant worker centres that exist in numerous countries and have effectively fused a migrant-led, community-based politics with a clear orientation to labour militancy and class politics. In other places, established trade unions have managed to successively incorporate migrant workers and effectively open space to rank-and-file activism by migrants themselves. This is critically important. Precisely because migrant workers tend to be found at the front edge of labour market deregulation and flexibilization – such as the increased use of temporary labour schemes, and the proliferation of subcontracting agencies – they often lead resistance to such measures *before* they rollout to wider sectors of the class.[83] As a result, migrant workers are increasingly 'defining the organisational form of workers and unions' and are 'a source of new forms of labour organising as well as a potential force to rethink and reshape traditional union politics'.[84]

What is striking about any survey of migrant worker experiences across the world is how much patterns and forms of organizing are dependent upon historical precedents, levels of militancy, and subjective conditions found in cities, workplaces, or individual union branches. Yet in all these spaces, successful examples of migrant worker organizing tend to confirm the importance of breaking with narrowly economistic models that are confined simply to the immediate workplace. Even more than non-migrants, the political and social conditions that migrants face in their wider communities and households – questions of racism, sexism, immigration status, threats of deportation, criminalization, and so on – are elemental parts to their lives as workers. These conditions of social existence are ultimately effects of the 'border imperialism'[85] on which the political economy of migration so crucially depends, and for this reason are a critical feature of migrant worker organizing and left politics more generally. Campaigns against border violence, deportations and detention centres; supporting migrants in legal matters and other day-to-day engagements with the state; ensuring access to services such as healthcare, education, childcare, language training, and so forth; and, perhaps most importantly, fighting for the regularization of status for those who may be temporary, undocumented or deemed 'illegal' – these are all issues *of* and *for* labour. 'Immigrant rights are worker's rights', as the old slogan reminds us.

All of these issues present substantial challenges to the left and traditional trade unions, particularly when they are considered on an international scale where the barriers to transnational organizing and solidarity are immense. But in this era of Trump and rising right-wing populism – movements that are in themselves organized globally – we cannot cede ground to racism and anti-migrant sentiment, nor retreat into views of 'the worker' that are blinkered by the bunkers of nationality and citizenship. Migration and the ways that borders function are fundamental to how class is both made and lived in contemporary capitalism. In this fact ultimately lies an opportunity – one that is a central to any renewal and growth of socialist politics today.

NOTES

1   Migration Policy Institute, 'Revving Up the Deportation Machinery: Enforcement and Pushback under Trump', MPI: Washington D.C., May 2018, p. 2.

2   W. A. Lewis, 'Economic Development with Unlimited Supplies of Labour', *Manchester School of Economic and Social Studies*, 22, 1954, pp. 139-91; J. Harris and M. Todaro, 'Migration, Unemployment and Development: A Two Sector Analysis', *American Economic Review*, 60(1), 1970, pp. 126-42.

3   The classic approach is the Harris-Todaro (H-T) model, which was originally developed in 1970 by two US economists to explain rural to urban migration. Since that time, the H-T model has undergone numerous refinements. In February 2011, the *American Economic Review* described the original article as one of the twenty most important and influential pieces the journal had published in one hundred years of its history.

4   International Organization of Migration (IOM), *World Migration Report 2018*, Geneva: IOM, 2017, p. 13.

5   Adam Hanieh, 'Overcoming Methodological Nationalism: Spatial Perspectives on Migration to the Gulf Arab States', in A. Khalaf, O. Shehabi and A. Hanieh, eds, *Transit States: Labour, Migration and Citizenship in the Gulf*, London: Pluto Press 2015, p. 65.

6   Some exceptions include Adam Hanieh, *Lineages of Revolt: Issues of Contemporary Capitalism in the Middle East*, Chicago: Haymarket Books, 2013; Hannah Cross, *Migrants, Borders and Global Capitalism: West African Labour Mobility and EU Borders*, London and

New York: Routledge 2013; Aziz Choudry and Adrian Smith, *Unfree Labour? Struggles of Migrant and Immigrant Workers in Canada*, Oakland: PM Press, 2016; David Bacon, *The Right to Stay Home: How Us Policy Drives Mexican Migration*, Boston: Beacon Press, 2013.

7   Bacon, *The Right to Stay Home*.

8   Cedric J. Robinson, *Black Marxism: The Making of the Black Radical Tradition*, Chapel Hill & London: University of North Carolina Press, 2000, p. 23.

9   Stephen Castles and Godula Kosack, 'The Function of Labour Immigration in Western European Capitalism', *New Left Review*, 73, 1972, pp. 3-21.

10   IOM, *World Migration Report*.

11   Dennis Arnold and John Pickles 'Global Work, Surplus Labor, and the Precarious Economies of the Border', *Antipode*, 43(5), 2011, pp. 1598-1624; Dae-Oup Chang, 'Informalising Labour in Asia's Global Factory', *Journal of Contemporary Asia*, 39(2), 2009, pp. 161-79.

12   Amaia Pérez Orozco, 'Global Care Chains', Gender, Migration and Development Series Working Paper 2, United Nations International Research and Training Institute for the Advancement of Women, 2009; Nicola Yeates, 'Global Care Chains: A State-of-the-Art Review and Future Directions in Care Transnationalization Research', *Global Networks*, 12(2), 2012, pp. 135-54.

13   Choudry and Smith, 'Unfree Labour?'

14   Gareth Dale, 'Leaving the Fortresses: Between Class Internationalism and Nativist Social Democracy', 30 November 2017, *Viewpoint Magazine*, available at: www.viewpointmag.com.

15   Robinson, *Black Marxism*, p. 24.

16   Choudry and Smith, 'Unfree Labour?', p. 24.

17   Sue Ferguson and David McNally, 'Precarious Migrants: Gender, Race and the Social Reproduction of a Global Working Class', in Leo Panitch and Greg Albo, eds, *Socialist Register 2015: Transforming Classes*, 2014, pp. 1-23.

18   Himani Bannerji, *Thinking Through: Essay on Marxism, Feminism and Anti-Racism*, Toronto: Women's Press, 1995.

19   Adam Hanieh, *Capitalism and Class in the Gulf Arab States*, New York: Palgrave-Macmillan 2011, pp. 177-180.

20   Aziz Choudry and Mondli Hlashtawayo, eds, *Just Work? Migrant Workers' Struggles Today*, London: Pluto Press 2016, p. 5.

21   Arnold and Pickles 'Global Work, Surplus Labor'.

22   Mondli Hlashtawayo, 'Xenophobia, Resilience, and Resistance of Immigrant Workers in South Africa: Collective and Individual Responses', in Choudry and Hlashtawayo, eds, *Just Work?*.

23   Yossi Harpaz and Pablo Mateos, 'Strategic Citizenship: Negotiating Membership in the Age of Dual Nationality', *Journal of Ethnic and Migration Studies*, 2018.

24   Aihwa Ong, *Flexible Citizenship: The Cultural Logics of Transnationality*. Durham, NC: Duke University Press 1999.

25   Harpaz and Mateos 'Strategic Citizenship', p. 4.

26   CBS News, 'Chinese Investors Spent $24B on 'Golden Visas' in U.S. and Elsewhere', 12 May 2017, available at www.cbsnews.com.

27   Transparency International, *Gold Rush: Investment Visas and Corrupt Capital Flows into the UK*, 2015, p. 11.

28   Rene Rodriguez, Jennifer Lu, and Glenn Garvin, 'These Visas May Vanish, Even Though They Have Paid For Lots of Miami Buildings', *Miami Herald,* 24 July 2017.

29   International Monetary Fund, 'Article IV Consultation and First Post-Program Monitoring Discussions, St. Kitts and Nevis', IMF: Washington, D.C, 2015, p. 8.

30   Notably, some prominent economists are now calling for all forms of migration to be commodified in this manner. Writing in the *Wall Street Journal*, Nobel laureate Gary Becker and Edward Lazear, the former chair of the president's Council of Economic Advisers (2006-09), recently argued for a 'market solution to immigration reform' through which the US would scrap its current immigration policy and make *all* citizenship available for sale. ('A Market Solution to Immigration Reform', *Wall Street Journal*, 1 March 2013.) US think tanks such as the Hoover and Bush Institutes have endorsed the idea, with the latter claiming that 'where demand for a resource [such as citizenship] greatly exceeds the supply of it, utilizing the price system is an efficient way to allocate the scarce resource. By selling the resource, those who value it the most highly will be willing to pay a high price … this ensures that the resource in question goes to where it is most valued, which is the efficient outcome.' See: Matthew Denhart, 'Becker and Lazear on Market-Based Immigration Reform', George W. Bush Institute, 13 March 2013, available at https://www.bushcenter.org. Similarly, other scholars have argued on philosophical grounds that such a market-based system for citizenship would provide the best allocation of scarce resources, even proposing that future income streams of migrants could be securitized and sold to investors prior to admitting prospective citizens to the country (Christopher Frieman, 'The Case for Markets in Citizenship, *Journal of Applied Philosophy*, 2017, p. 6).

31   Harpaz and Mateos, 'Strategic Citizenship', p. 8.

32   Nandita Sharma, 'Nation States, Borders, Citizenship, and the Making of 'National' Difference', in Deborah Brock, Rebecca Raby, and Mark Thomas, eds, *Power and Everyday Politics*, Toronto: National Education Limited, 2012; Sandro Mezzadra and Brett Neilson, *Border as Method, or, the Multiplication of Labor*, Durham, NC: Duke University Press, 2013.

33   Neil Brenner, 'Between Fixity and Motion: Accumulation, Territorial Organization and the Historical Geography of Spatial Scales', *Environment and Planning D: Society and Space*, 16(4), 1998, p. 469.

34   Paolo Novak, 'Back to Borders', *Critical Sociology*, 2016, p. 3.

35   Novak, 'Back to Borders', p. 4.

36   Nicholas De Genova, ed., *The Borders of 'Europe': Autonomy of Migration, Tactics of Bordering*, Durham, NC: Duke University Press, 2017, p. 6.

37   The growth in the number of walls over recent years has been astonishing – according to a report released on October 5, 2016 by the Migration Policy Institute (MPI) 'There weren't even five on the planet at the end of World War II; a figure which had risen only to 15 when the Berlin Wall fell in 1989 before jumping to nearly 70 today.'

38   De Genova, *The Borders of 'Europe'*.

39   Adam Baidawi, 'South Africa Says Australia Retracted Claims of "Persecuted" White Farmers', *New York Times*, 30 April 2018.

40   C. Dauvergne, *Making People Illegal: What Globalisation Means For Migration and Law*, Cambridge: Cambridge University Press, 2008.

41   N. P. De Genova, 'Migrant "Illegality" and Deportability in Everyday Life', *Annual Review of Anthropology*, 31, 2002, pp. 419-47.

42   M. Czaika and M. Hobolth, 'Do Restrictive Asylum and Visa Policies Increase Irregular Migration Into Europe?', *European Union Politics*, 17(3), 2016, pp. 345-365.

43   Mezzadra and Neilson, *Border as Method*.

44   D. Bigo, 'Frontiers and Security in the European Union: The Illusion of Migration Control', in M. Anderson, and E. Bort, eds, *The Frontiers of Europe*, London: Printer, 1988; A. Ceyhan, and A. Tsoukala, 'The Securitisation of Migration in Western Societies: Ambivalent Discourses and Policies', *Alternatives*, 27, 2002, pp. 21-39; G. Karyotis, 'European Migration Policy in the Aftermath of September 11: The Security-Migration Nexus', *Innovation: The European Journal of Social Science Research*, 20(1), 2007, pp. 1-17.

45   As Todd Gordon has recently noted, 'Unfreedom and coercion are systematic to capitalist market relations … and all wage labour, including that of formally 'free', is unfree.' Capitalism, Neoliberalism, and Unfree Labour', *Critical Sociology*, 2018, p. 2.

46   Julia O'Connell Davidson, *Modern Slavery: The Margins of Freedom*, Basingstoke, Hampshire: Palgrave Macmillan, 2015, p. 5.

47   Davidson, *Modern Slavery*, p. 5.

48   T. Gammeltoft-Hansen, and N. N. Sørensen, eds, *The Migration Industry and the Commercialization of International Migration*, London: Routledge, 2011.

49   Rachael Bade and John Bresnahan, 'House GOP, Trump Team Hatch Border Wall Plan', *Politico*, 5 January 2017.

50   Lydie Arbogast, *Migrant Detention in the European Union: A Thriving Business*, Brussels: Rosa Luxemburg Stiftung, 2016, p. 7.

51   Arbogast, *Migrant Detention*.

52   G. Lahav, 'The Rise of Nonstate Actors in Immigration Regulation in the United States and Europe: Changing the Gatekeepers or Bringing Back the State?' in N. Foner, R. G. Rumbaut, and S. J. Gold, eds, *Immigration Research For A New Century*, New York: Russell Sage Foundation, 2000.

53   Abdulhadi Khalaf, 'The Politics of Migration', in Khalaf, Shehabi, and Hanieh, eds, *Transit States*.

54   Ceyhan and Tsoukala, 'The Securitisation of Migration'; Jorrit Rijpma and Marise Cremona 'The Extra-Territorialisation of EU Migration Policies and the Rule of Law', *EUI Working Papers*, LAW, European University Institute, 2007.

55   Arezo Malakooti, 'Irregular Migration Between West Africa, North Africa and the Mediterranean', Altai Consulting for IOM, 2015, p. 52.

56   European Commission, 'A European Agenda on Migration', 13 May 2015, available at: https://www.ein.org.uk/news/european-commission-publishes-its-european-agenda-migration.

57   Parts of this section are adapted from Adam Hanieh, *Money, Markets and Monarchies: The Gulf Cooperation Council and the Political Economy of the Contemporary Middle East*, Cambridge: Cambridge University Press, 2018.

58   Author calculations from World Bank remittances data.

59   Author calculations from World Bank remittances data.

60   International Fund for Agricultural Development (IFAD), 'Sending Money Home: Contributing to the SDGs, One Family At a Time', IFAD, June 2017, p. 5.

61   IFAD, 'Sending Money', p. 186.

62   Human Rights Watch, 'Detained, Beaten, Deported: Saudi Abuses Against Migrants During Mass Expulsions', 10 May 2015.

63   Akhbar24, 'al-dakhli: tarhil 1.2 milyun makhalif wamukhalafa' [Interior Ministry: Deportation of 1.2 Million Violators], *Akhbar24*, 30 July 2015, available at www.akhbaar24.argaam.com.

64   Human Rights Watch reported that many 'returned to their home countries destitute and with no means to buy food or pay for transportation to their home areas', and that they faced 'arbitrary confiscation of their personal property, which authorities refused to allow them to take'. (Human Rights Watch, 'Detained, Beaten, Deported').

65   R. Anderson 'Illegal Workers in Saudi Face Prison, SAR50,000 Fine as Crackdown Begins', *Gulf News*, 30 July 2017, available at: gulfbusiness.com.

66   Calculated by author from Saudi Arabia Monetary Authority, Monthly Bulletin.

67   Hanieh, *Capitalism and Class*, pp. 177-80.

68   These aggregate figures also need to be differentiated on a subnational basis – certain geographical areas within countries tend to be much more tightly linked to Gulf labour markets than others. Remittances to India, for example, constitute a relatively low level of the country's overall GDP. But for the Indian state of Kerala, a major source of migrant workers to the GCC, remittances are estimated to make up more than 36 per cent of the net state domestic product and are a vital component of household consumption.

69   Sewell Chan, 'No End in Sight to Tide of Migrants Entering Europe, U.N. Says', *New York Times*, 25 September 2015; Danica Kirka, 'Tip of the Iceberg: No End in Sight to Migrant Wave', Associated Press, 4 October 2015.

70   James Cypher, 'The Debt Crisis as 'Opportunity': Strategies to Revive US Hegemony', *Latin American Perspectives*, 16(1), 1989, pp. 52-78.

71   Organisation for Economic Co-operation and Development, 'Jordan's Statement From the London Conference on "Supporting Syria and the Region" Held on 4 February 2016', 3 June 2016.

72   'Donors Pledge Around $40-billion Aid to Syrian Refugees' Hosts', *Jordan Times*, 8 April 2017, available at: www.jordantimes.com.

73   Supporting Syria and the Region Conference, 'Co-host's Statement Annex: Fundraising', 8 February 2016, available at: https://www.supportingsyria2016.com/news/co-hosts-statemtent-annex-fundraising.

74   Hanieh, *Lineages of Revolt*.

75   European Bank for Reconstruction and Development, 'Jordan's Statement at the EBRD 2016 Annual Meeting and Business Forum', London, 10-12 May 2016, p. 3, available at: www.ebrd.com/documents/osg/am-jor-eng.pdf.

76   Molly Anders, 'What the Refugee Crisis Means for Investment in MENA', *Devex*, 14 March 2016, available at: www.devex.com.

77   Katharina Lenner and Lewis Turner 'Making Refugees Work? The Politics of Integrating Syrian Refugees into the Labor Market in Jordan', *Middle East Critique*, 2018.

78   European Council, 'Decision No 1/2016 of the EU-Jordan Association Council of 19 December 2016 Agreeing on EU-Jordan Partnership Priorities [2016/2388]', Council of the European Union, available at: data.europa.eu.

79   Behzad Yaghmaian, 'How Not to Fix the Refugee Crisis – A Response to "Refuge"', 20 April 2017, available at: www.newsdeeply.com; Heaven Crawley, 'Why Jobs in Special Economic Zones Won't Solve the Problems Facing the World's Refugees', *The Conversation*, 6 April 2017, available at: theconversation.com.

80   Thomas Nail, *The Figure of the Migrant,* California: Stanford University Press, 2015, p. 236.

81   Of course, this should not be taken to imply that Western states hold sole responsibility for global displacement or are the single place where migrants end up. In many countries outside of the core, migrants face similar patterns of exclusion, xenophobia, and violence – the cases of South Africa and the Gulf Arab states are two prime examples. Similarly, the flight of Syrian refugees in the post-2011 period is largely an outcome of the Assad regime's attempt to crush the Syrian uprising, and has been facilitated by the support of Russia and Iran in this repression. The challenge is to build an effective solidarity with migrants that continues to oppose Western imperialism, but is simultaneously grounded in an analysis cognisant of the changing architecture of global capitalism – including the emergence of potential rivals to US hegemony, the role of sub-regional powers, and the ways in which authoritarian states operate within these shifting balance of forces.

82   For an excellent survey, see Choudry and Hlatshwayo, *Just Work?*

83   Aziz Choudry and Mostafa Henaway, 'Agents of Misfortune: Contextualizing Migrant and Immigrant Workers' Struggles Against Temporary Labour Recruitment Agencies', *Labour, Capital and Society*, 45(1), 2012, pp. 36-65.

84   Choudry and Hlatshwayo, *Just Work?,* p.10.

85   Harsha Walia, *Undoing Border Imperialism*, Washington, DC: AK Press, 2012.

THE CAPITALOCENE: PERMANENT CAPITALIST COUNTER-REVOLUTION

ELMAR ALTVATER AND BIRGIT MAHNKOPF

In the fetish world of modern capitalism, many people can more easily imagine climate collapse, the vanishing of bees and other insects, an extinction of a sixth of all species on planet Earth, the poisoning of the air in large cities, floods of biblical proportions, or indeed the downfall of humanity than the end of capitalism as a mode of production and political rule. As Günther Anders observed in his *Antiquatedness of Man*, people are 'blind vis-à-vis the apocalypse' and are 'more afraid of losing their jobs today than of losing tomorrow's existence, and the world the day after'.[1]

This blindness is not entirely new. In the eighth century before Christ, the Phrygian King Midas is reported to have begged the God Dionysus for everything he touched to turn into gold. Midas was foolish, for he had not taken into account that even food and drink and other use values necessary for survival would turn into abstract, golden, and thus eventually life-threatening wealth. Nothing would be left to quench his hunger and thirst, as exchange value supersedes use value. Not only are the benefits of things negated, Ernest Bornemann wrote about 50 years ago, but so too are their owners: 'He dies of money, he starves, thirsty, freezes on money … The daily, inevitable, inescapable transformation of all tangible values into intangible, interchangeable categories such as commodity, money, price and wage has changed the spiritual life of Man in capitalism completely.'[2]

The gods of Greek mythology responded to Midas in a knowing, rational and gracious manner. Dionysus advised Midas to take a bath in the river Patulous (in today's Anatolia), turning it into Asia Minor's most gold–rich river. Midas was economically clever and, as far as we know, used the wealth of gold he had just washed off to channel the river Patulous in order to irrigate his fields. He also allowed the riverbed to flow through to retrieve the deposited gold. The life-threatening wealth was thus recycled. The cycle was thereby completed, but nature – the river and the fields, forests and meadows – had transformed. Midas' soul was also affected. And there were consequences for the outward appearance of Midas: it is said that the god Apollo punished King Midas with long donkey ears.

However, we must consider not only the material form of abstract wealth (such as money and gold), but also the overall context of the production and circulation of wealth, including financial relations, with their tendencies towards autonomization going as far as to disembed the economic system from nature and society. Because of the complexity of the relations between nature, humans, society, and economy, the effect of washing off Midas' gold has been far too slight. The conditions of production in their entirety, including distribution, consumption, and financialization, would need to be changed in order to be free of the lethal clutch of exchange value. It is not enough to merely wash off the gold; it is essential to change the overall metabolic context. That is, the continuation of the 'Great Transformation' under contemporary conditions. Whether foolish Midas, so madly hanging on to gold, would be able to do so is doubtful.

Following Midas, humanity has produced far more abstract wealth while plundering resources that are becoming scarce everywhere on planet Earth. Economic and physical shortages are now inevitable. These shortages indicate that the yield of many raw materials, of mineral as well as energy and agricultural resources, has reached a peak: that is, the point in time when maximum extraction is achieved, after which terminal decline sets in. As limited as the resources of the planet are, garbage is simultaneously disposed of in abundant quantities, wreaking another form of ecological havoc. So-called 'pollutant management' is an attempt to keep such harmful substances away from humans. This involves the identification and isolation of toxins, dilution and drainage of wastewater, use of chimneys for smoke, creation of fire brigades, and much more. If nothing more can be extracted from the Earth's crust, its miners become unemployed; but at least they may find new work rummaging through the mountains of waste.[3] While some find work under relatively hygienic conditions using modern technology, many more 'mine' the mountains of rubbish of the major metropolises of Africa and Asia under pitiful social and ecological conditions.

But is this enough for a provident approach to the planet's riches? Midas is in distress. Dionysus would have to descend into our planetary ecosystems from Mount Olympus to teach people two lessons. First, to not only manage mining and its resulting pollutants, but also to be aware of how both are linked, and how pollutants again can become useful resources. The second lesson would be how to 'wash off' exchange value. The gods, however, having read Marx's *Capital*, know that exchange value is a social relation that cannot simply be washed off, that it can only be practically changed, transformed through reforms, or perhaps through a revolution in which the world is turned upside down. Midas, the gold and money fetishist with the donkey ears, shied away from revolutionary consequences. We cannot afford to do the same, given the trajectories of our own time.

Under the pressure of constant competition, capitalists have to reduce production and circulation costs, and therefore increase the productivity of labour. This has been the way of producing the 'wealth of nations' ever since the early days of capitalism. This is the reason capitalists have to replace living labour with machinery. Since the nineteenth century, machinery has been run mostly by fossil energy such as coal, oil, and gas. This machinery in fact processes agricultural as well as mineral raw materials into use values for the satisfaction of human needs. These materials must be transported from their location of origin, where they are mined, bred, or grown, to the locations where they are processed, and to where they are finally consumed. These supply chains running from the original nature of the earth (the pool of resources) to the economic, cultural, social, and political systems (in plural) of the earth, constitute the backbone of the global capitalist system.

The supply chains of energy and raw materials are in the hands of changing alliances among states and private corporations. It is not only natural laws that govern the flow of resources from their origins to the place of final consumption; rather, it is powerful economic and political actors who establish these chains to guarantee the supply of fossil energy and raw materials for modern economies. Due to unequal and uneven development – a contest among unequal partners, both internationally and also within nations – the struggle over energy and other primary commodities has been extremely chaotic.

The ideal of harmonious economic progress (as put forth by development economists, entailing a transition from a primary economy based on agriculture and mining via a secondary economy of diversified production to a tertiary service economy)[4] has turned out to be naïve. Even the virtual economy, using bitcoins as the medium of exchange, depends on using the physical resources of planet earth and the atmosphere as a sink for its inevitable emissions. The mining of bitcoins is extremely energy-intensive, and takes place only where the production of energy has decisive comparative cost advantages. The battles waged over fossil energy are actually about defending the capitalist-fossil mode of production and its accompanying way of life. It is a permanent counter-revolution against the industrial and fossil revolution, and an integral part of the 'Great Transformation' from pre-capitalist to the capitalist mode of production and beyond.

The dynamics of (exchange) value are bound in their manifold connections to the labour process, and to the production of use-values as varied as food, bricks, machinery, automobiles, computers, data networks, and security guards. Marx analyzed the concrete and the abstract side of value creation. The latter can grow without limits. Modern economic models suggest that, without external hindrance, abstract processes will not lead to 'limits to growth'. Potential limits to growth of course arise within these models, but they play a minor role, as material and energetic dimensions of 'factors of production'. The logic of capitalist production for exchange rather than use thus drives the expansion of fossil energy production as part of the production of material products and infrastructures 'for eternity'. Once this mechanism is set free, value keeps growing: it cannot acknowledge any limits to its growth.

The pollution on which this system of production and consumption is based suggest that we are approaching the *point of no return*: the 'tipping points' of bio-physical systems. Geologists have proclaimed a new age conditioned by measurable human-made changes of the atmosphere (such as the increase of the average temperature), the hydrosphere (in the oxidation of the oceans), and the lithosphere (with new solid pollutants absorbed into the crust of the earth). These scientists have termed the cumulative impact of such changes 'the anthropocene'. However, it might well be referred to as the capitalocene,[5] due to the fact that the moving drivers of these planetary transformations are profitability and productivity in maximizing the valuation of capital. Capitalism, we argue, is a *growth-machine* as long as it is not forced to acknowledge the limits of the material or use-value form.

While most of the rich industrialized countries still have at their disposal large amounts of raw materials and fossil energy, bottlenecks have emerged for all of them as well as for the middle-income industrializing countries. Whatever the decisive differences among advanced and other industrialized countries, these bottlenecks emerged as economic growth increased demand for raw materials, and as international competition on the primary goods markets has intensified. Furthermore, the ongoing trend towards the digitalization of economies entails numerous supply chain risks such as price increases, price volatility, and scarcity of the 'critical metals' upon which all promising new technologies depend (including those for renewable energy production, electric vehicles, digital manufacturing, 'smart' consumer products, and modern military systems). This means that the fight for primary materials is not over with the emergence of artificial intelligence and ubiquitous digitalization. On the contrary, this will likely intensify given the global nexus of land, water, food, minerals, and energy, and given that a few countries dominate the market for critical minerals.

As the anthropocene is human-made, humankind would seem to have the ability to overcome its negative consequences, such as climate collapse and species extinction. This essay contends that, under contemporary conditions, another 'Great Transformation' would require a change of the conditions of production in their entirety, including distribution, consumption, and finance. We show why we cannot base our hopes on a 'green narrative' promising to decarbonize the global economy, and explain why and how this promise has been more or less systematically broken. Today, we are faced with a renewal of geopolitics based on fossil-fuel production and large infrastructure projects to transport carbons of all kinds. This geopolitics pertains not only to oil and gas, but increasingly also to metals and minerals that have become 'strategic resources'. As we show, instead of the urgently needed 'revolution in energy policy' towards 100 per cent renewable energy production and substantial reduction in energy consumption, all signs point to a counter-revolution in energy transition. Further, we highlight some features of the global minerals and metals crunch, which has been stimulated by the race for a number of 'strategic materials' needed for many 'green technologies' as well as for the digitalization of the economy.

While in current debates, economic and geopolitical dimensions of resource scarcity receive broad attention, the impact of the physical scarcity of minerals on the geo-economy of global capitalism, and even more importantly on a 'post-fossil' future, are rarely attended to. Against this backdrop, we explore a number of unavoidable trade-offs between economic and ecological goals, including the shift towards a 'greener capitalism'. We argue that, according to the principle of capitalist accumulation, even a transition towards renewable energy technologies will result in a vicious circle between the energy and metal sectors. Moreover, in many countries (foremost in China), it would sharpen the already severe contradictions embedded in the nexus of water and energy, and therefore would also negatively affect food production. The conclusion confronts the reader with many uncomfortable insights; yet, we argue that the 'good life' must begin today.

THE GREEN NARRATIVE AND THE
NEW GEOPOLITICS OF ENERGY

A 'green narrative' seems to be the order of the day, with its objective to decarbonize the global economy and radically reduce the use of non-renewable as well as renewable resources in a short period of time, and within capitalism. Hopes are placed on technological breakthroughs and innovations that are supposed to increase sustainability in all sectors of the economy. In addition, intelligent macroeconomics (including huge investments in public infrastructure) and all kinds of market-based policies are recommended as necessary but also sufficient conditions to rescue human civilization from collapse. At the same time, it is common knowledge that transforming the green narrative into real change would require serious steps to cut the use of carbon. This would require leaving most of the available fossil fuels in the ground, and stopping the search for and exploitation of unconventional oil and gas resources. Indeed, such unconventional fuels are even more difficult and costly to produce, and usually even more carbon-intensive to process, than conventional fossil fuels. Furthermore, deforestation would have to be stopped, and reforestation started.

In 2017 the Intergovernmental Panel on Climate Change (IPCC) measured the highest record of CO_2 emissions in history (90 per cent of which stem from human activity). Now, heads of state, business leaders, and civil society organizations across the world are discussing in conference after conference, in special seminars and webinars, how to reduce emissions. However, instead of reducing carbon emissions across the planet by about 5 per cent annually, the 'emissions gap'[6] is in fact increasing. We are at the threshold of the survival of humanity (and millions of other species) as we have known it for several thousand years. But the prevalence of capital accumulation prevents a shared sense of the multidimensional crisis from emerging. Obviously, 'lifeboats' are still available for the global one per cent and for some of the upper-middle class in both North and South. The 'green narrative', therefore, is at best dishonest. It attempts to conceal its contradictions, pretending that a shift towards renewable energy sources and a 'smart economy' based on the digitalization of transport, housing, manufacturing, and all kinds of communication can avoid unwanted side effects, risks, and potentially serious conflicts in the near future.

In fact, the globalized world of the twenty-first century does not appear in a friendly green outfit. The international order is collapsing, regional conflicts are without solutions, a new arms race has started, and international law as established after World War II seems outdated. In the United States, government officials think out loud about nuclear war. These processes fuel fierce international competition for dwindling stocks of oil and natural gas, and increasingly for metals, minerals, water, and land as well. Despite all the 'green metaphors', global capitalism still depends on cheap oil. Its importance for meeting the world's primary energy needs may decrease over the next decades. But cheap oil is still the 'life blood' of transportation, the petrochemical industry whose outputs have become so essential to daily life, industrial agriculture, manufactured products, and modern war. Indeed, global transportation and military systems have become largely reliant on oil, to the extent that any disruption of oil markets can bring even the great powers to a standstill. This has turned the market power of energy suppliers into political power. It also explains why the US has been trying to free itself from the constraints of being an oil-importing nation, becoming in recent years a supplier of oil from unconventional sources.

In spite of all this, an international green governance structure may still be possible, in good part depending on whether global elites are inevitably antagonistic to its emergence or not. Notably, in order to maintain control over the supply and pricing of hydrocarbons, pipelines as well as harbours, refineries, and railroads continue to be constructed. As in the past, pipelines stretching for huge distances across land and water extend the reach of the most powerful states well beyond their own territories. This is the rationale that US president Trump follows when he encourages greater fossil-fuel consumption abroad (be it in Europe, India, or South Korea) or when he promotes even closer cooperation with Saudi Arabia: 'No other country, least of all an international community united behind the Paris climate accord, should be able to deprive the U.S. of its carbon fix'.[7] But also the Chinese 'Belt Road Initiative' (BRI) is designed to serve the new geopolitics of – still fossil fuel-based – energy. The initiative, which emphasizes building infrastructure, provides China with leverage to curtail or contain other nations' activities without even using arms. In fact, the BRI is a fossil-fuel driven project, aiming to build oil pipelines, oil refineries, and harbours to ship oil and other raw materials from Latin America, Africa, and Iran to mainland China.

As in the heyday of the old geopolitics of European imperialism, geography has acquired renewed relevance in the sense of control over other states' territories (with a special emphasis again placed on Eurasia). In addition, the relevance of geology has grown in the sense that not only oil and gas, but also metals and minerals have become 'strategic resources'. Today, these two elements of geopolitics coexist with geo-economics, which refers to market power and alliances that are strengthened via bilateral, regional, and even macro-regional free trade agreements and worldwide protection of so-called intellectual property rights and investments. Moreover, international politics still has a role to play, in the form of resource diplomacy, legislative methods for establishing and defending monopolies, various restrictive regulations; and, not to be forgotten, economic sanctions, the establishment of military bases and, at least for the declining hegemonic power of the United States, military interventions aiming at 'regime change'.

PROFITING FROM ECOLOGICAL DAMAGES

Although the evidence indicates that globally, one third of oil reserves, half of gas reserves, and over 80 per cent of current coal reserves should remain unused in order to meet the target of global temperature not exceeding 2°C above the pre-industrial average, we are on track to rapidly and completely exploit all conventional – and increasingly also unconventional – fossil fuel resources.[8] Global warming above the 1.5° C limit will multiply hunger, migration, and violent conflicts that could easily result in state collapse due to biophysical factors (such as droughts and water scarcity, but also declining revenues after 'peak oil'). Already today, a growing number of people are faced with the brutal consequences of living in a world of political, natural, and human insecurity. Nevertheless, we can safely assume that capitalist classes will continue to make money until the last moment, with the complicity and support of governments across the globe.

In the short term, capitalists will seek out – and can expect – profits even from the collapse of ecological systems and its economic and social repercussions. For some, the ecological disaster presents business opportunities: desalination plants and floating cities can be built in rich countries; precious land for agricultural planting can be bought and sold for high profit; insurance against catastrophes such as fires and floods may be sold. Business in genetically modified crops is booming. In addition, the field of so-called 'border-nomics'[9] is becoming a new sector of significant accumulation, be it in the area of wall-construction and all sorts of border security markets, or that of surveillance technologies and detention facilities for the growing numbers of people uprooted from their homes. Millions of people are displaced due to armed conflicts and environmental degradation, spawning political instability and extremism in some countries, populism and xenophobia in others. Useless, or if not, then inhuman borders are constructed and fences built between rich countries with heavy carbon footprints and huge consumption of raw materials, and poorer ones without any chance of ever becoming as polluting and resource grabbing as their neighbours. But even between poor countries (e.g. India and Bangladesh), walls factor in to what Christian Parenti has called the 'catastrophic convergence' of political, economic, and ecological crises.[10]

Certainly, some business leaders are worried about numerous factors linked to the transgression of 'planetary boundaries' threatening the value of their businesses and credit-worthiness.[11] They might worry about the impending water and hunger crisis causing social unrest, violent conflicts, and involuntary migration to places they deem to be their 'homeland security regions'. But many others view even climate change as a business opportunity. New transport routes will become accessible in the Arctic due to climate change, while new oil and gas fields that are difficult and expensive to access will become more attractive – such as the bitumen type resources in Venezuela and Africa, deep offshore oil in Brazil, or heavy oil in the rainforest of the Amazon. A new 'resource race' has already started over raw materials for the 'green economy' and the 'digitalization' of society. Furthermore, as the US Pentagon and other military agencies in Europe indicate, climate change is expected to have major implications for national security. It is likely to stimulate not only a new arms race in an age of 'asymmetric warfare' and 'cyber conflicts,' but also justify the application of unmanned air combat systems, including killing drones and other sorts of autonomous weapon systems. For the arms industry and their shareholders this is, in fact, good news.

Instead of applying existing laws and drafting new ones to finally phase out fossil fuels and shrink industries that are heavily dependent on them, advanced capitalist states provide billions of dollars for developing coal overseas in the form of export credit preferential loans. Not surprisingly, despite the growing concerns of investors over the risks climate change poses for their portfolios, plans for coal power expansion around the world are still underway.[12]

THE COMPETITIVE RACE
TOWARDS A COUNTER-REVOLUTION IN ENERGY POLICY

In many countries, renewable energy capacity has been expanded in recent years, and the share of renewables in the energy mix has increased rapidly. In the coming years, this expansion is expected to further accelerate, because electricity production from renewable energy sources globally has become less expensive than burning fossils. Some think-tanks echo predictions that the industrial era of centralized fossil fuel-based energy production and transportation will be over by 2030, hopefully complementing the phase-out of nuclear energy production. As a result, investors are worried about the longer-term risks associated with 'stranded assets'.

The European Union's (EU) shifting energy and environmental policy unfortunately provides a telling example of energy counter-revolution. A hundred per cent renewable energy is within reach. In the past, the objectives of the EU´s long-term energy and environmental policy had been anything but ambitious. But until 2014, legally-binding requirements for all member states were established with regard to the reduction of energy consumption, the share of renewable energy in the energy mix, and the increase of potential savings through technological innovation. Certainly, neoliberal enthusiasm for market forces never went so far as to leave the large power producers and the energy-intensive industries to their own devices. Subsidies, tax breaks, and other compensation mechanisms have always strengthened the competitiveness of nuclear and coal-fired power-plant operators. Meanwhile, under intense lobbying pressure, the legal constraints on energy policy objectives agreed to in Brussels have been lifted.

As a consequence, in the EU the balance looks gloomy. Its import dependence on oil, gas, and agro-fuels (as well as on the agricultural commodities needed for their production) did not decrease – even in the years of unintentional 'de-growth' after the 2008 economic crisis. Now all signs point in the direction of 'reverse', away from the always half-hearted course towards 'energy transition'. National concerns (or what influential lobby groups present to the political classes and respective governments as such) render even the laxest specification of EU energy policy as 'detrimental to the economy', threatening jobs within EU countries.[13]

This is unlikely to change in the near future. On the contrary, it is probable that geopolitical conflicts and international disputes over access to, and transportation of, all kinds of raw materials will undermine even modest attempts at cooperation. It is not only the US that is pursuing growing national protectionism. In the EU there is good reason to fear that one maxim will prevail: the cheapest and most easily accessible energy source, which for most EU states is still coal. Especially with regard to oil and gas, the EU is heavily dependent on imports of metals and minerals, with the highest net imports of resources per person worldwide. The share of EU imports for many 'strategic materials' is as high as 100 per cent.[14] In the words of former EU Trade Commissioner Peter Mandelson at the Trade and Raw Materials Conference in Brussels in September 2008, the EU needs 'to import in order to export … We are in a race'.[15] It is thus not surprising that the European Commission as early as 2006 addressed the changes imposed on the global economic order by the enormous scale of resource-intensive developments in China and India, with its 'Global Europe Strategy' followed in 2008 with its 'Raw Material Initiative' (reconfigured in 2011 into the 'Roadmap to a Resource Efficient EU').

On the other side of the Atlantic, it is highly unlikely that the US will ever be fully energy self-sufficient. The expansion to its production capacity due to the so-called 'shale revolution' might bring greater resilience to short-term shocks, but rising per-capita energy use means the country will suffer long-term energy cost increases. Nevertheless, for the time being the Trump administration, functioning as an extended arm of the finance-fossil-fuel military complex, seems to be fiercely determined to exploit all domestic reserves in order to gain 'energy dominance' by supplying fossil fuels to other countries.[16]

The US administration has also discovered that the country is 'heavily reliant on imports of certain mineral commodities and that this dependency creates a strategic vulnerability for both its economy and military to address foreign government action, natural disaster, and other events that can disrupt supply of these key minerals'.[17] Concerns relating to 'strategic vulnerability' are discussed not only among government agencies in the US and Europe, but also in resource-poor Japan. The continuation of these countries' technological leadership depends on constant and growing supplies of minerals and metals (at affordable prices), which are vital for a number of future technologies. In contrast, for Australia, which is a major global mineral exporter, the critical assessment depends more on the potential for its own resources to cover global demand.

The imperialist underpinning of the national resource strategy of the other energy-consuming giant, China, is less obvious. But just like the US, China will do anything to ensure continued energy flows (be they from the Middle East, Russia, or Africa). The main difference with the US goal of 'energy dominance' might be that China, at least for now, is more willing to hedge its vulnerability to resource constraints through policy choices beyond military action and exclusion of potential allies and trade partners. China therefore focuses more on building alliances to make long-term access deals, expecting greater dividends from cooperation than from confrontation.

But what is of utmost importance about today's resource nationalism is that its focus is not only on controlling the production and trade of dwindling stocks of oil, which gives a high energy return on investment (EROI),[18] and far more expensive unconventional oil and gas, extracting and processing of which requires huge amounts of energy and money to build refineries, pipelines, oil rigs, harbours, roads, and other infrastructure. In addition to this, access to 'critical raw materials' has become an ever more important strategic concern of all 'great powers', and even those in the second tier.

Against this backdrop, military forces, scientists, international organizations (such as the International Energy Agency), and think-tanks concerned with geopolitics (such as the Council of Foreign Relations in the US, the Netherlands Institute of International Relations Clingendael, Chatham House in the UK, and Price Waterhouse Cooper) are looking at the impacts of sharply rising demand for minerals and metals. In addition to the raw materials necessary for infrastructure development, fossil and nuclear-based energy production, the chemical industry, aerospace, medical equipment, and all sorts of advanced communication (such as GPS, space-based satellites and command systems, and signal amplification infrastructure), huge quantities of metals and minerals are needed for novel industries: *first*, for the 'green transition' towards renewable energy production; *second*, for the electric vehicles; *third*, for the so-called 'Fourth Industrial Revolution' based on digitalization and artificial intelligence; and, *fourth*, for different sorts of military systems[19] in which not only aircraft need masses of 'critical materials', but also other components of the systems, such as ground stations, data links, and control staff.

In almost all advanced industrial countries (but also in China), the integration of digital data processing into production processes has been developing – with key technology such as sensors, radio frequency 'IDentification tags', high-performance microchips, advanced display technologies, and fibre-optic cables demanding an increasing amount of particular metals and minerals. A study conducted in 2016 on behalf of the German Mineral Resources Agency (DERA) examined the global demand for raw materials for 42 different future technologies in 2013 and 2035, and compared the expected increasing demand to the global production volume of the respective metals in 2013. It found that for some raw materials (such as lithium, light rare earth metals, germane, indium, and gallium), it is already foreseeable that within a period of slightly over two decades demand will nearly double, treble (in the case of heavy rare earth), and even quadruple (tantalum). In some cases, the increase in demand would far exceed primary production in 2013 (lithium, dysprosium/terbium, and rhenium), while in others the increase would be even more tremendous (cobalt, copper, scandium, platinum).[20]

TRADE-OFFS BETWEEN ECONOMIC PURPOSES AND ECOLOGICAL CONSTRAINTS

The 'criticality' of raw materials is usually debated from an economic point of view, with the main focus on delivery delays and other supply risks. These are often linked to unstable raw material governance and the volatility of commodity prices. However, since the early 2000s geopolitical dimensions of scarcity (in terms of political barriers raised in producing countries, which have begun to protect their interests by means of export taxes and various trade restrictions) have moved into the foreground. In particular, China, where more than 90 per cent of rare earth elements were produced, has started to prioritize its own supply needs. Government officials argue that export taxes on raw materials are lower than those for finished products (such as magnets for renewable energy technology), and that illegal mining in the south of the country (where heavily polluting rare earth oxides are extracted) should be cleaned up. Furthermore, the prognoses for the state of China's rare earth metal industry are not promising: even though the country produces 95 per cent of the world's production, it only holds 23 per cent of the world's total quantity of minerals, sourced primarily at three sites in the south of China, already heavily depleted. Consequently, export restrictions are viewed as an appropriate instrument to protect Chinese 'green technologies'. Fear has been growing in both the US and the EU that their economies might lose technological leadership to the Chinese, particularly with regard to solar photovoltaic and wind turbine technologies. Today, the rush for leadership in artificial intelligence and digitalization of entire economies seems to be even more important than competition over 'green technologies'. This has the potential to stimulate trade wars between the West and China.[21]

In contrast to the economic and geopolitical dimensions of scarcity, the physical scarcity – and therefore also the geological and material character – of minerals is rarely considered as a serious threat, either in terms of the geo-economy of global capitalism or the ecological impact of mining. This reflects a systemically anchored ignorance, at least from the perspective of a 'post-fossil future'. Even though the crust of the earth contains huge quantities of mineral ore reserves, many widely used substances face depletion as a function of absolute scarcity in nature and current technological limits. From the point of view of thermodynamics, a resource can be seen as 'critical' when it surpasses a certain 'exergy threshold'.[22] As ore grade decreases, the energy required to extract the ore increases exponentially. This is already the case with copper,[23] an essential material for nearly every kind of electrical device. Compared to gasoline engine technology, electric motor vehicles need a fourfold amount of copper, in addition to a larger quantity of metals such as cobalt, lithium, and heavy and light rare earth elements.[24] If only every second fuel-based car already on the market were replaced by an electric vehicle, and current trends in global sales (which are expected to rise by 50 per cent in the next 25 years) are taken into account, the amount of metals needed for car production alone would accelerate deforestation as a result of mining, generating more ecological damage.

This illustrates that a trade-off is unavoidable. Without substantial findings of highly concentrated repositories, the production of various metals (that is, products needed for a future 'green economy') cannot increase, but will more likely decrease along with the concentration of existing sites. When the production of various metals does not increase at the same (fast) rate as demand, the price for the 'critical materials' will rise substantially in the near future. Under these conditions, even less concentrated repositories will look economically viable. But the lower the concentration of the material, the more residues will be generated, and the more toxic chemicals and massive amounts of water and energy will be necessary for extraction. In short, the more disruptive will be the impact on local nature, workers, and the population.

The 'new gold rush' targeting rich metal deposits with high concentrations of metals two to five miles below the surface of oceans (along the equator or in the Arctic Circle) provides another example of a trade-off between economic and ecological goals. Within the next few decades, the technological capability for deep-sea mining will improve, and recent funding difficulties for these types of 'adventures' will likely be resolved due to rising commodity prices. At that moment, active commercial extraction might begin, destroying the unique ecosystems of deep oceans before this common heritage of humankind is even understood and mapped.[25]

The half-hearted move towards a greener capitalism, with its main focus on renewable energy technologies, is a project based on a number of trade-offs and any number of unresolved contradictions. As long as the mechanism of capitalist accumulation based on the principles of private property and economic growth is taken as a given, and by implication the infinite creation of monetary wealth, a transition towards renewable energy technologies will result in a vicious cycle between energy production and metals. The 'water-for-energy' and 'energy-for-water' trade-offs are also significant. On the one hand, solar and wind technologies compared to coal consume less water in power generation. But when the entire life cycle of such technologies (including the manufacturing of solar panels and wind turbines) is taken into account, the water footprint of both is quite substantial. Energy is required to supply and treat water; as the water footprint of the energy sector increases and water becomes scarce (which will be the case not only in China but in many other regions of the word), more energy is required to supply and treat it.[26] Furthermore, since onshore solar photovoltaics (PV) and wind farms require large land areas – which are not available in countries and regions with high population density – more conflict over access to water, land, and food will result. Water, in particular, has the potential to soon become the most important cause of conflicts, as petrol has been for a long time.

In this context, the Chinese example is especially telling.[27] China has, on the one hand, become the biggest emitter of CO_2, and is responsible today for around 30 per cent of global carbon emissions. Its population is faced with unhealthy air pollution and a growing lack of clean water. This is due, first, to a huge number of coal power plants and widespread mining; second, the operation of extremely energy intensive and very dirty factories (such as steel and cement); third, millions of cars becoming central to daily transport; fourth, massive urbanization and an ongoing building boom; fifth, the detrimental ecological effects of industrial agriculture; sixth, the destruction of vast areas of forest; and seventh, a large proportion of electricity production based on hydropower. On the other hand, China has installed more renewable energy capacity than the EU or the rest of the Asia Pacific region, and has introduced quite ambitious environmental regulations. However, based on current plans, the share of renewable energy in China's energy mix may not rise to much more than 20 per cent by 2030.[28] Similarly to the US and Europe, China depends heavily on imports of key minerals (such as copper, iron ore, and oil) for its manufacturing. In parallel to policies applied within the EU, but with more power at hand and far more money invested, China is also strengthening low-carbon development at home – as long as it does not interfere with the profit-generating (and job-creating) principle. China has thereby caused both 'clean' (in terms of carbon emissions) and 'dirty' pollution in foreign countries, as the US and the EU have done for a long time. At the same time, as mentioned before, China is financing and constructing coal-fired power plants abroad as an important element of its 'One Belt One Road Initiative', be it in Egypt, Iran, Vietnam, or Pakistan.

The Chinese way of addressing some select dimensions of the environmental crisis by merely technological methods (in particular producing energy with solar photovoltaics (PV), wind turbines, and concentrated solar power) also illustrates stark trade-offs between water and energy production. The unintended consequences of taking steps towards an energy transition that focuses more on renewables have the potential to create environmental problems, stimulate social resistance, and even cause international conflicts. With regard to water resources, China resembles the Middle East more than the EU or the US. The country faces severe and growing water scarcity, in particular in its 'dry eleven' provinces where most of its coal reserves are located, where its steel production is concentrated, and where half of its GDP is created. Vast water inputs are required not just for the production of fossil fuel-based energy, but also for the manufacturing process (including the mining of numerous raw materials) and for the operation of renewable energy power generation technologies such as PV and wind turbines, and even more for concentrated solar power (which needs large amounts of water for cooling). More 'water-friendly' technologies like solar PV and wind turbines imply a very resource-intensive manufacturing process, which also translates into a huge water footprint – in this case, due to the indirect water costs inherent in mining and the use of chemicals with devastating environmental impact. It is not controversial that among all available technologies for energy production, solar offers the highest potential for water savings in dry regions. But in order to add more solar PV capacity, China would have to phase out other water-demanding energy sources, or in other words replace the still more than 60 per cent of energy production that is based on coal. Yet both solar and wind technologies will not only boost the demand for water, but also for steel and therefore coal (on which steel production depends). Even worse, the threat of water scarcity, and thus also the trade-off between water and energy, affects not only millions of people in China, but also in India, South and Sub-Saharan Africa, and the Middle East region.

Even more significant trade-offs are foreseeable with regard to so-called 'negative emissions technologies' that aim to suck carbon dioxide out of the atmosphere, either by increasing forest cover or by pumping underground the emissions from burning wood and other plants to generate electricity.[29] This is because both technologies would require large amounts of land, which would conflict with food production. Even more devastating are the prospective techniques for cooling the planet by reflecting heat into space: this could lower the average temperature in some parts of the earth, and also cause high drought risks in the Sahel and other places. Also, the technique of boosting CO_2 uptake in oceans by stimulating plankton growth could harm biodiversity, and would bring carbon into all food chains.[30]

OVERCOMING THE COUNTER-REVOLUTION

The Intergovernmental Panel on Climate Change, according to a leaked draft of its report to be published in late 2018, is expecting a global temperature rise around 1.9°C by 2050. The IPCC also argues that 'geo-engineering' will be unavoidable to push down rising temperatures by the end of the twenty-first century. The same scientists are fully aware that scaling up 'negative emissions' in line with the 1.5°C goal will clash with efforts to fight hunger and the resulting social conflict.[31] Geo-engineering is indeed becoming the new technological fix – to save capitalism by sacrificing future human life on earth. It is clearly the hour of climate engineers who try to ward off or encapsulate the secondary consequences of global warming: prevention and mitigation by building dams against floods, blocking the movement of ecological refugees, or removing CO_2 from the atmosphere. These geo-engineering measures do not address the mode of production and consumption. They avoid even minor systemic changes that would address the root causes of the problem. The world is upside down because nature and a majority of people are oppressed.

This is why a movement to reverse this situation is gaining momentum. It is a movement for an alternative mode of organizing production and reproduction through a transition from fossil to solar energies, for the introduction of cooperative forms of work and life, the creation of new forms of collective property, the transition towards a new combination of market mechanisms and planning on a planetary scale. It is not an easy endeavour to break away from the systemic logic that dictates the motion of capital. As a result, the temptation to adapt to capitalist power structures, and make compromises with the major corporations and with state power, is ubiquitous. A really Great Transformation would have to begin instead from some uncomfortable insights.

First, greenhouse gas emissions cannot to be reduced on the basis of profit maximization. Instead of an increase in the share of renewable energy sources in the energy mix of individual countries, the relevant indicator has to be an enormous decrease in emissions and raw material consumption, including the renewable resources land and water.

Second, technological progress, on which most of the transition scenarios developed by scientists rely, will not save the day. This is because all kinds of trade-offs will shift the problems from energy to other resources (such as metals, minerals, land and water) and each trade-off has its own losers, be it workers, peasants or businesses.

Third, it is highly unlikely that the industries based on fossil fuels (defence and military industries in particular) or the major financial interests will be weakened via political decisions rapidly enough, whether in the US, Europe, China, or India. Too many vested interests are too closely tied to the fossil-fuel-financial complex, both in countries producing primary resources as well as consumer countries. Large-scale voluntary divestment will, therefore, not happen. But even if it did, new investors would buy the shares of coal power plants sold by agencies at the national and local levels (including trade unions, universities, pension funds, and philanthropic organizations). Instead, we will see the use of marginal oil and gas on the rise, accompanied by a new scramble for the raw materials necessary to build so-called 'future industries'. Both tendencies will cause even more political tensions and even more severe geopolitical conflicts than we know today.

Fourth, the globalization of capital and trade must be retailored to the service of humankind without deploying populism, nationalism, or xenophobia on any scale. For this to happen, not only the old major powers but also those striving towards a (new) role in regional dominance would have to place global climate commitments ahead of domestic economic needs. Nor will it suffice to promote 'climate jobs'. Rather, a democratization of the economy and fairer distribution of income and wealth are needed, along the lines that trade unions in some countries and progressive social movements across the world are campaigning for.

Fifth, as long as energy overproduction is in the hands of the oligarchs, and private accumulation is considered as inevitable as the laws of nature, an alternative social logic has only a slim chance of developing and spreading.[32] Individual choices to behave more ecologically in terms of consumption and daily life, even though necessary, can stimulate only minor changes.

Sixth, increased recycling of raw materials and re-use of all kinds of materials would certainly be one of the most important steps in the right direction. If we would re-use all materials over and over, we could indeed limit the consumption of energy, metals, minerals, sand, soil, and water. We could even create a vast numbers of jobs, as the repair and re-utilization of resources would be very labour intensive. Although the recycling rates for many metals and minerals are so low that even a doubling or quadrupling will not have a significant impact, an increase in raw materials recycling rates would be very helpful. Still, even if new recycling technologies were developed, the process is usually energy intensive and results in new trade-offs between energy and raw materials. Most importantly, the devastating practice of discarding materials no longer used in advanced industrial countries to be repaired and reused in developing countries must stop. Tough regulations are needed to force large corporations to design equipment in a way that makes it easy to disassemble the materials contained therein. This would certainly interfere with corporate property rights. Longer product life cycles, improved repair and recyclability of products, and a consistent cycle of waste management are simply not compatible with capitalism. Corporations would lose control over the production process, and the production of goods across the economy as a whole would contract.

As a consequence of all the above, what appears to be necessary within capitalism in fact translates into a crisis of capitalism. In the long run, structural change that respects socio-ecological constraints on human action must establish some kind of 'dynamic equilibrium', something that is simply not possible within the capitalist world system. The laws of evolution and the main theorems of thermodynamics, the quantity restrictions on exhaustible resources, and the threshold values for toxic substances are like traps into which one inevitably falls if the preconditions of *buen vivir*, or the 'good life' (including the limits that nature puts on human action) are not observed. This 'good life' neither exists in a utopian land of milk and honey, nor will become reality in a sparse nirvana – which many believe is its only possibility. Rather, it is a rational mode for handling natural, social, economic, and cultural limitations and boundaries.

In capitalist society, however, rational practices are defined as those that respect the 'laws' of the market, derived from scarcity imposed by the social order. The moral resources of economy and society, which are indispensable to a 'good life,' are either underestimated or completely ignored. This arrogant stance towards nature has brought us perilously close to the 'tipping points' of bio-physical systems. The 'good life,' as an enlightened and mature way of dealing with the scarcities we humans have caused ourselves by deploying the capitalist mode of (re)production must be started everywhere immediately.

NOTES

This text was written, like many others preceding it, in collaboration between Elmar Altvater and Birgit Mahnkopf. But Elmar's life was threatened by the sword of Damocles since the beginning of this work. When the sword fell and Elmar died, the manuscript was still in an early state and would have needed the two of us to complete it. Unfortunately, one co-author had the sad task of finishing the text alone, to the best of her knowledge. The argument would certainly have succeeded better if Elmar had still had the chance to intervene. We thank Margit Mayer and Miriam Boyer for their careful English editing.

1   From the manuscript of the third volume of Günter Anders, 'Antiquatedness of Man,' FORVM, 428/429(Aug–Sept), 1989, p. 52. Of course, Fredric Jameson noted this peculiar blindness as well, as did other social critics such as Joel Kovel, Naomi Klein, and others.

2   Ernst Bornemann, Psychoanalyse des Geldes. Eine kritische Untersuchung Psychoanalytischer Geldtheorien, Frankfurt/Main: Suhrkamp, 1973.

3   Ugo Bardi, Extracted: How the Quest for Mineral Wealth is Plundering the Planet, White River, VT: Chelsea Green Publishing, 2014.

4   Jean Fourastié, Le Grand Espoir du XXe siècle. Progress technique, progress économique, progrés social, Paris: Pressess Universitaires de France, 1949; Colin G. Clark, The Conditions of Economic Progress, London: Macmillan, 1949.

5   Elmar Altvater, 'The Capitalocene, Or Geoengineering Against Capitalism´s Planetary Boundaries', in Jason W. Moore, ed., Anthropocene or Capitalocene? Nature, History, and the Crisis of Capitalism, Oakland: PM Press 2016, pp. 138-52.

6   UNEP, The Emissions Gap Report 2017, Nairobi: United Nations Environment Programme, 2017.

7   Michael T. Klare, 'America's Carbon Pusher-in-Chief: Trump's Fossil-Fueled Foreign Policy', 2017, available at http://www.tomdispatch.com.

8   Paul Ekins and Christophe McGlade, 'Un-Burnable Oil: An Examination of Oil Resource Utilization in a Decarbonised Energy System', Energy Policy, 64, pp. 102-112.

9   Ruben Andersson, Illegality, Inc.: Clandestine Migration and the Business of Bordering Europe, Oakland: University of California Press, 2014.

10   Christian Parenti, Tropic of Chaos: Climate Change and the New Geography of Violence, New York: Nation Books, 2011.

11   Johan Rockstroem, et al., 'Planetary Boundaries: Exploring the Safe Operating Space for Humanity', *Ecology and Society*, 14(2), 2009.

12   National pension funds, insurance companies, mutual funds, asset management companies, commercial banks, and most importantly sovereign-wealth funds based in the US, Japan, Malaysia, South Korea, India, and China, but also representing investors from Germany, Norway, the Netherland and the UK, are still channeling money into coal plant development. If built, these plants would increase the world's coal capacity by over 40 per cent. Among the institutional investors holding the largest stake in coal plants are those funds that announced (at the 2017 Climate Summit in Bonn) that they want to 'phase out coal'. However, this does not prevent them from investing in coal plant developers − because the threshold for their divestment only refers to companies that base more than 30 per cent of their power generation or revenues on coal. See Heffa Schücking, 'Investors vs. the Paris Climate Agreement', *Coalexit.org*, 2017, available at: www.coalexit.org.

13   Birgit Mahnkopf, 'Lessons From the EU: Why Capitalism Cannot be Rescued From Its Own Contradictions', in Gareth Dale, Manu V. Mathai, and Jose A. Puppim de Oliveira, eds, *Green Growth: Ideology, Political Economy and the Alternatives*, London: Zed Books, 2016, pp. 131-49.

14   European Energy Agency, *Material Resources and Waste: 2012 Update*, Copenhagen: EEA, 2012; PBL Netherland Environmental Assessment Agency, *Scarcity in a Sea of Plenty? Global Resource Scarcity and Policies in the European Union and the Netherlands,* The Hague: NEEA, 2011.

15   Peter Mandelson, 'The Challenge of Raw Materials', Speech at the Trade and Raw Materials Conference, Brussels, 29 September 2008, available at http://europa.eu.

16   Klare, 'America's Carbon-Pusher in Chief'.

17   US Department of the Interior, 'Draft List of Critical Minerals,' 2018, available at www.federalregister.gov.

18   Even though there is a lot of dispute about the exact EROI of the different energy sources, there is no doubt that the EROI for most 'green' energy sources (such as wind, solar photovoltaic, or ethanol) but also 'unconventional' oil and gas, is lower compared to conventional oil, gas, or coal.

19   Such as for aircraft parts, engines, missile guidance systems, and anti-missile defence, underwater mine detection, GPS for the entire communication system, electronic counter-maneuver, not to forget unmanned military systems (drones).

20   DERA (Deutsche Rohstoffagentur/German Mineral Resources Agency), '*Rohstoffe für Zukunftstechnologien*', Berlin, 2016. For a thorough analysis see: Andre Diederen, *Global Resource Depletion: Managed Austerity and the Elements of Hope*, Delft: Eburon, 2010: and essays by Werner Zittel, Ernst Schriefl, and Martin Bruckner, in Andreas Exner, Martin Held, and Klaus Kümmerer, eds, *Kritische Metalle in der Großen Transformation*, Berlin: Springer, 2016.

21   US Department of the Interior, 'Draft List of Critical Minerals.' The Department of the Interior indicates here that for strategically important raw materials, China was the leading producer of 15 of the 33 commodities listed as 'critical'.

22   This is a measure of the degree of thermodynamic distinction a piece of material has from its surrounding 'commonness'; the physical or thermodynamic rarity is accounted for by the energy costs required to obtain a mineral commodity from ordinary rock with prevailing technologies. See: Guidomar Calvo, Alicia Valerio, and Antonio Valerio, 'A

Thermodynamic Approach to Evaluate the Criticality of Raw Material Flows and its Application Through a Material Flow Analysis in Europe', *Journal of Industrial Ecology*, July 2017.

23   See the sources cited in note 28.

24   DERA, '*Rohstoffe für Zukunftstechnologien*'.

25   Rahyun Kim, 'Should Deep Sea Bed Mining Be Allowed?' *Marine Policy*, 82(August), 2017, pp. 134-37.

26   International Energy Agency, *World Energy Outlook 2016*, Paris: IEA, 2016.

27   Debrah Tan, Feng Hu, Hubert Thieriot, and Dawn McGregor, 'Towards a Water & Energy Secure China: Tough Choices Ahead in Power Expansion with Limited Water Resources,' available at http://chinawaterrisk.org; Hong-Hanh Dinh, 'The Role of Solar and Wind Energy in China's Water-Energy Nexus: The Water Footprint of Solar and Wind Expansion in China', Institute of Management, Berlin School of Economics and Law (MA Thesis), 2017.

28   International Renewable Energy Agency (IRENA), '*RE map 2030. A RE Roadmap*', Abu Dhabi 2014, available at www.irena.org/Remap. See also: Richard Smith, 'China´s Drivers and Planetary Ecological Collapse', *Real-World Economics Review*, 82(13 December), 2017.

29   Thomas Fatheuer, *New Economy of Nature: A Critical Introduction*, Berlin: Heinrich Böll Foundation, 2014.

30   ETC Group; *The Big Bad Fix: The Case Against Climate Geoengineering*, Montreal: HeinricBöll Foundation, 2017.

31   The leaked draft summary of the UN special report on the 1.5C climate goal is from the online magazine *Climate Home*, and is available at: www.climatechangenews.com/2018/02/13/leaked-draft-summary-un-special-report-1-5c-climate-goal-full.

32   Elmar Altvater and Birgit Mahnkopf, 'Der Begrenzte Planet und die Globalisierung des Einen Prozent', *Blätter für deutsche und internationale Politik*, 5, 2017, pp. 63-74.

TRUMP AND THE NEW BILLIONAIRE CLASS

DOUG HENWOOD

Donald Trump's ascension to the presidency was a shock that has still not worn off almost two years into his administration. It's a shock that has occupied not only the political portion of many minds, but has caused psychic distress (confirmed by interviews with psychoanalysts and bartenders) and strained friendships among most left-of-centre Americans. For someone like me, who watched his rise in New York from the early 1980s onward, it was especially shocking. That rise was fuelled by hucksterism, lying, vandalism, litigiousness, and multiple cycles of heavy borrowing and bankruptcy, all performed with consistent viciousness and vulgarity. To the cultural elite he was a repulsive joke, but he did have some fans among the working class, which can show a soft spot for a populist plutocrat. No one could have imagined, when he sued a brokerage analyst who wrote negative commentary on his casinos, or posed as a publicist to talk up his sexual prowess to the *New York Post,* or hosted a reality TV show featuring him declaring 'you're fired!', that he'd ever be president.[1] He'd toyed with the idea of running for president in 1988, 2000 (when he actually entered the California Reform Party primary), 2004, and 2012, but no one took him seriously. Nor did most people take him seriously when he made his formal announcement in June 2015. *Politico,* which loves the pose of knowing cynicism, played it for laughs, characterizing the speech as 'quixotic … discursive, pugnacious … bizarre … [and] entertaining', and ran a list of its ten best 'nuggets'. They included his pledge to repudiate the Iran deal, get tough on China, undo the Affordable Care Act, and build a wall to keep out drug runners and rapists crossing the border from Mexico. The list is familiar to anyone who's followed his presidency, and it sure doesn't seem funny now.[2]

It's hard to think clearly about Trump. In his book *On Television,* Pierre Bourdieu warns against the twin oversimplifications of sociological analysis: either something 'has never been seen before' or it's 'the way it always has been'.[3] Nowhere are those temptations as visible as in Trump studies. You've got a large set of critics screaming that he's our Hitler (or, for the Russophobes, Putin), a violator of all the ethical norms of high office. And there's a hearty band of ultras, less numerous than the alarmists, who assure us that Trump is little different from Obama (the deportation numbers are down, though there are technicalities involved). Is it too distressingly moderate to say that there's more continuity in Trump than the screamers say, but that he does mark a turn for the worse?

It's not like bombast, anti-intellectualism, and authoritarian urges are foreign to American life. Were Trump's ravings about unleashing 'fire and fury' on North Korea any more alarming than the boozy bellicosity of Richard Nixon, who once shocked Henry Kissinger, of all people, by suggesting the use of nuclear weapons on North Vietnam? Nixon's Defense Secretary James Schlesinger ordered his subordinates to ignore any nuclear launch orders coming from the president and check with him or Kissinger before pushing any buttons.[4]

But there *is* that turn for the worse. Decades of economic and geographic polarization have produced a harder, meaner edge to American politics (not that they were ever absent). The working class no longer enjoys the rapid income growth it did from the end of the Second World War to about the time Nixon resigned in disgrace. Entire regions – former industrial cities like Detroit, the inner suburbs of older cities, much of the hinterlands – are in varying stages of decay. The old WASP ruling class that ran the US into the 1970s has faded, replaced by a horde of new plutocrats who made their fortunes in tech and finance. The WASPs were a relatively coherent, stable formation, concentrated in the Northeast, married from the same pool, belonged to the same clubs, and had some capacity for thinking about the future. (It was this class that designed the post-Second World War structure of the American empire.) But their fortunes declined with the old-line industries and companies they were rooted in.[5]

The new class, which came into being with the boom of the 1980s – a milestone in its development was freebooting oilman and takeover artist Boone Pickens' 1983 attempt on Gulf Oil, a pillar of the old Pittsburgh corporate establishment – is a much less organic thing. It's more geographically and socially diverse and less inclined towards *noblesse oblige* than its predecessor. That new class – or class fraction, if you want to be wordy – has had a heavy role in transforming the Republican Party, once a coalition of liberals, moderate, and conservatives, into the rightmost mainstream party in the First World.

THE MAKING OF DONALD TRUMP

Trump has a lot in common with that arriviste demographic: brash, not as self-made as they'd like you to believe, less concerned with legitimation than earlier plutocrats like Carnegie and Rockefeller. But although he loves to present himself as a business genius, that case is hard to make. He managed to lose money on casinos, a business where the house always wins. (To be fair, he loaded them up with debt and extracted the proceeds.) He flopped at running an airline and peddling steaks. On his death in 1974, Fred Trump's real estate holdings were worth about $200 million. Divided among his five children, that means Donald's share was about $40 million. Had he simply invested the proceeds in a stock market index fund and reinvested the dividends (after paying taxes on them) he'd have $2.3 billion today. If you start the clock in 1982, when Trump's business career was just getting going and the stock market was emerging from its 1970s funk, he'd have $6.3 billion today. He's thought to be worth between $2.9 billion (Bloomberg) and $4 billion (*Forbes*), though Trump massively inflates everything – he claims he's worth 'in excess of TEN BILLION DOLLARS' (capital letters his) – and there are people who doubt he's even a billionaire.

According to *Forbes,* none of the 1,538 people who'd been on its 400 list between its inception in 1982 and 2015, when the article was written, has been as obsessed with his ranking as Trump. Of those who've bothered to question the magazine's estimate of their wealth, Trump was the only one who wanted to push it higher; the rest didn't welcome the attention it brought them. Not only was a big number important to his celebrity – it enabled him to get bigger loans.[6] He was the perfect embodiment of the kind of capitalist Marx wrote about in volume 3 of *Capital*: 'The actual capital that someone possesses, or is taken to possess by public opinion, now becomes simply the basis for a superstructure of credit.'

Trump came into office with nothing resembling a coherent political philosophy – not the technocratic centre-left politics of Obama, for sure, but also not a worldview like Reagan's, shaped by decades in movement conservatism. Yes, Reagan had some intellectual limitations, but if you read his speeches (no doubt written by professionals, and not the Gipper himself) to the Conservative Political Action Conferences (CPAC) in the 1970s and 1980s, you can see he cared about articulating a worked-out agenda. His 1977 speech comes in at an 11th-grade reading level, according to the Flesch–Kinkaid calculator.[7] Trump's inaugural address, largely a catalogue of woes that George W. Bush pronounced as 'some weird shit', comes in at an 8th grade reading level.[8]

Trump did have a few instinctive beliefs, mainly rooted in racism and xenophobia with a heavy seasoning of vengefulness, authoritarianism, and misogyny. Early signs of this were his behaviour during the so-called Central Park Five case. In 1989, five black and Latino teenagers were accused of raping a white woman in Central Park, Manhattan. Confessions, which turned out to be false, were extracted under hours of heavy police questioning, although there was no evidence linking the teens to the crime. Trump promptly spent $85,000 taking out full-page ads in all four of New York's daily newspapers calling for a return of the death penalty. 'Muggers and murderers should be forced to suffer and, when they kill, they should be executed for their crimes', he wrote in the ad. Anticipating his later tweeting style, he declaimed: 'How can our great society tolerate the continued brutalization of its citizens by crazed misfits? Criminals must be told that their CIVIL LIBERTIES END WHEN AN ATTACK ON OUR SAFETY BEGINS!' They served six to thirteen years in jail. Soon after the last was released, all five were exonerated by DNA evidence and a confession to the crime by a serial rapist – but Trump not only refused to apologize, he continued to insist they were guilty.[9]

Like father, like son? Fred Trump, Donald's father, was a developer who got rich building working-class housing in Brooklyn in the years after the Second World War, well before gentrification made the borough glamorous (parts of Brooklyn, at least). In 1927, when he was twenty-one, Fred was one of seven people arrested during a Ku Klux Klan riot in Queens, a fact reported in several newspapers at the time but which Trump denied during the 2016 campaign. It's not clear whether the elder Trump was a participant or a bystander – though two of the contemporary reports described all the arrestees as 'berobed' – but it did set a tone for decades to come.[10]

In 1973, the U.S. Department of Justice sued the Trump Organization, still headed by Fred but with Donald as president, alleging racial bias against renting to black tenants. (That practice was well-established enough that one of his tenants, Woody Guthrie, wrote a song denouncing Fred's drawing up a 'color line' and stirring up 'racial hate' in 1950.) Donald denounced the suit as part of a 'nationwide drive to force owners of moderate and luxury apartments to rent to welfare recipients'. The family's lawyer, Sen. Joseph McCarthy's former-aide-turned-fierce-litigator Roy Cohn, countersued, screaming that the government sought 'the capitulation of the defendants and the substitution of the Welfare Department for the management corporation!'[11]

Fred Trump lived in Queens and made his money doing real estate in Brooklyn, a mission in which he received great assistance from the borough's Democratic Party political machine. Fred passed along those connections, and to New York governor Hugh Carey, to his son, which greased his early rise. But despite those connections, Donald Trump – whom *Spy* magazine mocked during the late 1980s as a 'Queens-born casino operator' and a 'short-fingered vulgarian' – wanted to crack Manhattan society and never really made it. He was never part of the high-end real estate establishment (he wasn't even a member of the Real Estate Board of New York, the developers' trade association), and Wall Street distrusted him as a serial bankrupt. Even his alleged friends (though it's not clear he has any actual friends) speak scornfully of him. Buyout artist Carl Icahn, whom Trump cites frequently, ridiculed him privately and doubted he was a billionaire (a charge that Trump has sued people for).[12] Trump was able to transform his outer-borough resentment of the Manhattan establishment into an anti-elite pseudo-populism that lured millions of votes from busted ex-machinists and coal miners in the American heartland.

But such a reputation, whatever its electoral merits, is not the way to win elite approval for a presidential run. Trump never got that, but he was able to turn that to advantage by denouncing the upper orders in ways no major party candidate had ever done. It was half sham and half real, and sometimes it's still difficult to say which is which. One by one he disposed of the Republican establishment's favourites.

Politicians are ideologically flexible, but no candidate had ever been as ideologically un-anchored as Trump. For much of the campaign, and early in his presidency, Trump turned for political direction to Steve Bannon, the 'Che Guevara of American right-wing nationalism', in the words of *Bloomberg* reporter Joshua Green. Bannon was introduced to Trump several years before the 2016 campaign by David Bossie, a veteran right-wing operative and Trump friend who cut his teeth on investigating Bill Clinton's finances in the 1990s.[13] (Both Bannon and Bossie were close to hedge fund billionaire Robert Mercer, of whom more in a bit.) Before Trump appointed him as deputy manager of his campaign in September 2016, Bossie had been president of Citizens United, the conservative advocacy group most famous for having engineered the 2010 Supreme Court decision that lifted restrictions on political spending by moneyed interests, which opened the way for a fresh torrents of cash into the American electoral system (which never lacked for torrents of cash, but the *Citizens United* decision took it to a new level).[14] Bannon, Bossie, and Trump were all united by a contempt for the Clintons, not all of it of the delusional right-wing kind. As Green put it, Bannon saw Hillary Clinton, 'as 'a résumé', 'a total phony', 'terrible on the stage', 'a grinder, but not smart', 'an apple-polisher who couldn't pass the D.C. bar exam', 'thinks it's her turn', but 'has never accomplished anything in her life' – all pretty much true.[15]

What Bannon offered Trump was, in Green's words again, 'a fully formed, internally coherent worldview', an America-first nationalism that comported well with the mogul-candidate's instinctive worldview, but which Trump himself was too lazy and ignorant to develop on his own. For years before his presidential run, Trump had been something of a New York Democrat, which is the world he (and his father) emerged from. As late as early 2016, Trump praised the British National Health Service, and during his brief 2000 run on the Reform Party ticket, touted the Canadian single-payer system as a model for the US.[16] Bannon helped change all that.[17]

Over the course of decades, Bannon, a passionate autodidact steeped in reactionary Catholicism, had developed a political philosophy that saw the West as decadent and under siege by hostile forces, notably Islam, a force that was thought to have been defeated in Spain five centuries ago but which was back for revenge. He trembles before 'jihadist Islamic fascism'. Among his influences was the Italian fascist writer Julius Evola.[18] Bannon also brought with him a populist critique of Wall Street, which Trump used to good effect in the campaign but forgot upon taking office. But despite that reversal, Trump has stuck with his hostility to immigrants and Islam, and his paranoid view that foreign trade weakened the US.

It's hard to believe now, but Trump's reality TV show, *The Apprentice,* was highly popular with black and Latino viewers, and its audience was cherished by advertisers as a model of a multicultural America. But as soon as Trump began touting the theory that Barack Obama was not born in the US in 2011, his appeal to non-white audiences cratered – but his appeal to right-wing nationalists began to soar. Trump – who lives by ratings, be they for TV or Twitter – began to appreciate the power of xenophobic appeals. He always had at least a toe in that water, but he soon dove all the way in. The transformation was stark: Trump blamed Mitt Romney's loss to Obama in 2012 in part on his 'mean-spirited' attacks on immigrants; months later, Trump told the Conservative Political Action Conference that '11 million illegals' were an obstacle to 'mak[ing] America strong again'. And a year later, Trump decided that building a wall on the Mexican border was a great marketing gimmick for his campaign.[19]

Bannon had a patron in the reclusive hedge-fund billionaire Robert Mercer. Mercer had only recently become interested in politics, politics of a fairly standard right-wing billionaire sort, anti-tax and anti-regulation. Mercer, along with his daughter Rebekah, found his way into the orbit of the Koch Brothers, the right-wing philanthropists (of whom much more later), contributing $25 million to their efforts during the 2016 election cycle. Mercer also funded a network of media organizations (like *Breitbart*

News) and activist groups run by Bannon. One of the prime targets of that network was the Clinton family. Bannon steered Mercer money to Peter Schweizer, whose book *Clinton Cash,* though loathed by Democrats, painted an accurate if unattractive picture of Bill and Hillary's financial operations – the foundations, the speaking fees, and the board memberships that made them rich and corporate bigwigs feel important.[20] All this naturally appealed to Trump. And Bannon saw in Trump a political figure who could carry his nationalist agenda forward.

Mercer was not a Trump fan at first; he started the primary season as a backer of Ted Cruz. But when Trump won the nomination, Mercer began throwing millions into his campaign (something Trump himself didn't do) – and the anti-Clinton propaganda that Schweizer had assembled made for great off-the-shelf opposition research. Mercer's data operation, Cambridge Analytica, also contributed to the Trump campaign's strategy, though precisely how much is controversial.

Trump would later split with Bannon, because he resented his advisor being given too much credit as mastermind, and Mercer would drop Bannon, for the bad things he said about Trump to the journalist Michael Wolff for his book *Fire and Fury.*[21] A lot of Bannonism remains in Trump, however, particularly the nationalist dislike of immigration and foreign trade. Two of the nationalist advisors remain: Stephen Miller, the lead architect of Trump's immigration policy, and Peter Navarro, the Sinophobic guru on trade policy.

Having right-populist instincts and friends in the right-wing media world isn't much help in staffing an administration – especially when you don't expect to win an election. According to Wolff, Bannon was about the only member of Trump's inner circle who thought he could win, and many thought he shouldn't (they thought the campaign would be good for their careers in right-wing media or consulting – but that would work only if he lost).[22]

Little has been written on precisely how Trump staffed his administration – and re-staffs it, given the unprecedented level of turnover. (There are still a massive number of unfilled positions.) At first, it was a mix of Bannonites and more standard-issue right-wingers. The standard-issue right-wingers were a bit of a surprise, since he didn't campaign as one and most on the right distrusted him. *National Review,* a flagship journal of the right founded by William F. Buckley Jr, ran an 'Against Trump' cover feature in its 16 February 2016 issue, featuring anti-Trump screeds by nearly two dozen prominent conservatives. L. Brent Bozell III – the son of the co-author of Buckley's defence of Joe McCarthy and Buckley's sister, and a prominent moralizer and media critic in his own right – summarized his objections by saying that instead of 'walking with' the right, Trump had been 'distracted' for years by 'publicly raising money for liberals such as the Clintons; championing Planned Parenthood, tax increases, and single-payer health coverage; and demonstrating his allegiance to the Democratic party.'[23]

Key to Trump's right turn was his choice of Mike Pence as vice president. Pence, a six-term Congressman and then-Governor of Indiana, was an undistinguished if reliable conservative of the evangelical sort. The choice appeared to be a gesture of reassuracce to the Republican establishment and social conservatives and, importantly, a way of reaching out to the all-important Koch Brothers.[24] The Kochs were not Trump enthusiasts at first. They sat out the presidential election, and devoted the better part of their $750 million campaign budget to down-ballot races. (They'd initially planned to spend almost $900 million, but when Trump got the nomination, they cut their spending accordingly.)[25] Pence had numerous personal ties to the Koch circle, and they in turn held up his governorship as a political model.[26] Koch allies would soon be all over the new Trump administration.

THE KOCH BROTHERS POLITICAL NETWORK

Charles and David Koch are the core of a small but extremely rich network of right-wing plutocrats who have pushed American politics to the right at every level of government over the last few years. They organize regular (and secretive) conferences for the like-minded where they raise money and plot strategy, and their tentacles spread into every state in the country. Of course there have long been plutocrats financing the American right. But things have come a long way from the 1950s, when obscure machine tool makers in the midwest were funding the John Birch Society. There's just so much more money at the top to throw around now. As Jane Mayer put it, 'more billionaires participated anonymously in the Koch planning sessions during the first term of the Obama presidency than existed in 1982, when Forbes began listing the four hundred richest Americans'. She lists 18 regular participants whose combined fortunes amounted to $214 billion in 2015. The names included Sheldon Adelson, the passionate Zionist ($31.4 billion); Trump crony and energy advisor Harold Hamm ($12.2 billion); financier Steve Schwarzman ($12.0 billion); Charles Schwab, the discount brokerage magnate ($6.4 billion); and Richard DeVos, the Amway mogul ($5.7 billion).[27]

The Koch circle is heavy with financiers and fossil fuel magnates (with special emphasis on the dirtiest sources, like fracking and tar sands). Financiers like Steven Cohen, Paul Singer, as well as Schwarzman were drawn to the enterprise in the early Obama years, fearing he was a reincarnation of FDR about to crack down on their business models, though as it turned out he never did much more than call them 'fat cats', a remark that many on Wall Street never forgave him for. Schwarzman was incensed by Obama's brief flirtation with lifting a tax break enjoyed by the private equity and hedge fund businesses, a break that extends them a lower federal tax rate than what their secretaries pay. He likened the proposal to Hitler's invasion of Poland.[28] And the carbon moguls were afraid that he was actually serious when he said upon clinching the Democratic nomination in 2008 'this was the moment when the rise of the oceans began to slow and our planet began to heal'.[29]

They stayed mobilized throughout the Obama presidency. They did score huge gains in the 2010 midterm elections, but failed to dislodge Obama in 2012 with private equity centi-millionaire Mitt Romney. Aside from their wealth and the sources of their fortunes, several other features stand out about the Koch circle. One is a long history of legal problems, usually resulting from environmental or labour abuses. And another is the prevalence of private ownership of their businesses (as opposed to publicly traded corporations). [30] The formation deserves a close look. Charles and David Koch learned right-wing politics from their father Fred, founder of the family business. Fred did business with the Nazis in the 1930s, and, beyond the commercial connection, admired the labour discipline in Germany. 'When you contrast the state of mind of Germany today with what it was in 1925 you begin to think that perhaps this course of idleness, feeding at the public trough, dependence on government, etc., with which we are afflicted is not permanent and can be overcome', he wrote in 1938. Fred so admired the Nazi way of life that he hired a German nanny who was a passionate Hitler fan for his young sons; she ran the household with what Mayer described as an 'iron hand'.[31] The Second World War made Nazi sympathies inconvenient, but Fred joined the John Birch Society soon after its founding.

Charles has long been the brains of the operation, both its business and political sides, and stayed in Wichita. David, sometimes derided as a dim playboy, lives in Manhattan and is a generous patron of the arts; the home theatre of the New York City Ballet, although owned by the City of New York, was renamed after him in 2008 in return for a gift of $100 million. Although the Kochs dominate right-wing philanthropy now, they're certainly not without precedent. There were also characters like Richard Mellon Scaife (whose middle name tells all), Harry and Lynde Bradley (brothers who ran a machinery manufacturer, and created a foundation bearing their names), John Olin (chemicals and munitions, also with a foundation, and one that laundered money for the CIA in the late 1950s and early 1960s), the Coors family (brewers of tasteless but widely cherished beer, who hated gay people as much as they hated unions), and the DeVos family (founder of the multilevel marketing cult Amway).[32] Scaife financed a lot of the right's war on Bill Clinton, feeding all the lunatic stories about the 'murder' of Hillary's friend and former colleague Vince Foster, as well as the less lunatic but nonetheless exaggerated tales of corruption around Whitewater. Hillary Clinton famously dubbed these the product of a 'vast right-wing conspiracy', which was true, but it was nowhere near as vast as it would become. Most of those were largely twentieth-century phenomena; Scaife died in 2014 (though not before making peace with Bill Clinton), and the Olin Foundation – which financed a lot of the right-wing legal infrastructure that still operates today – shut down in 2005. The Bradley Foundation is still active, but it's small next to the Koch network.

The DeVos family has remained powerful into the twenty-first century – so powerful that one, Betsy DeVos, who is married to the son of Amway's founder, is Trump's Secretary of Education. (She's doubly right-wing royalty because she's the sister of Erik Prince, founder of the mercenary firm formerly known as Blackwater.) DeVos had been active in education reform in Michigan – 'reform' in this context means cutting spending and privatizing public schools, a cause dear to the entire Koch network – even though, as her confirmation hearing demonstrated, she knew nothing about education. It did not hurt her chances for Senate confirmation that she and her family had contributed nearly $1 million to twenty Senators over the years. As she said twenty years earlier, 'I have decided to stop taking offense at the suggestion that we are buying influence. Now I simply concede the point. They are right.'[33]

The Koch brothers have been involved in politics for four decades. In the late 1970s, Charles Koch decided he wanted to be the 'Lenin' of the libertarian movement.[34] It's striking how the right often speaks admiringly of the Bolsheviks and their organizational and ideological discipline. Steve Bannon, whom Joshua Green dubbed a Che Guevara figure, has described himself as a Leninist, and as I wrote in my essay in the 2016 *Register,* the many former Reds who turned to the right used their experiences in Communist and Trotskyist organizations as models for their takeover of the Republican Party.[35] Earlier right-wing heroes also cite the communist tradition. Michael Joyce, who was paid by the Olin Foundation to think for the right in the 1970s and by the Bradley Foundation in the 1980s, was a student of Gramsci; he directed the financing of conservative intellectuals as part of the ideological war. John Birch Society founder Robert Welch modelled his organization on the very techniques he attributed to the Communist Party – manipulation, deceit, and secrecy.[36] Charles Koch wanted nothing of the nutty reputation the Birchers earned; to win, his party had to be respectable. It's easy to read David's philanthropy as part of the scheme. But that – and the courting of academics, name bequests to theatres, and the use of misleading names for the various front organizations – is simply a higher form of duplicity than the bottom-feeding Birchers could manage. Ever since he got involved in politics, Charles has thought that secrecy and duplicity were essential to his project.

'Covert Actors', Jane Mayer's 2010 article in *The New Yorker,* first brought wide attention to the political activities of the Koch Brothers. (The brothers, unhappy with the attention, hired private detectives to find, and publicists to spread dirt about, her.) The Koch political network now consists of about 700 major donors who contribute at least $100,000 a year; it collectively spent $750 million during the 2016 election cycle as compared with $100 million in 2010, a third of it on front groups like Americans for Prosperity and Freedom Partners, and plans to spend up to $400 million during the 2018 cycle.[37] But it's not only electoral politics. The network, with Charles Koch as its general, supports professors, think tanks, publications, advocacy organizations, as well as political candidates – all as part of a coherent, long-term, ideologically rigorous strategy. There's nothing remotely like them on the liberal left.

That's not to say there isn't some big money on that liberal left – just not as much, and not as ideologically coherent. The closest liberals come is the Democracy Alliance, founded in 2005, which gets money from the likes of George Soros and less famous moneyed liberals. But it distributed only about $500 million in the first decade of its existence, less than the Koch network spends on a single election cycle. And unlike the Koch network, whose spending is tightly controlled by the leadership, DA members decide where to spend their money. Among its beneficiaries are Media Matters and the Center for American Progress, which were essentially puppets of the Clintons.[38] Since the 2016 election, the DA has been funding what is grandly known in liberal circles as The Resistance, a vague effort to counter Trump via a grab-bag of organizations. So far, success seems elusive, in no small part because the driving philosophy has little more content than 'We're not Trump'.[39]

According to Theda Skocpol's 'Shifting Terrain' project, there are substantial geographic and sectoral contrasts between liberal and conservative big money. A third of both camps – with the liberals defined as Democracy Alliance partners and the conservatives as Koch Seminar participants –

derive their fortunes from finance; the commanding heights of the industrial class structure are not only shifting but contested terrain. But below that, the sorting is neater. The reactionaries are powered by dirty industries like mining and manufacturing, politically fraught ones like health care, and low-wage ones like food services and retail, while the liberals emerge from professional and scientific services, information, and education, arts, entertainment, and recreation. This sectoral line-up is highly congruent with the political complexions of the two major parties. (Notably absent on the liberal side: anyone representing the working class.) So too is their geographical makeup, with the liberals concentrated on the coasts and the conservatives in the heartland and South.[40]

Insofar as right-wing groups like think tanks, outside funders, and 'constituency organizations' have grown in importance while the Republican party itself has declined,[41] they are mostly part of the Koch network. It's an immensely complex structure, involving scores of front organizations. Open Secrets, an organization that follows political cash, has a flow chart on its website that tracks the Koch money from its core operations, Freedom Partners and TC4 Trust, to a variety of organizations like Americans for Prosperity, the 60 Plus Association, Concerned Women for America, and the Club for Growth, to more established operations like the U.S. Chamber of Commerce, the National Rifle Association, and the National Federation of Independent Business.[42] The flowchart, while vertiginously informative, obscures how hierarchical the operational structure is.

For Charles Koch, following the model laid down by Hayek and the Mount Pelerin crowd, political ideas have a production chain. Richard Fink, whom the Kochs have paid generously to think on their behalf for decades, wrote a brief but influential essay on the topic.[43] Fink outlined an intellectual economy of producer goods and consumer goods – the intellectuals, often university-based, are the makers of the producer goods, ideas which are then transformed into intermediate goods by think tanks, and then into products for mass application by activists. Or, as Koch himself put it, 'libertarians need an integrated strategy, vertically and horizontally integrated, to bring about social change, from idea creation to policy development to education to grassroots organizations to lobbying to litigation to political action.'[44] Check book in hand, he's done a lot to make it happen.

Fink, then an economics graduate student at New York University teaching part-time at Rutgers, dropped in on Charles in Wichita one day in the late 1970s, and asked for money to fund an institute devoted to Austrian economics at Rutgers. At the time, NYU was one of the few universities in the US where Austrian economics was taught at all. Koch immediately offered $150,000 (just over half a million in today's dollars) to kick-start the programme. With that money, Fink – who dreamt of becoming the Malcolm X of the libertarian movement (those revolutionary leftists again!) – founded the Center for the Study of Market Processes at Rutgers and soon relocated it to George Mason University (GMU), where it became the Mercatus Center.[45] (Mercatus brags that it receives no government or university money: it's entirely supported by right-wing philanthropists despite its academic home.) A couple of years later, James Buchanan, the libertarian economist, relocated himself to GMU. And then in 1985, the Koch-funded Institute for Humane Studies moved from California to GMU. This sequence of events transformed a formerly obscure state university in the Washington suburbs of northern Virginia into the Vatican of libertarian intellectual life. GMU isn't the only recipient of Koch funds, however; there were similar arrangements at institutions across the country.[46]

Think tanks are the second stage in the production and dissemination of ideas. One of the most important has been the Cato Institute, founded in 1977 with Koch money. The name came from Murray Rothbard, the libertarian economist, who emphasized there was nothing 'conservative' about the Institute's mission: he dismissed conservatism as 'a dying remnant of the *ancien régime* of the preindustrial era, and, as such, it has no future. In its contemporary American form, the recent conservative revival embodied the death throes of an ineluctably moribund, fundamentalist, rural, small-town, white Anglo-Saxon America.' For Rothbard – like Koch and Cato – libertarianism is a revolutionary doctrine.[47] It must be noted that a lot of people who voted for Trump live in rural, small-town, white Anglo-Saxon America.

Koch money also funded the Reason Foundation, best known for its eponymous magazine. The magazine was founded by a Boston University student in 1968 and published out of his dorm room in its early days. A decade later, Charles Koch agreed to fund it as long as it remained 'uncompromisingly radical'. It's hard to imagine a program officer at a liberal foundation saying something like that, because radical is against everything they believe in – though just two years later, Koch funded a presidential run by Ed Clark on the Libertarian Party ticket that involved enough compromise to inspire Rothbard to denounce his agenda as 'treacle'. For that, and other acts of insubordination, Koch fired Rothbard, who was shocked to experience the coercive power of the boss under actually existing capitalism (rather than the paradise of liberty, equality, and Bentham that existed in his head).[48]

All these Koch-fuelled entities – GMU, Cato, *Reason* – busily schooled Republican politicians and operatives throughout the 1980s and 1990s on the wisdom of privatization and austerity. Buchanan himself became disillusioned by the whole enterprise's lack of academic rigor and the compromises necessary to wield political power, and ended up getting squeezed out of GMU.[49] But to the Kochs, the ivory tower was a means not an end.

I don't mean to slight the contributions of other magnates in the Koch circle. Foster Friess, a Jackson Hole, Wyoming-based mutual fund magnate, has a special fondness for funding candidates of the Christian right, notably Rick Santorum. He also provided start-up money for *The Daily Caller,* a website edited by Tucker Carlson.[50] (Friess isn't the only member of the Koch network with his own media outlet; Philip Anschutz owns *The Washington Examiner* and *Weekly Standard.*) According to a friend who lives in Jackson Hole, Friess tried to persuade, without success, a local art museum to mount an exhibit on its front lawn featuring dinosaurs and humans living peacefully together, a tenet of the fundamentalist doctrine. Friess argues that taxes on the rich should be cut because they 'self-tax' through philanthropy. He encapsulated his principles of political economy and taxation in a 2012 interview:

'Do you believe that the government should be taking your money and spending it for you, or do you want to spend it for you …? If you look at what Steve Jobs has done for us, what Bill Gates has done for society, the government ought to pay them … It's that top 1 percent that probably contributes more to making the world a better place than the 99 percent … I think we ought to honor and uplift the 1 per cent, the ones who have created value.'[51]

More importantly, Robert Mercer, the hedge fund billionaire who would later pump cash into the Trump campaign, was drawn into the Koch circle after he financed an Islamophobic vendetta against the Ground Zero mosque, the pejorative name for a proposed Islamic cultural centre near the former site of the World Trade Center in lower Manhattan. There was some speculation that Mercer financed the campaign not only out of bigotry, but also to ward off regulation of Wall Street by New York State by scaring Democrats with his cascade of then-anonymous money.[52]

Another important figure in the Koch circle is Art Pope, a North Carolina discount store magnate, who has been central to the transformation of that state, which once had a reputation as one of the South's more progressive, into a hotbed of reaction. Pope hates unions and minimum wage laws – and his stores are located mainly in poor neighbourhoods. His anti-labour policies actually help create new customers, by creating more poor people.[53]

There are some right-wing philanthropists outside the Koch circle. Among the most important, but far less known, is Richard Uihlein, a Wisconsin-based packaging supplies magnate. Most of his support goes to political candidates, though he does support some think tanks in the Midwest. He's been a major supporter of the war on public employee unions, supporting not only political candidates but also the so-called *Janus* case, a suit that would devastate the funding of such unions. Uihlein was also not originally a Trump supporter, though he did come around and contribute both to his campaign and his inauguration. His extreme politics does give some Republicans pause; Pat Brady, former chair of the Illinois GOP, complains that he damages the party's brand by supporting candidates who are 'fringe right, homophobic bomb-throwers'.[54]

Pope and Uihlein are a reminder that the Kochs and their friends have been very active at the state and local level, where Democratic losses have been especially stark. (During the Obama years, they lost 11 Senate seats, 62 House seats, 12 governorships, and 958 state legislative seats. After the 2016 elections, Republicans controlled governorships and state legislatures in almost half the states.)[55] Control of the states matters not only for policy, but also because they draw the district lines for seats in the House of Representatives, and thereby have a strong hand in shaping its partisan makeup.

Right-wing funders have scores of outlets around the US. The State Policy Network (SPN) has 66 affiliates and over 80 associates populating every state but North Dakota.[56] Founded in 1992 by the South Carolina industrialist Thomas Roe, who had set up the first of these think tanks in his home state six years earlier on a suggestion from Ronald Reagan, the SPN flock develops policies, disseminates propaganda, and trains personnel to 'strengthen working families and defend our rights by promoting policies that create a level playing field and safeguard personal freedom, economic liberty, rule of law, property rights, and limited government', which in practice means gutting regulations, cutting taxes and services, privatizing public schools and pension systems, destroying unions in both the public and private sectors.[57] According to a 2013 investigation by the Center for Media and Democracy, the SPN is funded by right-wing foundations including the Koch Brothers, the Bradley Foundation (a long-standing funder of the right), and the Walton family (of Wal-Mart fame) along with corporations like Microsoft, AT&T, Verizon, GlaxoSmithKline, and Time Warner.[58]

Although SPN-affiliated think tanks often have anodyne names to disguise their ideological leanings, like the James Madison Institute in Tallahassee,

Florida, under that surface lies a lot of odious stuff, including nostalgia for the Confederacy and a desire to keep black people from voting. A recent study by the activist group UnKoch My Campus showed that a Madison 'scholar', Marshall DeRosa, promoted a scheme that the restoration of voting rights of convicted felons be made conditional on completing a 'civics' course – such as one funded by Koch foundation and by GEO, a private prison operator. (GEO has contributed to Trump and other Republicans, and is getting contracts for housing detained immigrants.) Not coincidentally, a disproportionate number of ex-convicts denied voting rights – for the rest of their life, even after release – in Florida and many other states are black and likely to lean left politically. You can see the charm of this sort of program for the right. DeRosa is also affiliated with another think tank in the Koch orbit, the Ludwig Von Mises Institute (LVMI) at Auburn University. LVMI is closely associated with the neo-Confederate movement. It's striking how often you scratch a 'libertarian' and find a white supremacist lurking underneath.[59]

That's not a casual slur. As Nancy MacLean shows in *Democracy in Chains* – much to the annoyance of contemporary libertarians – the movement was energized in the 1950s and 1960s by resistance to federal attempts to integrate public school systems in the South. Liberty, in this view, was indistinguishable from the right of white people not to have to associate with black people. The intimate relationship between race and this conception of freedom goes back at least as far as John C. Calhoun, a figure revered among serious American conservatives.[60] In the 1960s, the young Charles Koch founded an all-white private school in Colorado; he named it the Freedom School.[61]

Closely associated with the SPN is the American Legislative Exchange Council (ALEC), which shares funders and agenda, but operates at the political ground level, writing bills, lobbying legislators.[62] Since state and local governments often operate in obscurity, with part-time legislators and thin staffs, having pre-written bills and trained politicians is a great lubricant to the right-wing agenda. ALEC draws funding from a wide variety of business interests, often by offering themselves as helpful on a very specific policy issue and then bringing the firms more permanently into the fold. ALEC also developed a longer-term political strategy, larger than the particular interests of individual firms and sectors, which explained the fiscal strains on states as coming from excessive spending rather than meagre revenues. They pushed for constitutional limits on state spending and legislative supermajorities to pass tax increases. To promote that agenda, ALEC framed public employees as an unjustly 'protected class' and placed their unions in the crosshairs.[63] As with the SPN, ALEC gets money (and personnel) from the Kochs and other right-wing foundations, but also from corporations pursuing specific sectoral interests, though the details are largely secret.[64]

Koch allies like Robert Mercer are also active on the state and local level. In 2014, Mercer's daughter Rebekah founded Reclaim New York, which not only pushes the standard right agenda in the state capital, but also gets involved in small-town politics in upstate New York, a region that most big players don't give much thought to.[65]

THE TRUMP PRESIDENCY

From the first, Trump – or, given his ignorance of policy, more likely Pence – turned to the Koch network for advice in staffing his new administration. A well-organized force is ideally suited to fill a vacuum. Unsurprisingly, given the family's material interests – among other things, Koch Industries handles about a quarter of the exports from the Canadian tar sands to the US – their presence was most prominent in the fields of energy and the environment.[66] To help staff the Energy Department, Trump – or whoever was thinking for him – drew on the expertise of Michael McKenna, among whose consulting clients was Koch Industries. Another Koch lobbyist, Michael Catanzaro, headed the 'energy independence' function for the transition team.

Heading the search for Environmental Protection Agency (EPA) staffers was Myron Ebell, a climate change sceptic out of the Koch-recipient Competitive Enterprise Institute. Koch Industries was one of only three US companies that had been listed by the EPA as a top-ten polluter of air, water, and the climate.[67] The EPA has proven to be one of the most effective arms of the Trump regime, lifting environmental regulations with vigour, despite a multitude of scandals surrounding its chief, Scott Pruitt. Pruitt's nomination was fervently supported by Koch-funded interests and Senators.[68]

And there are others, even apart from the already mentioned Education Secretary Betsy DeVos. Mike Pompeo, a Kansan nicknamed 'the Congressman from Koch', first headed the CIA and then moved over to run the State Department after the early departure of Rex Tillerson (himself a former CEO of ExxonMobil). Marc Short, who once worked for Pence and spent five years as president of the Koch Bros' Freedom Partners, is Trump's liaison to Congress, having moved into that role from being one of the 'Kochs' liaisons to Washington's professional conservative class.'[69] (Short left the administration in July 2018, citing 'diminishing returns', and took a fellowship at the University of Virginia.) The network's influence extends to informal advisors as well. Trump solicits advice on energy from pals like fracking magnate Harold Hamm, whom Mayer described as a 'charter member of the Kochs' donor circle', and Robert Murray, CEO of a privately owned coal mining company that bears his name. Because of declining demand for coal, the company is experiencing considerable financial distress; he's also been lobbying Trump to bail out the industry.[70] These guys are libertarians until their cheques start bouncing.

The Kochs have won a few victories in the Trump era – a conservative Supreme Court justice, Neil Gorsuch (son of the head of the Environmental Protection Agency during the Reagan years), lots of deregulation in energy, environment, and finance, and giant tax cuts. But there are frustrations: federal spending has hardly been cut overall, aside from small cuts to specific programs, and Congress failed to repeal Obamacare, though they and the executive branch are chipping away at it. And the tariffs and immigration restrictions are major losses.[71] Trump's rhetoric about immigration and Muslims were among the reasons Charles Koch refused to endorse Trump. Much of corporate America is not happy with that part of Trump's agenda either, but they seem unable to do much about it. This says something about the relative autonomy of the state: despite objections from internationalist elites, Trump is getting his way pretty often.

It's surprising how little business support Trump had for a Republican nominee. Hillary Clinton, though not deeply loved by big capital, was nonetheless the candidate they preferred over the loose-cannon Trump. With a few exceptions, Wall Street didn't like him. Nor did Silicon Valley, with the exception of the libertarian PayPal founder Peter Thiel (who also bought himself New Zealand citizenship and wants to set up an offshore libertarian state). As Michael Wolff reports in *Fire and Fury,* shortly after the election, a Valley delegation made the pilgrimage to Trump Tower. Afterwards, Trump called Rupert Murdoch, who asked him how the meeting went. 'Great, just great', Trump characteristically reported. Obama had them under his boot for eight years – 'too much regulation' – and they were looking forward to his help. Murdoch responded, 'for eight years these guys had Obama in their pocket. They practically ran the administration. They don't need your help.' Trump countered that they need H-1B visas, which the industry uses to bring in lower-wage foreign engineers. Murdoch reminded him that would difficult to square with his anti-immigrant positions. Trump, unconcerned, said he'd figure it out. After hanging up, Murdoch (whose approval Trump craved but never fully got) commented, 'what a fucking idiot'.[72] It's striking that Murdoch, who for decades has been a master of right-wing propaganda, and whose *New York Post* provided endless coverage of Trump's rise to fame, is not really part of Trump's business base. Murdoch held a fundraiser for

Hillary Clinton when she was running for Senate in 2006, and supported her in the 2016 election.

Silicon Valley does love those H-1Bs, and corporate America likes immigrant labour, skilled and unskilled. The upper bourgeoisie also likes immigrants to do the gardening and change diapers, as does the lumpen-bourgeoisie. They've been unable to stop Trump's xenophobic crackdown on immigrants. The bourgeoisie loves free trade, too. And they've been unable to block him from starting a trade war, or from undermining basic structures of the US empire, like NATO.

And what a trade war it is. It's unlinked to any economic plan, and seems slapped together with a mix of whim and Sinophobia. Imposing tariffs on steel and aluminum makes no sense at all; the industries are small, and raising the prices of these metals harms much larger sectors like autos, appliances, and machinery. Imposing tariffs on hundreds of Chinese imports will push up prices and provoke retaliation that would damage farming and manufacturing industries whose workers are part of Trump's electoral base. Trump is thought likely to impose tariffs on imported cars; he has a special animus for German cars and has reportedly said he doesn't want to see any more Mercedes on Fifth Avenue in Manhattan. He's apparently unaware that Mercedes, BMW, and Volkswagen all have large manufacturing operations in the US South, and not only are many of these offending vehicles made here, those factories export a substantial portion of their production.[73] His downscale voters work in those factories; his upscale voters drive their products.

It would be overdone to bring up Smoot-Hawley, as bourgeois pundits reflexively do in these situations, but a trade war would push up prices and distress the financial markets – not, in other words, in US capital's general interest. But capital wasn't able to stop his election. Tech companies have been reportedly lobbying Congressional Republicans to dial it back on immigration restrictions, but with little success.[74] Republicans, even those once loyal to big capital, who might be expected to do big capital's work in reining in Trump's xenophobia, have fallen in line with his agenda, thanks to his ability to promote primary challenges to Establishment-friendly incumbents. Trump is an ignoramus, but he does have some striking political skills.

THE NEW CLASS

So how should we conceive the New Class, or class fraction, that finds expression in, or at least affinities with, the Trump administration? As I argued in my essay for the 2016 *Register,* drawing on Benjamin Waterhouse's history of lobbying, the business coalition that came together in the 1970s to lobby for deregulation and tax cuts largely dissolved as a coherent force when it got what it wanted. Rather than a broad agenda, the business lobby narrowed to sectoral and individual corporate interests. The Chamber of Commerce, though purporting to speak for business-in-general, came to rent itself out to specific clients, often unsavoury ones. That original coalition was socially liberal – it had no interest in the Christian right's moral agenda. Nor were they nativist. Almost every Wall Street and Fortune 500 company has a diversity department, handling everything from antiracist training sessions to the corporate float for the annual Gay Pride parade. Their worldview is little different from Hillary Clinton's. But they're not passionately engaged in politics. They write checks, but profits are high and the tax rate they paid on those profits at the beginning of 2018 was the lowest since 1930.[75]

They're layabouts compared to the New Class, or class fraction, I'm describing, a gang made up of the owners of private companies as opposed to public ones, disproportionately in dirty industries. The financier wing comes largely out of 'alternative investments', hedge funds and private equity, not big Wall Street banks or Silicon Valley venture capital (VC) firms. The Kochs have their own VC operations, designed, among other things, to 'find, fund, and assist companies whose groundbreaking products, services, and innovations would otherwise be locked out of the marketplace by burdensome public policy barriers' – barriers they're helpfully paying politicians to dismantle. They're trying to win friends in the Valley, but with limited success.[76]

Most alternative investment operations are run as partnerships with a small staff, often under the direction of a single personality. Collectively they look like freebooters more than corporate personalities, and more like asset-strippers than builders, be it natural assets in the case of the carbon moguls or corporate assets in the case of the PE titans. Trump himself ran a real estate firm with a small staff and no outside shareholders. Like a private equity guy, Trump loaded up his casinos with debt and pocketed much of the proceeds. You might think it's hard for casinos to go bust – the house always wins – but Trump managed to steer his into a ditch, at great personal profit to himself (though with him you never know for sure). Trump met his Commerce Secretary Wilbur Ross when Ross, a buyout artist, helped him restructure his busted casino debt so that he could maintain a stake even though the bondholders – whom Ross was allegedly representing – could have frozen him out.[77]

The prominence of private ownership is striking, and politically reactionary. Lately, for example, some institutional investors have been lobbying energy firms to plan for a post-carbon future and start thinking of their fossil assets as financially doomed – a point endorsed by Mark Carney, governor of the Bank of England, in a 2015 speech warning that 'stranded' carbon assets represented a challenge to financial stability.[78] Since they have no outside shareholders, the Kochs, Bob Murray, and Harold Hamm are spared having to listen to this chatter.

This alliance between the private corporate form and political reaction is a reminder of Marx's observations on the topic. He described the emergence of the corporation, with its separation of ownership and management, as 'the abolition of the capitalist mode of production within the capitalist mode of production itself, and hence a self-abolishing contradiction'. Workers could hire managers as easily as shareholders, or maybe perform the task themselves. The stockholder-owned public corporation was a stepping stone to a truly public entity. And short of that ambition, public firms are more transparent and subject to outside pressure than ones controlled by a small, secretive circle of owners.

But, as we've seen, such owners have proven highly capable of organizing as a political force. Corporate America isn't averse to working with Koch organizations. Exxon and Microsoft worked with the Koch-heavy Citizens for a Sound Economy to push very specific agendas. But these are usually temporary, targeted crusades; none have the breadth, durability, and ubiquity of the Koch agenda. And that agenda has a substantial toehold on state power.

Trump himself, however, isn't always that agenda's most stable administrator. His volatility and impetuousness are the opposite of the corporate style of deliberative, bureaucratic rule. Trump would love to rule by decree; CEOs prefer more careful working out of details. Trump's nationalist obsessions around tariffs and immigration are shared with only a few advisors like Ross (who has a history of investing in domestic steel) and Peter Navarro. It's unwelcome to more conventional staffers like economic advisor Lawrence Kudlow (ex-Bear Stearns) and Treasury Secretary Steven Mnuchin (ex-Goldman Sachs). Although Silicon Valley would love to open up the Chinese market, there's no interest in doing so by beating the country over the head with a club. As Apple CEO Tim Cook has said, the company does business in China not so much for cheap labour as its substantial manufacturing and coding skills.[79] Cook tried to discourage Trump from imposing tariffs on Chinese exports; Trump tried to buy his assent by promising to exempt iPhones from duties, but Cook is worried about larger risks of a trade war.[80] But Trump imposed the tariffs anyway, and it looks like Cook and his comrades can do nothing to reverse it –

though should the protectionist turn end badly, Trump will be vulnerable. It's certainly straining relations with some of his popular electoral base, like soybean farmers in the Midwest hit by retaliatory Chinese tariffs. (China and the EU have selected their retaliatory targets carefully, so that they disproportionately hit Trump-voting areas.)[81] But so far, free-trading elites have yet to mobilize.

A striking thing about the economic agenda of the Trump administration is how snarling and backward-looking it is. Most American politicians trade in optimism about the future. Bill Clinton could never stop talking about building a bridge to the twenty-first century. Reagan could never stop talking about how our best days are ahead of us. Not Trump. His inaugural address was all about 'American carnage'. He seems to want to bring back the world of 1955, when coal and steel were powerful industries. It would make more sense − capitalist sense − instead to develop an industrial future, one manufacturing the infrastructure of a clean energy and transportation system, in the abandoned parts of the Midwest and South, regions suffering from poverty, isolation, addiction, and early death. But that would take major amounts of public investment and planning, things that Trump and his party are profoundly opposed to.

It's a government of, by, and for the asset strippers. Their climate denialism and financial recklessness are all of a piece. Live for today; tomorrow is someone else's problem.

NOTES

1   The 'vandalism' charge refers specifically to his destruction, in 1980, of limestone reliefs on the front of the old Bonwit Teller building, which were supposed to be preserved. He'd promised them to the Metropolitan Museum of Art, but then decided it would be too expensive to save them. They were jackhammered in the middle of the night by a crew of undocumented Polish workers, an interesting detail in light of his later hostility toward immigrants. They demolished the entire building, toiling for $4 an hour in 12-hour shifts, without gloves, hard hats, or masks, to make way for what would become Trump Tower. In 1998, Trump reached a settlement for $1.4 million in the case (though its terms were not revealed until late 2017). Just over a third of it went to a union benefit fund, and the rest to lawyers' fees and expenses. Christopher Gray, 'The Store That Slipped Through the Cracks', New York Times, 3 October 2014; Charles V. Bagli, 'Trump Paid Over $1 million in Labor Settlement, Documents Reveal', New York Times, 27 November 2017. Trump Tower was the developer's second major project. His first was a Hyatt hotel next to Grand Central Station in Manhattan, which opened in 1980. As a condition of the development, Trump was supposed to allow access to the subway; he reneged on that promise. The Hyatt was granted $360 million in tax breaks by the city, which was burrowing its way out of its 1975 fiscal crisis and desperate for a high-profile development. (Throughout his career, Trump has enjoyed

$885 million in such favors in New York City alone.) When Richard Ravitch, the head of the state's Urban Development Corp. and a major player in New York real estate and politics over the decades, said he thought the hotel should pay regular taxes, Trump threatened to have him fired. Trump's father was wired into the Democratic power structure in the city and the state, so that was probably not an idle threat; he was very friendly with then-mayor Abe Beame and then-governor Hugh Carey. The hotel was built by putting a glass and steel façade over an existing stone structure. Presaging decades of coming assaults on the aesthetic sense, Trump told one of the architects, 'I hate granite. I like shiny …' Charles V. Bagli, 'A Trump Empire Built on Inside Connections and $885 Million in Tax Breaks', *New York Times,* 17 September 2016; William Menking, 'Donald Trump's Grand Hyatt Hotel Illustrates What's Wrong With Development in New York', *The Architect's Newspaper,* 5 August 2016.

2   Adam B. Lerner, 'The 10 Best Lines From Donald Trump's Announcement Speech', *Politico,* 16 June 2015.

3   Pierre Bourdieu, *On Television,* Translated by Priscilla Parkhurst Ferguson, New York: New Press, 1998, p. 43.

4   Garrett M. Graff, 'The Madman and the Bomb', *Politico,* 11 August 2017.

5   The classic work is E. Digby Baltzell, *The Protestant Establishment,* New Haven, Connecticut: Yale University Press, 1987.

6   Dylan Matthews, 'Donald Trump Isn't Rich Because He's a Great Investor. He's Rich Because His Dad Was Rich', *Vox,* 30 March 2016; Josie Cox, 'Michael Bloomberg Implies Donald Trump Might Not Be a Billionaire', *The Independent,* 1 August 2017; Tina Nguyen, 'Is Donald Trump Not Really a Billionaire?', *Vanity Fair,* 31 May 2016; Randall Lane, 'Inside the Epic Fantasy That's Driven Donald Trump for 33 Years', *Forbes,* 29 September 2015.

7   Ronald Reagan, 'The New Republican Party', speech delivered at Fourth Annual CPAC Convention, 6 February 1977. A Flesch-Kincaid calculator is available at www. webpagefx.com.

8   Yashar Ali, 'What George W. Bush Really Thought of Donald Trump's Inauguration', *New York Magazine,* 29 March 2017; Donald Trump, 'Inaugural Address', Washington, D.C., 20 January 2017, available at www.whitehouse.gov.

9   Sarah Burns, 'Why Trump Doubled Down on the Central Park Five', *New York Times,* 17 October 2016; Amy Davidson Sorkin, 'Donald Trump and the Central Park Five', *The New Yorker,* 23 June 2014.

10   Philip Bump, 'In 1927, Donald Trump's Father Was Arrested After a Klan Riot in Queens', *Washington Post,* 29 February 2016; Mike Pearl, 'All the Evidence We Could Find About Fred Trump's Alleged Involvement With the KKK', *Vice,* 10 March 2016.

11   Wayne Barrett, 'How a Young Donald Trump Forced His Way From Avenue Z to Manhattan', *Village Voice,* 15 January 1979; Thomas Kaplan, 'Woody Guthrie Wrote of His Contempt for His Landlord, Donald Trump's Father', *New York Times,* 25 January 2016.

12   Michael Wolff, *Fire and Fury,* New York: Henry Holt & Co., 2018, p. 19.

13   Joshua Green, *Devil's Bargain: Steve Bannon, Donald Trump, and the Nationalist Uprising,* New York: Penguin Press, 2017, pp. xxi, 13.

14   Robert Costa, 'Trump Enlists Veteran Operative David Bossie as Deputy Campaign Manager', *Washington Post,* 1 September 2016.

15   For supporting evidence, see Doug Henwood, *My Turn: Hillary Clinton Targets the Presidency*, New York: OR Books, 2016.

16   Aaron Blake, 'Trump's Forbidden Love: Single-Payer Health Care', *Washington Post*, 5 May 2017.

17   Green, *Devil's Bargain*, pp. 59, 110.

18   Green, *Devil's Bargain*, p. 240.

19   Green, *Devil's Bargain*, pp. 131, 133.

20   Green, *Devil's Bargain*, pp. 141–7, 156.

21   Michael Wolff, *Fire and Fury: Inside the Trump White House*, New York: Henry Holt, 2018.

22   Wolff, *Fire and Fury*, pp. 9–10.

23   L. Brent Bozell III, 'Conservatives Against Trump', *National Review*, 16 February 2016.

24   Chris Cillizza, '5 Reasons Mike Pence Makes a Lot of Sense as Donald Trump's Vice President', *Washington Post*, 14 July 2016.

25   Jane Mayer, *Dark Money: The Hidden History of the Billionaires Behind the Rise of the Radical Right*, New York: Anchor Books, 2016, Kindle edition, loc. 136.

26   Kenneth P. Vogel and Maggie Haberman, 'Mike Pence's Koch Advantage', *Politico*, 8 August 2014.

27   Mayer, *Dark Money*, Kindle locs. 406–407, 7432.

28   Jacob Bernstein, 'The Man Who Bought New York', *New York Times*, 5 May 2018.

29   Barack Obama, 'Presumptive Democratic Nominee Speech', St. Paul, Minnesota, 3 June 2008, available at: obamaspeeches.com.

30   Mayer, *Dark Money*, Kindle locs. 545, 548.

31   Quoted in Mayer, *Dark Money*, Kindle locs. 743, 769.

32   Mayer, *Dark Money*, Kindle loc. 2171.

33   Emily DeRuy, 'What Betsy DeVos Did (And Didn't) Reveal About Her Education Priorities', *The Atlantic*, 17 January 2017.

34   Mayer, *Dark Money*, Kindle loc. 1205.

35   Ronald Radosh, 'Steve Bannon, Trump's Top Guy, Told Me He Was "A Leninist"', *Daily Beast*, 22 August 2016.

36   Mayer, *Dark Money*, Kindle locs. 915, 2139.

37   Matea Gold, 'Koch network seeks to defuse donor frustration over Trump rebuff', *Washington Post*, 1 August 2016; James Hohmann and Matea Gold, 'Koch Network to Spend $300 Million to $400 Million on Politics, Policy in 2018 Cycle', *Washington Post*, 28 January 2017.

38   Kenneth P. Vogel, 'Inside the Vast Liberal Conspiracy', *Politico*, 23 June 2014.

39   Kenneth P. Vogel, 'The Resistance, Raising Big Money, Upends Liberal Politics', *New York Times*, 7 October 2017.

40   'Maps and Charts', *Research on the Shifting U.S. Political Terrain*, available at: terrain.gov. harvard.edu/graphs-and-maps-0.

41   Theda Skocpol, 'The Koch Network and Republican Party Extremism', *Perspectives on Politics*, 14(3), September 2016, pp. 681-99.

42   Center for Responsive Politics, 'A Maze of Money', graphic located at: www. opensecrets.org/news/wp-content/uploads/2014/01/koch-descrip.png.

43   Brian Doherty, *Radicals For Capitalism: A Freewheeling History of the Modern American Libertarian Movement*, New York: Public Affairs Books, 2007, p. 410. Richard Fink,

'The Structure of Social Change', *Liberty Guide*, George Mason University Institute for Humane Studies, 18 October 2012. Fink's essay can be found at archive.org.

44   Doherty, *Radicals For Capitalism,* p. 410.

45   Doherty, *Radicals For Capitalism,* pp. 408, 430.

46   Over the years, the Kochs have given about $50 million – a third of what they've given to hundreds of colleges and universities between 2005 and 2015 – to establish GMU's economics programs and law school as bastions of right-wing thought. Documents dislodged through a lawsuit filed by student activists at GMU showed that from 1990 onward, the Kochs had enormous say in faculty hires in economics. Mayer, *Dark Money*, Kindle locs. 2871–2883; Erica L. Green and Stephanie Saul, 'What Charles Koch and Other Donors to George Mason University Got For Their Money', *New York Times*, 5 May 2018. The Charles Koch Foundation lists 349 colleges and universities as recipients of funding – see www.charleskochfoundation.org/our-giving-and-support/higher-education/list-of-supported-colleges.

47   See Nancy MacLean, *Democracy in Chains: The Deep History of the Radical Right's Stealth Plan for America*, London: Scribe, 2017, p. 139; and Murray N. Rothbard, 'Left and Right: The Prospects for Liberty', *Left and Right,* Spring 1965, pp. 4-22. The Rothbard essay dates from 1965, but was republished as Cato's first paper. It's striking how reminiscent the quoted passage is of this, from Emerson's 'Circles': 'I unsettle all things. No facts are to me sacred; none are profane; I simply experiment, an endless seeker with no Past at my back.' In the essay, Rothbard criticizes socialism, and Marx specifically, for being too 'conservative', though he expresses admiration for Lenin's eagerness to overturn things.

48   MacLean, *Democracy in Chains,* pp. 143–44, 147.

49   MacLean, *Democracy in Chains*, pp. 197–203.

50   Mayer, *Dark Money*, Kindle loc. 5130.

51   Chrystia Freeland, 'Money Demonized in U.S. politics, Millionaire Says', *New York Times,* 16 February 2012.

52   Ben Smith, 'Hedge Fund Figure Financed Mosque Campaign', *Politico,* 18 January 2011.

53   Mayer, *Dark Money*, Kindle locs. 5213–5216.

54   Maggie Severns, 'The Biggest Republican Megadonor You've Never Heard Of', *Politico,* 19 March 2018.

55   Matt Yglesias, 'The Democratic Party's Down-Ballot Collapse, Explained', *Vox,* 10 January 2017; Reid Wilson, 'Dems Hit New Lows in State Legislatures', *The Hill,* 18 November 2016.

56   See the State Policy Network website, at http://spn.org, for a directory, mission statement and number of affiliates.

57   Center for Media and Democracy, 'EXPOSED: The State Policy Network: The Powerful Right-Wing Network Helping to Hijack State Politics and Government', November 2013, available at: www.alecexposed.org/wiki/EXPOSED:_The_State_Policy_Network.

58   Center for Media and Democracy, *Exposed.*

59   The 'UnKoch My Campus' report details the racist history of the Koch family and their network of grantees. UnKoch My Campus, 'Advancing White Supremacy Through Academic Strategy', May 2018, available at www.unkochmycampus.org/los-preface.

60   See MacLean's prologue to *Democracy in Chains* for a detailed history. When I was in the Party of the Right at Yale in the early 1970s, 'John Caldwell Calhoun' – always all three names – was cited frequently as an authority. Calhoun was a Yale alumnus, and a residential college named after him was only renamed, after years of protest, in 2017.

61   Mayer, *Dark Money*, Kindle loc. 180.

62   Center for Media and Democracy, 'A CMD Special Report on ALEC's Funding and Spending', 31 July 2011, available at: www.prwatch.org/news/2011/07/10887/cmd-special-report-alecs-funding-and-spending.

63   Alexander Hertel-Fernandez, 'Explaining Durable Business Coalitions in U.S. Politics: Conservatives and Corporate Interests across America's Statehouses', *Studies in American Political Development*, 30(1), April 2016, pp. 1-18; Alexander Hertel-Fernandez, 'Who Passes Business's 'Model Bills'? Policy Capacity and Corporate Influence in U.S. State Politics', *Perspectives on Politics,* 12(3), September 2014, pp. 582–602.

64   Center for Media and Democracy, 'ALEC's Funding and Spending'.

65   Jon Campbell, 'How Robert Mercer Impacts Local Battles in New York', *lohud,* 9 November 2017, available at: www.lohud.com.

66   Mayer, *Dark Money*, Kindle loc. 1112.

67   Mayer, *Dark Money,* preface to the 2017 Anchor Books edition (2017).

68   Union of Concerned Scientists, 'Who's Backing Scott Pruitt to Head the EPA? The Koch Brothers', February 2017, available at: www.ucsusa.org.

69   Kyle Cheney and Matthew Nussbaum, 'Donald Trump's Man on the Hill', *Politico,* 18 January 2017; Kenneth P. Vogel and Tarini Parti, 'Inside Koch World,' *Politico,* 15 June 2012.

70   Soma Biswas, 'Murray Energy Opens Debt Talks with Bondholders', *Wall Street Journal,* 7 May 2018.

71   James Hohmann, 'Koch Network Growing Frustrated with the GOP's 2018 Agenda', *Washington Post,* 6 April 2018.

72   Wolff, *Fire & Fury*, p. 36.

73   Jackie Wattles and Charles Riley, 'Why President Trump's Obsession with German Cars is Misplaced', *CNN,* 31 May 2018.

74   Anna Palmer, Jake Sherman, and Daniel Lippmann, 'POLITICO Playbook: Senate GOP Outside Group Starts to Wallop Donnelly in Indiana', *Politico,* 15 June 2018.

75   US Department of Commerce Bureau of Economic Analysis, national income and product accounts, table 1.14, line 28 divided by line 27, available at: www.bea.gov.

76   Alana Abramson, 'A New VC Firm Tied to the Koch Brothers Plans to Take on Government Regulations', *Fortune,* 31 January 2018; Nancy Scola, 'Tech's New D.C. Partner: Charles Koch', *Politico,* 10 December 2017.

77   Max Abelson, 'Wilbur Ross and the Era of Billionaire Rule', *Business Week,* 26 January 2017.

78   Mark Carney, 'Breaking the Tragedy of the Horizon – Climate Change and Financial Stability', speech given to Lloyd's of London, 30 September 2015, available at: www.bankofengland.co.uk.

79   Glenn Leibowitz, 'Apple CEO Tim Cook: This is the Number 1 Reason We Make iPhones in China (It's Not What You Think)', *Inc.,* 21 December 2017.

80   Jack Nicas and Paul Mozur, 'In China Trade War, Apple Worries It Will Be Collateral Damage', *New York Times,* 18 June 2018.

81   See for example Maureen Linke and Josh Zumbrun, 'Chinese Tariffs Hit Trump Counties Harder', *Wall Street Journal,* 6 July 2018.

LOCATING TRUMP: PALEOCONSERVATISM, NEOLIBERALISM, AND ANTI-GLOBALIZATION

RAY KIELY

'Capitalism, an economic system driven only, according to its own theory, by the accumulation of profit, is at least as much the enemy of tradition as the NAACP or communism.'[1]

The title of the article from which this quote is derived was 'Capitalism, the Enemy', but it was not written by any kind of socialist. The positive reference to tradition and the negative references to the NAACP do give us some clue. Indeed the article was published in the American paleoconservative journal *Chronicles* in 2000, and was written by the late Samuel Francis, a paleoconservative thinker who was an advocate of white nationalism, if not white supremacism. It was written as a protest against the decision of the South Carolina House of Representatives to remove the Confederate flag from the state capital building. One might add that it also reflects a longstanding southern tradition that is in some respects hostile to capitalism, in which the likes of John Calhoun and George Fitzhugh defended slavery on the grounds that it was based on a paternalism in which 'natural masters' looked after their inferiors, in contrast to capitalism in which wage slaves simply had to find work in order to live.[2]

Even after capitalism became dominant in the US, conservatives like Theodore Roosevelt and Brooks Adams worried that the cash nexus, individual self-interest, and abstract liberal principles were insufficient guarantors of social cohesion. Like much of the European (and especially German) conservatives right before and after World War I, they made the case for imperial expansion. In the post-World War II era, European conservatism in many respects made its peace with capitalism in the face of the threat of 'totalitarianism'.[3] In the United States it gave rise to 'fusionism',[4] which combined suspicion of the New Deal state with support for its robust deployment against (perceived and real) communism, and in support of 'traditional values' such as family and religion. A conservative-libertarian fusion into 'neo-conservatism' energised the Goldwater presidential campaign in 1964 and the victorious Reagan presidencies in the 1980s. The Cold War was important for post-war American conservatism in reconciling these two things. Neoconservatives had significant doubts about the Great Society program and the ways in which welfare increasingly undermined the nuclear family and the male breadwinner, so that the 'masculine welfare state' of Roosevelt was displaced by the 'feminine' welfare state of Lyndon Johnson.[5] This gave rise to the neoconservative-neoliberal alliance in challenging a welfare state that was not only providing social safety nets to the deserving poor, but was showing compassion for the undeserving poor, and thus encouraging welfare dependency.[6] Neoconservatives hoped that welfare reform and the promotion of supply side economics would restore the virtue of the individual entrepreneur, though there remained an ongoing tension between market individualism and social cohesion. But crucially, like neoliberals, neoconservatives believed that the spirit of competition was essential for the resurgence of the entrepreneur, and that this included the promotion of free trade and the end of protectionism as well as financial liberalisation, as occurred in the Reagan era and beyond. After the Cold War, the decadence of the 1990s was replaced by the post-2001 renewal of what amounted to empire through a 'neo-Reaganite' foreign policy, so that republican virtue could exist alongside the so-called free market.[7]

But even neoconservatives – the conservative faction most supportive of capitalism and indeed neoliberalism – worried that while capitalism promoted both the (supposed) freedom of the individual and efficiency through wealth creation, it was far less successful at promoting virtue. This was necessary for society to cohere around shared values, rather than individual market calculation.[8] In other words, conservatives still feared that the republican tradition was under threat because of capitalism's excessive individualism, relativism, and expansion, which undermined tradition, established order, and the nation. As expressed most militantly, this came to be known as 'paleoconservatism'. Although one survey of American conservatism suggested as recently as 2016 that 'paleoconservatism presently appears to be a spent force',[9] this failed to capture the ways paleoconservative concerns to reconcile capitalism with tradition, so that private vices can give rise to public virtue, could resonate.

Paleoconservatives had little problem with anti-communism in the Cold War but were far more suspicious of interventionism and internationalist commitments in the post-Cold War world. In particular, while private enterprise and capitalism were to be supported, free trade and internationalism were seen to have undermined the republic and republican virtue. Samuel Francis thus argued that American identity had been undermined by an alliance of a managerial elite and multinational companies, neither of whom put America first.[10] While inter-war European conservatives decried the impact of pluralism on the mass state, leading to weak states like the Weimar Republic, the American paleoconservatives argued that the post-war managerial state remained strong.[11] On the face of it, this could be regarded as a critique of the New Deal and Great Society, and thus compatible with neoconservative and neoliberal critiques which focus on a self-interested new class of state elites. However, paleoconservatives contended that this liberal managerial elite retained control of the state *after* Reagan and the end of the Cold War, promoting globalization in alliance with rootless multinational companies that invest overseas and outsource production, while encouraging immigration and multiculturalism. The end result is deindustrialisation and the undermining of traditional American culture, squeezing white 'Middle America' between a cosmopolitan corporate elite and poor ethnic minorities.[12] State elites themselves may claim to be the prisoners of various interest groups, but in fact these liberal social planners 'hide rather than flaunt the power they exercise. This however does not render their power any less real, though it is not individuals but a class of experts who speak out against inequality and monopolize this rule.'[13]

In the 1990s, the paleos had their national hero in Patrick Buchanan, who tried unsuccessfully to be the Republican candidate for the 1992 and 1996 presidential elections. He particularly gave voice to the disappointment that the economic liberalism of the 1980s coincided with the rise of social liberalism, which came to be epitomised by the loathed Clinton administrations of the 1990s. Talking in terms of the need to win the 'culture wars',[14] Buchanan emphasised the need to save America from foreign do-gooders, bureaucrats, and corporate elites, so that the market could re-embed itself within virtuous conservative traditions, while ensuring that governments avoided becoming embroiled in liberal wars of intervention and leave burdensome international agreements. This 'anti-globalization' abroad should also lead to 'anti-globalization' at home, as Buchanan warned that multiculturalism was a threat to the US cultural heritage just as free trade threatened its economic strength. The US' cultural heritage needed to be restored, and this meant promoting a white, European, Christian nationalism. Against 'free trade', Buchanan invoked the spirit of an older republican tradition, such as Alexander Hamilton's case for protectionism to develop American manufacturing,[15] arguing that 'no nation has risen to pre-eminence through free trade'.[16] He also suggested that immigration was changing the cultural cohesion of the US, and by 2011 could still be found apocalyptically talking of the suicide of a superpower and the threat of the end of white America. To prevent this, he called for ending all immigration as well as removing 'illegal' immigrants, closing military bases overseas, massively cutting government spending, introducing economic protectionism, and undertaking a conservative counterattack in the culture wars.[17]

Much of this sounds like Donald Trump's programme during his presidential campaign. Indeed, Buchanan himself called Trump 'Middle America's Messenger'.[18] Although the *National Review*, the conservative intellectual magazine founded by William Buckley Jr. in 1955, contended that 'Trump is a philosophically unmoored political opportunist who would trash the broad ideological consensus within the GOP in favor of a free-floating populism with strongman overtones',[19] this reflected an understanding of conservatism which reduces it to a pragmatic acceptance of, and cautious adaptation to, the status quo. A better appreciation of what Trump represented may be captured in terms of the distinction that maverick conservative Samuel Huntington usefully made between *positional* conservatism, which adapts to the status quo in times of relative stability, and *doctrinal* conservatism, which emerges in times of perceived reversal and decline.[20] Seen in this way, Trump and the paleos stand in a long line of doctrinal conservatives who have attempted to reconstruct the US in the context of the loss of the true republican tradition.

RESENTMENT AND TRUMP:
LINKING PALEOCONSERVATISM TO NEOLIBERALISM

Many have argued, with good reason, that much of the world has been neoliberal since the 1980s, as reflected in the widespread, if uneven, shift toward investment, trade, and financial liberalisation. This is unremarkable, but it has spawned the facile deployment of the term neoliberalism, not least by its critics on the left, which has led to all kinds of confusion. Thus, David Harvey argues that:

(t)he neoliberal label signalled their adherence to those free market principles of neo-classical economics ... Neoliberal doctrine was therefore deeply opposed to state interventionist theories ... Neoliberalism is in the first instance a theory of political economic practices that proposes that human well-being can best be advanced by liberating individual entrepreneurial freedoms and skills within an institutional framework characterized by strong private property rights, free markets, and free trade.[21]

In this account, the role of the state is to create and preserve an institutional framework appropriate to such practices. This includes for example, the quality and integrity of money as well as the military, defence, police, and legal structures required to secure private property rights and guarantee, by force if need be, the proper functioning of markets. The argument is that neoliberal theory believes states play a part in creating markets, but beyond this foundational role the state should allow for the (spontaneous) functioning of free markets. Such a definition leads to the obvious objection that the state is hardly 'limited' in its intervention across the world today, and indeed state spending as a proportion of GDP is generally higher now than it was in 1945. Thus, for Talbot '(w)e are no nearer the "neoliberal state" now than we were in 1980. Neoliberalism is therefore a bogeyman invented by leftists to oppose various conservative attempts to rebalance state-market relations.'[22]

Those who equate neoliberalism with limited government and the 'night-watchman state' on the one hand, and the free market and neo-classical economics on the other, both fail to capture what is distinctive about neoliberalism. To properly understand Trump, it is very important to recognize that this supposed separation of state and market is mistaken, and that '(f)ar from trying to preserve society against the unintended consequences of the operations of markets, as democratic liberalism sought to do, neoliberal doctrine instead set out actively to dismantle those aspects of society which might resist the purported inexorable logic of the catallaxy, and to shape it in the market's image'.[23]

Seen in this way, neoliberalism is based less on the separation of the economic sphere (the market) from the political sphere (the state), as in classical liberalism, and more on the marketization of not only the state, but all spheres of society, right down to constructing all individuals as entrepreneurs.[24] The neoliberal paradox is that it must always rely on the state to carry out this political project.[25] This marketization of society is visible in the case of public sector reform, where, in the name of consumerism for the customer and entrepreneurialism for the public servant, bureaucratization has increased in order to both measure and administer reforms (developing and implementing key performance indicators, targets, and so on). Through this process, the 'enterprise must replace bureaucracy whenever possible and, when this is not possible, bureaucrats must as far as possible conduct themselves *like entrepreneurs*'.[26] This point applies right down to the specific individual, but also – and this is where Trump is relevant – to the country as a whole, whereby competitiveness becomes central to national security.[27]

In this way, the neutrality of the market and of money is associated with de-politicization. However, de-politicization is itself a (political) project, and there is an on-going danger that vested interests will undermine the neutrality of this market order. While never able to fully deliver, neoliberalism promises freedom and spontaneity through the neutral market order. In this respect, there is significant overlap with the American republican promise of independent producers, free markets, and the reconciling of private vice and public virtue. But just as the (supposedly) spontaneous market order can be corrupted by external actors, so too can the American republican tradition.[28] It is precisely at this point that we meet a further manifestation of the neoliberal paradox, which is, as Martijn Konings puts it, '(t)he fact that capitalist life is often so patently at odds with the republican image of the market has often not occasioned a revision of that image but has rather heightened the felt importance of ensuring its realization.'[29]

From the financial crisis of 2007-8 to Trump's election in 2016, much of the left imagined that neoliberalism was in crisis because of the active role of the state in bailing out private financial companies and the nationalizations that followed.[30] This reflected the mistaken definition of neoliberalism rejected above, namely that it is all about limited government and free markets. A similar left fallacy is to locate a resurgence of neoliberalism with companies 'recapturing' the state. This is not necessarily entirely wrong, but it mirrors the paradoxical nature of neoliberalism, as one of its central arguments is that regulation is counter-productive because regulators are generally 'captured' by such vested interests.[31] One might point out, quite correctly, that in fact regulation is necessary for so-called free markets to operate in the first place, but in some respects this argument misses the point. Neoliberals can always point to the promise of the pristine market. Such a market can never be fulfilled, but it is *the promise, and the failure to deliver on its promise*, which goes to the heart of the neoliberal paradox:[32] the neoliberal explanation for failure is that some people and interests cheat on this promise. And even though these people – in a nutshell, third way Democrats and Republican neoconservatives – actually promoted trade, investment, and financial liberalization; reform of the state to make it operate more like an imagined market; cut welfare payments for individuals, and promoted mass incarceration for those that 'chose' not to play the market game; they have also cheated on the promise of the neutral market and the republican ideal. This, in Trump's words, is 'the swamp': promoting globalization, multiculturalism and political correctness while essentially ignoring the concerns of 'middle America.'

This argument was given a strong paleoconservative twist by Steve Bannon as early as 2009, linking technocratic social engineering, as well as political correctness and the social irresponsibility of Wall Street, with the nihilistic culture that emerged in the 1960s.[33] Seen in this way, the rise of Trump was in good part a response to both longer-term trends of de-industrialization and the growth of precarious work,[34] and a shorter-term response to the fall-out from the financial crisis. Trump, then, represents the rise of Middle American Radicals[35] against the swamp of state and corporate elites. For all its supposed libertarian principles, much of the Tea Party that emerged in 2009 switched their support to Trump in 2016,[36] not least because of hostility to the liberal managerial state.

This argument parallels those suggesting that Trump's victory owed much to the support of the white working class, which is racist and/or has been betrayed by a Democratic Party no longer interested in the concerns of white manual workers. Yet in terms of relating this resentment to the white working class and then to the vote for Trump, there is a need for considerable caution. Voting data suggests that Trump enjoyed very high support among higher income groups, while the lowest income groups and unionised workers who actually voted tended to opt for Hillary Clinton, albeit by small margins, and were less pro-Democrat than in the past.[37] What was significant however was the continued low turnout in the election, coupled with continuing loss by the Democrats of their former working-class base, particularly in rustbelt states. Trump was more successful in winning votes among those who had an unfavourable view of both candidates (around half of whom had a favourable view of Obama).[38] Insofar as sections of workers supported Trump and had an impact on the election, it was significant above all in Michigan, Wisconsin, and Pennsylvania, where a swing at the margins helped Trump to victory in all those states.[39] Although there was a 16 per cent national shift among poorer voters to Trump, in the Rustbelt Five (Iowa, Michigan, Pennsylvania, Ohio and Wisconsin) a 10.6 per cent swing to Trump was significantly less than the 21.7 per cent swing away from the Democrats in the same states.[40] Clinton's support fell among all ethnic groups, and not just white voters – indeed the 13 per cent decline for Clinton among rustbelt white voters was almost matched by the black, indigenous, and people of colour vote in the same territories, which saw an 11.5 per cent decline. In the Rustbelt Five, Clinton lost 1.35 million votes and only 590,000 shifted to Trump, while the rest either voted for a third candidate or stayed home.[41] There was limited expectation that President Trump in office would lead to social improvement, and given that these people had very little to lose in the first place, they often expressed a kind of negative solidarity whereby if they have to suffer, then so should everyone else.[42]

Whereas Inglehart and Norris find that support for Trump is best explained not by rising economic insecurity but rather by a cultural backlash against progressive social change,[43] at one level the Trump election reinforces Thomas Frank's[44] long standing argument that the culture wars have provided an ideological cover whereby workers vote against their own (self/class) interests. As Frank suggests, in government the Democrats have offered workers little more than the Republicans. But much of this argument – on both sides of the debate – is couched in a methodologically individualist account of voting behaviour, with one side reducing culture to the revealed preferences and 'authoritarian tendencies' of voters, and the other side regretting that voters do not vote for their economic self-interest. This is ironic given that this methodology mirrors precisely the technocratic neoliberalism, based on rational choice models and revealed preferences in the (political) market, which is at the source of resentment and protest. The idea of 'uneducated whites' is often used as a proxy for the white working class, but this downplays the large numbers of small business owners in this category. Furthermore, some definitions of the white working class lead to very odd conclusions. Thus, Joan Williams' book on the white working class defines it as those on an annual median income of $75,144, which gives room for those on an income of between $41,005 and $131,962 a year. This excludes the poor, and perhaps even more problematically, much of the educated cosmopolitan elite could fit into this income bracket – even though it is precisely this group that is supposed to be the source of resentment among the white working class.[45] This might suggest that the source of resentment is not economic but cultural, though this begs a number of questions about the timing of any cultural backlash and the rise of 'authoritarian values', why this is concentrated in certain places, and why these places are often areas of relatively low migration.

Rather than explanations based purely on economic or cultural variables, it is more fruitful to explore how these two factors overlap and reinforce each other. Thus, the decline of communities does exist as a social reality, but also as a 'social resource' in which a narrative of decline is constructed whereby even better off members of these communities blame urban elites more interested in Wall Street or liberal wars of intervention, while regulation hits small business far more than the corporate elite. We thus have the growth of a politics of resentment, such as a 'rural consciousness' that believes that rural areas are being ignored, marginalized, and misunderstood by urban elites.[46]

Hochschild shows how in Louisiana, where people directly experience the destruction of the environment, there is rage less against environmental polluters, such as large corporations, and more against the hypocrisy of the federal government, which is seen as rewarding and facilitating joblessness and delinquency. These attitudes are indicative of a worldview in which life is seen as harsh, but the American dream would exist if people were prepared to 'wait in line' to reap their rewards. The dream has been undermined by the growth of those who are thought to jump the queue, such as welfare recipients, immigrants, and 'privileged' identity groups, all encouraged by a Washington elite that instructs outsiders to show empathy and endorse political correctness.[47]

That these are myths is in many respects less significant than the fact that these are *powerful* myths, and indeed ones that accord closely with the paleoconservative worldview. They are powerful precisely because there are significant levels of despair in the US. Chetty et al estimate that the rate of absolute mobility, defined as the ideal that children will have a higher standard of living than their parents, has declined from around 90 per cent for children born in 1940 to around 50 per cent for children born in the 1980s.[48] Indeed, economic *anxiety*, rather than income per se, appears to have been a significant factor in the election. Trump's support was stronger than Romney's in 2012 among those with low credit ratings; and it was even stronger in counties where men have stopped working, where people had sub-prime loans before 2008, or where more residents now received disability payments.

The areas where Trump's support was significant[49] were those where the future holds out little prospect of hope, except insofar as it can become one in which a mythical past is recaptured, where security and freedom may be 'reconciled' through what the late Zygmunt Bauman called 'retrotopia':

> the future is transformed from the national habitat of hopes and rightful expectations into the sight of nightmares: horrors of losing your job together with its attached social standing, of having your home together with the rest of life's goals and chattels 'repossessed', of helplessly watching your children sliding down the well-being-cum-prestige slope and your own laboriously learned and memorized skills stripped of whatever has been left of their market value.[50]

This is the reality of the 'end' of the American dream, not only for those groups always excluded, such as African-Americans and native Americans, but also increasingly (if still unequally) for all sections of the population.

This is not so much a revolt of the white working class, but rather a revolt – both cultural and economic – that cuts across classes. Indeed much of its ideological appeal can be considered middle class, as it rests on precisely the image of rugged individualism and the republican ideal.

TRUMPING THE TENSIONS BETWEEN NEOLIBERALISM AND PALEOCONSERVATISM

But it is precisely here that we can see some of the tensions between (and within) paleoconservative and neoliberal ideals, and the reality of the US (and indeed global) political economy. In one respect, Trump represents a re-politicization of the world in the face of the technocratic de-politicization of actually existing neoliberalism since the 1980s. This also feeds into the populist discourse in which technocratic economism has existed alongside competition, so that the losers in this competitive game – individuals, localities, even countries – are somehow less worthy precisely because they have lost.[51] Seen in this way, there is indeed a populist backlash, but one in which recourse to notions of the white working class oversimplifies.

But if Trump represents a re-politicizing response to neoliberal de-politicization, then does his presidency represent a break with neoliberalism? A clear, black-and-white answer cannot be provided because neoliberalism is itself ambiguous. As we have seen, while neoliberalism carries the promise of spontaneity, freedom, and the market, it continually relies on constructing markets, and the state is central to carrying out this project. Even the project of marketization always relies on something outside of the market, such as the sovereign state. While technocratic neoliberalism has been dominant in recent years, neoliberalism can also involve de-politicization through authoritarian rule. There are some parallels here with the radical conservatives of 1930s Germany, as Trump can be seen as an attempt to re-enchant a world of bureaucratic rationalisation (albeit this time one where the rationalization has occurred through the market).[52] Ordoliberalism emerged in the 1930s as an authoritarian liberal response to Weimar and an alternative to the Nazis. A number of ordoliberals shared views close to Schmitt's case for the sovereign to exercise exceptional power in response to the politicization of the economy.[53]

Neoliberalism promises a truly free market based on free producers working and exchanging independently of the state. But it requires the state to realize that goal, and so can never escape the reality of regulation. However, cases of market failure are perpetually explained by the existence of regulation, and so the neoliberal promise is, potentially at least, continually renewed. What is clear is that the Hayekian promise of spontaneity *always* relies on constructing markets, and thus on something outside of these markets. For instance, technocratic neoliberalism relies on the state, as the response to 2008 makes clear.[54] But – and here the overlap with Schmitt is significant – this applies also to neoliberalism and the authoritarian liberalism that is associated with the neoliberal project of depoliticization. But we might go further than this, for the search for re-enchantment is not simply about a strong leader exercising executive power, because there is also a neoliberal discourse of heroic entrepreneurs constantly innovating in the economic sphere and thereby challenging bureaucracy. This idea is present in the turgid novels of Ayn Rand, in neoliberal management studies, and indeed in Third Way discourses of a new, socially liberal, socially conscious capitalism. Thus the kind of managerial capitalism that Schumpeter, Burnham and the paleoconservatives decried might be re-enchanted by entrepreneurial rule. Seen in this way, Donald Trump is the heroic head of a new state, which will make America great again through entrepreneurialism and running the US as if it was a business. In this scenario, Trump is literally the CEO of 'America Inc.'. In this way, technocratic neoliberalism is displaced by an authoritarian neoliberalism, which offers re-enchantment through the recovery of the founding ideas of the republic.

The question remains of where this leaves the republican ideal. It is here that we can briefly explore some tensions both within and between neoliberalism and paleoconservatism, and in doing so identify the real area of tension between the two, namely globalization. First, in terms of paleoconservatism there is a clear tension between Patrick Buchanan's support for a conservatism based on 'the patriotism of Theodore Roosevelt' on the one hand, especially for his strong advocacy of empire, and the decentralized 'humane economic vision of Wilhelm Ropke on the other', based on his hope for a society based on free and independent producers. This would appear to conform to the republican ideal and the neoliberal promise of free markets. At the same time, Buchanan also talked of his admiration for the capitalists of the Gilded Age, rejecting the notion that they were robber barons and instead suggesting that they were patriotic Americans, even though[55] this ignored both the giant corporations these capitalists created and indeed their own proto-globalization strategies. Moreover, Buchanan's case for protectionism for manufacturing rested less on a defence of the Old Right conservatism and its links with the South, and rather more on the Union's case for protection for manufacturing in the North before and after the civil war. Indeed Buchanan's favourable view of Hamilton contrasts sharply with that of paleoconservative thinkers like Francis, who argues that Hamiltonian nationalism undermined tradition in the nineteenth century.[56]

This inconsistency is reflective of a conservative tradition which claims support for small businesses – those Middle American Radicals – that are so important to Trump, but which often in effect support large corporations. Moreover, as we have seen, this gap between rhetoric and reality is a central feature of neoliberalism – for example ordoliberal support for small business, echoed in places by Chicago and Hayek after 1945, but which (via Coase and Becker) ended up rejecting anti-trust laws and developing a theoretical case for private monopoly.

This leads us to consider the most significant difference between paleoconservatism on the one hand, and neoliberalism on the other. This is the question of protectionism against free trade, the latter of which was of course an important part of the Reagan administration, the legacy of which both sides claim allegiance to, albeit with some qualifications.[57] In contemporary political discourse, this is a tension between ('small') paleo anti-globalization and ('large') neoliberal globalization.

ANTIGLOBALIZATION?
TRUMP AND THE LIBERAL INTERNATIONAL ORDER

The area in which Trump the candidate threatened the most significant shift away from neoliberalism was in the international order and the promotion of 'globalization'. Neo-conservatism was often allied with neoliberalism because the former was committed to the US playing a leading role in the liberal international order; its disagreements with liberal internationalists were over the way US hegemony should be exercised in this order, not the order itself. Some of Trump's pronouncements both before and after he became President – over the Trans Pacific Partnership, NATO, NAFTA, relations with China, the United Nations, environmental agreements, and liberal wars of intervention among others – suggested a significant shift away from the US' international commitments. The practice has to date been somewhat more limited, but it does in part reflect tensions between Trump's supposed isolationism on the one hand, and continued US involvement in the liberal international order on the other. Steve Bannon was in many respects the key figure associated with the 'alt-right' movement[58] and paleoconservatism, both of which are committed to a white nationalist isolationism. However, this ethno-nationalist worldview begs a number of questions around how 'separate' ethno-cultures can peacefully coexist with each other. Indeed Bannon has argued that the West faces a war against multiculturalism, including against 'jihadist Islamic fascism'.[59] How this supposed war sits alongside separate cultural development is not clear. Moreover, it implies that the problem of Islamist terrorism is not one based on politics but on cultural difference. For all their differences with the paleos, neoconservatives also explain the rise of Islamist terrorism in purely cultural terms, ignoring the ways in which this is linked to Cold War US and Soviet policies, and indeed US policy in the post-Cold war world.[60] In both cases peaceful coexistence is precluded on cultural terms, and therefore, seen in this way, the appointment of neoconservative fellow traveller John Bolton as National Security Adviser in 2018 is not so surprising. This is because for all its supposed isolationism and ethnonationalism, paleoconservatism cannot avoid an engagement with the international order, and therefore if there has been a significant shift, it is less in terms of one from 'globalization' to 'isolationism' and more one from multilateralism to bilateralism, as we will see.

These geopolitical issues are probably less important, in terms of the Middle American Radicals (MARs) deemed so central to Trump, than the promise of Making America Great Again through the return of secure jobs that have been 'lost' through globalization. Liberal wars of intervention and their disastrous failure might matter to the MARs, but less in terms of the significance of foreign relations, and somewhat more in terms of high casualty rates in regions already neglected by the liberal managerial state.[61] This again feeds into the narrative of resentment, but it forces stark questions about the feasibility and the desirability of Trump's pronouncements of isolationism and protectionism, given his commitment to a corporate capitalism which is at the same time portrayed as part of the 'swamp'.

First it should be noted that many of Trump's appointments – above all from Wall Street and oil interests – were straight from the swamp and his administration is full of billionaires.[62] Second, Trump remains critical of NAFTA but has toned down at least some of his earlier criticisms of China, both of which were central to rhetoric about bringing back American jobs. Seen in this way, Buchanan's contradictory stances on decentralized political economy on the one hand, and protectionism for large scale manufacturing on the other, are being replayed in Trump's vacillating positions, and tensions in his administration between protectionists on the one hand and so-called 'globalists' on the other.

Trump the candidate argued that China is 'stealing our jobs, they're beating us in everything, they're winning, we're losing'.[63] The abandonment of the planned Trans-Pacific Partnership is relevant here. The East Asian region, and China in particular, is a central part of the liberal international order, but at the same time its integration into this order is far from complete.[64] While China's incorporation takes place in part through its role in global production networks, at the same time it still protects its national champions, whereby 26 sectors prohibit foreign capital investment and a further 38 insist on joint ventures with foreign capital.[65] There is also concern that China's protection of foreign intellectual property rights is too lax, with the result that many cheap copies of foreign goods are available in the Chinese market. None of this means that China represents a 'state capitalist' alternative to the neoliberal international order, or a Beijing Consensus alternative to the Washington or post-Washington Consensus. Rather, China simply wants a bigger slice of the pie in the existing order, and is prepared to accept foreign investment in some sectors while trying to build national capacity elsewhere.

It is in this context that we need to understand so-called trade deals, from NAFTA to the Trans-Pacific Partnership. These were always more about the consolidation and extension of global, above all American, corporate power than about trade per se. The aim is the promotion of 'universal' standards which in effect mean adopting US style regulatory measures on finance, investment, and so on, particularly as regards intellectual property rights and the extension of the ability to pursue lawsuits against governments to challenge regulations. These deals then often promote a global capitalism with the US at the summit, and in this regard the US withdrawal from the TPP was (despite China not being a signatory) a defeat for US capital.

Like the paleoconservatives, Trump and advisers like Peter Navarro argue that 'globalization' has not worked for the interests of the United States.[66] The Navarro/Trump/paleo position is that free trade does not work for the US *today*, and treats trade as simply a zero-sum game in which one participant wins (has trade surpluses) entirely at the expense of the other (deficit countries). Much was therefore made of the fact that after NAFTA, the US moved from having a trade surplus with Mexico to a trade deficit, and of particular political significance was Trump's claim shortly after his election to have secured a pledge from the Carrier Corporation to abandon plans to move jobs to Mexico, even if [67] this was subsequently reversed by the company. Much more telling may have been the March 2017 G20 meeting in Germany shortly after he was inaugurated, where newly appointed Treasury Secretary Steven Mnuchin, formerly of Goldman Sachs, blocked the collective endorsement of 'free trade' in the G20 communiqué, an argument in effect repeated in response to G7 condemnation of tariffs in June 2018. In fact, the picture is more ambiguous than this. Despite steadfast verbal commitments, the US adherence to free trade was always rather selective, sometimes promoting free trade for others but not for itself. (Indeed, in the period from 2008 to 2016, the US employed far more protectionist measures than any other G20 country).[68]

But the issue goes far deeper than this, relating to the feasibility of a pro-capital administration that rhetorically rejects globalization. At a visit to Boeing's North Charleston factory in North Carolina in early 2017, Trump made his usual pronouncements about protecting manufacturing jobs. However, while the new Boeing 787-10 Dreamliner may have been assembled in South Carolina, it relied heavily on components from a numbers of countries, including Japan, South Korea, India, Italy, France, Sweden, Canada, Mexico and Australia. The planes assembled in the US are delivered to over 60 airlines throughout the world, and international suppliers account for about 30 per cent of the plane's components. The Chinese market will be particularly important for Boeing over the coming years. Moreover, contrary to simplistic assumptions about globalization, the suppliers are not easily replaceable, and some are full partners that have invested significant capital and are locked in through the whole life of the programme. Shifting suppliers of the wings and batteries would involve granting billions of dollars in compensation to Japanese companies, searching for an American equivalent, and massive new start-up costs.[69]

These observations reflect the reality of trade in an increasingly globalized world. Around 60 per cent of world trade is composed of the transfer of intermediate goods between different parts of the same firm or between firms that have entered subcontracting agreements. The Boeing case is thus far from exceptional. According to the US Census Bureau, 26.6 per cent of US imports from Mexico in the period from 2007 to 2016 were made up of consumer goods, but as much as 28.1 per cent were oil, raw materials, and industrial inputs, while 35.6 per cent were investment goods. Any attempt to impose a blanket tariff of 40 per cent on Mexican imports would therefore increase the price of US goods, including exports, with likely detrimental effects on employment.[70] Furthermore, the decline of manufacturing long pre-dates free trade agreements like NAFTA. Manufacturing accounted for around 30 per cent of non-farm jobs in 1950, and around 25 per cent by 1970. The figure for 2016 of slightly less than 10 per cent suggests an acceleration since 1970, and indeed the period from 2000 to 2010 saw a sharp decline in manufacturing employment. But the point about long term manufacturing employment decline also applies to manufacturing powerhouses like Germany, even when allowing for the effects of reunification.[71] Following NAFTA, there was no sharp increase in unemployment, and indeed in the automobile industry, employment actually increased in the period from 1994 to 1997. It is true that since 1994, manufacturing employment as a percentage of total employment has fallen, but this is also true of Mexico and indeed many countries of the South. In contrast to arguments that suggest an unambiguous new international division of labour in which a race to the bottom has encouraged capital to take advantage of cheaper labour and other costs,[72] and therefore manufacturing has left the core countries for the periphery, Rodrik has identified a process of 'premature de-industrialisation' in much of the South. In this scenario, countries are de-industrialising at low rates of per capita income compared to the developed world, and moving into low paid service work and a massive informal sector of urban marginality.[73] The North-South gulf remains massive, and indeed one of the most striking features of the rise of middle income countries from the South is the high rates of inequality and expansion of low paid, insecure work, rather than the supposed rise of higher wage secure work 'stolen', in Trump's eyes, from the United States.[74]

Thus deindustrialisation appears to be a concern for North and South alike, which suggests a more complex scenario than the zero-sum game envisaged by Navarro and Trump. For manufacturing *output* in the US, apart from exceptions such as the period following the 2008 crash, there has been a consistent upward trend. There have been some sectoral declines, such as in furniture, wood products, and printing, but these have been more than compensated for by increases in machinery, motor vehicles and parts, other transport equipment, food, beverages, and tobacco. Labour productivity from 2006 to 2013 increased in all manufacturing by an estimated 90 per cent, and although a great surge in the computer and electronics sector is a significant part of this story, there were still high rates of productivity increases in sectors like motor vehicles, other transport, electrical equipment, and apparel. Hicks and Devaraj estimate that in the period from 2000 to 2010, 88 per cent of job losses were accounted for by productivity increases rather than trade deals.[75] While such a stark contrast between productivity and trade as explanation is problematic, not least because the former might in part occur because of the latter, it is also true that any account that simply blames trade deals for US jobs losses is *extremely* problematic.

Moreover, even in sectors where there has been a decline in both employment and output – such as steel and aluminium – it is far from clear that protectionism will actually protect manufacturing jobs. For all his free trade rhetoric, George W. Bush introduced tariffs on steel in 2002. While it is difficult to establish straightforward causality, not least in the context of widespread falls in manufacturing employment, it is true that this did not save jobs in manufacturing. In fact, some estimates suggested that it led to losses in employment in steel-using manufacturing industries to the tune of 200,000 jobs, including in rustbelt states like Pennsylvania, Ohio and Michigan. The 2018 tariffs should be seen the context of a US labour force which employs 60 workers in steel using industries for every single worker in steel itself.[76]

This argument feeds into much wider debates over US decline, usually linked to concerns over declining US shares of world GDP, and more recently US (trade and budget) deficits and growing debt, the fiascos in Afghanistan and Iraq, the 2008 financial crisis and its aftermath, and the rise of China. But these argument fail to account for the specific nature of US hegemony and its central role in the making of global capitalism.[77] Seen in this way, US hegemony has not so much declined as globalized. US capital and the US state continue to enjoy significant advantages in the international order, including low rates of interest on its debt, higher rates of return on its overseas investment, and advantages gained from the international role of the dollar.[78] US MNCs continue to dominate in most sectors in the *Forbes* 'Global 2000'.[79] Though China has undoubtedly had some success in 'climbing the value chain', it continues to play a subordinate role in global production networks, which are still led by US companies.[80] According to Credit Suisse's 'Global Wealth Report' of 2015, the US accounts for 46 per cent of the world's millionaires, compared to China's 4 per cent, which reflects the fact that many of these make their money through overseas investment.[81] Figures such as these might suggest that in fact Trump, Navarro, and the paleoconservatives have a point. American millionaires are increasingly making their money outside of the United States and the relocation of jobs does take place in global production networks. It is indeed true that some sectors have suffered from relocation and/or closure through heavy trade competition, and there is evidence that Trump received significant support in these areas. In politicizing globalization, Trump challenges Third Way technocratic neoliberal treatment of it as an irreversible fact of life, and something that exists outside of politics. But Trump and Navarro represent a kind of mirror image of this approach, suggesting that the inevitable but supposedly costless globalization envisaged by the Third Way can be replaced by an inevitable but costless 'de-globalization' for the United States. At best, this would involve bringing back low paid manufacturing jobs, not the relatively secure well paid manufacturing jobs of the 1950s. Moreover, *in the aggregate* job losses in manufacturing reflect technological change more than relocation.

In any case, much of this project sounds like an attack on globalization as the outward *movement of capital* rather than an attack on neoliberalism, let alone on *capital per se*. US capital benefits enormously from its global operations, and it is locked into deals with foreign suppliers that would carry enormous costs if these were broken. Moreover, heavy tariffs on imports could raise consumer prices on finished goods in the US market or export prices in the case of more expensive imported inputs. This would carry risks in terms of inflation and competitiveness, and so hit workers in terms of purchasing power or jobs. It is therefore not surprising that movement towards a process of economic nationalism has been far more limited than Trump's rhetoric suggests.

In his first year in office, Trump claimed success in any case where jobs appeared to have been saved from relocation, even though these investment decisions pre-dated his presidency – this included investment by Ford, General Motors, Wal-Mart, Intel, Sprint and Lockheed Martin, all of which date back to the Obama era. Indeed, there are good reasons why productive capital continues to invest in the developed world, including access to final markets, a more developed infrastructure (at least compared to parts of the developing world), the clustering of economic activity, and so on. Some companies have indeed sourced back to the US, and the rate of offshoring appeared to slow down in the period from 2015 to 2017.[82] But none of this is enough to bring back secure jobs to American workers on the scale envisaged by Trump. Much the same point applies to coal mining, where Trump promised to restore jobs in the face of supposedly anti-job environmental regulations. Even the tariffs on solar panels introduced in 2018 were likely to lead to job losses, as most employment in that sector is in distribution and not production.[83]

CONCLUSION

Much of Trump's rhetoric and appeal is rooted in right-wing anti-globalization discourses that promise to lock (American) capital down, leading to a new golden age of investment in the US.[84] But this is not feasible, particularly when one considers the way in which Trump represents not only continuity with, but in some respects the culmination of, neoliberalism: namely, that he will supposedly Make America Great Again by running the country as if it was a business. Seen in this way, and for all the talk of freedom, neoliberalism is simply another form of elitist paternalism[85] -- albeit one that relies on the leadership of property owning 'entrepreneurs' who claim their authority from money, as opposed to traditional conservative elites who claimed their authority from God. Given the tendency of capital to concentrate, centralize, and indeed globalize, it is hardly likely that such a leader will, notwithstanding rhetoric to the contrary, attempt to significantly hinder the movement of capital. Similarly, Trump's rhetoric on free trade agreements does not mean that widespread protection of manufacturing jobs will be introduced. Rather, Trump (wrongly) believes that rapid bilateral trade deals can be done that by-pass the bureaucracy that multilateral trade deals depend upon, and thus get a 'better deal' for the US. In fact, multilateralism is better for capital, not least by reducing transaction costs and ensuring conformity on standards which are necessary in the context of trade between different parts of global value chains.

The focus on Trump as a business leader also tells us a great deal about his authoritarianism. Arguments claiming that he represents a simple return to the 1930s miss what is distinctive about Trump.[86] His narcissistic character, his lack of interest in and incapacity to understand detail, and his belief that there are easy and fast solutions to complex problems, actually reflect his business-centric view of the world, and this explains why Trump is not only a potential authoritarian, but an incompetent one (though this in itself carries a number of dangers). His failure to deliver on his promises will however carry great risks as well as opportunities, not least because the Democrats are divided, and especially because most are in denial, still appearing to believe that there is a prospect of returning to pre-2007-8 business as usual once Trump is defeated. Given the very substantive causes of resentment, even Trump's failure in the absence of a real alternative could simply exacerbate the poisonous, dangerous political trends of which Trump himself is culmination and symptom.

NOTES

1   Samuel Francis, 'Capitalism: The Enemy', 2000, available at www.chroniclesmagazine. org.

2   See Peter Kolozi, *Conservatives against Capitalism*, New York: Columbia University Press, 2017, chapter 1.

3   Friedrich Hayek, *The Road to Serfdom*, London: Routledge, 2001.

4   See William Buckley, *God and Man at Yale*, Chicago: Henry Regnery, 1951; and Frederick Meyer, *The Conservative Mainstream*, New York: Arlington, 1969.

5   See Irving Kristol, 'The Two Welfare States', *Wall Street Journal*, 19 October 2000.

6   See Daniel Moynihan, *The Negro Family,* Washington D.C.: Department of Labor, 1965.

7   See in particular William Kristol and Robert Kagan, 'Toward a Neo-Reaganite Foreign Policy', *Foreign Affairs*, 75(4), 1996, pp. 18-32. It should be noted that this call for a neo-Reaganite foreign policy is based on selective memory on the part of neoconservatives, some of who accused Reagan of appeasement of the Soviet Union in the early 1980s. See for instance N. Podhoretz, 'Appeasement By Any Other Name', *Commentary*, 76(July), 1983. For representative neoconservative views of Trump, see William Kristol, 'Our Trump Problem', *Weekly Standard*, 19 May 2017, and Max Boot, 'Donald Trump is Proving Too Stupid To Be President', *Foreign Policy*, 16 June 2017.

8   See for instance Irving Kristol "When Virtue Loses Her Loveliness' – Some Reflections on Capitalism and the 'Free Society", *The National Interest*, 31, 1970, pp. 3-15.

9   See George Hawley, *Right Wing Critics of American Conservatism*, Kansas City: University of Kansas Press, 2016, p. 178.

10   See Samuel Francis, *Leviathan and its Enemies*, New York: Radix, 2016. See also Paul Gottfried, *After Liberalism*, Princeton: Princeton University Press, 1999.

11   This argument owes a great deal to James Burnham's contention that a managerial revolution had taken place that undermined the virtue of the entrepreneur, and indeed his later argument that the liberalism espoused by the managerial class represented self-destructive suicide for the western world. See James Burnham, *The Managerial Revolution*, New York: Praeger, 1972 [1940], and *Suicide of the West*, New York: Encounter, 2014 [1964].

12   See Samuel Francis, 'Outsourcing: the Economic Equivalent of Ethnic Cleansing', *VDare.com*, 2004.

13   Gottfried, *After Liberalism*, p. xi.

14   Patrick Buchanan, 'Republican National Convention Speech', 1992, available at www.buchanan.org.

15   Patrick Buchanan, 'Death of Manufacturing', *American Conservative*, 11 April 2003.

16   Patrick Buchanan, 'The Isolationist Myth', 1994, available at: www.buchanan.org.

17   See Patrick Buchanan, *The Death of the West*, New York: St Martin's, 2002, and *Suicide of a Superpower*, New York: Thomas Dunne, 2011.

18   Patrick Buchanan, 'Trump: Middle America's Messenger', *American Conservative*, 23 February 2016.

19   *National Review*, 'Against Trump', 15 February 2016, pp.14–16.

20   Samuel Huntington, 'Conservatism as an Ideology', *American Political Science Review* 51(2), 1957, pp. 454-73; see also the characterisation of conservatism in Corey Robin, *The Reactionary Mind*, Oxford: Oxford University Press, 2018, second edition; and Ray Kiely, *Conservative (Anti-) Globalization*, London: Agenda/Columbia University Press, forthcoming.

21   David Harvey, *A Brief History of Neoliberalism*, Oxford: Oxford University Press, pp. 20, 22.

22   Colin Talbot, 'The Myth of Neoliberalism', 2016, available at colinrtalbot.wordpress.com.

23   Philip Mirowski, 'The Political Movement that Dare not Speak its Name', INET Working Paper no.23, 2014, pp. 8, 12.

24   Michel Foucault, *The Birth of Biopolitics*, Basingstoke: Palgrave, 2008 [1978/9].

25   See Ray Kiely, *The Neoliberal Paradox*, Cheltenham, UK: Elgar, chapters 2, 4 and 12.

26   Pierre Dardot and Christian Laval, *The New Way of the World*, London: Verso, 2014, p. 238.

27   August Cole, *American Competitiveness: A Matter of National Security*, Washington: National Security Foundation, 2012.

28   This argument is well made by Martijn Konings, 'From Hayek to Trump: the Logic of Neoliberal Democracy', in Leo Panitch and Greg Albo, eds, *Socialist Register 2018: Rethinking Democracy*, London: Merlin, pp. 48-73.

29   Konings 'From Hayek to Trump', p. 63.

30   None of this was new, and indeed Pinochet's Chile saw bailouts and nationalizations.

31   See George Stigler, 'The Theory of Economic Regulation', *Bell Journal of Economics and Management Science*, 3, 1971, pp. 3–18.

32   Kiely, *The Neoliberal Paradox*.

33   See the 2009 documentary produced, written, and directed by Steve Bannon, *Generation Zero*, available at www.youtube.com.

34   The debate on the rise of precarious work is a large one, and there is not space to consider it in detail here. Guy Standing exaggerates the rise of precarity while Kevin Doogan appears to deny that it has occurred at all. See Guy Standing, *The Precariat*, London: Bloomsbury, 2011; and Kevin Doogan, *New Capitalism?*, Cambridge: Polity, 2009. In fact, in the US, part time workers constituted around 20 per cent of the labour force in 2015, compared to 15 per cent in 1968, and if other forms of non-standard employment are factored in, this figure rise to 40 per cent in 2015. See Aaron Benanav 'Precarity Rising', *Viewpoint Magazine*, 15 June 2016.

35   Samuel Francis, 'Message from MARs', in G. Schneider, ed., *Conservatism in America Since 1930*, New York: NYU Press, pp. 300-317.

36   A CNN poll in February 2016, suggested that 16 per cent of Tea Party affiliates supported Ted Cruz, while as much as 56 per cent supported Trump. See K. Aronoff, 'Trump and the Tea Party', *Jacobin*, 26 March 2016. The 1990s also saw something of a paleoconservative-libertarian alliance and support for Buchanan in 1992, with both sides hostile to immigration, the libertarian side because immigrants support more statist policies. See the discussion in George Hawley, *Right Wing Critics of American Conservatism*, Kansas City: University of Kansas Press, 2016.

37   See Charles Post, 'How the Donald Came to Rule', *Jacobin*, 10 February 2017.

38   Perry Anderson, 'Passing the Baton', *New Left Review*, II(103), 2017, p. 42; Joshua Mound, 'What Democrats Must Do', *Jacobin*, 30 September 2017.

39   Michael McQuarrie, 'Trump and the Revolt of the Rustbelt', 2016, available at blogs. lse.ac.uk.

40   Konstantin Kilibarda and Daria Roithmayr , 'The Myth of the Rustbelt Revolt', *Slate*, 1 December 2016.

41   Kilibarda and Roithmayr, 'The Myth of the Rustbelt Revolt'.

42   William Davies, 'Brexit Will Make Things Worse. Is That Why People Voted For It?', *Washington Post*, 1 July 2016.

43   Ronald Inglehart and Pippa Norris, 'Trump, Brexit and the Rise of Populism: Economic Have-nots and Cultural Backlash', 2016, Harvard Kennedy School Working Paper 16-026.

44   Thomas Frank, *What's the Matter With America?*, London: Secker, 2004.

45   See Joan Williams, *White Working Class*, Cambridge: Harvard Business Review Press. For a critique see David Roediger 'Who's Afraid of the White Working Class?: On Joan Williams' 'White Working Class: Overcoming Class Cluelessness in America'', *Los Angeles Review of Books*, 17 May 2017.

46   See Katherine Cramer, *The Politics of Resentment: Rural Consciousness in Wisconsin and the Rise of Scott Walker*, Chicago, University of Chicago Press, 2016.

47   Arlie Hochschild, *Strangers In Their Own Land*, New York: New Press, 2016, p. 145.

48   Raj Chetty, David Grusky, Maximilian Hell, Nathaniel Hendren, Robert Manduca, and Jimmy Narang, 'The Fading American Dream: Trends in Absolute Income Mobility Since 1940', available at inequality.stanford.edu/sites/default/files/fading-american-dream.pdf.

49   Ben Casselman, 'Stop Saying Trump's Win had Nothing to do with Economics', *Five Thirty Eight*, 9 January 2017; and James Hohmann, 'The Daily 202: The Reagan Democrats Are No longer Democrats. Will they Ever Be Again?', *Washington Post*, 11 November 2016.

50   Zygmunt Bauman, *Retrotopia*, Cambridge: Polity, 2017, p. 6.

51 See William Davies, *The Limits of Neoliberalism: Authority, Sovereignty, and the Logic of Competition*, London: Sage Publications, 2014.

52 See David Graeber, *The Utopia of Rules*, London: Melville, 2015.

53 Though Hayek was often dismissive, his case for market freedom was similar to Schmitt's view. Schmitt's argument rested on a distinction between general legal norms and specific commands, and he claimed that only the former could satisfy the condition of upholding the rule of law. His problem with the Weimar Republic was that as a pluralist party state it led to rule through specific discretionary demands. The state was the prisoner of powerful interest groups that undermined the rule of law and the constitutional order. For Schmitt, 'only a strong state can depoliticize, only a strong state can openly and effectively decree that certain activities ... remain its privilege and as such ought to be administered by it, that other activities belong to the ... sphere of self-management, and that all the rest be given to the domain of a free economy.' Carl Schmitt, *The Concept of the Political*, New Jersey: Rutgers University Press, 1976[1932], pp. 226-7.

54 Konings suggests that for this reason the focus on Schmittian exceptionalism misses the point, because neoliberalism contains within itself an 'internalist' critique of regulation. This is true, but only up to a point. The idea of a state of exception refers less to a temporal phenomenon, and more to the (ongoing) existence of something beyond the market which is necessary for its operation. See Konings, 'From Hayek to Trump'.

55 Buchanan, *The Great Betrayal*, pp.93-4.

56 Samuel Francis, 'Nationalism, Old and New', *Chronicles*, June 1992, p. 18.

57 For the paleos there was the failure to undertake a cultural revolution and for the neoliberals there was the failure to tackle state spending, above all massive increases in budget deficits.

58 The alt-right movement includes a variety of patriot and white supremacist movements. It also has a significant online presence, which has drawn on counter-cultural ideas usually associated with the New Left. Indeed, the Frankfurt School critique of capitalist conformity and the culture industry has in effect been co-opted by a certain strand of far right would-be hipsters critical of the liberal conformity associated with political correctness and a certain strand of identity politics. Paleoconservative intellectuals are themselves not unaware of this cultural Marxism – see Paul Gottfried, *The Strange Death of Marxism*, Columbia: University of Missouri Press, 2005. On the alt-right movement see David Niewert, *Alt-America*, London: Verso, 2017; and the online culture wars involving the alt-right are discussed in Angela Nagle, *Kill All Normies*, London: Zero, 2017.

59 Cited in Lester Feder, 'This is how Steve Bannon Sees the Entire World', *Buzzfeed*, 15 November 2016.

60 See Jean-Francois Drolet, *American Neoconservatism*, London: Hurst, chapter 5.

61 Philip Weiss, 'Clinton Lost Because PA, WI, and MI Have High Casualty Rates and Saw Her as Pro-War, Study Says', *Mondoweiss*, 6 July 2017.

62 Nina Burleigh, 'Meet the Billionaires Who Run Trump's Government', *Newsweek*, 14 April 2017.

63 Marc Thiessen, 'Why, Despite His Insults, the Chinese Love Trump', *Newsweek,* 2 June 2016/

64 Ray Kiely, *The BRICs, US Decline and Global Transformations*, Basingstoke, UK: Palgrave, 2015.

65   See Sean Starrs, 'China's Rise is Designed in America, Assembled in China', *China's World*, 2(2), 2015, pp. 9-20.

66   Peter Navarro, *Death by China,* New York: Prentice Hill, 2011.

67   Interestingly many of these jobs were held by African-American workers and indeed Burmese immigrants, but the symbolic significance of saving manufacturing jobs played into the wider narrative about the US' manufacturing past where white workers had secure and well paid jobs. Steven Greenhouse, 'Is Trump Really Pro-Worker', *New York Times*, 2 September 2017.

68   CEPR 'The US Pursues Selective Protectionism not Free Trade', 2017, available at cepr.net.

69   Benjamin Zhang, 'Trump's 'America First' policies are catapulting Boeing into dangerous territory', *Business Insider*, 4 February 2017.

70   J. W. Mason, 'What We Get Wrong When We Talk Trade', *Jacobin*, 28 January 2017.

71   J. Bradford De Long, 'NAFTA And Other Trade Deals Have Not Gutted American Manufacturing', *Vox*, 24 January 2017.

72   See Folker Frobel, Jurgen Heinrichs, and Otto Kreye, *The New International Division of Labour,* Cambridge: Cambridge University Press, 1980; and Roger Burbach and Bill Robinson, 'The Fin de Siecle Debate: Globalization as Epochal Shift', *Science and Society* 63(1), 1999, pp.10-39.

73   Dani Rodrik, 'Premature Deindustrialization', Cambridge: Harvard University, unpublished paper, 2015.

74   See Mike Davis, *Planet of Slums*, London: Verso, 2004; Andrew Sumner, *Global Poverty*, Oxford: Oxford University Press, 2016.

75   Michael Hicks and Srikant Devaraj, 'The Myth and the Reality of Manufacturing in America', Ball State University Center for Business and Economic Research, 2015.

76   Annie Lowrey, 'Trump's 'Smart Tariffs' Don't Make Economic Sense', *The Atlantic*, 1 March 2018; Jessica Halzer, 'Trump's Steel Tariffs are a Surefire Way to Hurt the Rustbelt', *Foreign Policy*, 4 May 2017.

77   Leo Panitch and Sam Gindin, *The Making of Global Capitalism*, London, Verso, 2012.

78   See Pierre-Olivier Gourinchas and Helene Rey, 'From World Banker to World Venture Capitalist: US External Adjustment and the Exorbitant Privilege', 2005; and Kiely, *The BRICs, US Decline and Global Transformations*.

79   See Sean Starrs, 'American Economic Power Hasn't Declined – It Globalized! Summoning the Data and Taking Globalization Seriously', *International Studies Quarterly* 57(4), 2013, p.823; and Sean Starrs, 'The Chimera of Global Convergence', *New Left Review* II(87), 2014, p.87.

80   Starrs, 'China's Rise', pp. 15-16.

81   Starrs, 'China's Rise', p. 20.

82   Jeffrey Rothfeder, 'Why Donald Trump is Wrong About Manufacturing Jobs and China', *The New Yorker*, 14 March 2016.

83   See O. Milman, 'Donald Trump Tariffs on Panels Will Cost US Solar Industry Thousands of Jobs', *The Guardian*, 23 January 2018; C. Bown, 'Trump's Steel and Aluminium Tariffs are Counterproductive: Here are 5 More Things You Need to Know', Peterson Institute for International Economics, 7 March 2018. Employment in coal mining fell from around 138,000 in 2008 to 98,000 in 2015, and coal's contribution to US electricity provision fell from around 52 per cent in 2009 to 30 per cent in 2017. But coal mining bankruptcies and closures have far more to do with competition from

cheap shale gas and technological change rather than regulation, a point accepted even by Robert Murray, the US' largest private coal owner. See also Valerie Volcoviel, Nichola Groom, and Scott Di Savino, 'Trump Declares End to 'War on Coal' But Utilities Aren't Listening', *Reuters,* 5 April 2017.

84   It was Steve Bannon who was most closely associated with this anti-globalization rhetoric, but we should be careful not to over-estimate the significance of Bannon. His removal is just one of many in a chaotic administration, albeit the one most closely associated with paleoconservative ideas. In any case, Bannon is not the strategic genius that some – above all Bannon himself – think. As we have seen, the idea that the election was won by a wholesale, rather than marginal, shift of white working-class voters attracted by 'economic populist' policies , as envisaged by Bannon, does not correspond with the facts. Moreover, when in office his ideas were not always endorsed, above all his calls for an increase in the marginal tax rates for those earning over $5 million a year, which were ignored in favour of tax cuts for the rich. The dismissal of Bannon did not mean the end of the influence of paleoconservative ideas within the administration, but as we have argued throughout these do not promote a politics which will overcome profound grievances within the US.

85   See Robin, *The Reactionary Mind*; Kiely, *The Neoliberal Paradox*; and Kiely, *Conservative (Anti-) Globalization*.

86   See for instance Timothy Snyder, *On Tyranny*, Harmondsworth: Penguin, 2017.

CHINA'S NEW GLOBALISM

LIN CHUN

The traditions of communist revolution and socialist internationalism, which once defined the People's Republic of China, have today faded into the distant past. The programme of 'reform and opening' market integration that began in 1978, intensified especially since 1992, has now evolved into an all-round globalism that guides China's domestic and foreign policies. Free trade is promulgated in a peculiar rhetoric of socialism that embraces a 'common destiny for the human community' along with a cooperative relationship between the 'G2'. At the Chinese Communist Party's (CCP) 19th National Congress in October 2017, President Xi Jinping declared that 'socialism with Chinese characteristics has entered a new era'.

What exactly is new and aspirational about this era? The 'two centenary' goals first proposed in the 15th Party Congress in 1997, and elaborated in the 18th Congress in 2012, remain in place: By 2021, the 100-year anniversary of the founding of CCP, China will have built itself into a fully-fledged *xiaokang* (moderately prosperous) society by doubling its 2010 per capita income while eliminating poverty. By 2049, the 100-year anniversary of the founding of PRC, China will have become a 'strong, democratic, civilized, harmonious, and modern socialist country'. How these lofty characterizations might be substantiated is a real question, as current policies do not seem oriented toward achieving them.

What does appear unconventional is the 'fifth generation' leadership's 'going out' plan (apart from domestic escalation of repressive control). This marked the complete end of the Maoist internationalist and anti-imperialist worldview, a process begun with Deng Xiaoping's ineffective war to 'teach Vietnam a lesson' in 1979 to signal China's pro-US shift. Deng's pragmatic strategy of keeping a 'low profile' in the next three decades has been replaced by Xi's more assertive posture in pursuing the 'great rejuvenation of the Chinese nation' and demanding a place at the center of the global stage: 'Scientific socialism is full of vitality in twenty-first century China, and the banner of socialism with Chinese characteristics is now flying high and proud for all to see.' Chinese approaches to solving the problems facing mankind, from conflicts to eco-crises, were declared here to be globally applicable.

This global optimism in the name of its own brand of socialism, however, contradicted China's subordination to the logic of capitalism at home and abroad, and may now be tested by an aggressive US trade war. Xi's speech at the Boao Forum for Asia in April 2018 struck a much less confident and more conciliatory tone. Stressing that countries should stay committed to openness and mutual benefits, he reconfirmed China's commitment to more comprehensive economic liberalization, including relaxing controls on the financial sector. China would 'significantly expand market access' by: immediately (or soon) stepping up imports, further opening its financial market and service industries, raising foreign equity limits in securities, insurers and banks, lowering auto tariffs, easing restrictions on foreign ownership in manufacturing (e.g. ships, aircraft and autos), and enforcing intellectual property rights. Here the contrast between China's economic vulnerability and foreign policy boldness, as between autocratic political control and neoliberal-style economic policies, is uniquely striking, even as China apparently remains determined to stick to its flagship Belt and Road Initiative (BRI) as well as its pledge to be a 'responsible big country'.

This essay, after a brief background account of China's departure from socialist internationalism and global repositioning, will critically assess the dominant official ideological justifications for globalism in China. Along the way, three propositions are advanced. First, China's partially dependent development since undertaking market reforms is unsustainable and cannot be emulated by others. Second, China must address its own serious problems before it can offer the world anything morally appealing or practically feasible: the success of China's overland and overseas adventures will depend on the creation of a humanly and environmentally sound domestic social model. Third, China's outward quest for energy and other resources comes with serious perils amidst the *realpolitik* of American hegemony and militarism. It is in this context that the essay concludes by asking whether China can reasonably be expected to regain the ability to positively reshape the global political economy.

FAREWELL TO THIRD WORLD INTERNATIONALISM

Revolutionary China's socialist internationalism had two dimensions: defending national sovereignty based on internal ethnic equality and solidarity, and externally supporting other countries in the socialist and third world camps. The new China of the 1950s saw the modern world in terms of overcoming the challenges of uneven capitalist development, in which a 'privilege of backwardness' could enable a country at the margin to catch up or even surpass the centre through learning and leaping. Such ascendance was seen to be conditional on the subjugated peoples breaking free from imperialist chains, that is, from the capitalist extraction, domination, and sabotage which not only hampered independent development, but entailed profound and anguishing disadvantages associated with economic backwardness.

Despite its relatively advanced status before 1800, the Chinese experience of semi-coloniality, whereby the collusion between foreign powers and a local comprador-bureaucracy achieved no imitation of the West but only prevented any substantive attempt at modernization.   The lessons the Communists drew from this explains the dual character – both nationalist and socialist – of the revolution of 1949. Oriented to fashioning an independent developmental state wherein revolutionary nationalism and third-worldist internationalism were dual markers of Maoist foreign policy. The victorious revolution in China was never merely Chinese in the postwar realignment of global politics. Nationalism was a form of internationalist identification with other oppressed peoples in a twofold commitment to national liberation. Chinese nationalism was also tied to socialism which was intrinsically internationalist.

This internationalism confronted a global capitalist system, in which the independent survival of any socialist regime would depend on the sustenance it could draw from wider resistance to that system. Despite its own acute difficulties, China thus aided anti-colonial movements and postcolonial developments beyond its borders, often in the complicated circumstances of an international united front replete with internal tensions. China's assistance to its socialist neighbours and communist guerrillas in Southeast Asia, support for nationalists and socialists in the Arab world, and solidarity with civil rights and black liberation movements in America and Africa, were all predicated on its own security as well as its internationalist duties. The third world, in Mao's map, constituted a broad area of popular struggles that challenged what he increasingly came to characterize as two hostile camps dominated by the competing super powers. Proudly self-reliant, China was able to create precious autonomy and diplomatic room for manoeuvre in an extremely treacherous geopolitical context. On an anti-imperialist platform – Soviet 'social imperialism' included – Maoist internationalism embraced the nonaligned nations that had initially rallied together at the 1955 Bandung conference, as well as the rebellious and antiwar generation of 1968 in the West. This anti-hegemonic stance was asserted with no little panache against the narrow logic of the Cold War adversaries, although the rigidity of China's opposition to the Soviet Union resulted in serious errors, with some damaging effects not only on the Communist bloc but also the developing world.

Socialism, third-worldism and internationalism were, at the most basic level, natural allies. Based on the 'five principles of peaceful coexistence' earlier codified between China and India in their agreement concerning trade and communication in the Tibetan region, the Bandung Conference adopted 'ten principles' of national independence and integrity, equality of all races and nations, and non-interference in international affairs. Later the nonaligned movement (NAM), initiated by Yugoslavia, India, and Egypt, became an important political force, especially once it entered a more radical phase following the 1959 Cuban revolution, which led to the participation from Latin America.

Indeed, China was highly visible among progressives throughout the three continents, spanning its support for struggles ranging from Congolese independence and the Algerian revolution to the Chinese-designed and financed TAZARA, the single longest railway in sub-Saharan Africa, connecting Tanzania and Zambia and completed in the early 1970s. Indeed, China maintained a large aid programme and friendly diplomacy with third world countries, offering grants, interest-free loans, and direct building, training and service projects that involved technology transfer, especially in agriculture. China's international conduct was exemplary of an alternative practice to the prevailing first-third world relationship.

In 1964, after China's relations with the Soviet bloc (and India following the 1962 border war) had gone sour, Mao did not miss the occasion to support anti-US protest in Panama in calling for the 'broadest united front' to 'counter American imperialist aggression and war policies and defend world peace'.[1] Without getting into the Sino-Soviet debate over fundamental theoretical questions or relationships among the communist parties, suffice it here to note that in the more militant Chinese view, 'revisionist' Soviet policies amounted to a betrayal of Marxism and world revolution. Overlooked was the very existence of a USSR constraining the Atlantic powers, and thus functioning as a brake on capitalist war and money machines – something that could be truly appreciated only after the fact. It was in this sense that Eric Hobsbawm described the collapse of the Soviet Union as 'an unmitigated catastrophe'.[2] In other words, China's preoccupation with counter-hegemony led to a categorical misjudgment, similar to the error in domestic politics of confusing the 'two kinds of contradictions' (as Mao put it in 1957) by mistaking 'contradictions among the people' for those between enemies. This form of 'left infantilism' eventually trapped China in impossible isolation. To relieve itself, and counterbalance the Soviet threat,[3] China turned to the US after having rebuffed American entreaties in 1968-69 when the war in Vietnam heavily involved Chinese weapons and undercover field troops. The shift from waging a united struggle against global capitalism to an anti-hegemonic alliance poisoned by sectarianism or from socialist to nationalist principles, compromised the class nature of the third-worldist version of proletarian internationalism.

Consequently, the impact of China's foreign policy and international relations involuntarily became mixed, if not outright detrimental, in relation to the internationalist cause.[4] Communist infighting spread from the Sino-Soviet split, fracturing parties everywhere and resulting in 'an ever more accelerated disintegration of the internationalism of the classical communist movement', with the exception of Cuba as an icon of internationalism.

The nationalist impulse, however, was an almost inevitable response to capitalist crusades against communist regimes since 1917, as exemplified by the contrast in Asia between the blockading of communist states and the nurturing of anti-communist ones, which have enjoyed extravagant aid and market access from the US and Japan. Problems associated with internal bureaucratization of the Eastern bloc were somewhat curbed by the wars in Ho Chi Minh's Vietnam, redressed in Mao's experiments in China, and fairly kept at bay in Cuba. Yet in addition to the centralization, and often personalization, of power that subverted revolutions, conflicts among comrades and allies demoralized and exhausted both the socialist and third worlds. Internationalism, socialism, and third-worldism went down together.

In the aftermath of the breakdown of Bretton Woods and the oil crisis and abandonment of the gold standard, as the developing countries found themselves even more deeply dependent economically, the 1970s witnessed the gradual transformation of the 'third world' from a politically transformative agent to merely a developing economic enterprise. This was marked by the formation of the G77, which was confined to a growth agenda implemented under the monopoly of the G7, the IMF and the World Bank. China showed growing ambivalence toward the NAM due to its own enmity towards the USSR, signing a reversion of its third-worldism. The responsibility of China for the passing of an age of raging popular mobilization for global equality and justice is especially regrettable because China itself belonged to the third world. Its traverse, from being fiercely independent to opportunistically leaning toward the US, followed the same

Cold War logic of détente originated in the Yalta deal – that of a 'balance of terror'.

An important clarification is in order. If revolutionary China's rapprochement with the US through Mao's tactical acceptance of the American olive branch in the early 1970s was still a conditional strategic move, reformist China was subsequently fully willing to play the rules of capitalist domination. The Maoist endeavour was to weaken a bipolar world order and strengthen China's defence and economy by pitting the two superpowers against each other. By contrast, a globalizing China has today largely abandoned anti-imperialism in joining a unipolar world. Obvious continuities notwithstanding, the two eras represent different Chinese identities: between socialism and 'socialism with Chinese characteristics'; between internationalism of class/national liberation and globalism of *jiegui* or 'getting on the track'; between independence and subordination; and indeed between revolution and counter-revolution. If Mao momentarily deviated from socialist and internationalist propositions, he and his colleagues retained them in their long-term principles. His successors, on the other hand, became cynical about socialism altogether and simply removed 'internationalism' from the official vocabulary. This great transformation was of momentous significance: by fuelling global capitalism with its enormous workforce and vast market for capitalist expansion and financialization, China actually helped extend and sustain the global capitalist system.[5]

CHINA'S GLOBAL INTEGRATION 2.0

China's turning itself into a 'rule-taker' and capitalist growth centre not only meant providing capitalism and its global division of labour with a vast new space of exploitation and reconfiguration. Politically, it also meant that the world's most populous state became no longer identified with the loosely rallied anti-capitalist left of the world. While ecologically, it led to the largest developing country, albeit one producing goods primarily consumed abroad, to overtake the developed economies in pollutant emissions and resource depletion. But above all, market reforms in China, in tandem with global neoliberalism, deeply transformed Chinese culture along with its class, gender, ethnic and regional relations. The nominally communist regime has sponsored what is depicted inside China as a partial bureaucratic-capitalist restoration, which continuously inflicts calamities upon society and nature. This is a polarizing process. It has evidently reduced absolute poverty while reproducing it in other ways due to the marketization of public services and creating a degree of consumerist homogeneity amidst all kinds of social disparities. Tens of millions of children 'left behind' by their parents work as rural migrants in faraway cities, often in precarious, low wage jobs allowing only the most meagre of living conditions – this alone tells the inhumanity of China's 'economic miracle'.

If China's globalism 1.0 was a project of reform and opening intended to utilize foreign capital, managerial skills, and technologies to build an advanced sovereign national economy, that 'shallow', selective and self-protective 're-linking' has long been outdone by a more thorough integration. Continuing the trend, globalism 2.0 is premised on *shengai* ('deepening the reform'), thereby pointing to China's comprehensive global participation. The agenda is unprecedented: privatizing state firms and commodifying the land, loosening financial regulation for foreign investors, and liberalizing the 'commanding heights' of national industries.

Xi's latest interpretation of the *Communist Manifesto* serves as ironic ideological packaging for this agenda. In a Political Bureau study session on 23 April 2018, he applied Marx's characterization of a rising capitalism conquering the globe in claiming that China must strive to 'multi-polarize the world, globalize its economy, informationize its society, and pluralize its culture' so as to allow the benefits and opportunities brought about by globalization to be better shared. Bearing Xi's personal name, this upgraded globalism demands unreserved consent from not only party officials, but also common citizens. Any critical voice is stifled.

A fundamental reversal of Maoist self-reliance, globalism 2.0 resembles elements of the earlier cases of dependent development yet is also unconventional. It has two interrelated defining features. One is a considerable degree of dependence on foreign capital, markets and technology as a result of unequal exchange, and inadequate economic self-protection; the other is capital exportation as a result of overcapacity and the quest for energy, as well as by virtue of excessive foreign reserve holdings and capital flight through individual transfers of funds abroad by the new rich.[6] The first, entailing heavy labour exploitation, resource extraction, and environmental degradation, is more or less within the analytical scope of dependency theory. The second dimension is less anticipated, as it entails a peripheral economy competing with the core economies in the capitalist concentration and financialization of assets.

The first feature of China's new globalism is the amplification of its flawed reform model. Attempts to change it have not succeeded. It was quite unexpected by the initial reformers that, in comparison with the typical East Asian developmental states, foreign dependency has been reinforced rather than phased out as the Chinese economy has grown exponentially. Not without large gains, of which some are short-term, this trajectory has proven very costly. As top companies in most industrial sectors in China are already infused with foreign capital and control,[7] a trend only reinforced by the current policy of further opening, the initial hope to 'exchange market access for technologies' is being dashed. In the same vein, nothing seems able to halt the inroads made by multinationals seeking super-profits and rents, some are also moving away from China to seek still cheaper labour.

This pattern emerged as a result of extraordinarily preferential policies toward foreign investors: reductions to, or even exemption from, regular taxation applied to Chinese firms in various periods and forms; and the double failure of Chinese regulators to enforce conditions on foreign investment for technological transfer and diffusion, on one hand, and to rein in 'casino capitalism' and prevent investor short-termism, on the other. If such policies were rationalized at a time of China's capital shortage, their reinforcement today is hardly justifiable, not only politically but also economically. This is all the more puzzling given that the government has repeatedly pledged to 'rebalance' and move China up the value chain. Since Hu Jintao's 'scientific conception of development' proposed in 2006 and emphasizing innovation, China has focused on its large state firms for technological capacity building while leaving smaller enterprises in the export sector to sustain a trade surplus.

In 2015, the national 'Made in China 2025' agenda promoted R&D in ten strategic industries to develop a knowledge economy equipped with mostly Chinese-made components. But the current deficit in sovereign determination and control over the Chinese economy risks sabotaging these efforts. The importance of China becoming technologically independent is mirrored in current US trade blockages, ranging from Section 301 tariffs to threatening a wholesale trade war (the first announced in June 2018 with tariffs on some 1300 Chinese goods valued at about $50 billion for US imports, and a second list valued at about $100 billion being prepared).[8] In April, the US Department of Commerce suspended the supply of key chips to China's leading telecom company, Zhongxing Telecommunication Equipment Corporation (ZTE), instantly paralyzing the company's operations (before rescinding them shortly after under new US supervision of its activities). Another tech giant, Huawei, has also faced limits on its exports to the US (and several US ally states as well). In response, the Chinese government announced in June 'special opening-up measures' to further widen market access for foreign investment in twenty-two key fields including finance, transportation, services, infrastructure, energy, resources, and agriculture.[9]

As events unfold, questions will be raised about just how much leverage China has. The one certain thing is that reliance on foreign supply and markets undermines national self-determination, as well as financial and cyber-security in an age of global standardization. Washington's policing deals with China to protect American advantage alone negates the myth of 'free trade' that the Chinese state holds dear. Shocking inequalities in liberalization are demonstrated by massive agricultural subsidies in the West, and the blocking of Chinese FDI in the US and Europe.

All this is in spite of the major concessions China has made through the marketization of its state sector, both for WTO accession as well as currently in the form of addressing its trade surplus (of which a huge trunk is attributable to foreign and joint ventures). The contrast between Apple's astronomical profits and its Chinese subcontractors' thin margins is notorious, not to mention the miserable conditions faced by Chinese workers assembling iPhones. Multinationals producing in China for the world market (while factored into Chinese GDP) also weaken China's fiscal and monetary tools, which are already constrained by dollar primacy and attendant capital liquidity requirements. Although barely at a middle income level in comparison to other states, it is exceptional that China has become a net exporter of assets and wealth. While it will surely not return to the bad old days of its semi-colonialism as some worry, China is indeed the only large economy that has permitted its sovereignty and security to be so seriously compromised. Introducing foreign 'strategic partners' into Chinese state banks with large shares as well as voting rights, for example, is an astonishing cession of control to foreign capital – capital which at times is even formally connected to foreign governments.

The second feature of the new Chinese globalism (though developed from such projects as 'developing the west' and 'going out' since the late 1990s) is more novel, and decorated with both nationalist and transnational or cosmopolitan slogans like 'national rejuvenation' and 'common human destiny'. The mega-idea of the Belt and Road Initiative, first announced in 2012, is to create new economic corridors and networks linking over 70 countries, 70 per cent of the world's population, and three-quarters of known global energy reserves, by constructing highways, railroads, mines, pipelines, dams, ports and trading routes, using the image of ancient Silk Road by land and sea. Eurasian integration is extended to the Caucasus and Western Europe, while the maritime side of the BRI is to embrace the Indian Ocean and the Mekong and Oceanic nations, as well as Africa and Latin America. It aims to export capital, commodities and entrepreneurship as well as broader social goods like schools, medical facilities, poverty alleviation programmes, and agricultural cooperation. As a state priority of both economic and political-diplomatic importance, the newly-founded Asian Infrastructure Investment Bank (AIIB), the China Development Bank, and other institutions support the BRI financially. And by pursuing 'intra-regional local currency convertibility' – making the Renminbi a common hard currency, beginning in Central Asia – the BRI also hopes to be a financial project that can pave the way for China to gain a footing under the dollar monopoly, while simultaneously yielding more influence on major international organizations.

But it was the economic imperative of channelling China's excess capital and overcapacity that immediately explained the launch of the BRI. The massive stimulus undertaken to protect growth and employment following the 2008 financial crisis triggered by the US subprime meltdown has had lasting consequences. Debt-financed overinvestment in the built environment and 'forced urbanization' on an unparalleled scale are explosive: 'The Chinese who have absorbed and then created an increasing mass of surplus capital now desperately seek a spatial fix.'[10] The BRI, then, is an ideal representation of China's position in a global economic structure in which any upward movement faces a contradiction between overaccumulation and underconsumption. As such, the Chinese project of investing abroad is both an economic necessity that stems from capital's expansive tendencies as it searches for new resources and markets, as well as a politically and culturally inspired ambition to promote 'globality, connectivity, equality, sharing and commonality'.

A SOCIALIST VISION OF GLOBAL EQUALITY?

Remarkably, the official discourse of BRI bears no trace of the internationalist legacy of the earlier socialist third-worldist tradition. A representative summary indicates five strategic changes in Chinese growth that follow from the conviction that development is enabled by the opening up of national economies for global integration by moving from: 1) a focus on foreign capital to a dual emphasis on both the inflows and outflows of FDI; 2) an export-orientation to encouraging growth in the volume of trade from both exports and imports; 3) opening the coastal areas to the coordinated incorporation of the inland regions as well; 4) trading within the WTO framework to more bilateral and multilateral FTAs; and 5) a 'rule-taker' in relation to global governance to active participation in 'rule-making'.[11] The BRI project, with its lavish elaborations by mainstream intellectuals and inflected with a nationalist appeal to a youthful middle class, enjoys solid support in China.

Even more critical socialist arguments tend to be, at once, both defensive and wishful. Lured by such notions as growth for all, equal partnership, and shared prosperity and security, critics imagine aligning the BRI with local needs and designs across the globe through 'people-to-people interactions'.

This would, apparently, nurture trust and peace as well as cooperation and interdependence, while enabling China to play a leadership role in pushing for a new world order. The key concept in this imaginary is a globalizing equality right to be applied to both domestic and international relations. The politics of equality, born of the Chinese revolution and its internationalist commitments, is what distinguishes the BRI from familiar stories of oppression, exploitation, and war-prone power rivalries. As an alternative to the capitalist world system of polarizing inequality among nations, a rising China with a global vision would lead a new politics of equality – equality in difference, equal recognition of diversities, and socialist egalitarianism with an international dimension. Most optimistically, uninfected by imperialist and colonialist intention and methods, China would counter the US-Japan maritime dominance in the region while reshaping the entire global system away from an unequal north-south divide.[12] The significance of the BRI, on this interpretation of it, is not only material but also broadly political and spiritual: 'It must not be a plan of territorial expansion but one of connectivity, exchange and communication, and a plan of transcending historical capitalism while recreating civilization.'[13]

Another argument in a similar vein asserts that China has an advantage in the 'real economy', as opposed to speculative financialized capitalism, despite its own credit and asset bubbles. By defying financial imperialism 'the most unnatural stage of decayed capitalism', China can stimulate an international united front to fight the dominance of financial capital and its local comprador financiers.[14] Since, according to this view, the expansion of the BRI is neither profit-driven, nor a contemporary version of the Marshall Plan, it can pursue productive socialization by means of automation, digitalization, and financial cooperation.[15] The AIIB is put forward as China's first attempt to form a post-Bretton Woods framework through which the international allocation of funds may serve both market and non-market considerations, resulting in peaceful co-development.

While Chinese lending involving both state and private commercial banks (currently at a low annual interest rate of 2-3 per cent for 15-20 years, including a grace period of five to seven years) entails foreign liabilities, at least the state lenders also conduct periodic evaluations to reduce or even cancel debts. Moreover, China rarely imposes IMF-type conditionalities on borrowers. Equally true, however, is that 'when providing loans and finance, the AIIB must remain flexible regarding labor and environmental standards' in order to remain compatible with 'the limited financial capacity of less affluent countries'. China is also strongly against adding labour protections into bilateral trade agreements.[16]

The 'Chinese alternative' would also be hard-pressed to identify any pillars of a socialist circle of commerce operational in an overridingly capitalist global order. From its own collective memory, China knows only too well the catastrophe of colonialism, and just how impossible it is for the poorer countries to achieve the 'surplus retention' necessary for development. Moreover, unbridled business, clutching resources and making money, attract state as well as private capital, with inadequate public supervision at both dispensing and receiving ends.

Conspicuously absent from these sympathetic explanations is a class analysis of the Chinese state and its projected foreign relations. What is the class content of the BRI? Is it in the fundamental interest of the rulers and elites, Chinese and otherwise, or of the labouring and common people – unless it can be argued that these interests are broadly identical? Without a political and conceptual justification for the project in class terms, it is also difficult to refute the charge of China's own 'neo-' or 'sub-'imperialism, which, from a Marxist perspective, is intrinsic to accumulation and capitalization in a globalizing economy. At stake is regime legitimacy in uncharted waters; ultimately, the question of whether China can refashion globalization on its own terms cannot be answered without an answer to the prior question of what kind of society China is building for itself in the first place. Without a morally appealing domestic model, as the foundation for so-called soft power, any image China offers to the world will be tarnished.[17]

This is precisely where the country's vulnerability emerges. Side-by-side with its immense economic achievements, its radicalized market transition has borne witness to severe social inequalities, environmental destruction, rampant corruption, and an ever more repressive atmosphere for the constitutionally protected rights of labour, ethnic minorities, and political dissidents left and right alike. As the super-rich and bureaucratic tycoons sit in the National People's Congress, and anti-corruption campaigns end up strengthening autocratic power, socialism sounds hollow inside and outside China. The fact that 'maintaining stability' takes the largest slice of Chinese national spending speaks for itself.[18]

CONFUCIAN UNIVERSALISM GOES GLOBAL?

A highly influential traditionalist interpretation of China's new globalism relies on an idealized Confucian conception of *tianxia,* or 'all under heaven'. Unlike the conventional culturalist sinological conservatism that simply overturns communist negation of traditional Chinese values, the *tianxia* discourse is politically conscious while simultaneously crafting a depoliticized language of universal harmony. It presents an ethnically and religiously insensitive cosmology of a grand amalgamation of races and cultures – within fluid identities and frontiers, without stable or definable boundaries. The constant internalization of the external results in a boundless realm of *wuwai*: literally, 'nobody/nothing being outside'. 'Inventing world politics' anew, *tianxia* in the contemporary era signifies a globalist worldview that understands human society all inclusively, and is thus at odds with the anachronistic Westphalian nation-state system. It also confirms the normative ideal of moral rule by the 'mandate of heaven', underscoring the ancient wisdom of equal sharing of land/wealth, and the 'people as the foundation' of government (Mencius).

As an 'ontology of coexistence' and a worldview of 'compatible universalism', *tianxia* is claimed to have transcended the Kantian doctrine of perpetual peace.[19] This blending of an old harmonious imaginary with a new blueprint for a silk road makes it impossible to repeat colonial conquests and exploitation. This is a unique spatial politics that is couched in an apolitical narrative of 'civilization' and 'empire without imperialism' as a cure for the immorality of global ills. The renewal of a splendid pre-modern system can catalyze a groundbreaking reformation that transcends the capitalist and imperialist logic of nation states. China in the twenty-first century, carrying the residues of its former self – as an empire, or civilization, or in any case a worldly entity – might well 'slip loose' of its boundaries once again, all for a good cause.[20]

As traditionalism is inflected to serve a legitimizing function, China's new globalism is at pains to appear as an attractive path to enhancing south-south cooperation and equality among nations in a non- or post-capitalist fashion.[21] But this is a fantasy. For one thing, it was repressive hierarchy rather than equality that characterized the Confucian social norms as well as the Sino-centric regional order. Equality existed only in the demands of peasant uprisings and utopian social thinking. For another, the claim that the 'civilizational state' was non-hegemonic is questionable, not only because imperial territories had doubled under the Qing rule, but more subtly because of Han domination. Even minority dynasties protected their own elites, while pursuing reverse assimilation toward the majority. It was not until the communist revolution that the issue of ethnic inequality was directly addressed through a socialist ideological and institutional reorganization.

Historically, the Chinese 'pacified empire', in Max Weber's depiction, rarely engaged in military aggression perhaps due to an inward-looking worldview and agrarian-based physiography. By and large, 'in sharp contrast to the European powers and their colonial-settler descendants, China did not seek to construct an overseas empire'.[22] But neither was historical 'China' ever singularly intelligible without floating frontiers, as it continued to absorb new territories and vassals. This inheritance of the modern *zhonghua minzu* or Chinese nation could be as much a blessing as a curse. If once categorically distinguishable from the capitalist colonial powers, it is no longer obvious that Chinese capital abroad today is not primarily motivated by profit and resources, or is a convenient diversion from domestic discontent.

China's 'farewell to revolution' and its international repositioning to court the US constitute an intertwined political logic. Domestically, ethnic tensions have sharpened with invading market forces, which have changed local demographic composition and eroded minority cultures. External agitation and state oppression make things worse. Globally, as the third world is replaced with 'emerging markets', the aspiration of rectifying an unjust world system has vanished. The fact that revolutionary China's double mission of overthrowing foreign domination as well as Han chauvinism at home has now indefinitely halted also indicates the failure of *tianxia-ism*, or Chinese universalism, as a rival to realist theories of international relations. This is not so much because nations and their unequal or conflicting relationships are formidable realities as because nationalism and inclusive universalism are acutely different normative frames. However unwillingly, the image of *Pax Sinica* is tainted by the impossible thesis of a 'clash of civilizations'.[23] Furthermore, Confucian universalism, as 'the art of co-existing through transforming hostility into hospitality',[24] is toothless when facing a global order sustained by a powerful capitalist industrial-financial-military complex. The most glaring weakness of traditionalist theories, then, are their neglect of the state and the unavoidable need to win sovereign, autonomous, and democratic popular power across the developing (and indeed developed) world. Capturing state power is a prerequisite for achieving significant progressive goals at the global level.

From a modern socialist point of view, Confucianism, however modernized, is pre-socialist (and non- rather than necessarily pre-capitalist). Its conservative teachings, from belittling women to endorsing gentry-scholar elitism and undemocratic hierarchies, render it hopelessly reactionary and obsolete. Its most radical element – the moral right and legitimacy of rebellion against tyranny – is convincingly suppressed in its official promotion of a ruling ideology. Sophisticated and eloquent though it may be, the philosophy of a uniformly benevolent, ascendant, globalizing Chinese tradition cannot rival either liberal or realist theories of great power politics, which also extend into the public sphere and mass media. Nothing less than the practical renewal of socialist internationalism presents a real alternative. To be sure, traditional culture comprising a rich array of intellectual resources can be re-appropriated, from the nature-friendly idea of unity between heaven and people and 'methodological relationism' over individualism to the wisdom of economic management, market regulation, and disaster relief. But it is the 'revolutionary break with the past' that has defined China since 1949, completely recasting its internal and external relations. In this light, Confucian revivalism signals a politics of defeat and escapism. The bizarre scene of party secretaries kneeling to a statue of Confucius in an ancestral temple or an educational campus indicates a political crisis. It is a sign of ideological bankruptcy that official China should have found it necessary to appeal to an ancient saint.

LOST IN ACCUMULATION: CRISES AND ILLUSIONS

Neither a socialist reinterpretation of China's new globalism as heralding a monumental shift in global capitalism, nor a neo-Confucian universalism envisioned to be reordering international relations, can overcome the contradictions in China's current position: China is simultaneously a beneficiary and victim of market transition, exploited by foreign capital and multinationals while arguably also engaged in exploitative relations with even more peripheral states; suffering dependency on foreign markets and technologies while also exporting capital and labour; disciplined by global powers yet possessed of a rising economic and diplomatic influence that is seen as a threat by competitors and neighbours; and espousing a nationalist discourse that champions globalization and free trade. The contrast between its socialist rhetoric and substantially neoliberal-style policies is also striking – especially given that the latter includes a pro-management labour regime, and gross inequalities in basic public provision and social services.

These two romantic approaches share an additional fundamental flaw. They leave the developmentalist core of Chinese globalism intact, at least concerning its sustainability in terms of its resource-environmental, financial, and foreign relations implications. It is only too easy to liken China with the old colonizers.[25] However, as the world's largest importer of a variety of essential commodities, China is indeed in the game of a global scramble for resources, from minerals to land and water. This, in turn, increases carbon emissions and pollution, worsening climate change and other ecological problems. It is dubious that the BRI can be environmentally conscious as geography and geology are being altered. Joining other global buyers, Chinese demand affects price and stock volatilities in both global and national markets. China's macro financial system also suffers a debt problem at both the central and local levels, although denominated in its own currency. The same pattern is repeated by a 'cheque-book diplomacy' that risks repayment crises and bankruptcies. More generally, the dystopia of GDP growth-at-all-costs, 'creative destruction' of organic communities and the eco-world, and the predictable panorama of bubble bursting and bank runs are neither morally sound nor practically viable.[26]

The constant need for new spaces to accommodate endless accumulation is also geopolitically perilous. The scope and manner of China's global adventures is a central question of *realpolitik*. For capital to source profits and rents globally, as it proceeds with its concentration, centralization, monopolization, and financialization, it needs to be backed by military strength. The existing world system cannot tolerate another growing economy of China's size, or the emergence of new global powers. The imperialist law of value requires technological monopolies and protection of a rentier oligarchy.[27] Since the BRI is packaged in liberal ideology, its silky discourse may superficially minimize certain political sensitivities, but it cannot eliminate them.

Despite China's devotion to market globalization in line with the capitalist world order, for those who retain a perpetual cold war mentality, any prospect of a 'communist' China becoming a financially and technologically independent economy is anathema. Yet even merely ensuring its supply of energy appears unrealistic without some Sino-US parity in geopolitical capacities, as more than half of Chinese imports and exports pass through straits and waterways that are within reach of the US Navy (and that the West has controlled for centuries). Under the Pentagon's strategic encirclement of China, the economic and security objectives of China disturb the American-secured regional balance. Tensions have risen in the Himalayas, the East and South China Seas, and other more distant places. The Chinese geo-strategic notions of a 'String of Pearls' in the Indian Ocean and the 'Nine-Dash Line' in the South China Sea are fiercely contested. So far the Chinese objectives of 'strategic mutual trust' and 'win-win cooperation' remain elusive.

Instead of believing in its destined 'marriage' to the US, as declared by more than one government minister in Beijing, China should break free of American containment by guarding its hard-won independence. Expanding investments overseas, it needs to reinstate its founding principles of egalitarianism and democracy as the basis for any foreign policy. If Chinese economic and financial foundations lack the ability to fend off turmoil in global markets; if basic needs are still unfulfilled in national food sovereignty and securely funded public services for all; and if the poor, migrants, and certain minority groups are deprived of full citizenship and welfare rights; then are there not less wasteful and less risky forms of development that should be pursued instead of investing massively abroad? Operating globally may also escalate a vicious race to the bottom in addition to depleting resources, draining reserves, piling up debts, and spreading pollution through both production and consumption.

The point is that China doesn't need growth at such costs, especially when facing immense tasks at home – from resolving tech-bottlenecks to advancing toward its pledged 'ecological civilization'. Greener industries can, in turn, assist agricultural productivity on the basis of collective land ownership and cooperative family farming. A new type of moral economy of rural and urban commons would aim at production for need rather than profit through a socialized market. This path would be both more ambitious and more realistic, if only because in the whole background is the incurable disease, historical impossibility, and structural inability of capitalism to provide for the vast majority of the world's population.[28] The colossal destruction entailed by plundering land and people through the system of endless accumulation and crisis forces on us, more urgently than ever before, a non-choice as sharp as 'socialism or barbarism'.

This is by no means to repudiate internationalism. On the contrary, the argument is that without a domestic class power oriented toward socialism, no global vision or foreign policy can be truly internationalist. Reorientation within China is required before it can reshape globalization as an alternative to, rather than enhancement of, the capitalist global system. Any socially and internationally credible project here must also be part of an international front of popular struggle. The question would then be how China might forge a new path to reconstruct the global economy by organizing a scheme to aid national development and transform socioeconomic conditions in the global south in particular, while heeding the warning against forming a 'sub-imperialism'.

In the most robust attempts to blend socialist and *tianxia*-ist ideas for China's new globalism, the premise is the 'unity of three traditions' – classical Confucianism, Maoist socialism and Dengist market pragmatism.[29] This is a straightforward narrative of China 'standing up' under Mao, 'getting rich' under Deng, and 'becoming powerful' under Xi. The confidence in offering the world a 'Chinese solution' and 'Chinese wisdom', as supporters see it, has a great deal to do with the depth of China's cultural traditions. In one blatant formulation, Xi's new era is 'not adding Chinese characteristics to an already defined "socialist framework." Rather, it uses China's lived experience to explore and define what, in the final analysis, "socialism" is.' And this definition is to be 'universally recognized throughout the entire world'.[30] Indeed the Chinese outlook has always been worldly and universalist, as shown in historical East Asia where 'the *tianxia* order and the tribute system made up a universal system of diversity within unity, capable of absorbing different peoples, cultures and religious beliefs'. To expand such a Chinese civilization is 'the greatest historical mission of the Chinese people in the Xi Jinping era'.[31]

In another interpretation based on a more profound analysis of world history and spatial politics, the concept of 'supra-state' is introduced as a creative agency to delineate China's historical potential. Critical of 'the loss of meaning, abstraction of the life-world, and the rationalization of unequal relations' entailed by capitalism, this formulation relies on culturalist foundations to articulate a different political vision. The Chinese 'supra-state', based in a vast, complicated, and boundless civilization, begs the ultimate question of how to spatially and substantially define 'China' and its everyday internal and external relations. Answering this question requires a shift in our conception of history, so that the BRI can be situated within a civilizational imaginary. Given that China has evolved into an intrinsically 'supra-civilization of civilizations' against the singularization or homogenization that breeds conflict and oppression, 'the practice of One Belt One Road can reestablish mutually respective social relations in a dynamic process'. It is thus a plan of global communicative inter-subjectivity, blending a traditional civilization and modern socialism, particularity and universality, difference and equality. It is 'a plan of great harmony that differs from capitalism'.[32]

Here the leading Chinese scholars have deconstructed the traditionally intertwined concepts of socialism and internationalism – even rendering the latter conceptually impossible within a discourse of an all-encompassing civilization that invalidates the international. As such, 'class' is analytically nullified and cannot animate politics. The party theory of 'three represents' to accommodate the pluralized values of a market society proposed in 2001 is to 'allow the CCP to represent the political interests of newly arisen social strata, successfully avoiding the crisis of representation that would occur if the party were only to represent the interests of workers and peasants'. This observation is astounding, coming as it did at the very time when traditional socialist conceptions of representing the labouring classes were in devastating retreat. The replacement of a classless cultural 'nation' as what is to be represented by the CCP is grounded in 'its indigenous, national nature, its authentic Chinese nature, rather than in the Party's class nature'.[33] At the same time, China's desire to make a contribution to humanity is believed to 'prove that the great revival of the Chinese people is not nationalistic, but cosmopolitan'. Again culturalist in essence, the roots of this cosmopolitanism are in Confucian universalist declarations that 'when the Way prevails, *tianxia* is shared by all', as well as in the communist belief in human emancipation. Displacing internationalism, this conflation of Confucianism and communism turns the stigma of empire into an advantage. Superseding nations and other societal units, the notion of a 'supra-state' might be compatible with those of the 'global', 'transnational', and 'cosmopolitan', but not the 'international'.

Unexpectedly perhaps, anti-capitalism is then displaced by the struggle for global supremacy, and the politico-economic opposition between socialism and capitalism is converted into the culturally-based shift of the global centre of gravity toward the East, bringing Western hegemony to an end. In this perspective, any criticism of imperialist or expansionist menace is precluded, especially given that no territorial dispute is insolvable if 'shared sovereignty' and other innovative institutional means can be explored. The fact that China is being globalized, and that the participating capital in the BRI is no longer limited to Chinese capital, does, to say the least, further complicate the issue.

THE SPECTRE OF SOCIALISM

Does China have a global grand strategy to achieve socialism? Officially, the country is celebrating the 40th anniversary of its initial market reform this year. In retrospect, undoubtedly the reforms have been a march toward capitalist global integration, rather than a temporary strategic retreat analogous to the New Economic Policy in Soviet Russia nearly a century ago. Many see China's presence as a commanding fact on a planetary scale – not just in terms of the betterment of the lives of one fifth of the world's population, but even in the sense that the epoch of ruthless capitalist dominion over miserably subjugated peoples seems to have come to a close.[34] The irony, however, is that the resilience of capitalism is nowhere better vindicated than in China's participation in the system. The People's Republic is losing its original substance and distinction along the way, as the growth model it champions becomes ever more socially and ecologically indefensible. With the ruling ideology (whether in its deformed Marxist or Confucian discourses) as well as social consciousness so entrenched in the fetishisms of commodities and money, China has remade itself into an unlikely carrier of the torch for neoliberal globalization with authoritarian and bureaucratic characteristics.

The transformation of Communist China from outside challenger to dutiful participant in global capitalism marks a world-historical defeat for socialism no less significant than the collapse of the Soviet Union. Yet, these former 'two great hybrids' in the process of modernization[35] need not remain stuck where they have arrived. In particular, the Chinese success in capitalist terms means that a reorientation towards reviving socialism in China would inevitably affect the whole globe. Socialism, after all, is the only assurance of equality against chauvinism and expansionism. The theoretical indivisibility of socialism and internationalism means a practical incompatibility between domestic departure from socialism and foreign advance in line with internationalism.

China's search for its future is wide open. It depends on the development of a transformative politics from above, which is not totally inconceivable so long as there is a strong impetus for this from below. The potential for such a political fusion may be seen in the ongoing movements of striking workers and protesting veterans, villagers and civic activists, as well as young Marxist reading groups and bloggers defying censorship and repression. Any project of reclaiming the party and state can critically draw on still active Chinese revolutionary and socialist legacies. Only such a project will allow China to take the long view, and lead the way in restricting capital, socializing monopolies, and de-financializing economic management the world over. Socialism and internationalism remain the two indispensable aspects of contemporary Chinese ambition whose success will ultimately be measured by overcoming capitalism and imperialism.

NOTES

1   Such a front should encompass 'the peoples of the socialist camp, of Asia, Africa and Latin America, of every continent of the world, of all the countries in love of peace and all the countries suffering from aggression, control, intervention and bullying from the US'. See: Mao, 'The Chinese People Firmly Support Patriotic Struggles for Justice by the Panama People', *People's Daily*, 12 January 1964.

2   Eric Hobsbawm, quoted in Perry Anderson, *Spectrum: From Right to Left in the World of Ideas*, London: Verso, 2007, p. 313.

3   Also suspicious of US interest in a Soviet military attack on China, Mao confronted Henry Kissinger in one of their meetings in 1973 and proposed a 'horizontal line' of the US, Japan, China, Pakistan, Iran, Turkey, and Europe to counter the Soviet Union. See *The Chronology of Mao, Vol.7*, Beijing: Central Document Press, 2014.

4   Ralph Miliband, *Class War Conservatism and Other Essays*, London: Verso, 2015, p. 232; Vijay Prashad, *The Darker Nations: A People's History of the Third World*, New York: The New Press, p. 174; Fred Halliday, 'Marxist Analysis and Post-Revolutionary China', *New Left Review*, 100(November-December), 1976, p. 2.

5   David Harvey, *A Brief History of Neoliberalism*, Oxford: Oxford University Press, 2005, chapter 5.

6   According to Yu Yongding, an expert from the Chinese Academy of Social Sciences, net outflow of capital in China's balance sheet of international payments amounted to an annual 6 per cent of GDP in recent years. In 2015-16 alone, it reached to $1.28 trillion. See: 'China Is Very Likely to see Some Serious Capital Flight in the Next Few Years', *Xinlang Finance*, 21 September 2017, available at http://finance.sina.com.cn/china/gncj/2017-09-21/doc-ifymesii4798476.shtml.

7   See Gao Liang, then the director of the State Capital Research Centre in China's Development and Reform Commission: 'A Summary of Foreign Acquisition of Chinese firms', 28 June 2007, available at http://www.xici.net/d54430863.htm. See also Jia Genliang, '"Post-Listianism' or a Model of Dependency?', *South China Quarterly*, 2, 2015.

8   'Trump Has Approved $50 billion in China Tariffs as the Superpowers Inch Toward a Trade War,' *Fortune*, 15 June 2018; 'What's at Stake in US-China Trade War: The Full List,' *Financial Times*, 19 June 2018.

9   'China Loosens Investment Curbs as Trade War Looms', *Financial Times*, 30 June 2018; 'China Focus: China Unveils Shortened Negative List for Foreign Investment', *Xinhuanet*, 29 June 2018; 'China's substantial relaxation of market access for foreign investment', *ChinaNewsnet*, 29 June 2018.

10   David Harvey, *The Ways of the World*, London: Profile Books, 2017, pp. 2-6, 246-50. Harvey notes: 'China consumed some 60% of the world's copper and more than half of world's output of iron ore and cement after 2008' (p. 2). See also Hyun Bang Shin, 'Economic Transition and Speculative Urbanization in China: Gentrification versus Dispossession', *Urban Studies*, 53(3), 2016.

11   Huang Qifan, 'The New Characteristics of China's Opening Shaped By the Belt and Road Project', Speech at the Chinese Academy of Social Sciences, BRI International Thinktank Inauguration Conference, May 2018.

12   Yin Zhiguang, 'The Concept of "Chinese Nation" in Political Practice', *Open Times*, 2, 2016; Yin Zhiguang, 'The Internationalist Moment: The Chinese Perspective on the National Independence Movements in the Arab World and the Making of the Chinese Third-World Internationalism', *Open Times*, 4, 2017; Wang Hui, 'The Taiwan Question in the Great Change of Contemporary Chinese History,' *Beijing Cultural Review*, 1, 2015.

13   Wang Hui, 'Civilization Between the Pacific and Atlantic,' *Economic Herald*, 9, 2015.

14   Zhang Wenmu, 'The Three Changes of Postwar Global Political Structure and the Emergence of Historical "Breaking Point"', *World Socialism Studies*, 1-3, 2017.

15   Wang Shengsheng and Li Bangxi, 'Cycling Alteration or Historical Transcendence?', *Open Times*, 2, 2017, pp. 90-92.

16   *Beijing Review* article by Zheng Xinye, 'The AIIB Must Buck Financing Trends to Improve the Forturns of Nations along the Belt and Road', published in *The Economist*, 2017, available at: chinafocus.economist.com. China's Ambassador to Canada, for example, said China stood strongly against adding any conditions to protect labour into the bilateral trade agreement: the Canadian 'progress trade agenda' has no place in free trade. See: Radio Canada International, 10 April 2018, available at: chinascope.org.

17   Joseph Nye's concepts of soft and hard power and notions of sharp and smart powers are fashionable in China's international relations discourse. Nye calls for democracies to respond to China's sharp power, which he sees as 'information warfare' that 'helps authoritarian regimes compel behavior at home and manipulate opinion abroad'. 'China's Soft and Sharp Power', *Project Syndicate*, 5 January 2018.

18   Adrian Zenz, 'China's Domestic Security Spending: An Analysis of Available Data', *China Brief*, 18(4), 2018, available at: jamestown.org/program/chinas-domestic-security-spending-analysis-available-data.

19   Zhao Tingyang, 'All-Under-Heaven and Methodological Relationism', in Fred Dallmayr and Zhao Tingyang, eds, *Contemporary Chinese Political Thought: Debates and Perspectives*, Frankfort: University Press of Kentucky, 2012, pp. 46-51, 62-65.

20   Xu Jinyu, 'The Geopolitical Economy of China's 'One Belt One Road': Inclusive Tianxia or Exceptional Space?', *Open Times*, 2, 2017; He Guimei, 'How Has Traditional Culture Become a "Consensus" Among Different Social Forces in China', *Chinese Social Sciences Today*, 28 January 2016.

21   For Giovanni Arrighi, the East Asian models of growth are perceived as alternatives to Western models and can be widely emulated. China with a commitment to a more equal global order would in particular reorient the world. See his *Adam Smith in Beijing*, London: Verso, 2007.

22   Max Weber, *The Religion of China*, trans. and ed. by Hans Gerth, New York: Free Press, 1964 [1951]; Peter Nolan, 'Imperial Archipelagos: China, Western Colonialism, and the Law of the Sea', *New Left Review*, 80(March/April), 2013; David Schweickart also notes that China, 'unlike the major European states, has not tried to colonize areas of the world's poorer or weaker than itself'. And, 'unlike pre-World War II Japan, it has not waged ruthless warfare against its neighbors. ... Unlike the United States, it has not set up military bases all over the world. ... Unlike the Soviet Union, it has not engaged in a massive arms race with the world's other 'superpower,' nor has it installed client governments in nations on its border.' See: *After Capitalism*, Lanham, MD: Rowman & Littlefield, 2011, p. 174.

23   William Callahan, 'Chinese Visions of World Order: Post-Hegemonic or a New Hegemony?', *International Studies Review*, 10, 2008, p. 756.

24   Zhao Tingyang, 'Can this Ancient Chinese Philosophy Save Us from Global Chaos?', *The Washington Post*, 7 February 2018.

25   See: Ching Kwan Lee, 'The Specter of Global China', *New Left Review*, 89 (September/October), 2014; Ho-Fung Hung, 'The Tapestry of Chinese Capital in the Global South', *Palgrave Communications*, 4, 2018; Deborah Bräutigam, *The Dragon's Gift: The Real Story of China in Africa*, Oxford: Oxford University Press, 2011; Deborah Bräutigam, *Will Africa Feed China?* Oxford: Oxford: Oxford University Press, 2016; Barry Sautman and Yan Hairong, *East Mountain Tiger, West Mountain Tiger: China, Africa, the West and 'Capitalism'*, Maryland Monograph Series in Contemporary Asian Studies, 186, Baltimore: University of Maryland School of Law, 2006.

26   Harvey, *The Ways of the World*, p. 5; Sam Moyo, Paris Yeros and Praveen Jha, 'Imperialism and Primitive Accumulation: Notes on the New Scramble for Africa', *Agrarian South: Journal of Political Economy*, 1(2), 2012.

27   Samir Amin, 'The Surplus in Monopoly Capitalism and the Imperialist Rent', *Monthly Review*, 64:3, 2012; John Smith, 'Imperialism in the 21st Century', *Monthly Review*, 67:3, 2015.

28   Aijaz Ahmad, *In Theory*, London: Verso, 1992, pp. 315-17; Utsa Patnaik and Sam Moyo, eds, *The Agrarian Question in the Neoliberal Era: Primitive Accumulation and the Peasantry*, Oxford: Pambazuka Press, 2011.

29   Gan Yang, *Unify The Three Traditions*, Beijing: Sanlian Publisher, 2007.

30   Jiang Shigong, 'Philosophy and History: Interpreting the 'Xi Jinping Era' Through Xi's Report to the 19th National Congress of the CCP', *Open Times*, 1, 2018. See also the introduction of this text by David Ownby and Timothy Cheek from the Australian

Center on China in the World, *The China Story*, 11 May 2018, at www.thechinastory.org.

31   Jiang, 'Philosophy and History.'

32   Wang Hui, 'Civilization between the Pacific and Atlantic,' a synthesis of his earlier discussions of nation vs. empire, 'region as method', and bridging 'society of inter-systems' and 'supra-societal systems' (borrowed from Marcel Mauss). He uses China's ethnic minority regions as an example to show how an intercommunicative and inclusive inter-systemic society can be undermined by inequalities mediated by market forces of augmenting trans-border production and consumption ('Equality of What? II', *Beijing Cultural Review*, 12, 2011).

33   Jiang Shigong,'Philosophy and History.'

34   If the Chinese reforms in the 1980s can be seen as a gigantic NEP 'determined to maintain the political independence and achieve the technological autonomy of the country, to enable China to advance towards a socialist society and alter the balance of world power', then the post-1989 radicalization of reform has thoroughly changed this course. David Broder, 'Eastern Light on Western Marxism', *New Left Review*, 107(September/October), 2017, 145.

35   Goran Therborn, *Cities of Power: The Urban, the National, the Popular, the Global*, London: Verso, 2017, pp. 30-31.

CAN CHINA UNMAKE THE AMERICAN MAKING OF GLOBAL CAPITALISM?

SEAN KENJI STARRS

If the United States made global capitalism in the twentieth century,[1] can China unmake this American making in the twenty-first? If global capitalism was made by integrating the West under the aegis of American hegemony, then can China construct an alternative world order by integrating the East? This essay argues that there are severe contradictions constraining China's capacity to successfully challenge a global capitalism that continues to be centred upon the United States, including in East Asia. The most important contradictions lie in the nature of China's nationalist discourse and its economic integration with Western – particularly American – capital. Any sober assessment of China's new mission of challenging the United States in the twenty-first century needs to be made in the light of these contradictions, with their unknowable domestic consequences.

Nevertheless, while China may not succeed in making an alternative global capitalism in the foreseeable future, it will certainly not be for want of trying. The period of China following Deng Xiaoping's dictum of 'biding our time and keeping a low profile' in the 1990s and 2000s was decidedly over by 2013, with President Xi Jinping announcing a new era of China 'striving for achievement'.[2] Previous taboos have now been shattered, with Xi explicitly proclaiming that China is returning to its 'natural' place of centrality in Asia and that 'it is for the people of Asia to run the affairs of Asia' – a pointed reference to American hegemony.[3] Of course, Xi is not the first to proclaim that China is now standing up. Beginning with Mao's famous proclamation atop the Gate of Heavenly Peace across from Tiananmen Square on 1 October 1949 at the dawn of the People's Republic, the question many Chinese elites have long debated is not *whether* China should challenge American hegemony, but *when*. Even as China transformed from a version of state socialism to a version of state capitalism in the 1980s and 1990s and deeply integrated with American-centred global capitalism, the assumption behind Deng's dictum was that China should keep a low profile until such time that it is powerful enough to no longer need to do so. Many Chinese elites believed that this time had come in the aftermath of the 2008 Wall Street crash and ensuing global financial crisis, with the West on its knees, and China becoming increasingly assertive in the last term of President Hu Jintao.[4]

These trends were significantly ramped up with the appointment of President Xi Jinping in fall 2012. Where Hu was more risk-averse and ruled collectively in China's opaque governance system, Xi took great political risk with his 'anti-corruption campaign' and consolidated his power to become China's strongest leader since Deng, if not Mao. On his path to becoming China's 'core leader' – a moniker not bestowed upon Hu Jintao – contrarian positions (and sometimes people) were eliminated. The debate on whether China is ready to stand up to the United States was thus concluded by 2017, when Xi enshrined his 'thoughts' in the Constitution, rendering them effectively unchallengeable. And since Xi removed China's decade-long presidential term limit in February 2018 and can now rule for life, it is worth delving deeper into his thoughts and how they are being put into action – with the contradictions sprouting faster than a black lotus after a monsoon.

WHAT IS XI JINPING THINKING?

In a land known for clunky slogans, Xi Jinping can compete with the best of them. At the Nineteenth Party Congress in October 2017, a new clause was inserted into the Chinese constitution on 'Xi Jinping Thought on Socialism with Chinese Characteristics for a New Era'. At this seminal Party Congress, Xi gave a marathon nearly three-and-a-half-hour speech laying out these thoughts, verbosely entitled 'Secure a Decisive Victory in Building a Moderately Prosperous Society in All Respects and Strive for the Great Success of Socialism with Chinese Characteristics for a New Era'.[5] The 'new era' signifies China's return to the global stage, of what Xi calls 'The Great Rejuvenation of the Chinese People' forever banishing 'The Century of Humiliation' (1839-1949) to the dustbin of history. To fulfil (or control) the aspirations of the rising urban middle class, Xi places much emphasis on the 'Chinese Dream', a mix of individual material advancement akin to its American counterpart but placed in the context of national prowess and rejuvenation (under the tutelage of the Chinese Communist Party). Xi employs the phrase quite flexibly, for example when he urges his comrades to 'work together to create a mighty force for realizing the Chinese Dream and the dream of building a powerful military'. In essence, Xi decrees that national rejuvenation (including of its military) is the dream of the Chinese people, and even an 'historic responsibility'. To dispute this is now anti-constitutional.

Note that 'national rejuvenation' means more than simply economic growth and development, the more limited goals of previous leaders since Deng. Rather, it refers to China regaining its historical place at the centre of East Asia before the onset of Western imperialism from 1839, which necessarily implies a substantially diminished regional role for the United States. This national rejuvenation entails restoring China's international status and moral standing (from a Confucian perspective of 'moral leadership'), so that, Xi declared, Chinese people can feel 'the pride of a strong and prosperous China', instead of 'humiliation' at the hands of foreigners. In fact, national rejuvenation is so central to 'Xi Jinping Thought' that he has re-written the history of the Chinese Communist Party (CCP) as being founded in 1921 upon the principle of national rejuvenation against 'feudal rule and foreign aggression'. Mao's goal of world socialist revolution has been erased from history – even if the over 2,000 delegates of the Nineteenth Party Congress still sang the *Internationale*.

Further note that Xi has an expansive view of who the 'Chinese people' are, based on ethnicity, not citizenship, as he avows that 'blood is thicker than water' in reference to never allowing Taiwanese independence. For Xi (and many other Chinese elites), the Chinese people are bound by a common civilizational heritage of 5,000 years no matter where one is currently geographically located in a world divided by Eurocentric nation-states. Rather, Chinese elites make reference to the ancient system of *tianxia* (suzerainty) that encompasses 'all under heaven'. This harks back to China's centrality in Asia's imperial tributary system before its dismantling by Western imperialism in the nineteenth century, which Xi calls a 'historical tragedy'. Indeed, for Yan Xuetong, one of the most prominent international relations scholars in China today, 'national rejuvenation as a phrase literally refers to resuming China's historical international status as the world's most advanced state during the period of Zhenguan Prosperity (627-649 AD) in early Tang Dynasty (618-907 AD)'.[6] With Xi now able to rule for life, the period of 'Xi Prosperity' may last longer than this 22-year period at the supposed pinnacle of Chinese power almost 1,400 years ago.

In this vein, during his speech at the Nineteenth Party Congress, Xi gave a timeframe for these goals. He already proclaimed that the 'Chinese nation, with an entirely new posture, now stands tall and firm in the East', and that the 'trends of global multipolarity ... are surging forward'. This 'entirely new posture' is China's increased assertiveness under Xi, including over its territorial claims in the South China Sea (SCS). By 2021 (the centenary of the founding of the CCP), Xi wants China to become a 'moderately prosperous society', and between 2020 and 2035 a 'global leader in innovation'. Between 2035 and 2050, Xi plans for China to 'become a global leader in terms of composite national strength and international influence ... making China a great modern socialist country in every dimension'. Especially in the context of national rejuvenation – making China great again relative to its historical system of *tianxia* – this can only mean the end of the American-centred world order by 2050, according to Xi's plan (by then he would be 97 years old).

WHAT IS XI JINPING DOING?

How has Xi implemented these thoughts on national rejuvenation? For starters, since 2012 China has become more internationally engaged than any of its historical predecessors since the founding of the Qin Empire two millennia ago. In Xi's first five years he visited many more countries – fifty-six on five continents – than any other CCP leader.[7] By comparison, his predecessor Hu visited seven countries in ten years, and Barack Obama, the most well travelled US president ever, visited fifty-eight countries in eight years. Xi also hosted more foreign leaders than any other Chinese leader in history and has so far organized seven major international summits including APEC, the BRICS Summit, the G20, and the Belt and Road Forum for International Cooperation in May 2017 (China's largest international gathering since the 2008 Beijing Olympics). In 2013 David Shambaugh called China a 'partial power' largely because of its limited foreign policy activism despite having trade and investment relations around the world.[8] But under Xi, China is arguably now second only to the United States in global diplomatic engagement and vision – a stunning transformation in merely five years.

This increased international activism is clearly designed to bolster China's global influence, which in the medium-term would *not* necessarily come at the expense of American influence, for example in international infrastructure investment. Over the long-term (by 2050), however, the goal is to do nothing short of 'reOrienting' the post-1945 American hub-and-spoke system in the Asia-Pacific towards China as hub for at least a sizable share of trade, investment, and eventually security links stretching across Eurasia and Africa. The first major initiative under Xi in this regard was the decision in March 2013 at the South Africa BRICS Summit to create a 'BRICS Bank'. By its establishment over a year later it had become known as the New Development Bank (NDB), with headquarters in Shanghai (despite originally being an Indian idea; the compromise was that its first director would be Indian). It should be stressed, however, that the NDB was explicitly created to complement, not compete with, the incumbent Western-led financial institutions. Article 1 of the NDB's Articles of Agreement states its purpose as 'complementing the existing efforts of multilateral and regional financial institutions for global growth and development', and they have since agreed to co-finance projects with the European Bank for Reconstruction and Development (EBRD), the Japan-led Asian Development Bank (ADB), and World Bank, among others.[9] If many of NDB's projects are co-financed with Western-led institutions, then this increases the overall financing pool without threatening the latter.

More striking from the perspective of offering an alternative to the American-centred system was the establishment of the Asian Infrastructure Investment Bank (AIIB) in 2015, headquartered in Beijing. There was great fanfare over the circumstances of its founding because the United States lobbied its allies to refuse to join the AIIB, but even its closest allies joined anyway. Australia, Canada, Germany, France, the Netherlands, South Korea, and most significantly Britain (the first Western nation to join, sparking a cascade) joined the AIIB. By 2018 the AIIB had 84 members, with the continued glaring absence of regional rivals Japan and the United States. This marks the first major rift in the West regarding the rise of China – that is, the first time key American allies such as Britain and South Korea have gone against American foreign policy and instead apparently sided with China. Surely this is one of the most embarrassing diplomatic flops suffered by the United States in East Asia since the withdrawal of US troops from Vietnam. Naturally, many commentators saw this as stark evidence of the decline of American hegemony in the face of China's rise.

While the AIIB is still new, it has been very underwhelming in its first two years of existence. It was planned to disperse $10-$15 billion per year in its first five years, but as is common for Chinese commitments of massive investment around the world, the actual values dispersed are only a fraction of initial public announcements. In 2016 the AIIB only approved $1.1 billion and $3.3 billion in 2017 (figures on actual loan dispersal have not yet been released).[10] Tellingly, 56 per cent of the total value of projects in its first two years are actually led by Western-centred financial institutions such as the ADB and EBRD – with 11 of 24 total projects so far being co-financed with the World Bank. In contrast, the ADB alone dispersed $17.5 billion in 2016 and $19.1 billion in 2017. Strikingly, China has received more in loans from the ADB than it has dispersed via the AIIB. For that matter, China remains the largest recipient of World Bank loans, receiving $2.4 billion in 2017.

And both the NDB and AIIB disperse all funds in US dollars, not RMB – the more international institutions that use the US dollar, the stronger will be the dollar's role as global reserve currency. Like the NDB, then, the AIIB has acted as a complement to the existing US-centred financial system, not as an institution bent on overturning it as many declared in 2015.

Xi inaugurated a potentially much bigger game, however, with the launch of the 'Silk Road Economic Belt and the 21st Century Maritime Silk Road', or 'Belt and Road Initiative' (BRI).[11] A wide range of loose investment pledges have been reported in the media under this Silk Road umbrella concept, from over $100 billion to eventually up to $8 trillion, mostly in infrastructure projects across Eurasia and Africa. The BRI has become Xi's signature foreign policy project, as he has directly claimed authorship of its creation multiple times (including in his 2017 speeches at the World Economic Forum and BRI Summit). It has become one of the core components of national rejuvenation. In 2016 it was the most cited concept in the *People's Daily*, the biggest circulation newspaper in China and official mouthpiece of the CCP. Numerous institutes are now set up to study and promote BRI (including the University Alliance of the Silk Road with 135 member universities in 36 countries), and it is already the topic of thousands of conference papers and journal articles, with academic careers striking gold on this new Silk Road. In various speeches Xi has even urged a 'Silk Road spirit' of 'peace and cooperation, openness and inclusiveness, mutual learning and mutual benefit'.[12] If Xi's plan for global leadership is to be accomplished by 2050 (especially 'reOrienting' trade and investment links towards China), then the success of the BRI over the next couple decades will be crucial. But the contradictions are many, as we shall see below.

In 2017 Xi Jinping also did not hesitate to attempt to fill the apparent void left by the US's alleged withdrawal from global leadership under President Trump's 'America First' platform. Xi became the first Chinese leader to attend the World Economic Forum in Davos, Switzerland, and gave the keynote address to capitalists of the world four days before Trump's inauguration, entitled 'Jointly Shoulder Responsibility of Our Times, Promote Global Growth'.[13] In his speech, Xi chided those who 'blame economic globalization for the chaos in the world … [since] many of the problems troubling the world are not caused by economic globalization'. He also asserted that globalization is historically inevitable, taking the liberal position that it 'is a natural outcome of scientific and technological progress, not something created by any individuals or any countries'. Nevertheless, he insinuated that countries *do* have control as he promised that China would continue to 'offer opportunities to business communities in other countries' by keeping its 'door wide open'. Thus Xi presented himself as defender of globalization, and delivered similar sentiments at other venues such as APEC. The irony of one of the most highly protectionist state-owned political economies in the world still ruled by a Communist Party trying to position itself as a defender of global capitalism should not be lost.

Xi has also increased China's military activity and diplomatic assertiveness – making use of a giant pile of carrots as well as by now the world's second largest stick (by military budget). Again, the trend of increasing Chinese assertiveness abroad began post-2008 during Hu's second presidential term. Nevertheless, Xi significantly ramped up China's assertiveness compared to Hu, especially in East Asia. In November 2013 China announced a new air defence identification zone (ADIZ) in the East China Sea that overlaps with Japan's existing ADIZ over the Senkaku Islands (which Taiwan also claims). Unlike Japan's ADIZ or Taiwan's (or even that of the US), which do not require anything of aircraft that do not intend to land within their zones, the Chinese Ministry of Defence requires all airliners entering its ADIZ to identify themselves and their flight path, reserving the right to shoot down any aircraft that do not comply. Japan ordered its airlines to refuse compliance (as did South Korea), and there have been regular scramblings of Japanese fighter jets as the Chinese airforce has regularly flown in this contested air space ever since. Meanwhile, the US has reiterated multiple times that the Senkaku Islands fall under the Japan-US Security Treaty. Regardless, five years after China announced its new ADIZ – and despite continual air and coast guard incursions – Xi has not been able to change the status quo in the East China Sea as Japan's control of the Senkaku Islands remains firmly entrenched.

Xi Jinping has, however, substantially altered the status quo in the South China Sea. Both China and Taiwan claim virtually the entirety of the SCS with the infamous 'nine-dash line' (sometimes ten or eleven dashes), first used on Republic of China maps in 1947 to demarcate the then-ruling Kuomintang's territorial claims (with US-backing). This nine-dash line cuts into the exclusive economic zones of Vietnam, Malaysia, Indonesia, Brunei, and the Philippines. Moreover, China has never clarified the coordinates of the dashes nor how to connect them. The controversy had origins before Xi, as in 2009 China first submitted the nine-dash line map to the United Nations and started sending naval patrol ships around the South China Sea. Also, in 2010 China announced that the SCS is a 'core interest', parallel to Tibet, Hong Kong, and Taiwan (meaning that China reserves the right to use military force to defend this territory), and in 2012 the nine-dash line map was emblazoned in Chinese passports for the first time.

But Xi changed the facts on the ground by actually building new ground, in late 2013 initiating a massive construction project transforming reefs and rocks (some of which were submerged) into artificial islands. Much of the construction is concentrated in the Spratly Islands, various parts of which are also claimed by the Philippines, Malaysia, Brunei, Indonesia, and Vietnam, as well as the Paracel Islands, claimed by Vietnam. The land reclamation was largely complete by 2017 with a combined 13 square kilometers of new artificial land, and China continues to build various facilities (including airports and dredging deep water ports) on what US Admiral Harris has called a new 'great wall of sand'. In 2015 Xi promised Obama that he would not militarize the Spratlys, but a year later started doing just that, installing anti-aircraft and anti-missile systems. Nevertheless, Obama drew a red line over the Scarborough Shoal (also claimed by the Philippines) in 2016, and China has yet to construct anything there.

There has also been a surge in Chinese military activity under Xi Jinping. China gained the capacity for long-range aircraft in 2015 from Russia, after the latter partially relaxed their ban of certain high-end military exports to China due to concerns over intellectual property theft. Hence China started flying patrols over the South China Sea – at first four times a year, then several times a month by 2017.[14] China and Russia have inaugurated joint naval exercises: for the first time in 2015 they conducted exercises in the Sea of Japan and the Mediterranean Sea (China's first ever naval exercise in southern Europe); in 2016 they staged their first ever joint-naval exercise in the South China Sea; and in 2017 a series of joint exercises in the Baltic Sea (China's first ever in northern Europe), the Sea of Japan, and the Okhotsk Sea north of Japan (another first for China).[15] Moreover, in 2017, China completed its first overseas military base in 700 years (with funds from BRI), in Djibouti on the Horn of Africa; strategically vital for the Arabian Sea and Suez Canal, Djibouti also hosts, apart from the French, America's only permanent base in Africa and Japan's only overseas military installation.

While military ties between China and Russia have grown closer than they have been since the 1950s, before the Sino-Soviet split – encouraged by Western sanctions on Russia in 2014, driving President Putin into Xi's embrace – in 2017 relations with India plunged to their lowest point since China invaded India in 1962. To stop the Chinese from constructing a road, there was a seventy-two-day standoff in July-August between the two militaries in Doklam, an area claimed by both China and Bhutan (which India regards as its protectorate). No shots were fired, but bizarre videos were released showing soldiers from both sides shoving each other with their chests. Chinese relations with South Korea also plunged from 2016, when the latter ignored Chinese protests and allowed the US to install its anti-ballistic missile system (with a powerful radar that can reach deep into China), the Terminal High Altitude Area Defense. In response, China closed down South Korean factories and department stores, banned South Korean pop stars from touring China, and forbade Chinese package tourists to South Korea.

In any case, while more instances of growing Chinese assertiveness could be mentioned, the crucial questions are: has the rest of Asia appreciated China's intensifying regional activism? Does this bipolar posture of distributing financial incentives and punishments increase China's influence and status in Asia? Does it convince neighbouring countries to nudge the US out of the region?

CONTRADICTION #1: REGIONAL BACKLASH

Overall, judged by its own goals, China's mounting assertiveness in Asia has been very far from a spectacular success. Regional tensions have reached a level not seen since the Cold War. China's relations have soured with almost all neighbouring countries (including North Korea and Myanmar), with a few exceptions (Russia, Laos, and Cambodia), to such an extent that a number of countries have called for an increased American presence in the region – the exact opposite of what China wants. No country in the East and South China Seas has accepted an inch of China's expansive territorial claims, regardless of Xi's island-building and military intimidation. And certainly no other country is pining for a rejuvenation of the pre-1839 Sino-centric East Asian order. No country is sufficiently charmed by China to dream of returning to an era in which they were considered barbarian vassal states in a tributary empire, even if Cambodia and Laos may be heading in this direction out of desperation for investment. Unlike the American dream, the Chinese dream does not so enthrall non-Chinese people.

Therefore, one of the core contradictions of China's attempt to eventually challenge American hegemony in East Asia is the nature of its ethno-centric nationalist discourse. Like most Asian countries, Chinese national identity is defined by blood and ethnicity, but coupled with the additional historical baggage of assuming cultural superiority and centrality within Asia. This identity is in the very language that China uses – for example 'peripheral diplomacy' (*zhoubian waijiao*) to refer to its relations in the region, implying a Sino-centric order, which is in fact what the Chinese characters for China (*Zhongguo*) mean ('Country in the Centre', often translated as 'Middle Kingdom'). Unsurprisingly, other countries in the region are at best suspicious of a rejuvenated Sino-centrism, not least because it runs up against their own nationalist orientations that have also become more assertive.

This is a conundrum from which Chinese elites will not likely be able to extract themselves in the foreseeable future. Indeed, the ethno-centric nature of Han Chinese nationalism has only become more important for Chinese elites since the 1980s (including for the repression of non-Han minorities in northern and western China). The social dislocations affecting over a billion people since that decade is on a scale rarely seen in human history. One of their consequences was over a million people protesting in Tiananmen Square and elsewhere in 1989, with the demonstrations being brutally crushed. Since then, and as China overturned more and more aspects of Maoist socialism, Chinese elites have increasingly relied on constructing a nationalist discourse that centres on three main components. First, it involves a rehabilitation of Confucianism, which the CCP's founders maligned as a reactionary authoritarian ideology pushed by feudal class enemies of the people.[16] Second, Chinese nationalist discourse has evolved in designating Japan as the premier 'humiliator' of China, so as to encompass a constant stream of multimedia on Japanese war crimes in the 1930s and 40s (textbooks, film, television dramas, literature, events, exhibits in museums, memorials, and so on).[17] And third, as discussed above, Xi increasingly emphasizes that national rejuvenation entails not simply material advancement and economic development, but also the Chinese dream of once again being the centre of Asia, forever overcoming the Century of Humiliation. In short, the less relevant the principles of Marxism, communism, and revolution are to the deeply exploitative state capitalism of contemporary China with its hyper-materialist nouveau riche, the more relevant is nationalism as a social glue to keep a rapidly changing society from tearing itself (and the ruling class) apart.[18]

As a result of China's new nationalism – based on addressing historical grievances coupled with increasing diplomatic and military assertiveness – there have been numerous calls for greater US engagement to hedge against or contain what many perceive to be the rise of Chinese aggression. There is rarely a clearer manifestation of Lundestad's 'empire by invitation', a phrase he coined in reference to American hegemony in Europe, but speculated in the 1990s could also be applied to East Asia.[19] Of course, Japan has been under the umbrella of US hegemony since 1945, as has South Korea, where the US still has wartime operational command over its military. Around the South China Sea, almost all countries have called for United States diplomacy and military to play a greater role in the region. This includes Vietnam, Malaysia, Singapore, Indonesia, and the Philippines all supporting more frequent 'freedom of navigation operations' (FONOPS) in which, beginning in 2015, the US Navy sails past these artificial islands to contest China's claims. The US Navy, Air Force, and Coast Guard have also stepped up joint exercises in the SCS with Vietnam, Cambodia, Thailand, Malaysia, Singapore, Brunei, Indonesia, Timor-Leste, and the Philippines, both bilaterally and multilaterally.

A number of countries in the region have also granted the US greater access to their military facilities or even agreed to host US troops semi-permanently, such that the US now has a greater military presence in East Asia than at any other time since the end of the Cold War – again, the exact opposite of what China wants. In 2015, over 1,000 US Marines began rotating through a Darwin, Australia military base every six months, as part of a new agreement expiring in 2040. In 2015 Singapore signed an enhanced defence agreement that allows US spy planes, which are flown over China's artificial islands, to be based in Singapore, along with up to four US Navy littoral combat ships (that can sail in shallow waters near atolls). Most strikingly, however, in 2013 Vietnam publicly invited the US to play a greater role in the South China Sea, and in 2016 (after President Obama fully lifted the US ban on lethal weapons exports to Vietnam) allowed US Navy warships to return to the most strategically important deep-sea port, at Cam Ranh Bay, for the first time since 1975. These port visits expanded by March 2018 to include over 5,000 US troops – the most on Vietnamese soil since 1975 – when a US aircraft carrier visited Da Nang for the first time in decades. This is a remarkable reversal in US-Vietnamese relations and is a direct result of China's increasing assertiveness.

Furthermore, under the auspices of the Enhanced Defense Cooperation Agreement (EDCA) signed in 2014, US troops returned to forward deployment (on a rotational basis) in the Philippines in 2016, after being kicked out in 1992 (US military occupation was made illegal in the post-dictatorship 1987 constitution). The US gained access to five bases across the Philippines and is able to construct new facilities on them, which began in early 2018. While newly-elected President Duterte in 2016 promised to rip up EDCA, 'separate' with the US, and announced that if China and Russia were creating a new world order then the Philippines would gladly join,[20] in reality Duterte has done very little to substantively follow through on these threats. Instead, relations with the US have deepened, for example in June 2017 when US Special Operations Forces, for the first time in years, engaged in joint operations with the Philippine military against Islamist separatists in the southern island of Mindanao, Duterte's home-base where he was mayor for 22 years. In May 2018 his foreign minister even threatened war if China continues to encroach on Philippine claims.[21] The Philippines is a core component of what is known in Chinese strategic thinking as the 'First Island Chain' (the others being Japan, Taiwan, and Indonesia) that could potentially inhibit the Chinese Navy from accessing the Pacific Ocean. Since 2016 the United States military has become more entrenched there than at any other time in the post-Cold War period. Therefore, these regional counter-moves represent significant blowback from China's increasing assertiveness.

Nevertheless, despite an increasing US military presence, all these countries perform a delicate balancing act in order to avoid alienating their giant neighbour. China is now more powerful than the majority of its Asian neighbours, and every country wants access to the Chinese domestic market and a piece of China's financial largesse. Herein lies a core contradiction, as, for example, the countries of ASEAN (or for that matter the EU) are consistently unable to form a consensus position on China's actions in the South China Sea, even when in 2016 the UN tribunal ruled that China's territorial claims have no legal basis and are invalid. Over the years, Cambodia, Laos, Indonesia, and since Duterte's election the Philippines (even though the previous government brought the legal complaint to the UN in 2013 and decisively won), as well as Hungary and Greece in the EU (both of which have received sizable Chinese investment), have all prevented citing a collective regional concern over Chinese actions in the South China Sea. In this more limited sense (compared to the failure of preventing an increased US military presence), China has been successful, and Xi's 'great wall of sand' is by now a fait accompli as many countries have quietly forgotten the 2016 UN ruling.[22]

In addition to this geopolitical failure vis-à-vis the United States in China's own backyard, there are increasing signs that Xi's signature foreign policy, the BRI, is already cracking at the seams. One of the core contradictions of the infrastructure investment-driven growth model is that if there is insufficient domestic consumer and/or export demand to actually use this infrastructure then ultimately the growth model is unsustainable, with mounting debt and inadequate revenue to pay it off. To aggravate matters, Chinese loans have a higher interest rate than the Bretton Woods institutions, even if sometimes after an initial grace period, and are tied to Chinese state-owned enterprise contracts that often bring their own suppliers and even Chinese labour (which they can more easily control).[23] An increasing number of people in recipient countries characterize these Chinese practices as 'neo-colonialism', creating new relations of dependency while offering limited knowledge transfer or even jobs to locals. And many in the region now see what happened in Sri Lanka in December 2017 as a wake-up call. Sri Lanka leased its southern port Hambantota to China for 99 years after defaulting on its crippling Chinese debts, amassed to build the unprofitable port in the first place (highly symbolic, since the leasing of Kowloon, Hong Kong to Britain for 99 years is a core component of China's 'Century of Humiliation'). In May 2018 the 92-year old Mahathir Mohamad staged an upset victory ending 60 years of Barisan National Party dominance in Malaysia, on a platform questioning Malaysia's participation in BRI-linked rail projects, citing the case of Sri Lanka, and has vowed to renegotiate all 'unequal treaties' with China. Similar misgivings have been expressed in Cambodia, Indonesia, Myanmar, Nepal, Thailand, and Vietnam. It is also difficult to see a positive future for Laos' high-speed rail investment when debt from building the single line through Laos to connect China and Thailand is now almost half of Laos' $14 billion GDP.[24]

Indeed, China's own debt-fuelled investment-driven growth is itself slowing since 2013, which is one of the impetuses of the BRI in the first place: to provide overseas opportunities for its behemoth SOEs and reduce their chronic overcapacity in heavy industry. China is essentially trying to transfer the costs of its slowing growth model onto its neighbours, without anywhere near its level of consumption or export-driven production. It is unlikely Chinese firms would be encouraged to fill this gap by shifting their production overseas in the foreseeable future, since this could result in millions of lost jobs which would be counter-productive to the primary short-term purpose of BRI (to boost Chinese growth). And while Chinese domestic consumption is growing in importance, it is still not enough to compensate for declining infrastructure investment – hence China's overall growth rate continues to decline since 2013. If China's domestic market of over 1.3 billion people still cannot adequately drive Chinese growth after over three decades of the largest export and infrastructure boom the world has ever seen, then the chances for BRI to drive sustainable long-term growth in much smaller countries in Eurasia and Africa seem rather slim.

Finally, even if over the next couple decades China is able to gain increasing support from its neighbours for CCP leadership and secure their accommodation to the Chinese dream of national rejuvenation, and even if the BRI successfully 'reOriented' a significant proportion of diplomatic, investment, trade, and even cultural and popular linkages towards China as hub, this would not necessarily decouple China (let alone the region) from the US. This is because East Asia will likely remain open to foreign capital and global supply chains; moreover, Western, and especially American, corporations will likely remain dominant forces.[25] As we shall see, currently Chinese-controlled firms do not even dominate in their own export sector, so there is little reason to believe that Chinese firms will be able to out-compete Western transnational corporations (TNCs) in neighbouring markets. Hence, even if Chinese SOEs build the infrastructure across the region, it is Western TNCs that remain best situated to use this infrastructure to shift production, drive exports, and compete in growing local consumer markets.

CONTRADICTION #2: CHINESE INTEGRATION INTO GLOBAL CAPITALISM

The second core contradiction concerning China's potential capacity to unmake the American making of global capitalism is China's very integration into that system. In fact, China was the first major political economy to rise in the era of American-centred globalization in the 1990s (China's share of world GDP actually declined in the 1980s) and one cannot appreciate the nature of one without the other. The broad strokes for understanding the capitalist rise of China are by now well known, with its reliance on foreign investment and technology in special export zones, exporting particularly to the US and EU. But what is far less commented upon is the extent to which China's export-driven boom is not only dependent on integrating into global capitalism, but is actually *driven* by foreign capital in key respects. This is where the capitalist rise of China has diverged from the earlier rises of Japan and South Korea pre-1990s globalization, where production and exports were and remain predominantly driven by domestic, not foreign, firms. Japan and South Korea followed the classic path of development by protecting their 'infant industry' (a concept employed as far back as Alexander Hamilton in 1791 to protect the new republic against British competition), and today have globally competitive firms in a variety of advanced technology sectors. By contrast, China's rise is the first of any major country to be predominantly driven by the globalization of production via Western TNCs shifting their low- and then later medium-value production to countries with much cheaper labour. China has been the primary recipient of this kind of foreign direct investment in the short history of contemporary globalization, with implications on its capacity for challenging American hegemony.

As we dig deeper into the data and move beyond the common assumption that national accounts measure the activity only of national firms, the integration of China into and indeed dependence on global capitalism is illuminated. Figure 1 shows the enterprise types of China's exporters from 1995-2017, and we can see that 'foreign-invested enterprises' (FIEs) – which include both fully foreign-owned enterprises (FOEs) and joint ventures with Chinese firms – initially drove China's export boom from the 1990s. Concomitantly, the exports of state-owned enterprises (SOEs) collapsed. By 2006 FIEs reached a peak in accounting for almost 60 per cent of all Chinese exports before stabilizing after 2014 at around 44 per cent. The exports of Chinese privately-owned enterprises (POEs) surged as China joined the WTO, and by 2014 also stabilized at around 44 per cent of total Chinese exports, neck-and-neck with foreign firms. This may give the impression that Chinese POEs have learned from (or copied) the world's top TNCs, and have technologically upgraded to already match foreign firms exporting from China.

Figure 1. Enterprise Type of China's Total Exports, 1995-2017

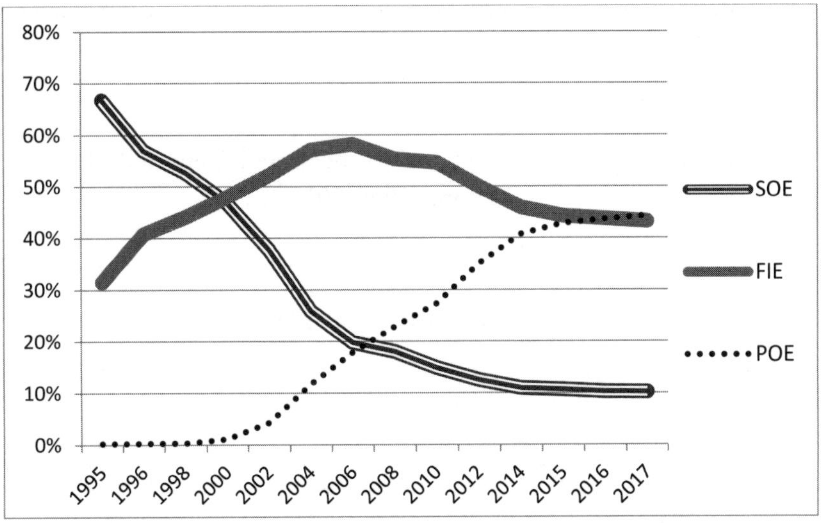

Note: SOE=State-Owned Enterprise; FIE=Foreign-Invested Enterprise; POE=Privately-Owned Enterprise.
Source: Author's Calculations from China's Customs Statistics, 1995-2017.

But the majority of these exports by POEs remain in low-value sectors, such as clothing and cheap consumer goods. Figure 2 shows the enterprise types for the most dynamic and technologically advanced of Chinese exports, what China Customs classifies as 'process with imported materials exports'. These exports are at the heart of China's integration into the global value chains of the world's top TNCs, and are at the low-end of final assembly with high-value imported components. For example, these exports include the iPhone, as Apple subcontracts other firms to coordinate the importation of various components produced in different countries to be assembled in China and then re-exported to the rest of the world. In 2017, these exports accounted for $679 billion, or about a third of all Chinese exports. Like China's total exports, the share of SOEs has collapsed, while foreign firms drove the initial surge of these high value exports, reaching a staggering 80 per cent by 2003. What is more astonishing, however, is that the share of FIEs has not dipped below 80 per cent ever since – almost 15 years. The FIE share even recently increased, to 85-86 per cent since 2015. And as we can see, the majority of the FIE share consists of fully foreign-owned enterprises, at 65 per cent in 2017 – the highest so far in this 22-year period. By contrast, the Chinese POE share has struggled to surpass 10 per cent, with only a handful of overseas success stories such as Huawei and Lenovo (although the latter has declined in recent years, with Hewlett-Packard regaining the top spot for PC-maker). The dominance of foreign capital in China's most technologically advanced exports is staggering, especially when considering that most observers continue to assume that Chinese exports are exported by Chinese firms.

Figure 2. Enterprise Type for China's 'Process with Imported Materials' Exports, 1995-201

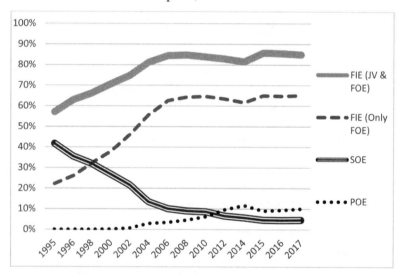

Note: FIE=Foreign-Invested Enterprise; JV=Joint-Venture; FOE=Foreign-Owned Enterprise; SOE=State-Owned Enterprise; POE=Privately-Owned Enterprise.
Source: Author's Calculations from China's Customs Statistics, 1995-2017.

Table 1 shows the top ten exporting firms from China by value in 2015. China's largest private employer with over 1 million workers is by far China's top exporter, larger than the next two combined: Hon Hai Precision Industry, better known by its tradename Foxconn. Around half of Foxconn's profit stems from assembling Apple's iPhones, while it also subcontracts for a slew of other Western TNCs. More broadly, nine of the top ten exporting firms are electronics manufacturers (the only exception is the Chinese SOE oil company, Sinopec). Hence electronics are China's most important, dynamic, and among its most technologically advanced exports – and China was already the world's largest exporter of electronics by 2004. But as we can see in Table 1 (and Figure 2), the overwhelming majority of China's top electronics exporters are foreign firms (especially Taiwanese and South Korean – only Huawei makes the top ten). Samsung and LG perform their own final assembly in China, but Western TNCs (including increasingly Japanese) prefer to outsource their lower value production to Taiwanese firms operating in China. These six Taiwanese subcontractors account for 71 per cent of the total value of exports by the top ten exporting firms from China, which themselves account for 11 per cent of all of China's $2.3 trillion of exports in 2015. In other words, in China's most dynamic and technologically advanced export sector – so crucial for the Chinese state to accumulate US dollars which then fuel its vast development projects – foreign firms continue to dominate after two decades of China's capitalist rise.

Table 1. Top 10 Exporting Firms from China by Total Value (US$), 2015

China Rank	Forbes Global 2000 (2016) Rank	Firms (Firm Type)	Nationality	Value (US$bn)
1	117	Hon Hai Precision Industry (FOE)	Taiwan	78.91
2	19	Samsung Group (FOE)	ROK	36.48
3	843	Quanta Computer (FOE)	Taiwan	33.53
4	864	Pegatron Corporation (FOE)	Taiwan	28.80
5	N/A	Huawei Technologies (POE)	China	20.38
6	1,467	Compal Electronics (FOE)	Taiwan	18.77
7	1,688	Wistron Corporation (FOE)	Taiwan	13.11
8	825	LG Corporation (FOE)	ROK	9.82
9	31	Sinopec (SOE)	China	8.42
10	1,874	Inventec Corporation (FOE)	Taiwan	7.63
		Total		255.83

Note: FOE=foreign-owned enterprise; POE=privately-owned enterprise; SOE=state-owned enterprise; ROK=South Korea.

Source: Author's calculations from SSFERTC (2016); Forbes Global 2000 (2016).

Another key aspect of China's integration into global capitalism is the extent to which foreign firms not only dominate China's chief export sectors, but also lead in numerous sectors in China's increasingly important domestic market. The extension of foreign capital's linkages both between China and global capitalism and within China's domestic market itself has some parallels with American capital's earlier expansion into Western European markets in the 1960s and 1970s. This earlier wave of expanding north Atlantic capitalist linkages was a source of concern for some Europeans, notably Jean-Jacques Servan-Schreiber who published *The American Challenge* in 1967, at the time the bestselling post-war nonfiction book in France. Half a century later, these worries have turned out to be prescient as much of Europe's information-technology sector is dominated by American TNCs, especially in computers, the internet, software, and telecommunications equipment.

The Chinese Communist Party is keenly aware of the potential pitfalls of foreign investment leading to foreign dependence and has been trying for over three decades to compel foreign technology transfer via joint-ventures and other mechanisms (including cyber-theft of intellectual property). These efforts have a mixed record over the decades. On the one hand, there are some notable successes, such as high-speed rail (copying Japanese technology); stealth fighter jets (copying Russian technology, although they have yet to be tested in battle); and renewable energy, especially solar panels (copying American and German technology) and wind turbines (copying American and Danish technology); among others. Chinese smartphone companies, particularly Huawei and Xiaomi, have successfully copied Apple and Samsung and now outcompete them in the Chinese market (Apple's iPhone is now fifth by volume in China). In 2017 Apple still dominates by profit, however, with an 87 per cent profit-share despite maintaining a market-share by volume of 11 per cent. Of the Chinese smartphone brands, only Huawei is profitable; Oppo, Vivo, and Xiaomi continue to be loss-making on razor-thin margins, despite all selling more units than Apple.

Additionally, China's internet economy is thriving and second only to Silicon Valley, with three giants straddling the domestic market: Alibaba, Baidu, and Tencent. China is now a world leader in mobile payments and online retail. But these domestic firms thrive in sectors that are ensconced behind the second most protectionist and censored internet in the world (only North Korea controls its internet more). These firms remain untested beyond the 'Great Firewall of China'[26] and there remains very little indication that they could compete with their American counterparts abroad. In fact, they cannot even out-compete Facebook and Google in Hong Kong and Taiwan, two territories that the CCP considers to be part of China.

On the other hand, in other key sectors China's record has been poor in terms of learning from foreign capital in order to build national champions to eventually out-compete them. The most notable is in automobiles, especially compared to Japan and South Korea where domestic national firms remain dominant at home and have become global competitors abroad. Over three decades since China implemented its industrial policy on automobiles, Chinese auto firms have had no such success, despite the Chinese auto market becoming the world's largest by 2009. Foreign automobile firms wanting to operate in China have been forced by the Chinese state to enter into joint-ventures with a Chinese SOE – the first being Shanghai Automotive Industry Corporation's (SAIC's) joint-venture with Volkswagen in 1985. Nevertheless, after three decades the Chinese brands of these SOEs still struggle to compete with their foreign partners. For example, the number one Chinese auto firm is SAIC, ranked number nine in the world by profit in 2016, in between Nissan and Honda. But, SAIC's joint-ventures with General Motors (GM) and Volkswagen accounted for 95 per cent of its sales, with its own brand cars accounting for 3 per cent.[27] As of 2014, foreign auto firms collectively held a 78 per cent market-share of passenger sedans in China,[28] which indicated that after three decades Chinese industrial policy had still not established Chinese-controlled auto firms that can compete with foreign firms in China (let alone abroad). Thus, while by 2016 Chinese auto production exceeded that of the US and Japan combined, this has been more a boon for foreign firms than domestic Chinese firms. In 2017 GM's Cadillac sold more units in China than in the US for the first time, and GM sells 550 per cent more Buicks there (for two decades one of the most popular brands in China) than it does in the US.

There are a variety of other sectors in which American TNCs lead in the Chinese domestic market while nonetheless reflecting the importance of global – and especially US – integration. Comprehensive market-share data across a wide range of sectors is not publicly available, so we rely on collecting a rag-tag of various sources from different years as reported in the media, with the original market research firm reports generally being publicly unavailable. Table 2 displays Chinese market-share data of selected American TNCs from a variety of sectors ranging from the years 2014-2018. Notably, despite officially exiting the Chinese market in 2010 due to its rejection of government censorship, Google still maintains an over 70 per cent Chinese market-share in smartphone operating systems with its Android software, the 'brain' of this ubiquitous consumer technology. (As of July 2017, China had 243 million of the planet's 728 million smartphones, the largest domestic market in the world). Together with Apple's iOS, these two Silicon Valley firms have a 99.8 per cent market-share in China, with most of the rest (0.2 per cent) going to Microsoft, which has a 90 per cent market-share in desktop operating systems. Despite Huawei's encroachment on Cisco's overall market-share in telecommunications equipment, Cisco maintains a 55 per cent Chinese share in ethernet switches. In advanced medical equipment, a sector that will only grow in importance as China's population is one of the most rapidly aging in the world, General Electric is a leading firm (along with European firms Siemens and Phillips). As for airplanes, in 2016 Boeing's 45 per cent market-share is second to Airbus' 49 per cent, but this duopoly switches back and forth over the years.

Table 2. Market-Shares of Selected US Firms in China, Various Years

Firm	Market-Share (Rank)	Sector	Year (Quarter)	Source
Google	71.2% (#1)	Smartphone Operating System	2016 (Q4)	Kantar World-panel
Apple	28.6% (#2)	Smartphone Operating System	2016 (Q4)	Kantar World-panel
Microsoft	90% (#1)	Desktop Operating System	March 2018	Statacounter
Intel	11% (#1)	Semiconductors	2015	PwC Report
Cisco	55% (#1)	Ethernet Switches	2017 (Q1)	IDC
Oracle	56% (#1)	Database	2015	IDC
General Electric	20%	Installed Capacity of Large Hydro Equipment	2016	GE Website
General Electric	39% (#1)	Nuclear Medicine	2014	Ipsos
General Electric	32% (#1)	Computed Tomography	2014	Ipsos
General Electric	34% (#2)	MRI Scans	2014	Ipsos
Boeing	45% (#2)	Airplanes	2016	CARNOC.com
DuPont	4% (#1)	Coating	2017	Maigoo.com
Wal-Mart	5.3% (#3) [China South 9.2% (#1)]	Grocery Stores	2017	Kantar World-panel
Proctor & Gamble	36% (#1) 16% (#1)	Haircare Oral Care	2016 2016	Euromonitor
Pfizer	5% (#1)	Prescription Medicine	2016	QuintilesIMS
Coca-Cola	63% (#1)	Carbonated Soft Drinks	2014	Euromonitor

Pepsi-Cola	30% (#2)	Carbonated Soft Drinks	2014	Euromonitor
Nike	19% (#1)	Sportswear	2016	Euromonitor
Yum Brands	30% (#1)	Fast Food	2015	Euromonitor
McDonald's	14% (#2)	Fast Food	2015	Euromonitor
Starbucks	55% (#1)	Coffeeshops	2016	Euromonitor
Las Vegas Sands	25% (#1)	Casinos	2015	GGRAsia

Table 2 also shows that in the still highly fragmented supermarket sector, Wal-Mart with its over 420 stores is third overall and first in southern China, which encompasses the country's largest province (Guangdong) and richest city (Shenzhen).[29] Furthermore, American firms lead in a variety of consumer goods, such as Proctor & Gamble in hair and oral care, Coca-Cola and Pepsi-Cola with a combined 93 per cent in carbonated soft drinks. Strikingly, despite China being the world's largest producer and exporter of clothes, indigenous brands cannot rival Nike's leading share of 19 per cent in sportswear. In addition, the first Western fast food company to enter China was KFC in 1987 (on Tiananmen Square's southwestern corner), and a year later this outlet already became KFC's largest restaurant in the world by volume. Three decades later, its parent company Yum Brands China manages over 7,685 KFC, Pizza Hut, and Taco Bell restaurants in 1,100 cities in China, well ahead of second-place McDonald's (which arrived in 1990, now with almost 3,000 restaurants). Starbucks entered the tea-drinking nation relatively later in 1999, but by 2017 was opening an outlet every 15 hours, including the world's largest in Shanghai in December 2017 with a gargantuan 29,000 square feet. Also selling the American dream to China's aspiring middle class, Las Vegas Sands leads with a 25 per cent market-share in casinos (all in Macau), owned by the Republican Party's top donor, Sheldon Adelson.

In sum, China's deep integration into global capitalism is complex. Careful assessment of its greater autonomy in certain respects and greater dependence in others is required. The Chinese state has greater autonomy than most states to try to carve out its own protected niche within global capitalism and develop indigenous technology. These efforts are proving successful in certain sectors, at least in terms of dominating their own domestic market (whether they can leverage this domestic monopoly to compete abroad has not yet been tested). But in a variety of other sectors, ranging from the most advanced technology of aerospace and medical equipment to automobiles and consumer goods such as soft drinks, sportswear, and fast food restaurants – foreign firms dominate to an extent that is greater than in many other major countries. The Chinese political economy is a hybrid of some of the most protectionist and some of the most open trade policies of any major country in the world, depending on the sector. In the key export sectors that determine China's integration into global value chains as 'workshop of the world' – the *sine qua non* of China's capitalist rise – foreign firms dominate to a degree that is rarely seen in other major countries (and never in hegemons). These particular economic dependencies do not make China a vassal state of the US as China remains relatively geopolitically independent in comparison to other states (and quite unlike Japan). But the nature of China's integration certainly proscribes its ability to challenge American hegemony, especially as the CCP desires above all the domestic social stability crucial to its power and influence within China.

China's constrained capacity and integration into the American-led global order can also be seen in other respects. Most sharply, after various Chinese elites championed efforts to move beyond the US dollar-based international system in the immediate aftermath of the global financial crisis, prompted by then-Central Bank Governor Zhou Xiaochuan in 2009, China's actions in subsequent years exhibited the exact opposite tendency. China more than doubled its stockpile of US Treasury Bills from $504 billion in June 2008 to $1.3 trillion by June 2011. And while China has made some attempts to internationalize its own currency, the RMB, these efforts reversed in the face of China's 2015 stock market crash and subsequent capital flight over the next two to three years (the RMB dropped back below the Canadian dollar as a global reserve currency, despite Canada having roughly a tenth of China's GDP). When faced with the choice to internationalize – and therefore at least partially liberalize – its currency or control its financial market, the latter won, and will always win for as long as the CCP maintains power in China (for which state control of finance is crucial).[30] At the same time, regardless of the fanfare over the NDB and AIIB, China has continued to actively support the leading international financial institutions, in 2009 pledging to boost its contribution to the IMF's budget by $50 billion and in 2014-15 actively lobbying for the RMB to be included in the IMF's basket of 'special drawing rights' in order to increase its credibility and role (as well as integration) in global finance. In 2018, the IMF opened a research centre in China to train more Chinese in neoclassical economics, for all of Xi's rhetoric of promoting Marxism.

China's continued technological dependency on the US became clear when the US Department of Commerce banned ZTE from all US suppliers for seven years due to US sanctions violations in Iran and North Korea. Due to its complete dependence on American advanced technology with no conceivable replacement suppliers on the scale required for the Chinese market, ZTE, China's second and the world's fourth largest telecommunications company, was forced to cease operations in May 2018 until Trump repealed the ban.[31] As for the Trump administration's efforts to reduce China's giant trade surplus and challenge its industrial policy (especially Xi's signature 'Made in China 2025' aimed at global leadership in ten advanced sectors) – it is too early to tell whether US Trade Representative Robert Lighthizer will be as successful as he was during the Reagan administration's negotiation of Japan's 'voluntary export restraints' a generation earlier. While China is more geopolitically independent than Japan, it is even more structurally dependent on the US in terms of technology and trade.

None of this is to say that the contradictions of China's integration into global capitalism, and its particular external vulnerabilities, will lead to its collapse anytime soon, as some doomsayers maintain.[32] China will continue to grow, even if more slowly than before, and its middle class will continue to expand and get richer, even if hundreds of millions will remain too poor to join the consuming class (due to structural reasons discussed below). China will continue to advance its national capacities to develop technology in certain niche sectors, and may lead the world in some of them (as Germany and Japan do today). But these vulnerabilities *do* mean that China will most likely not have the structural capacity to challenge the multi-faceted nature of American hegemony underpinning global capitalism along the lines of Xi's plan by 2050. To the extent that China continues to gradually (albeit unevenly) liberalize one sector after another, this structural dependence will likely only increase. For as long as the CCP's number one priority is to stay in power, the Chinese state cannot risk the fundamental disruption to its state-directed investment and foreign-driven export growth model (upon which directly or indirectly hundreds of millions of jobs depend) that a serious challenge to American hegemony would entail. Indeed, very little short of a revolution in China would be able to potentially alter these structural conditions, as the wealth of so many newly minted millionaires and billionaires depends on the particular manner in which China has integrated with global capitalism since the 1990s.

ASIAN ASPIRATIONS

In order to chart possible futures, given the above constraints and contradictions, it is vital to be clear-eyed about the nature of the Chinese political economy, including whether it is more state socialist or state capitalist. On the one hand, Xi Jinping Thought has muddied the waters by insisting that China remains 'socialist with Chinese characteristics' and Xi has consistently called for a reassertion of 'Marxism' over Western liberalism in the halls of the establishment, including in university curricula. In 2018 China held the largest events in the world commemorating the 200th anniversary of Marx's birth, during which Xi called upon his comrades to take *The Communist Manifesto* seriously.[33] Whether or not inspired by Marx, Xi has also reeled in some of the most freewheeling of China's billionaires, detaining among others flamboyant Xiao Jianhua (extra-judicially abducted from his hotel in the middle of the night in Hong Kong at the beginning of Chinese New Year 2017).[34]

On the other hand, while some in the Western Left might envy such trends, the fact that workers' rights and unions are better protected in the United States – the heart of global capitalism (let alone in northern Europe) – than in China reveals how intellectually and morally bankrupt Xi's version of 'Marxism' is. Xi has done nothing to end wage-labour and capitalist exploitation (whether by private owners or SOEs), especially of the hundreds of millions of rural migrants that have filled the factories, construction sites, warehouses, delivery vehicles, and mines of eastern and southern China, often in conditions that rival what Engels described in mid-nineteenth century Manchester. While several hundred million now comprise the urban middle class, this is on the backs of hundreds of millions of super-exploited rural migrants with no access to social welfare (with Mao's 'Iron Rice Bowl' having been dismantled by the 1990s) or even education for their children due to their rural household registration (*hukou*).[35] Hence, Xi's version of Marxism, with all references to class struggle removed, is left with the shell of single-party dictatorship and state ownership as marking 'socialism'. Instead of striving for the emancipation of the working class from capitalist exploitation, and lambasting the obscene profits of China's nouveau riche as a burgeoning bourgeoisie and the greatest inequality in the world, Xi exhorts Chinese 'entrepreneurialism' and 'poverty reduction'. He even turns the world upside down by defending global capitalism at the World Economic Forum against critiques from both Donald Trump and Marine Le Pen on the right and Bernie Sanders and Jeremy Corbyn on the left. Without freedom of speech or assembly, coupled with Xi's crackdown on all manner of dissent that would 'disturb social order', it is difficult to see a positive path forward.[36]

But no matter how arduous the path ahead, anything that is socially constructed can be socially deconstructed and reconstructed, and there is no better embodiment than China itself over the past 150 years of the maxim that 'all that is solid melts into air' – several times over. Xi's regular references to Marxism do indeed open opportunities to discuss Marx's ideas and their relevance to contemporary China (and the world),[37] even if deviations from Xi's interpretation are suppressed.[38] As China's growth continues to slow, decent jobs become scarcer, deadly levels of pollution persist (killing over two million a year), families are torn asunder as impoverished millions continue to be dislocated in the name of 'economic development', and housing becomes ever more unaffordable (especially in Tier 1 megalopolises) – opportunities to bring class consciousness back will surely increase. Moreover, anecdotally, some Chinese youth are becoming less hyper-materialist and are questioning the prioritization of economic growth above all other goals in the human condition, perhaps akin to the coming of age of Western youth in the 1960s – and the radicalism that ensued.

Finally, as the only part of China where freedom of speech and assembly are still more or less protected, Hong Kong can play a special role, where these ideas can be more freely discussed to crack the stifling dogma of Xi Jinping Thought. Hence Hong Kong is the final refuge of labour, environmental, and other social activist NGOs due to Xi's repression on the Mainland since 2015.[39] As Xi's authoritarianism has intensified, the youth of Hong Kong are also becoming more politicized – and some increasingly radicalized with massive inequality lorded over by monopolistic tycoons – especially since the 2014 'Umbrella Movement'. And if the more nativist elements in Hong Kong can be overcome, social movements forming linkages across the Mainland would only strengthen the possibilities for positive change. While predicting revolutions is a fool's game, it is clear that without one, China will not be able to unmake the American making of global capitalism. Both intentionally and unintentionally, Xi Jinping has been advancing China's integration into global capitalism. But if contradictions and struggle drive change, then history is by no means over in China.

NOTES

The author gratefully acknowledges the Hong Kong Research Grants Council for fully supporting the empirical research in this essay, Grant #21615915, and Mingtang Liu for invaluable research assistance and comments. I also thank Lamma Island adventurers Peter Beattie, Keegan Elmer, Mike Haack, and Chuangcn.org for very useful discussions on the nature of the Chinese political economy.

1   Leo Panitch and Sam Gindin, *The Making of Global Capitalism: The Political Economy of American Empire*, London: Verso, 2012.

2   Xuetong Yan, 'From Keeping a Low Profile to Striving for Achievement', *The Chinese Journal of International Politics,* 7(2), 2014.

3   From a 28 May 2014 Xi speech cited in Astrid Nordin and Mikael Weissmann, 'Will Trump Make China Great Again? The Belt and Road Initiative and International Order', *International Affairs*, 94(2), 2018, p. 246.

4   Nien-Chung Chang Liao, 'The Sources of China's Assertiveness: The System, Domestic Politics or Leadership Preferences?', *International Affairs*, 92(4), 2016.

5   Full text available at www.xinhuanet.com.

6   Yan, 'From Keeping a Low Profile to Striving for Achievement', p. 164.

7   Jonathan Kaiman and Yingzhi Yang, 'China's President is the Country's Most-Traveled Leader Since Communism – And Maybe the Strongest', *The Los Angeles Times*, 25 December 2015; Xie Tao, 'Chinese Foreign Policy with Xi Jinping Characteristics', Carnegie Endowment for International Peace, 20 November 2017, available at carnegieendowment.org.

8   David Shambaugh, *China Goes Global: The Partial Power*, New York: Oxford University Press, 2013.

9   World Bank, *World Bank Group, New Development Bank Lay Groundwork for Cooperation*, 9 September 2016, available at: www.worldbank.org; Asian Development Bank, *Asian Development Bank, New Development Bank Meet to Discuss New Project Cofinancing*, 13 October 2017, available at: www.adb.org.

10   Values in this paragraph from Salvatore Babones, 'China's AIIB Expected to Lend $10-15B a Year, But Has Only Managed $4.4B in 2 Years', *Forbes*, 16 January 2018.

11   Note that the CCP no longer endorses the English translation of 'One Belt, One Road', but its Chinese name has remained the same since 2013.

12   Nordin and Weissmann, *Will Trump Make China Great Again?*, p. 240. As the authors point out, does this mean that if countries reject the Silk Road then they are against peace, cooperation, mutual learning, and benefit?

13   Full speech available at america.cgtn.com. Interestingly, Xi's profile on the WEF website states his 'Degree in Marxist Theory' at Tsinghua University, possibly the first to address the capitalists of the world with such a degree.

14   Jamie Seidel, 'Photos Reveal China's South China Sea Island Fortresses are Complete', *News Corp Australia Network*, 7 February 2018.

15   Ankit Panda, 'Chinese, Russian Navies Hold Exercises in Sea of Japan, Okhotsk Sea', *The Diplomat*, 21 September 2017.

16   Mao famously opined, 'If the Communist Party has a day when it cannot rule or has met difficulty and needs to invite Confucius back, it means we are coming to an end'. Anti-Confucianism reached a fevered pitch during the Cultural Revolution, when Red Guards dynamited Confucius' grave.

17   In 2012 alone, more than 200 anti-Japan films were made in China, and one estimate claims that 70 per cent of drama on Chinese television, most of it state-owned, is about what the CCP calls the 'Chinese War of Resistance Against Japanese Aggression, 1931-1945' (the author can certainly attest to this from his experience channel-surfing in hotel rooms around China). Note that official Chinese sentiment towards Japan was much more positive in the early 1980s, as Japan was China's largest aid donor and Japanese corporations were among the first to enter China as Deng opened up. In the 1960s and 1970s, researching or publishing about Japanese war crimes was actually censored, because Mao was courting Japan in an effort to displace both US and Soviet influence from East Asia. The anti-Japan animus was in full swing by 2000, when a film that won the Cannes Grand Jury Prize (Jiang Wen's pointedly titled *Devils on the Doorstep*) was banned in China for showing a Japanese prisoner of war in too positive a light. David Lague and Jane Lanhee Lee, 'Why China's Film Makers Love to Hate Japan', *Reuters*, 25 May 2013.

18 Nevertheless, Xi Jinping has also been re-embracing 'Marxism', as discussed below.

19 Geir Lundestad, "Empire by Invitation' in the American Century', *Diplomatic History*, 23(2), Spring 1999.

20 Manuel Mogato, 'The US will Upgrade and Build Facilities on Philippine Military Bases this Year', *Reuters*, 26 January 2017.

21 John Reed, 'Philippines Claims It Would 'Go to War' Over China Incursions', *The Financial Times*, 29 May 2018.

22 Nevertheless, it is questionable whether this is a significant military victory since China still does not have the capacity to prevent US FONOPS (which have increased under Trump) and still cannot break out of the First Island Chain. Moreover, with the US Navy now having access to both Vietnam's Cam Ranh Bay and Subic Bay in the Philippines (as well as an increased presence in Australia and Singapore), China's supply routes between the Mainland and Spratly Islands are highly vulnerable.

23 One of the first and still most important BRI projects is the Gwadar port in Pakistan – which is attracting increasing protests since 91 per cent of the port's revenues go to the SOE, Chinese Overseas Port Holding Co., Adnan Aamir, 'China's Belt and Road Plans Dismay Pakistan's Poorest Province', *The Financial Times*, 14 June 2018.

24 China's own high-speed rail system is loss-making, hence reliant on massive subsidies that few other countries could afford.

25 Sean Kenji Starrs, 'The Chimera of Global Convergence', *New Left Review*, 87(1) 2014.

26 Or 'Golden Shield', the English translation of its official Chinese name. I am grateful to Chuangcn.org for pointing this out.

27 Date for profits is 2015, for sales 2016. See SAIC Motor, *Annual Report 2015*, 2016, p. 14, available at www.saicmotor.com/english/investor_relations/annual_report/index.shtml.

28 Tom Mitchell, 'Foreign Marques Surge Ahead in China Car Market', *The Financial Times*, 12 January 2015.

29 These figures do not include Wal-Mart's controlling share of the Taiwanese supermarket, Trust-Mart. I thank Chuangcn.org for pointing this out.

30 Sean Kenji Starrs, 'A Crash with Chinese Characteristics', *Jacobin*, 30 July 2015.

31 On 13 May, two days after a Chinese SOE approved over half a billion dollars of financing for Trump's Indonesia resort and the day after Xi made a personal phone call, Trump repealed the ZTE ban via Tweet because 'Too many jobs in China lost' (a substantial departure from Trump's repeated proclamations that China is 'raping' the US). But at the time of writing, Congress is attempting to pass a bill to maintain the ZTE ban.

32 Most famously, Gordon Chang, *The Coming Collapse of China*, New York: Random House, 2001; more than a decade later this prophecy of doom persists. See also David Shambaugh, 'The Coming Chinese Crack-Up', *The Wall Street Journal*, 6 March 2015.

33 Nectar Gan, 'A New Class Struggle: Chinese Party Members Get Back to Communist Manifesto Basics', *South China Morning Post*, 29 April 2018.

34 Don Weinland and Lucy Hornby, 'Tycoon Abducted by China Works with Authorities to Sell Assets', *The Financial Times*, 10 June 2018. Most strikingly, Wu Xiaohui, CEO and founder of formerly one of China's largest 'private' conglomerates, Anbang (now taken over by the government), was sentenced to 18 years in prison. 'Private' is problematic, since there is no separation between public and private in China à la Anglo-Saxon liberalism, neither *de jure* nor *de facto*. See, Sean Kenji Starrs, 'The Global

Capitalism School Tested in Asia: Transnational Capitalist Class vs. Taking the State Seriously', *Journal of Contemporary Asia*, 47(4), 2017; Nana de Graaff and Bastiaan van Apeldoorn, 'US-China Relations and the Liberal World Order: Contending Elites, Colliding Visions?', *International Affairs*, 94(1), 2018.

35   For an argument that in the Maoist period of the 'Iron Rice Bowl' the non-agricultural and capital stock growth were actually higher – even if total growth was lower – than post-1978, see Anton Cheremukhin, Mikhail Golosov, Sergei Guriev, Aleh Tsyvinski, 'The Economy of the People's Republic of China from 1953-2012', *National Bureau of Economic Research*, NBER Working Paper No. 21397, July 2015, available at www. nber.org.

36   For important counter-arguments, see Michael Roberts, 'China Workshop: Challenging the Misconceptions', 7 June 2018, available at: thenextrecession.wordpress.com; Giovanni Arrighi, *Adam Smith in Beijing: Lineages of the 21st Century*, New York: Verso, 2007.

37   Yue Xin, a student labour activist at Peking University and a prominent proponent of #MeToo in China, personally inspired by Marx's original texts (rather than vacuous CCP reinterpretations), offers an illustration of how this opening can meld with globalization from below. See Jun Mai, 'Why Beijing Isn't Marxist Enough for China's Radical Millennials', *South China Morning Post*, 25 May 2018.

38   The 2017-18 'Eight Young Leftists' case has received international attention, as they were persecuted for organizing a Marxist reading group at Guangzhou University of Technology that discussed the existence of a capitalist class in China, contravening Xi Thought (in the 2013 leak of 'Document 9: Communique on the Current State of the Ideological Sphere' detailing the 'Seven Unmentionables', China's censors are instructed to eliminate any mention of a 'privileged capitalist class in China'). See Chuangcn.org, 'Let the People Themselves Decide Whether We're Guilty', 14 June 2018, available at chuangcn.org.

39   Hong Kong is even the last refuge for Maoists to protest Chinese state capitalism. See Jun Mai and Chi-Yuk Choi, 'The Last Maoists in China Find Refuge in Capitalist Hong Kong', *South China Morning Post*, 25 May 2018.

DECOUPLING IS A MYTH:
ASIAN CAPITALISM IN THE GLOBAL DISARRAY

JAYATI GHOSH

The last decade has demolished a myth widely perpetrated during the earlier boom: that of 'decoupling', or the divergence of growth in some major emerging markets (such as China, India and Brazil) from that of the advanced economies. This over-optimistic perception derived from only a very short period in the 2000s, essentially from 2002-08. Over this period, the advanced economies expanded by around 2 per cent per annum, while the emerging markets and developing countries grew faster and at accelerating rates. But the 'Global Financial Crisis' that then erupted put paid to that, and this brief divergence turned out to be an aberration from the longer historical trend. Both the global crisis and the subsequent period have unfortunately confirmed the continued economic dependence of the periphery on the capitalist core of the world economy. The unfolding of this global crisis was perhaps the most striking example of this: while it originated in the United States and then spread to Europe, it immediately affected the emerging markets in the developing world, even those with current account surpluses and other signs of economic strength, by impacting on cross-border capital flows. Since then, GDP growth rates of these two categories of economies have generally moved together. Indeed, because emerging and developing countries had higher growth rates earlier, they have experienced sharper slowdowns subsequently.

The period of the boom was clearly associated with some structural shifts in the world economy, which may yet turn out to have systemic implications. But in essence, they still conformed to the earlier pattern of demand in the North (and particularly in the United States) driving capitalist expansion in the rest of the world. In the 2000s, growth in the United States and some large advanced economies was sustained by a combination of financial liberalization and loose monetary policy that enabled households and companies to consume and invest beyond their means through borrowing.

This credit-driven boom enabled other advanced economies, especially in Europe, as well as some developing countries (certainly China and other "emerging" economies in Asia, but then across all developing regions) to expand on the basis of increased demand for their exports from the core capitalist countries. Therefore, almost all developing countries adopted an export-led growth model, requiring the containment of wage costs and domestic consumption for the sake of international competitiveness and growing shares of world markets.

This in turn led to a particularly startling development: the net transfer of financial resources from the South to the North[1] driven precisely by the behaviour of relatively unregulated goods and capital markets. Essentially, capital flowed uphill. As more and more countries – both developed and developing – sought to achieve current surpluses, the need to maintain relatively low exchange rates that would generate greater external competitiveness became stronger. This was one factor in the substantial accumulation of foreign exchange reserves that followed upon current account surpluses.[2] The other factor was the perceived necessity for self-insurance against balance of payments crises resulting from sudden changes in investor experience, as in the numerous developing country financial crises in the 1990s. Therefore, central banks (particularly but not exclusively in developing Asia) accumulated large amounts of reserves which then had to be stored in the safest of places. What could be safer, despite the US' own large external deficits, than US Treasury Bills? As a result, all developing regions sent their net savings to advanced economies, most of all to the United States. This in fact implied investment rates lower than could have been achieved in these countries given levels of domestic savings, which was doubly surprising since in most of these economies the development project was far from complete. Nevertheless, it locked the major developing country exporters like China with major advanced economy importers like the US into an awkward tango of mutual dependence. The current account imbalances that were subsequently seen as one of the 'causes' of the global crisis were in fact utterly necessary for the prior much-celebrated boom, which could not have occurred in that form otherwise.

This peculiar configuration essentially meant that global expansion relied on a credit driven boom in the US that was financed by capital inflows from other regions of the world, including the Global South. This served, at least for a time, to disguise the aggregate demand deficiency associated with wage stagnation in most of the developed economies as well as much of the periphery. The boom was also associated with other, more damaging imbalances: very adverse environmental consequences and increasing internal inequalities.

While the crisis raised expectations that there would be significant substantive attempts to reform and restructure the systems and structures of global capitalism that rendered it so especially fragile, such hopes were belied. Post-crisis attempts at financial regulation were relatively limited in both the US and Europe, and even those moves, such as the Dodd-Frank Act in the US, are being revised and undermined in a return to more deregulated and re-empowered private finance. As a result, financial fragility and vulnerability to future crises are just as great if not greater than they were in 2007. Meanwhile, the political economy configurations within nations have become even less conducive to the reduction of the inequalities that were associated with the boom. Labour protection in any form has become even further eroded, and states across the world have become even more aggressive in their support for large capital. All this obviously creates problems of insufficient demand within economies, which is further accentuated by the increasing implausibility of widespread and co-ordinated implementation of macroeconomic policies that would generate more demand. Most governments remain opposed to expansionary fiscal policy and continue to emphasize austerity measures and fiscal consolidation. This in general means constraints on and reductions to public expenditure, as the continued lobbying power of large corporations and moneyed elites prevents any substantial cross-country effort at raising tax revenues by curbing tax evasion and avoidance strategies.

The pursuit of incredibly loose monetary policies in the advanced economies operated to keep them afloat to this point, and contrary to standard monetarist predictions they did not generate significant inflationary pressures for a decade. But neither did they succeed in creating conditions for a real and sustained recovery along the kind of growth trajectory experienced earlier. Even if governments chose to adopt proactive fiscal stimuli, they would rapidly falter, as it would be difficult if not impossible for individual countries to 'go it alone' and indulge in expansion without prompting capital flight.

This policy combination of suppressing internal demand and relying on external demand for expansion is potentially toxic for capitalist accumulation on a global scale. Figure 3 shows how this has been expressed in changing current account balances. The United States economy acted as the engine of global growth in the 1990s and then again in the 2000s boom, running relatively large current deficits up to 2008. After this strategy exploded in the sub-prime financial crisis, the US current account deficit declined quite sharply, and since then has remained at only around 0.5 per cent of global GDP. However, other advanced economies that are systemically important did not reduce their surpluses. Indeed, European surpluses expanded further to reach nearly 1 per cent of global GDP, as Germany increased its own surplus and the 'Troika' (of the ECB, the IMF and the EU, significantly influenced by Germany) was increasingly able to force strategies that generated export surpluses even out of the European peripheral economies in crisis. Chinese surpluses did come down, but have remained volatile around a flat trend since 2011, while those of Japan and advanced Asia fell from 2011 but then recovered to earlier levels. The surpluses of the oil exporters declined but they still fell to near balance. Other developing and transition countries in the aggregate did show larger deficits, but given their overall size and general balance of payments difficulties, this was both unsustainable and simply not enough to generate much net demand stimulus in the world economy.

Figure 1. World GDP, 2000-2017 (constant prices, $US billions)

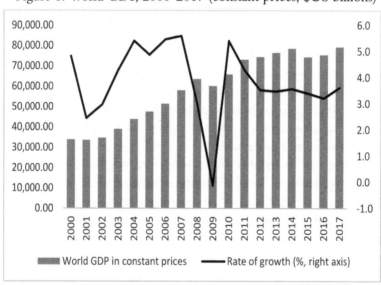

Source: IMF, World Economic Outlook, April 2018.

Over the past ten years, the world economy expanded at an estimated average of 3.3 per cent per annum, compared to 4.5 per cent in the period 2000 to 2007.[3] The years since 2014 have seen virtual stagnation, with more volatility accompanied by increasing inequality. Moreover, the much-vaunted 'recovery' touted by various international organisations (ranging from the IMF to the World Economic Forum) is limited, fragile and

Figure 2. Real GDP Growth, 1990–2017 (per cent per year)

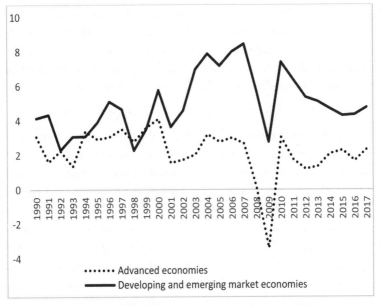

Source: IMF, World Economic Outlook, April 2018.

Figure 3. Current Account Balances, 2002–2017
(per cent of global GDP)

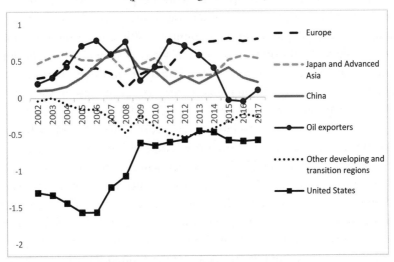

Source: IMF, World Economic Outlook, April 2018.

unsteady. Simply put, therefore, current macroeconomic strategies across the world are generating a zero sum game in which beggar-thy-neighbour strategies are emerging as the only option, with predictable results for international economic instability. As long as this fundamental problem of low growth and inadequate aggregate demand cannot be resolved, it is unlikely that the global economy would get on to a sustained growth trajectory, notwithstanding periodic evidence of 'green shoots'.

THE EXACERBATION OF INEQUALITIES

One significant change in this phase of global capitalism has been the decline of the 'labour aristocracy' in the North. The opening of trade, and with it a global supply of labour, meant that capital in the advanced economies at the core of global capitalism was no longer as interested in maintaining a social contract with workers in the 'home' country. Instead, it could use its greater bargaining power to push for ever-greater shares of national income wherever it operated. This was accentuated by the greater power of mobile finance capital to increase its own share of income as well. This process (which began in the United States in the 1990s) was greatly intensified during the global boom of the 2000s, when median workers' wages stagnated and even declined in the global North, even as per capita incomes soared. The increase in incomes, therefore, was captured by stockholders, corporate executives, financial rentiers, and the like.

The political fallout of this has now become glaringly evident. Increasing inequality, stagnant real incomes of working people, and the increasing material fragility of daily life have all contributed to a deep dissatisfaction among ordinary people in the rich countries. While even the poor among them are still far better off than the vast majority of people in the developing world, their own perceptions are quite different, and they increasingly see themselves as the victims of globalization. A recent report suggests that such a perception is not unfounded.[4] In 25 advanced economies, 65-70 per cent of households (540-580 million people) were found to be in the categories of the income distribution whose real incomes were flat or had fallen between 2005 and 2014. This was significantly higher than in the earlier period (1993-2005) when less than 2 per cent, or fewer than ten million people, experienced such real income declines. In Italy, for example, as much as 97 per cent of the population had stagnant or declining market incomes between 2005 and 2014. The equivalent figures were 81 per cent for the United States and 70 per cent for the United Kingdom. The worst affected were young people with low educational attainment, women and single mothers in particular.

Figure 4. Indicators of Global Inequality, 1960-2015

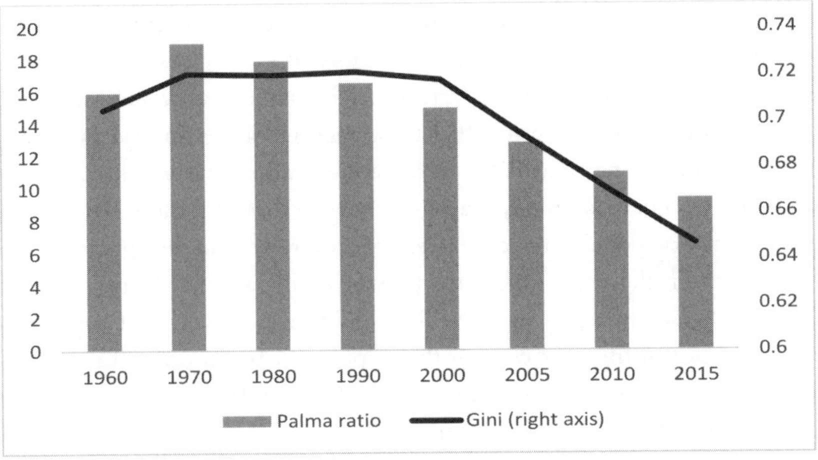

Source: Lucas Chancel, et al., World Inequality Report, 2018.

This deterioration of material conditions among working people in advanced countries has generated the mistaken perception that their own decline has been accompanied by the rise of the 'South', whereby workers in emerging and developing nations have benefited at their expense. In some ways, such perceptions are reinforced by academic discussions on global inequality, in which there tends to be general agreement that, whatever else may have happened, within-country inequality has increased in most cases, even as between-country inequality has come down. But overall, the recent emergence of countries with large populations like China and India has actually led to some reduction in global inequality, as a result of increasing incomes in the 'middle' of the global distribution. Figure 4 shows that, whether measured by the Gini coefficient (a measure of the dispersion of incomes across the population) or the Palma ratio (the ratio of the share of income of the top ten per cent of the population to the bottom 40 per cent), inequality has declined especially since the turn of the century.

This is what gave rise to the famous 'elephant curve',[5] which described percentage changes in income across different deciles of the global population. This showed a strong percentage growth in the middle of the global income distribution (the back of the elephant), much lower growth in the second decile, and a higher growth in the top decile (the trunk of the elephant). But there are two important caveats to this. First, the 'elephant curve' is based on proportionate increases in per capita incomes of each percentile – and obviously, the proportionate increase will be greater the lower the initial income. If incomes are lower to start with, a higher proportionate increase may amount to much less increase in absolute terms.[6] So it is worth looking at absolute changes in income, to see how the income gaps have really moved. When absolute changes are considered, the middle hump of the elephant disappears: the graph looks more like a hockey stick, with very little increase except for the top groups, which show very sharp increases. A second important concern is that these incomes are estimated in terms of purchasing power parity (PPP) exchange rates rather than market exchange rates (MER). There are many reasons to believe that PPP measures overstate the incomes of people in poor countries, thereby underestimating global inequality.[7] Further, the difference between PPP and MER has increased significantly over the past decades. The difference between the top ten per cent and bottom fifty per cent of the population was around 5 percentage points more in MER terms than in PPP terms in 1980, but by 2015, this difference had doubled to ten percentage points. So the extent of international inequality is likely to be substantially more than is indicated by measures based on PPP exchange rates.

Figure 5. Share of Emerging Markets and Developing Economies, 2000-2017 (per cent of world GDP at current prices)

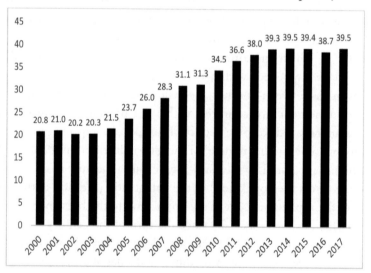

Source: IMF, *World Economic Outlook*, April 2018.

Consider, therefore, the share of global GDP of all emerging and developing countries taken together since 2000 (i.e. the period when they are generally perceived to have become so much more significant), but now measured at market exchange rates in current US dollars, as shown in Figure 5. This is clearly a more relevant indictor when assessing the distribution

Figure 6. Share of Global GDP, 1970-2010
(per cent at current market exchange rates)

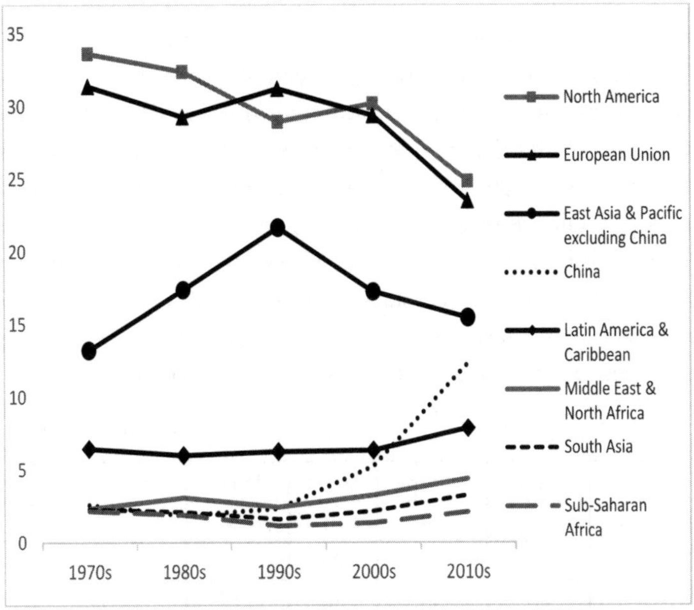

Source: World Bank, *World Development Indicators*, 2018.

of global economic power. Even though they accounted for nearly two-thirds of global income growth since 2009, developing countries' share of global GDP increased, then stagnated, after the global crisis. Indeed, Figure 6 indicates that in current market exchange rates, the decline in the share of North America was quite gradual, over a volatile trajectory, and more marked only after 2005; while for the European Union, the decline in share was really evident only from 2009 onwards.

But what may be more striking is the overall absence of convergence other than for a few countries in Asia. This is of even longer provenance: since the late 1960s, the only region to show notable increases in share of global GDP was East Asia and the Pacific. All the other regions, covering most of the developing world, showed little or no increase in shares of global GDP over this entire period. Given that population growth rates were typically higher in these regions than in North America and Western Europe, the differences in per capita income would have been even greater. Even the greater dynamism of East Asia was largely due to only two countries: first Japan until the late 1980s, and then China in the current century. China's share increased from less than 3 per cent in 1968 to nearly 15 per cent in 2016, with most of that increase occurring only after 2002.

Furthermore, even in the more dynamic developing regions, in general the bulk of the people did not benefit from the increasing incomes. Table 1 shows the share of income increases in the period 1980 to 2016 going to different segments of the population in major countries as well as in the world as a whole. Once again, it was only in China that the middle 40 per cent of the population (below the top decile) garnered slightly more than 40 per cent of the income increase, roughly similar to the gains taken by the top 10 per cent. In all other regions, the top decile clearly got away with the lion's share of income growth. Russia's trajectory bordered on the obscene, with the top decile getting more income increases than the country as a whole, at the cost of the bottom half whose incomes declined absolutely. But India's experience was also stark: the top 10 per cent got two-thirds of income increases, and just the top 1 per cent got 28 per cent – suggesting changes in inequality equivalent to those in North America.

Table 1. Share of Income Growth, 1980-2016

	China	Europe	India	Russia	US-Canada	World
Bottom 50%	13	14	11	-24	2	12
Middle 40%	43	38	23	7	32	31
Top 10%	43	48	66	117	67	57
Top 1%	15	18	28	69	35	27

Source: Lucas Chancel, et al., *World Inequality Report* 2018.

This stagnation of incomes at the bottom was driven by increased inequality within countries, much of which is encompassed within wage incomes because the top end of wage and salary earners – the managers – are essentially capitalists getting some shares of profits and rentier incomes as well. In recent years, incomes of managers and top executives have exploded relative to wages of ordinary workers. For example, in South Africa, the top 10 per cent of workers received half of all wage income, while the bottom half of the work force received just 12 per cent of all wages. A CEO in the US earned the same in just above one day of work as an ordinary worker in that country earned over the whole year. When national and gender differences are included, the contrast is even sharper. A CEO from any one of the top five multinational companies in the garment sector could earn in just four days as much as an ordinary Bangladeshi woman worker earns in her entire lifetime.[8] So the much-vaunted global income convergence seems much more like a coming together of elites in rich and emerging market economies, excluding the bulk of the population everywhere.

CHANGING PATTERNS OF GLOBAL TRADE

If there has been one big change in the nature of the global economy in the second decade of this century, it is in global trade. In the first decade of this century, especially in the period 2002-08, cross-border trade grew much more rapidly than total world output, and the integration of countries through greater exchange of goods and services essentially became the primary engine of growth. It is true that the explosion of financial activity that has become such a prominent feature of contemporary capitalism added substantially to income growth – and indeed generated the bubbles that were then expressed in more trade. But whatever the origins, this period was also the apogee of trade globalization.

In the process, a few developing countries – particularly China – emerged as major beneficiaries of such trade expansion, and then brought about a significant increase in what was known as South-South trade. The geographical relocation of production and the emergence of global value chains generated significant increases in intra-industry trade among developing countries, which were often directed to final demand in advanced economies, but simultaneously enabled income and demand expansion in the periphery. As noted earlier, the associated growth of several emerging economies was more rapid than in the core, giving rise to theories of global income convergence and even of the 'decoupling' of some countries in the periphery (particularly those in developing Asia) from the growth poles in the North.

The global financial crisis put paid to the latter theory, even as the arguments about greater income convergence were shown to be overly based on a very limited number of 'success stories' in the developing world. But the pattern of trade in the decade after the crisis has shown the fragility of that trade expansion. As indicated in Figure 7, the period after 2010 in particular has been marked by a significant deceleration of world trade in goods and services. Most of this was because of price collapses, as volume changes have been much less marked. While trade volumes grew by an average of 5 per cent per annum over 2000-09, they decelerated only marginally to 4.9 per cent in the period 2010-17. However, changes in world trade prices slowed down from 3.4 to 0.5 per cent per annum in the subsequent period, causing the growth in world trade values to fall below global output growth for the first time in the period of globalization (that is, after 1980). Indeed, in the years 2012-16 world trade prices fell, sometimes sharply, driven by the end of the commodity cycle that meant falling oil and primary commodity prices. The slight recovery in 2017 still left global trade values around 15 per cent below those prevailing in 2011.

Figure 7. World Trade in Goods and Services, 2008-2017 ($US billions)

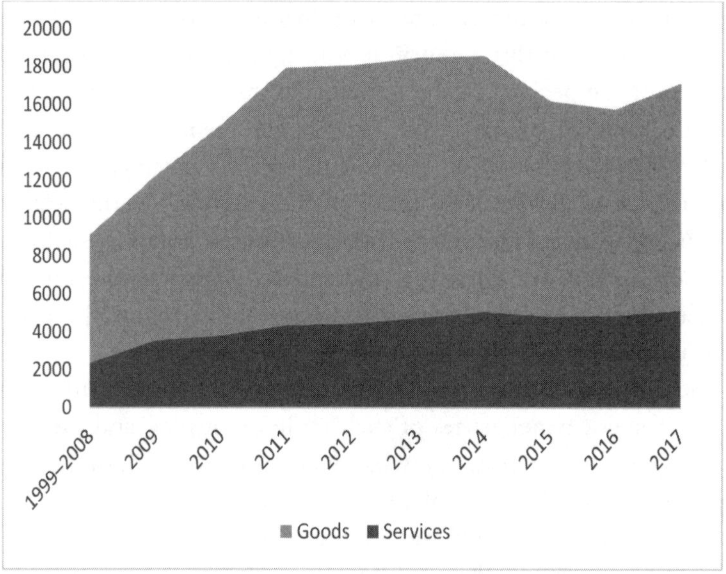

Note: The first data point is the average for the period 1999-2008.
Source: IMF, *World Economic Outlook*, Statistical Appendix, April 2018.

Price deflation (in US$ terms) or stagnation (in SDR terms) impacted differently on various groups of countries. From 2012, emerging and developing countries experienced worsening terms of trade and were only able to sustain aggregate trade values by substantially increasing trade volumes, essentially export volumes, which increased by 17 per cent between 2012 and 2017. Oil exporters were the worst hit, but even non-fuel exporters among developing countries were affected, and tried to cope with stagnant or falling export prices by significantly pushing out export volumes, which increased for this group by 21 per cent between 2012 and 2017.

So the picture of global trade is one of deceleration if not stagnation, where developing countries desperate to boost trade revenues in an environment of still-slow growth raise export volumes by reducing prices to an extent where the value of trade remains below what it was in the immediate aftermath of the crisis. This kind of competitive pressure – involving the well-known race to the bottom – generates tendencies for cost cutting and especially wage restraint, which in turn end up adding to the global problem of deficient demand. Since so much of the growth experienced by developing countries during the boom was export-led, this slowdown and even decline in trade has had obvious implications for their growth strategies. In the aggregate, there were absolute declines in export values (in US$ terms) for developing countries from January 2014. Much of this decline was due to South-South trade: while exports to the advanced economies declined by 20 per cent over this three-year period, those to developing countries fell by 25 per cent. One of the most striking features has been the dampened significance of China as an important market for developing country exports, discussed in more detail in the next section.

From January 2018, the recovery in global oil prices was seen by some observers as a sign of a more widespread economic recovery underway. In mid-May 2018, prices of Brent Crude oil (which is used as a global benchmark) crossed $80 a barrel in some markets. Like other primary commodities, average oil prices dropped very sharply after June 2014, falling by more than 70 per cent from their earlier peak in 2012, and then remaining at relatively low levels until January 2018 (Figure 8). This reflected the general deflationary atmosphere prevailing in the global economy, subdued demand in the face of significantly increased supply because of the shale boom in the US, and more production in countries like Iran as sanctions were lifted.

Figure 8. Average Petroleum Spot Price, 2011-2018

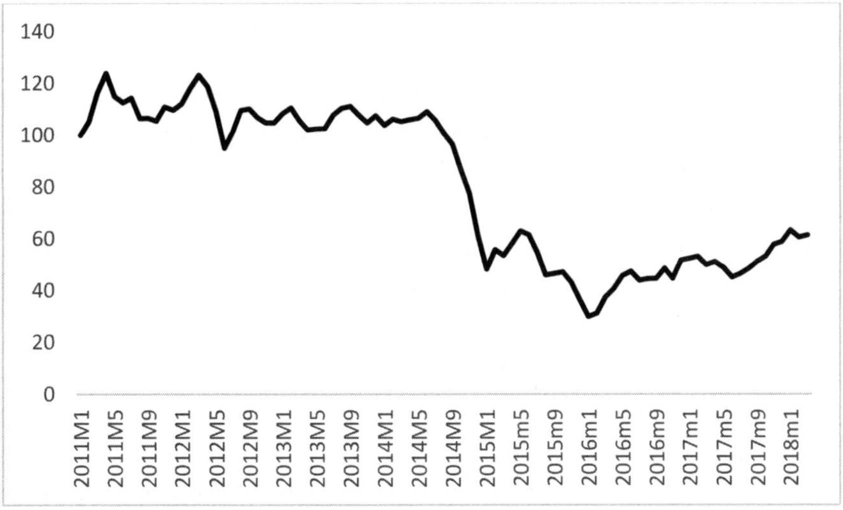

Index: January 2011 = 100

Source: IMF, *World Economic Outlook*, April 2018.

Several oil-importing countries were major beneficiaries of this decline. The top 15 importing countries (including China, India, Germany and Japan) all managed to increase the volumes of their crude oil imports between 2013 and 2017 without any increases in the value of imports, and some of them actually saw oil imports fall in value. In fact, several of them benefited from significant declines of oil import value.[9] But by mid-2018 the situation looked very different, as the price of the OPEC reference basket went up by 27 per cent (in the three months up to May 15) – and continued to increase at an even faster pace.

Several factors were behind this price surge, mostly unrelated to revived economic activity. One big factor was the willingness of Saudi Arabia (which had earlier refused to cut production hoping that low prices would force out the US shale producers) to change its tactics and join other members of the OPEC cartel in limiting production to stabilize and increase oil prices. In addition, from December 2017, Russia and 10 other non-OPEC countries joined forces with OPEC to effect an additional supply cut of more than 500,000 barrels a day. But other factors driving the price increase were more volatile: the uncertainties created by the Trump administration walking out of the Iran nuclear deal and re-imposing sanctions; the ongoing instability in the other countries of the Middle East; the difficulties in Venezuela, the largest producer in Latin America. Once prices start increasing, speculative activity also enters the picture. With greater uncertainty, there is naturally more speculation, so prices were driven higher in a febrile market that was volatile around a rising trend.

For the oil-importing developing countries that were reaping the benefits of low oil prices, this had quite an impact even in that relatively short period, generating larger import bills, potential balance of payments concerns for some, and inflationary fears. Obviously, the first direct impact tends to be on the balance of payments, as import bills that were contained by the low oil prices will now increase. There will also be inflationary consequences, as the oil price increase has a cascading effect on other prices. If this in turn affects investor confidence, there could also be adverse impacts on capital flows and other domestic investment.

THE ASIAN CENTURY?

This is supposed to be the 'Asian century'. The spectacular rise of China and the overall dynamism of the Asian region created the widespread perception that Western capitalism is stagnant and moribund, unlike Asian capitalism that will show rapid growth and create a new geo-economic balance. Developments in the wake of the global financial crisis appeared to confirm this: while growth rates in Asia (and in the largest economies of China and India) dipped in 2009 just as they did in most of the world, the recovery was rapid and subsequent rates of growth remained higher than elsewhere.

But the optimistic view of the new emerging growth pole in the East missed the evidence noted earlier that the greater dynamism of Asia was mostly due to a tiny set of countries: first Japan, then South Korea until the late 1980s, and China in the current century. And Chinese exceptionalism has been just that – exceptional, based on the astute use of heterodox economic policies by a highly centralised and controlling state. More to the point, since the global crisis, the recovery and expansion in almost all the major economies of Asia has been heavily based on debt. Even in China, debt-to-GDP ratios have more than doubled since before the crisis, and in many other Asian economies certain forms of debt (especially in housing and personal finance as well as corporate loans) have reached alarming proportions. In Asia – perhaps even more than in the advanced economies – the strategy of inducing recovery through credit expansion has increased fragilities (like asset price inflation and debt-driven cycles) that could generate another crisis in the future. This is already evident in India, where the overhang of bad corporate loans has become a drag on bank lending and on private investment, leading to absolute reductions in investment over the past few years.

One of the most widely remarked features of recent world trade has been the dramatic emergence of China as a substantial player in global trade, not only because its exports have penetrated nearly all countries' markets, but because it has become a major destination for developing country exports, raw material and intermediate exports in particular. Rapid export-led growth in China was the most significant factor behind the growth acceleration in large parts of the developing world from 2002 onwards. By generating a wide set of global value chains that drew in raw materials and intermediate goods imports from large parts of the developing world across hemispheres to enable processing for export to the developed countries, China played something of the role of the lead goose in the much-discussed 'flying geese model'. For developing countries, this affected both volumes and values of merchandise exports. China's demand drove up the prices of many primary products, leading to terms of trade improvements that contributed hugely to increased incomes in primary exporting countries.

The growing weight of China in world trade and investment had major effects globally: China became the biggest source of manufactured goods imports for most countries, whether developed or developing. Its voracious demand for raw materials and intermediate goods to be processed into exports largely meant for Northern markets changed the terms of trade and volume of exports for many primary-product (agricultural and mineral raw materials) producing countries and brought more countries into manufacturing value chains. Even though, simultaneously, cheaper manufactured goods from China did flood markets not only in advanced countries but also across developing nations, affecting their rates and patterns of industrialisation, the overall effect on income growth in developing countries was definitely positive.

In addition, partly because of the ability to channel the foreign exchange surpluses built up through years of positive net exports and significant capital inflows, Chinese capital became a significant player in the ongoing struggle for control over economic territory across the world. Some of these moves on the capital account certainly benefited developing countries, as China's aid, loans, and FDI into emerging markets and developing countries dwarfed the relatively small and declining contributions of advanced economies. A significant part of Chinese foreign aid (described as funds for development co-operation) was directed to infrastructure projects, especially in Southeast Asia, Latin America, and Africa, and these had direct and indirect effects on growth prospects in the recipient countries. By 2014 the China Development Bank and the China Eximbank had become among the most active development lenders, dwarfing traditional lenders like the World Bank with total loans of $1.2 trillion and $300 billion respectively, a significant part of which was directed to developing countries.[10] Since the mid-2000s, Chinese direct and indirect financing of infrastructure investment in sub-Saharan Africa has dominated over all other external players, including G7 countries.[11] Unlike the foreign aid and capital flows from the northern advanced economies, Chinese investment, aid, and loans have been overwhelmingly directed towards infrastructure expansion, particularly in the transport and energy sectors.

Such a pattern clearly suggests the potential for China to become a significant global economic player. But the hyperbolic accounts of Chinese economic strength risk overstating its current significance. In 2017, China accounted for less than 9 per cent of global output on the basis of market exchange rates at constant 2005 US dollars. Despite dramatic increases in income, its per capita GDP was only around 45 per cent of the global average, and still just a fraction of the average for the major advanced capitalist economies (for example, only 15 per cent of US per capita income at market exchange rates).[12] In relative terms, China remains a 'poor' country. The sheer size of its population nevertheless means that its potential as both a supplier and a market for goods in global trade is undoubtedly immense.

This was clearly evident during the boom of the 2000s. But some years after the global crisis, and more specifically in the period from 2014, China's share (as destination) of total exports from developing countries declined. It recovered only slightly in early 2018, while over this period, the European and US markets maintained or increased their shares slightly. This reflected changes in China's own external trade strategy. As the Chinese economy rebalanced towards more domestic demand-led growth rather than export-led growth, it required less imports from developing countries to use in processing for further export. In fact, the focus of the Chinese strategy has been toward internal rather than external rebalancing. The investment rate declined from 48 per cent in 2011 to 44 per cent in 2016, while China's current account surplus fell from a peak of more than 10 per cent of GDP in 2007 to only 2 per cent in 2011 – a very marked decline.[13] But since 2013, current account surpluses have started rising again – not because of more exports but because imports have decelerated or declined faster. This explains partly why, even as Chinese exports to developing countries were volatile but still remained largely at the same level from January 2014, imports from developing countries fell quite sharply in early 2015 and since then stagnated at the lower levels, as shown in Figure 9.

Figure 9. China's Trade with Emerging and Developing Countries, 2014-2017 ($US billions)

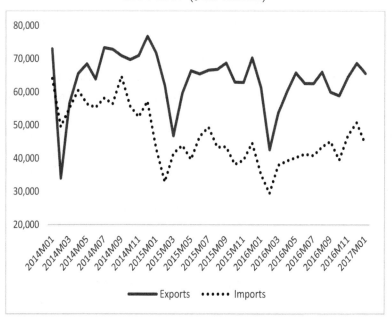

Source: IMF, *Direction of Trade Statistics*, 2018.

What this suggests is that China is unlikely to play the same role of providing a much-needed demand impetus for developing country exports that it played in the earlier decade, based on incorporation into larger global value chains directed to serving core capitalist economies. The possibility of Asia becoming a viable alternative growth pole for the world economy is also thereby undermined unless a completely new strategy can be put in place that actually provides China and other peripheral economies with ways to engage that do not rely on Northern expansion.

The basis of such a strategy would in effect have to be something resembling the mid-twentieth-century Marshall Plan through which the United States provided generous funds to enable the recovery and reconstruction of western Europe. This has been described as an early expression of 'Global Keynesianism' whereby the US as the dominant player provided capital and other resources to European nations not only for their reconstruction, but to enable expansion that would in turn provide a market for US exports over time, in a mutually beneficial synergy. While there were clear economic reasons for this, the geo-strategic considerations of the Cold War and the need to present capitalist western Europe as a viable and successful economic system were clearly also significant. There is no doubt that such considerations helped to make the Marshall Plan and associated US moves in that period particularly generous, with large scale and rapid speed of assistance that have not been observed thereafter with respect to any other region or country.

There is some evidence that such a new strategy is indeed being considered by the Chinese government, even if not in so many words. It is expressed in various initiatives, including the regional and pluri-lateral projects like the New Development Bank of the BRICS countries and the Asia Infrastructure Investment Bank, but most of all through the ambitious Belt and Road Initiative (henceforth BRI). The plan of the BRI is certainly ambitious. Harking back to the 'Silk Route' that was established two millennia earlier and became the primary trading route linking the Chinese empire with other civilisations of the time, it explicitly aims to connect more than 60 countries, with around two-thirds of the world's population. This would be done through infrastructure establishing transport and other connectivity links, facilitating trade and investment, and other forms of co-operation, with China as the hub rather than just one end of the trail.[14]

The initiative is confusingly named, since the 'Belt' refers to physical roads and overland transport, while the 'Road' actually refers to maritime routes. The Belt is intended to link China to Russia and the Baltic European countries through Central Asia and Russia; go through Central Asia to connect China with the Middle East, the Persian Gulf and the Mediterranean countries; and establish seamless transport links between China and Southeast Asia, South Asia, and the Indian Ocean. The Road would develop the links of Chinese coastal ports to Europe through the South China Sea and Indian Ocean, and to the countries of the South Pacific Ocean through the South

China Sea. Six 'international co-operation economic corridors' have been identified to start with, each of which is hugely ambitious in terms of the new infrastructure required and the physical and political difficulties of the terrain to be covered.[15] Each of these also requires developing particular regions in China in ways that would further these links, which would help to reduce regional inequalities within China. The corridors typically require not just railways and roads, but airports and seaports, oil and gas pipelines, power transmission routes with co-operation in creating and maintaining regional grids, cross-border optical fibre connectivity, and so on. The plan is not only to offer rail-to-rail freight transport along the entire route, but also eventually to move towards the convenience of 'one declaration, one inspection, one cargo release' for any cargo transported. Considering that this seamless freight transport is still not possible even after the trade facilitation agreement of the WTO, this clearly involves very bullish expectations about reducing/eliminating customs and border inspection across the participating countries.

So unlike the Marshall Plan, which was essentially confined to Western Europe, the BRI is much more extensive in its geographical coverage, which in turn means that significantly more resources would be required to make it meaningful. This makes the question of financing this set of projects an important one. This is where a second important difference with the Marshall Plan becomes evident: both in terms of the total resources planned, and the nature of the financing which is much less generous, the BRI falls short. The declared goals would require several trillion US dollars over the next few years. To start with, the funds are largely expected to come from recent development financing initiatives that China has been involved in leading, such as the Asia Infrastructure Investment Bank and New Development Bank of the BRICS countries. Both have total capital of $100 billion each, but they will lend to a range of projects in different countries, not just those connected to the BRI. The Silk Road Fund set up exclusively for the BRI by China has $40 billion. These are not just trivial amounts compared to the scale of the investment required, but even smaller than the current levels of investment in other developing countries enabled by the China Development Bank and the China Eximbank. The expectation is that other sources of funding will be mobilized in the form of Public-Private Partnerships (surprising though it may be that the Chinese have fallen for this much-utilized but failed warhorse of neoliberalism). So too are other governments involved in these plans supposed to make commitments and investment guarantees – after which the investment would still finally depend on the inclinations of private parties, who are notoriously hesitant and fickle with respect to infrastructure investment. All this means that the investments that fructify will be less significant relative to the size of the host economies. Further, the time period over which these are being envisaged is fairly long, and so the investments would not generate immediate dramatic impacts in the manner of the Marshall Plan. In any case, the amount of expected co-financing required in several projects makes them less generous and less affordable for the recipient countries.[16]

The Chinese BRI strategy appears to have bought into several features of neoliberal globalization, including deeper financial integration, protection of various kinds for private investors through 'investment facilitation,' and very extensive trade liberalization proposed for all partner countries.[17] This is surprising, given that China's own development success has been based on a much more heterodox and state-controlled approach. So, it may generate some growth in partner countries, but it will also accentuate inequalities. And, if such an approach does indeed become the norm, then the BRI and similar strategies spearheaded by China would not be enough to meet the challenge of injecting anything like sufficient demand into the world economy.

CONCLUSION

This is the context in which geopolitical uncertainties are adding to the economic fragilities created by global stagnation and increased inequality. To a significant extent, the two tendencies feed upon one another: the social and political tensions created by material insecurities and inequalities then create pressures for inward-looking political and economic strategies that generate further tendencies to instability. The potential eruption of possibly major trade wars is just one expression of this; on the geo-strategic side, the prospective arenas of violence have never appeared to be so many and so fraught with global implications.

For capitalism as a global system, the risks are compounded by the ultimate success of finance capitalism in permeating all corners of the globe. As a result of this, global stock markets have shown much more synchronized movement in recent years than in the past. In the run-up to the global crisis, the flow of liquidity primed both advanced economies and (mainly Asian) emerging markets. And once the 'easy money' response to the financial crisis was put in place, financial markets across the world turned buoyant once again. Several emerging markets in Asia and Latin America became the targets of the carry trade (that exploits differences in interest rates across countries), as speculative investors moved in backed with cheap capital and benefited from both equity price inflation and domestic currency appreciation because of large foreign capital inflows. As a result, markets in South Korea, India, and Thailand have been febrile and volatile, vulnerable to violent swings. The legacy of these bull runs is large accumulation of foreign financial capital investments in both equity and bond markets. In such conditions even the slightest economic or non-economic news can lead to capital flight, triggering steep currency depreciation, balance of payments difficulties, and internal financial problems. So even 'the flapping of a butterfly's wings' in a distant part of the world can cause economic tornados, such as financial crises in Asia, as it is already close to doing in some emerging markets in Latin America. It seems that the economic roller coaster ride may have only just begun.

NOTES

1   See for example: Bank for International Settlements, *Annual Report* 2008 and *Annual Report* 2010, Basel, Switzerland; *Trade and Development Report 2010: Employment, Globalization and Development, and Trade and Development Report 2014: Global Governance and Policy Space for Development,* Geneva: UNCTAD.

2   *Trade and Development Report 2015: Making the International Financial Architecture Work for Development,* Geneva: UNCTAD.

3   Based on calculations from data in: IMF, *World Economic Outlook,* April 2018.

4   McKinsey Global Institute, *Poorer Than Their Parents? Flat or Falling Incomes in Advanced Economies,* July 2016. The report is based on a study of income distribution data from 25 developed countries; a detailed dataset with more information on 350,000 people from France, Italy and the United States and the UK; and a survey of 6,000 people from France, the United Kingdom and the United States that also checked for perceptions about the evolution of their incomes.

5   First described by the economist Branko Milanovic and developed further in his *Global Inequality: A New Approach for the Age of Globalization,* Cambridge: Harvard University Press, 2016.

6   For example, a 20 percentage point increase of a per capita income of $1000 (approximately the fifth decile, or the middle) would generate an additional $200, but that would be only 1 percentage point increase of a per capita income of $20,000.

7   Jayati Ghosh, 'A note on estimating income inequality across countries using PPP exchange rates', *Economic and Labour Relations Review, Special Issue in Memory of Anthony B. Atkinson,* 29(1), 2018, pp. 24-37.

8   Lucas Chancel, Facundo Alvaredo, Thomas Piketty, Emmanuel Saez and Gabriel Zucman, *World Inequality Report 2018,* Paris: World Inequality Lab, 2018.

9   Chief among these beneficiaries was India, with nearly a 60 per cent fall in the value of crude oil imports between 2013 and 2017, but obviously others like China, Japan, Germany and the UK also gained in this way. In the US, while the oil import bill came down dramatically, the fallout of low oil prices was more complicated because it affected the viability of the nascent shale oil industry.

10   *Trade and Development Report 2015: Making the International Financial Architecture Work for Development,* Geneva: UNCTAD.

11   Jeffrey Gutman, Amadou Sy, and Soumya Chattopadhyay, *Financing African Infrastructure: Can the World Deliver?*, Washington, D.C: Brookings Institution, 2015.

12   Based on World Bank, *World Development Indicators*, at wdi.worldbank.org.

13   Data calculated from CEIC database, accessed on 12 March 2018.

14   Peter Cai, *Understanding China's Belt and Road Initiative*, Lowy Institute for International Policy, March 2017.

15   For example, the China-Pakistan Economic Corridor (slated to extend from Kashgar in Xinjiang Province of China to Gwadar port in southern Pakistan) has already become a bone of contention between China and India, since it involves a road being built through Pakistan-occupied Kashmir, recognised by India to be part of its own territory illegally occupied by Pakistan (over which several wars have been fought).

16   The dangers for recipient countries have been highlighted by the experience of Sri Lanka, which built a massive port in Hambantota (the constituency of the then President Rajapakse) at an estimated cost of $1.3 billion, using credit from Chinese state-owned banks. The port failed to take off and has been running losses, making debt servicing very expensive for the Sri Lankan government. In December 2017, the port was handed over on a 99-year lease to the Chinese state-controlled company China Merchants Port Holdings. See Kiran Stacey, 'China signs 99-year lease on Sri Lanka's Hambantota port', *Financial Times*, 11 December 2017.

17   See, for example, The State Council, The People's Republic of China, *Action Plan on the Belt and Road Initiative*, 30 March 2015, at   http://english.gov.cn/archive/publications/2015/03/30/content_281475080249035.htm.

AMPLIFYING THE CONTRADICTIONS: THE CENTRIFUGAL BRICS

ANA GARCIA AND PATRICK BOND

The formation of the Brazil-Russia-India-China-South Africa (BRICS) network is one of the main features of twenty-first century geopolitics, far exceeding in scope the investment strategy in BRIC economies that was identified by a senior Goldman Sachs banker, Jim O'Neill, in 2001. O'Neill may have kick-started this process as part of the standard Goldman Sachs approach to investment 'churning' (by 2013 the bank shut down its BRIC fund after poor returns), but it took on a life of its own. In 2006, a meeting between BRIC countries took place on the margins of the United Nations General Assembly. However, it was with the global financial crisis that the economic role of the BRICS gained prominence, especially insofar as financial bailouts and currency printing initially failed to restore growth, leaving the Chinese and Indian economies as drivers of global capitalism.

After two decades of unprecedented growth, it certainly appeared that China's economy would challenge the dominant position of the US, Europe, and Japan. The G8 countries expanded into the G20 in late 2008 in part to raise $750 billion in new resources for the IMF. In 2009, the first BRIC heads-of-state summit took place in Russia, launching a succession of annual gatherings of leaders that gave body and content. South Africa was incorporated as an African member at Beijing's request in 2010, and BRICS went through a process of institutional densification, drawing thousands of participants not only for inter-governmental events but also in business, academic, cultural, youth, labour, and civil society exchanges.[1]

The Indian National Congress party's loss to the Hindu-nationalist Bharatiya Janata Party (BJP) in 2014 did not disrupt the BRICS, although 2017 border battles between India and China caused enormous concern. By this time, the Chinese president who gave BRICS muscle, Hu Jintao, was succeeded by Xi Jinping in 2013, and within four years consolidated his power to Mao-like levels. Likewise, the control Vladimir Putin exercised in

Russia and his allegiance to the BRICS both grew stronger after Moscow's 2014 invasion of Crimea and capture of territory from Ukraine, as the other G7 powers expelled Russia from the G8. Notably, Brazil's 2016 congressional coup d'etat by Michel Temer, which ended Workers Party rule after 13 years, did not substantially affect the BRICS' agenda, nor did a more popular palace-coup replacement of South Africa's President Jacob Zuma (who had served since 2009) by his deputy Cyril Ramaphosa in February 2018, 15 months ahead of schedule.[2]

Through all this political turmoil, grand claims have been offered about the way BRICS will rebalance the world and ensure good global governance. This essay considers the opposite, namely that a resurgent imperialism is being facilitated by BRICS politics. This functions in three ways. First, global capitalist crisis tendencies are amplified by *centrifugal* forces emanating from BRICS economies. Second, the neoliberal character of multilateral institutions, especially in the spheres of finance, trade, and climate politics, is also amplified as the BRICS gain a seat at the table. Third, BRICS-based corporations, along with their states acting in a subimperial manner, are vital forces in super-exploitative accumulation within their respective regions and beyond. In our view, the centripetal forces supposedly pulling the world more tightly together through globalization had by 2018 reached their limits, and centrifugal pressures had begun to emerge. The BRICS were now very much part of a world turned upside down, and in many respects driving the process.

BRICS AS *CENTRIFUGAL* NOT *CENTRIPETAL*

Xi's 2015 promise at the BRICS Ufa Summit to boost 'the centripetal force of BRICS nations, tap their respective advantages and potentials and carry out cooperation in innovation and production capacity' now faces extreme political, economic, and ecological contradictions. The most obvious geopolitical wedges have been pushed into the BRICS not by Washington, at least for now, but are instead Sino-Indian border conflicts, especially in Pakistani-held Kashmir. There, the transport infrastructure needed by China to link its far western region to the Indian Ocean is a central component of the Belt and Road Initiative. In September 2016, India's Prime Minister Narendra Modi lost a showdown while hosting the Goa 2016 BRICS Summit, when he unsuccessfully tried to have Pakistan declared a terrorist state. Both China and Russia refused.

In mid-2017, an even higher-profile fight unfolded at the site where India and China share a border with Bhutan. When the Chinese built a small road on contested ground, Indian soldiers initiated fisticuffs. In late

August, just days before the BRICS Xiamen summit was to begin, India backed down and withdrew its troops, but not before Modi's staff hinted he would boycott Xiamen, just as he had China's Belt and Road Summit in May. The Chinese state mouthpiece *Global Times* ran a column headlined, 'New Delhi may disrupt BRICS Summit to blackmail Beijing'.[3] At the same time, the Chinese government also issued two travel advisories to its citizens visiting India: 'Pay close attention to the local security situation, improve self-protection awareness, strengthen security and reduce unnecessary travel' (the very opposite of the BRICS' stated objective: 'increasing people-to-people links'). In the end, Modi went to Xiamen and there have been no further disruptions on the scale of 2016-17.

Figure 1. Rise and fall of BRICS and world trade (imports and exports), 1997-2017:

High point ratio and 2017 ratio, as percentage of GDP

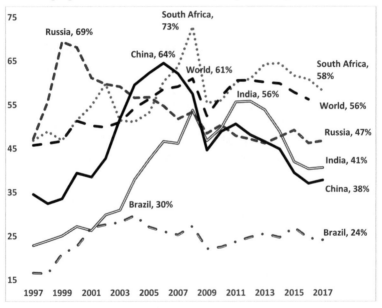

Source: World Bank Data Catalogue,
https://data.worldbank.org/indicator/NE.TRD.GNFS.ZS?end=2017&locations=CN-BR-
ZA-IN-RU-1W&start=1997&view=chart

There are deeper economic processes unfolding beneath the geopolitical tensions and rising internal repression. The motors to expand capitalism rapidly – in China and everywhere – were meant to be foreign investment, trade, and finance. But even as Xi praised them, all are running out of steam, or even veering towards collapse amidst soaring indebtedness. Indeed, financial assets invested in other countries fell from a level of 58 per cent of world GDP in 2008 to just 38 per cent in 2016, in spite of fast-rising flows into high-risk (high-return) emerging markets and notwithstanding capitalism's growing overall indebtedness. According to the 2018 UN Conference on Trade and Development (UNCTAD) *World Investment Report*, the BRICS accounted for 19 per cent of global investment inflows and 23 per cent of the world GDP in 2017. But Foreign Direct Investment (FDI) into the BRICS fell in 2017 to $266 billion, a decline of $10 billion from 2016, amidst a global decline of 23 per cent, to $1.43 trillion.[4] Global trade peaked at 61 per cent of world GDP in 2012 and then fell to 2016's 56 per cent, but the BRICS suffered faster declines in relative trade than the world as a whole (Figure 1). Hence contrary to Xi's ambitions for BRICS centripetality, the Standard Bank of South Africa issued a June 2018 critique of existing linkages, arguing that,

> the BRICS must find ways to elevate their commercial relevance to one another. Unfortunately, the commercial relevance of the BRICS to one another is minimal. Intra-BRICS trade has actually fallen, from $342 billion in 2013 to $312 billion in 2017. Furthermore, taken as a share of their respective trade, the BRICS share has plateaued, after doubling from 6 percent in 2003 to 12 percent in 2011. In fact, it fell sharply in 2016. The trade data is simple; for each of the BRICS, China is a large trade partner; just 20 percent of BRICS trade excludes China. The trade relation is therefore unbalanced. China is exporting manufactured goods to the other BRICS in proportions consistent with their relative GDP, whilst importing mineral products from Russia, Brazil and South Africa, and prepared foodstuff from Brazil.[5]

In addition to unevenness in trade, excessive financialization – both debt and equity over-valuation – is the Achilles Heel. The next recession – which HSBC, Citigroup and Morgan Stanley economists in mid-2017 already suggested was imminent due to vastly overpriced stock markets and unprecedented corporate indebtedness[6] – will confirm how capital has become overexposed locally, even while losing appetite for global markets. This makes credible in this case the warnings of conservative journalist Ambrose Evans-Pritchard:

> The world has never been so leveraged, and therefore so sensitive to a monetary squeeze. The Institute of International Finance says world debt

reached 318 percent of GDP at the end of 2017, 48 percentage points higher than the pre-Lehman peak. Emerging market debt has jumped from 145 percent to 210 percent. That is where the trouble is brewing. It is a near mathematical certainty that the currency crisis in Argentina and Turkey – already nibbling at Brazil, South Africa, and Indonesia – will spread to the rest of the emerging market nexus if the Fed goes ahead with its 'dot plot' guidance of five further rate rises by late 2019.[7]

Driven by financialization, the centrifugal forces ripping apart not just the BRICS but in fact all of contemporary world capitalism – first globalizing, now deglobalizing – can be traced back to the metabolism of economic cycles yielding ever more intense bursts of crises since the economic stagnation first hit the US, Europe and Japan in the 1970s. The 2008 crisis delivered a rude shock within this long cycle (as had the traumatic 1998-2001 period for Russia, South Africa, and Brazil), for even the ever-higher levels of world debt and the central banks' loose-money strategies have proven unable to restore growth and debt ratios to previous levels.

It was initially hoped that, as the *Financial Times* put it in 2010, these 'building BRICs' would 'change the economic order' by marshalling both their own raw resource production and manufacturing capacity to achieve sufficient weight to in turn reduce unfairness in world trade and finance.[8] But against such overblown theories of virtuous-cycling centripetal capitalism, whether from Xi or the *FT,* the centrifugal contradictions manifest in overproduction, over-indebtedness and deglobalization appear to be ending those fantasies. The only recent relief came from the Chinese state's massive urban construction investments (leaving scores of near-empty cities), perhaps to be repeated through its Belt and Road Initiative in coming years, as well as India's service sector-led boom. But the other three BRICS suffered recessions once the 2015 commodity price crash hit home, with South Africa not yet emerging into positive per capita GDP growth even in 2018. Under these circumstances of extreme intra-BRICS unevenness, Xi's centripetal strategy has become a centrifugal force spiralling out of control.

Xi and other Chinese leaders committed to pro-corporate globalization expect that their Belt and Road mega-infrastructure will push manufactured exports and pull energy imports through a restructuring Eurasia. But the BRICS' financial short-term fixes – massive debt and stock market speculation – continue, too, as stock markets bubble in South Africa (today 90 per cent higher than in 2010), India (70 per cent) and Russia (50 per cent). China's stock exchanges were in the same league, but just as the yuan was made an IMF-acceptable global currency reserve, the Chinese markets lost more than $5 trillion in two share bubble bursts in 2015-16.

Within this general decline in global flows, FDI inflows to the BRICS countries were still net positive, but as overaccumulation crisis hit China and overcapacity levels reached critical mass, FDI stocks of *outflows* rose by 21 per cent in 2016 to $2.1 trillion.[9] China became a net outward direct investor in 2016, and the second largest global investor (after the US), accounting for $183 billion in outward FDI.[10] But as shown below, if successful, this drive will entail much greater extraction of minerals and agricultural commodities, with associated ecological destruction and land grabs 'wrecking the landscape all around the world,' as Harvey remarks.[11] Moreover, global governance cannot address the conditions for restored capital accumulation, not if the past decade of reforms continues, in part because of the way BRICS are amplifying the contradictions.

MULTIPOLARITY RELEGITIMIZES IMPERIALISM

The standard argument of multilateral optimists was offered in 2016 by former Director of the OECD's Development Co-operation Directorate Richard Carey:

> The fact that the BRICS are such strong supporters of the G20 and of the 2015 United Nations agreements is no small matter. It is a highly significant evolution, reflecting the emergence of a multipolar international system which has made possible the striking shift from an era of ubiquitous North-South conflict to the current universal agreements in the UN development fora, on the basis of common objectives and differentiated responsibilities.[12]

But while demanding reforms in the Bretton Woods financial institutions, specifically concerning voting quotas at the IMF during 2010-15, in the course of which the BRICS committed $75 billion in recapitalization (of which more than half came from China), BRICS leaders also created their own new institutions. At the 2014 Fortaleza summit, the New Development Bank (NDB) was initiated to finance infrastructure, and the Contingent Reserve Arrangement (CRA) was built to lend to countries facing balance of payment problems. For those who considered the BRICS challengers to status quo neoliberal ideology, to US economic supremacy and to the postwar world financial order sustained by World Bank and IMF, there was initially great optimism in 2013-14.[13]

However, the leading NDB personnel were drawn from the most conservative elements within the five countries' pool of financiers (with the brief, partial exception of Brazil during Workers Party rule). The NDB operational arrangements mimicked those of the World Bank and other multilateral banks, even to the extent of explicit staff sharing and project co-financing arrangements in 2016-18 memoranda of understanding. And by 2018, notwithstanding rhetoric about sustainable lending cribbed from its advisors Joseph Stiglitz and Nick Stern, the NDB's non-consultative strategies led to credits for conflict-ridden, environmentally damaging projects (e.g. a controversial irrigation scheme in India and expansion of the Durban port-petrochemical complex). The NDB's social-environmental framework seeks to differentiate responsibilities by giving a greater role to the borrowing states' national socio-environmental protection and risk management systems (the so-called 'country system').[14] On the one hand, the policy of strengthening national systems complies with principles of non-interference in internal affairs and thus preserves the scope of action of national states, unlike policies pursued by traditional multilateral financial institutions such as the World Bank. On the other hand, there is a risk that the bank will precipitate a widespread downgrading of standards given the lack of environmental and social safeguards that were already won in struggles with other multilateral banks. Notably, these standards are left for national institutions to decide, implement and monitor, without the responsibility for lack of transparency, public consultation, human rights violations, corruption, and environmental disasters. Consequently, national social-environmental standards may be put to global competition to attract investors.[15]

Moreover, although the CRA facility has not been drawn down – mainly because Brazil, Russia, and South Africa have appeared set to exit their respective 2015-17 recessions without suffering a foreign debt repayment crisis – the CRA actually strengthens IMF leverage. The CRA articles of agreement compel any borrower to acquire an IMF structural adjustment package after receiving just 30 per cent of its lending quota (in order to access the next 70 per cent). And as for IMF voting reform, the new investments raised by the BRICS had the effect of disempowering most poor countries by lowering their ownership share (e.g. Nigeria and Venezuela by 41 per cent and even South Africa by 21 per cent), so that China's could rise by 37 per cent, Brazil's by 23 per cent, India's by 11 per cent and Russia's by 8 per cent.[16] As for the benefits of a greater 'voice', the BRICS directors failed to promote a candidate for managing director from within, as they not only voted unanimously for the French conservative finance minister Christine Lagarde in 2011, but in 2015 extended her term and even approved continuance of her controversial reign in 2016 on the day she was convicted in French courts of negligence in a $430 million corruption scandal. During this period, there was no change in the neoliberal Washington Consensus philosophy that has proven so adverse to poor economies, societies and environments.

With respect to trade, at the 2015 Nairobi WTO summit, agricultural subsidies and hence food sovereignty were slated for abolition, thanks to crucial alliances made between negotiators from Washington and Brussels, facilitated by Director General Roberto Carvalho de Azevêdo, a Brazilian. To the dismay of many observers, the deadlock that had characterized the WTO over the prior dozen years was broken, mainly by the Brasilia and New Delhi representatives, with China, South Africa, and Russia compliant.[17] This gave some credence to Xi's celebrated World Economic Forum speech two years later, deploying what might well have been the most hackish pro-market rhetoric ever heard in Davos:

> The problems troubling the world are not caused by economic globalization … Any attempt to cut off the flow of capital, technologies, products, industries and people between economies, and channel the waters in the ocean back into isolated lakes and creeks is simply not possible …
>
> We must remain committed to developing global free trade and investment, promote trade and investment liberalization. We will expand market access for foreign investors, build high-standard pilot free trade zones, strengthen protection of property rights, and level the playing field to make China's market more transparent and better regulated … China will keep its door wide open and not close it.[18]

The reality was rather different. During six months starting in mid-2015, Beijing had imposed stringent exchange controls, stock market circuit breakers and financial regulations to prevent two Chinese stock market collapses from spreading (beyond $5 trillion in estimated losses).[19] Moreover, within 18 months of his speech, Xi authorized a set of trade restrictions on US products in retaliation for Trump's protectionist tariffs.

With respect to the other main UN reforms at the global scale, in late 2015 the BRICS signed the Paris Climate Accord, but did so mainly because it is non-binding, unambitious, and outlaws climate-debt lawsuits by victims of Western and BRICS emissions. More evidence of assimilation was provided at the July 2017 G20 summit in Hamburg, where BRICS leaders were even more callous about the economic damage to poorer countries they are inflicting in alignment with the G7 (and especially the 'G1' – the US empire). A genuinely anti-imperialist climate change strategy would have entailed, at minimum, calling for a global carbon tax, with an initial focus on the United States.[20]

After the 2017 G20 summit, at least three seasoned political economists who in the past had firmly favoured the BRICS appeared to reverse positions. According to Ravi Kanth of the influential Malaysian NGO Third World Network,

> For the first time, the Doha Development Agenda (DDA) or the unresolved Doha issues were not even mentioned in the G20 leaders' communiqué because of opposition from the United States as well as other major industrialized countries. China, India, Brazil, South Africa, and Indonesia who negotiated the Hamburg declaration along with their developed country counterparts seemed to have allowed the erasing of DDA [i.e. which Kanth considers meets poorer countries' balanced trade interests].[21]

Others went further. Yash Tandon, former head of the South Centre, claimed: 'At the G20 Hamburg meeting, Africa was officially represented by only one country – South Africa, which was obsequiously behaving like a neo-colony that it is.'[22] And the Filipino founder of Focus on the Global South, Walden Bello, used this occasion to conclude that the whole export-oriented development strategy had reached a dead end:

> The stagnation of the once dynamic centers of the global demand – the U.S., Europe, and the BRICS – has made this model obsolete. It was, in fact, the non-viability of this once successful model of rapid growth in current global circumstances that pushed China, under Hu Jintao and Wen Jiabao, away from an export-oriented path to a domestic demand-led strategy via a massive $585 billion stimulus program. They failed, and the reason for their failure is instructive. In fact, a set of powerful interests had congealed around the export-oriented model.[23]

The BRICS assimilation into imperialism's main power bases has sparked a discussion on the character of subimperialism at the beginning of the twenty-first century. In 2018, former BRICS supporter Vijay Prashad conceded,

> The BRICS bloc – given the nature of its ruling classes (and particularly with the right now in ascendency in Brazil and in India) – has no ideological alternative to imperialism. The domestic policies adopted by the BRICS states can be described as *neoliberal with southern characteristics* – with a focus on sales of commodities, low wages to workers along

with the recycled surplus turned over as credit to the North, even as the livelihood of their own citizens is jeopardized, and even as they have developed new markets in other, often more vulnerable, countries which were once part of the Third World bloc ... In fact, the new institutions of the BRICS will be yoked to the IMF and the dollar – not willing to create a new platform for trade and development apart from the Northern order. Eagerness for Western markets continues to dominate the growth agenda of the BRICS states. The immense needs of their own populations do not drive their policy orientations.[24]

That eagerness for Western markets is mediated by multinational corporations. In 2015, the South African Reserve Bank recorded net profit flows from abroad ranging within three broad categories: above 100 per cent were Western countries; in the 15-60 per cent range were large middle-income countries; and below 15 per cent were poor, exploited countries. The BRICS were all in the 18-20 per cent range, except South Africa whose ratio was closer to 45 per cent (Figure 2).

Figure 2. Net profit flows, 2012-14
(average dividend receipts as a percentage of dividend payments)

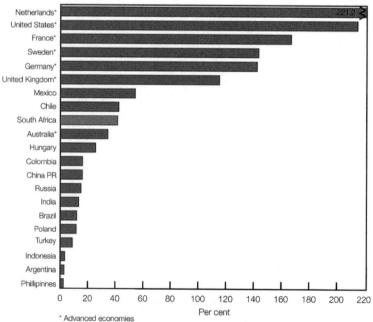

* Advanced economies

Source: South African Reserve Bank, *Quarterly Economic Bulletin,* 2nd Quarter
2015, p.39, https://www.resbank.co.za/Lists/News%20and%20Publications/
Attachments/6776/01Full%20Quarterly%20Bulletin%20%E2%80%93%20June%202015.pdf

This is a consistent indicator of the surplus extraction process, although corporate misinvoicing and other tax dodges make both the inflows and outflows to and from the BRICS even greater than formally recorded. The United Nations Economic Commission for Africa estimated that $319 billion was transferred illicitly from Africa during the commodity super-cycle, from 2001 to 2010. The United States was the leading single destination for this hot money with $50 billion in inflows; but China, India, and Russia were together responsible for $59 billion (Brazil is not recorded in the top 17 and South Africa is not included).[25] BRICS countries are also five of the top seven countries to lose Illicit Financial Flows, at a rate from 2004-13 of $340 billion annually.[26]

Following the brief 2009-11 post-crisis commodity boom – mainly driven by China's mega-project infrastructure projects (including its infamous ghost cities) – commodity prices peaked, and in 2015 crashed by more than 50 per cent in most sectors. This had an especially damaging role on Africa's and Latin America's current account balances and ability to repay foreign debt. Chinese contributions to both fixed capital and financial capital inflows waned in most of the major African and Latin American borrowing countries. With commodity prices recovering in 2016-18 but still very far from previous levels the potential for China to collect collateral is already becoming a source of potential conflict among the BRICS.

Certainly China's period of 'non-interventionism' appears to be ending. This is evident in Zimbabwe, where Beijing's military command played a vital role in the coup that ended Robert Mugabe's presidency in November 2017. The Chinese relationship with the local army included $15 billion in allegedly missing diamonds (according to even Mugabe in 2016). The other BRICS also appear to be supporting a relatively liberalized agenda – including increased imposition of bilateral investment deals – that will further weaken most poor countries' economic resilience in a world economy careening out of control.

SOUTH-SOUTH EXPLOITATION WHEN THE BRICS 'GO OUT'

David Harvey has insisted correctly that a rigid, fixed concept of 'North-South imperialism' cannot account for ever-more complex 'spatial, interterritorial and space-specific forms of production, realization and circulation' of surplus capital which has overaccumulated in emerging economies, especially China.[27] After the investment wave of the 1980s-90s in Asia's smaller Newly Industrializing Countries ebbed, global uneven development gave the BRICS an unprecedented opportunity to host a new round of capital accumulation. The export of capital by BRICS corporations was firmly supported by neoliberal interstate relations, especially Bilateral Investment Treaties (BITs). In many respects, the details provided below of how BRICS have assisted their firms' entry to Africa and Latin America suggest a subimperialism that could, in many cases, be characterized as even more exploitative than traditional Western multinational corporations.

Starting with the most important, China is Africa's main trading partner and the biggest investor in the continent, surpassing the US and overtaking the European Union.[28] Beijing's 'Go Out' strategy now puts investment and aid to African countries in the same Forum for China-Africa Cooperation 'package', linked to credit to infrastructure projects. China's main development bank created a specific subsidiary, the China–Africa Development Bank, to facilitate deals. The 2002-11 race for raw materials led to a boom of Chinese investment in African mining, energy, and oil sectors. Besides large and medium-sized state-owned companies, there are many Chinese small businesses spread through the African continent, along with more than a million Chinese residents of Africa.[29]

To be sure, there is danger of overstating China's African footprint, especially given the chaotic character of commodity demand. By far the largest investment proposal is in Egypt: the China Fortune Land Development company's $20 billion capital city, which if approved would turn 'a 700 square kilometer swath of desert into a modern hub for government buildings, foreign embassies and major companies'.[30] The firm had a 35 per cent profit rate in 2017. Yet in part because of extreme profiteering and illicit financial flows that these and other corporations are used to getting away with in Africa, the states that they loot don't have enough funding to build the supportive mega-project infrastructure (for example, the over-indebted al-Sisi regime desperately borrowed $12 billion from the IMF in 2018 to avoid default).

As a result of the 2015 price crash, the commodity-extractive investment envisaged in strategies such as the African Development Bank's 2010 Programme for Infrastructure Development in Africa hasn't materialized. The largest is the $100 billion Inga Hydropower Project in the Democratic Republic of the Congo, aiming to produce 43,200 megawatts of electricity. China had in 2014 attempted to get US government co-financing support but was turned down by the Obama administration and then the World Bank in 2016, leaving the project shelved until mid-2018. Together, the China Three Gorges Corporation and Actividades de Construccion y Servicios of Spain bid for $14 billion of start-up work, and it remains to be seen whether this will create an economically viable project.[31]

In Latin America, the Chinese presence rapidly increased from the mid-

2000s. Between 2005-16, nearly 80 per cent of loans to Latin America and the Caribbean came from China's development bank, far surpassing credits from the Inter-American Development Bank. Almost half of these went to Venezuela (44 per cent), but also to Brazil, Ecuador, and Argentina, especially for infrastructure and energy projects led by oil.[32] Most lending included a currency exchange agreement to promote local currencies and the renminbi. Nearly three quarters of Latin American exports to China are primary products, whereas to the rest of the world exports are diversified with a balance including low-technology manufactures.[33] In terms of FDI, however, Latin America has only 4 per cent of the total Chinese FDI, which still goes mainly to the US and Europe. It is heavily concentrated in infrastructure and mining.

China has largely protected its multinational corporations through 128 Bilateral Investment Agreements around the world (fewer only than Germany). Since the 1990s, it has signed 34 BITs in Africa and 15 BITs in Latin America and the Caribbean, in addition to other Free Trade Agreements with Costa Rica, Chile and Peru.[34] China reproduces the 'new Lex Mercatoria,' which provides transnational corporations with binding commercial and investment rights, against which international human rights law is fragile.[35] Chinese investment protection agreements resemble those established by Western powers, and Beijing participates in the World Bank's International Center for Settlement of Investment Disputes (ICSID), established to enable corporations to bring a recipient country to international arbitration.

While Chinese multinationals have captured large market shares and moved up in global manufacturing value chains (mainly chemicals, electronics, automotive and aircraft), Indian investments are linked into regional value chains and infrastructure networks.[36] Indian FDI peaked in 2008 at $21 billion, falling to $7.5 billion in 2015.[37] India has signed 73 investment agreements around the world, including 12 BITs with African countries and three with Latin America, in addition to two other economic framework agreements with Mercosur and with Chile.[38] India's efforts to build closer relations to the African continent have entailed cooperation and technical assistance, participation in peacekeeping missions and cultural relations.[39] Diplomatic, financial, and legal incentives; linguistic and cultural similarities have been supported by the Indian diaspora in Africa (about three million people of Indian origin live on the continent, of which 1.3 million are South Africans whose lineage dates to mid-nineteenth century indentured labour immigration). Indian FDI has been backed by direct credit lines from its Exim Bank,[40] as well as different diplomatic initiatives from the Indian government.[41] In Latin America, Indian FDI has grown through mergers and acquisitions in oil and gas, sugar, pharmaceuticals, and mining.

Among leading Indian companies in Africa and Latin America are Tata Group,[42] Infosys, Essar Group, Reliance Communications, Mahindra, Bharti Airtel, different Pharmaceuticals (Sun, Torrent, Glenmark), Oil and Natural Gas Corporation (ONGC), Jindal Steel and Power, Coal India, Ranbaxy Laboratories, Shree Renuka Sugar and Apeejay Shipping.[43] There are also two major Indian-owned but European-headquartered companies that are most active in extractive accumulation, Anil Agarwal's Vedanta and Lakshmi Mittal's Arcelor-Mittal.

Indian trade with Africa and Latin America is dominated by raw materials and energy commodities sent to India, while India supplies pharmaceuticals – including vitally important generic anti-retroviral AIDS medicines – and low- and medium-technology products.[44] India has entered Africa's agricultural sector, buying land through its public and private companies.[45] It is estimated that India is the fifth largest land investor in Africa, which is the source of numerous conflicts between local populations and private investors.[46]

South Africa joined the BRICS only in 2010 as a representative of the African continent. It is a regional 'economic powerhouse', and the second BRICS country after China in terms of economic presence on Africa. Johannesburg and Cape Town firms' investments are concentrated in telecommunications, retail, manufacturing, mining, banking and construction. Currently South Africa is party to 39 BITs and 10 other agreements around the world, 18 of which are with African countries and 3 in Latin America and the Caribbean.[47] Despite occasional nationalist rhetoric and the cancellation of European BITs due to complaints about state-imposed (affirmative-action) shareholder participation by local black residents, South Africa seeks to remain 'attractive' to foreign investors. Its regular appeal to multinational corporations – revived when Ramaphosa took over the presidency – highlights investment protection mechanisms. In that sense its relationship with global capital is yet another case of 'talk left, walk right'.[48]

In uneven ways, South Africa has played a subimperial role in Africa since the 1960s, first during the apartheid alliance with dictators in Malawi and Zaire, and after apartheid ended in 1994, aiming to expand business. For example, the South African-initiated New Partnership for Africa's Development was deemed 'philosophically spot on' by George W. Bush's State Department in 2002.[49] Pretoria located the national interest between those of the Western and BRICS powers and numerous poor, yet resource-wealthy countries. In Mozambique, the colonial-era Cahora Bassa power plant built by the Portuguese on the Zambezi River has exported large amounts of energy through Eskom into South Africa at very low prices. Aggressive accumulation by mining companies such as Anglo American (which by 2018 was 20 per cent owned by Agarwal), De Beers, and African Rainbow Minerals, as well as the oil company Sasol, give South African capital an often-predatory role in the region.[50] South African and Chinese capital often act together to exploit natural resources and dominate African markets.[51] In Zambia, for example, the retailer Shoprite has imported products (many of Chinese origin) from its South Africa suppliers in a manner that has crowded out local producers.[52] But the largest FDI in Africa's history was a 20 per cent stake by the Industrial and Commercial Bank of China (the world's largest) in South Africa's Standard Bank in 2007. In turn, that led the Chinese to intervene in Zuma's 2015 decision to replace his finance minister with one much closer to the Zuma family – an intervention that succeeded in immediately reversing Zuma's choice.[53]

The Russians are increasingly active in Africa, as well. Despite economic restrictions imposed by the European Union after the 2014 Crimea invasion, Russia is the main Eastern European recipient of FDI. As an external investor, Russia promotes firms mainly in natural resources and infrastructure related to extractive projects. Russia is undergoing a new privatization programme, selling parts of large multinationals such as the VTB bank, the shipping company Sovcomflot, Novorossisk Commercial Seaport, the giant diamond mine Alrosa, as well as part of the state-owned oil company Rosneft.[54] Russia has 79 BITs and six investment agreements around the world, 11 of which are in Africa and six in Latin America and the Caribbean.[55] Russia has signed the Washington Convention to access the World Bank's ICSID for investor to state arbitration, where the Russian state has been filed in over 20 cases.[56] The main sectors of Russian FDI are oil and gas, mining, natural resources, metallurgy, infrastructure, telecommunications, fishing, and security. Some of the leading Russian multinationals – Lukoil, Alrosa diamonds, Sintez conglomerate, Gazprom, Rosatom, InterRao, and RusAl – are in Africa and Latin America.[57]

Russia's engagement with Africa dates back to the time of the Soviet Union and its support for the liberation movements. It kept extensive diplomatic and diverse relations with Africa, which range from investments projects to peacekeeping missions.[58] In Latin America, besides its historical relations to Cuba, it renewed its engagement since the late 2000s with the ALBA members Venezuela, Ecuador, Bolivia, and Nicaragua, and extended its interests in Brazil, Argentina, and Peru.[59] Russia is today especially strong in military cooperation with African and Latin American countries. Its arms market deals in Africa were worth $66.8 billion in 2011.[60] During the Cold War, many African armies became dependent on Russian supply and military technology.

Between Russia and Latin America, arms sales reached $14 billion in 2013.[61] Russian companies are involved in conflicts, such as in Zimbabwe, where there are various claims against DTZ-OZGEO (Private) Limited, a joint venture between DTZ-Development Trust of Zimbabwe (DRZ) and the Russian Econedra Limited, engaged in the extraction of gold and diamond. There, Alrosa, Ruschrome, Rostec, and the Vneshekonombank bank control large diamond and platinum mining projects. The operations of DTZ OZGEO in the Penhalonga region have caused major environmental and social impacts.[62]

Brazil is the main recipient of FDI in Latin America and also a major investor in its own region. Brazilian trade and investment relations with Africa and Latin America grew significantly during the Lula da Silva government, with its priority orientation to 'South-South relations' which accompanied Brazil's more proactive position in multilateral arenas such as the WTO. But relations with African countries ceased to be a priority under Dilma Rousseff's administration (2011-2016) due to the economic and political crisis, thus revealing the fragile nature of its ties of cooperation with Africa.[63] The impeachment process against Dilma in 2016 and establishment of a right-wing government under Temer weakened these relations further. Brazil's South-South relations lost the 'solidarity' label and began to focus on commercial purposes, while Brazilian foreign policy prioritized relations with the world superpowers – primarily the US, European Union and China.[64] Brazilian outward FDI grew over 100 per cent between 2009 and 2014, until the political and economic crisis hit the country. The 'Car Wash' investigations affected mainly investments by the oil company Petrobras and construction companies led by Odebrecht, whereas a significant amount of Brazilian capital deposited in tax havens was repatriated after the government launched a tax relief programme.[65]

All BRICS investment agreements follow the traditional BITs model, ensuring national treatment to foreign investors, most-favoured nation rules, and prohibition of nationalization and expropriations without prompt, adequate compensation.[66] Even though Brazil never ratified a BIT in the 1990s, it continued to pass national laws to guarantee the sanctity of inward FDI. However, with the increasing international expansion of Brazilian multinationals, the country changed its stance and elaborated a new model, the Agreement on Cooperation and Facilitation of Investments

(ACFI).[67] This was not designed to attract multinational corporations to invest in Brazil, but to promote and protect Brazilian investments in other developing economies. Different than traditional BITs, this agreement did not provide for 'investor to state' arbitration in the event of conflict: the Brazilian state (and not the corporation responsible for a conflict) would negotiate a solution with the host state. ACFI consolidates the tendency of mixing public policies with private interests.[68] From 2015-18, Brazil signed four ACFIs in Africa and other four in Latin America, in addition to an investment protocol within MERCOSUR and an economic framework agreement with Peru, all containing the same ACFI clauses.[69]

Brazil's FDI goes mainly to extractive sectors, equipment, food and beverage, textiles, and construction. They go prior to, and are more diversified in, North and South America, while in Africa the general rate is small but very concentrated in construction and mining.[70] The Brazilian National Social-Economic Development Bank (BNDES) is the main source of funding for international projects and the export of construction services by Brazilian multinationals.[71] The global mining company Vale has faced many kinds of social, environmental and labour conflicts inside and outside of Brazil, including coal extraction from Mozambique's Tete Province.[72] Mozambique's Nacala Corridor is also a site for massive soybean production ('ProSavana') involving Brazilian and Japanese investors, which has also led to accusations of land grabbing.[73] In South America, Brazilian construction companies have been active in Peru and Bolivia, where an uprising took place in 2011 concerning BNDES-financed road building within a fragile environmental area ('TIPNIS'). Bolivia also depends on Petrobras as its major operator and gas importer through the Gasbol pipeline to different provinces in Brazil.[74]

This overview of BRICS FDI in Africa and Latin America captures part of the capital accumulation process, but most subimperial-imperial flows are between the BRICS and the world's core centres of accumulation. All BRICS remain recipients of FDI from US, European, and Japanese multinational corporations, and as noted above, this occurs on such adverse terms that four of the BRICS can claim rates of return only one-fifth as much as they repay dividends and profits to Western FDI owners. The capitalist development of BRICS took place, in the last decades, by creating and facilitating conditions for accumulation of foreign capital within their territories, supported (among other mechanisms) by the framework of investment protection agreements for foreign capital to come and stay 'in', as well as drawing profits inwards to the BRICS from their hinterlands.

Thus the rise of BRICS has generated new cycles of capital accumulation and new expropriations in other countries and regions of the South. The BRICS reproduce within South-South relations an imperialist logic of competition over natural resources, labour power, and market access. Whereas the BRICS governments seek to assert themselves as a cohesive group in multilateral forums, in Africa and Latin America, multinational corporations and states have their own competitive strategy and approach, producing new power hierarchies within the 'South and East'.

CONCLUSION

The nefarious effects of neoliberal globalization, having pushed the world into an uneven economic crisis, have yielded political consequences that are also uneven. The new far-right politicians, parties, and movements have come to power either through democratic or more dubious ways, with the 2016 parliamentary coup in Brazil an example of the latter. Curiously, Trump's election in the US and his shift towards economic protectionism places China in a new position: leading defender of open markets and globalization, notwithstanding its own powerful tools of protectionism and regulation. Thus, the international left faces a paradoxical situation: anti-globalization discourses – which, a few years ago, shaped transnational liberatory struggles against the multilateral institutions, perhaps most famously the Seattle WTO summit of 1999 – emanate from the extreme right, alongside the xenophobia and racism that are anathema to the left. And although many observers were understandably confused in the early years of the BRICS, today, as their governments have become promoters of home corporations above all, it is impossible to talk about a real alternative for a fairer world order coming from the BRICS' ruling elites.

In previous works, we identified ideological positions that help present BRICS through at least a rudimentary class analysis: 'BRICS from above' (the position of governmental and business leaders); 'BRICS from the middle' (the position of the generally pro-BRICS academics, think tanks, NGOs and trade unions); 'BRICS from below' (grassroots movements in struggles within those countries and beyond them, that may one day create strong linkages between struggles and build transnational solidarity); and, finally, the pro-Western businesses and their intellectuals, who remain adherents to old-order capitalism no matter the chaos within US-EU circuits, who still fear the rise of the BRICS.[75] To understand the BRICS beyond the narrow phraseology at heads-of-state summits requires familiarity with all these viewpoints.

From a realist, state-centric perspective of disputes between the great powers (a look 'from above'), it is obvious that the BRICS rulers seek to accumulate economic and political capacities, which in the future might also translate into military capacity. Yet even if this corresponds to some aspects of reality (e.g. Russia in Syria), it is insufficient and could encourage us to draw dangerous political conclusions. Considered from a more horizontal viewpoint, it is easy to identify convergences and disputes, differences and inequalities within and between the BRICS. And it is even more necessary to change our angle vertically to see the BRICS from below, understanding their relations with other countries and regions in the 'South,' and with (and often against) their subjects – especially workers and the environment, as well as women, youth, and other subalterns. From these combined angles, only in official rhetoric do the BRICS function as a centripetal force. Understood within a broader framework of capital accumulation/overaccumulation and class struggle, expanding to incorporate disputes over natural resources and access to labour that is increasingly cheap and overexploited as a result of gendered power relations, the centrifugal tendencies become obvious.

Additionally, if we look at the BRICS states in their expanded sense, we can better understand classes and social forces in dispute for certain models of development and for the ascendancy of new ideologies – especially now being crafted by the BRICS Academic Forum and Think Tanks. Finally, the central challenge will be the articulation of social struggles 'from below': local communities, peasants, and workers who face and resist major projects carried out by BRICS corporations and financial institutions operating in their territories, as well as women, youth, and other groups suffering from official discrimination, claiming their own liberations in alliance with others.

Although battling the BRICS is far removed from the reality of social movements in each of these countries (Johannesburg in 2018 being a case in point), this may change as BRICS institutions, especially the NDB, reinforce the environmentally-predatory development model that destroys their territories' natural life and the work of their peoples. In other words, international solidarity and processes of articulation and strengthening of 'BRICS from below' will take place in the inevitable processes of class struggle, with the challenge ahead being – as everywhere – to connect the dots and identify sites of structural weakness for insurgent opportunities.

NOTES

1   Leonardo Ramos, Ana Garcia, Diego Pautasso, and Fernanda Rodrigues, 'A Decade of Emergence: the BRICS Institutional Densification Process', *Journal of China and International Relations*, 6(1), 2018.

2   This occurred just five months before South Africa hosted the BRICS summit, with Zuma begging on national television to be permitted to stay through August, 'to

remove the perception out there that Zuma is being elbowed out'. SA Broadcasting Corporation, 'President Jacob Zuma speaks to SABC News,' 14 February 2018.

3   Liu Zongyi, 'New Delhi May Disrupt BRICS Summit to Blackmail Beijing', *Global Times*, 15 August 2017.

4   United Nations Conference on Trade and Development, *World Investment Report 2018*, Geneva, 2018, available at unctad.org.

5   Jeremy Stevens, 'Africa Macro: The BRICS Summti,' Standard Bank Resaearch Brief, Johannesburg, June 26, 2018, available at research.standardbank.com.

6   Sid Verma and Cecile Gutscher, 'Wall Street Banks Warn Downturn is Coming,' *Bloomberg News,* New York, 22 August 2017.

7   Ambrose Evans-Pritchard, 'A Worldwide Financial Storm is Brewing as Central Banks Pick Their Poison,' *Sydney Morning Herald,* 18 June 2018.

8   Helen Warrell and Steve Bernard, 'Building Brics: Changing the Economic Order', *Financial Times,* 15 January 2010.

9   United Nations Conference on Trade and Development, *World Investment Report 2017*, Geneva, p.18, available at unctad.org.

10   According to this report, 'Chinese multinational enterprises invested abroad to gain access to new markets and to acquire assets that generated revenue streams in foreign currency'. UNCTAD, *World Investment Report 2017*, p. 14.

11   David Harvey, 'Realities on the Ground: David Harvey Replies to John Smith', *Review of African Political Economy*, 5 February 2018.

12   Richard Carey, 'The BRICS Role in Today's Multipolar World', *Opinion,* Institute for Development Studies, Brighton, 22 December 2016.

13   Radhika Desai, 'The BRICS are Building a Challenge to Western Economic Supremacy', *The Guardian*, 2 April 2013; Walden Bello, 'The BRICS: Challengers to the Global Status Quo', *Foreign Policy in Focus*, 29 August 2014.

14   BRICS New Development Bank, 'Environmental and Social Framework', Shanghai, 2016, available at: ndb.int.

15   Paulo Esteves, 'Preface', in 'Country Systems and Environmental and Social Safeguards in Development Finance Institutions: Assessment of the Brazilian System and Ways Forward for the New Development Bank,' Conectas Direitos Humanos, 2018, available at: www.conectas.org.

16   In contrast, in the 2018 World Bank recapitalization, Russia deigned to participate, as it was under Crimea-related sanctions and hence not eligible to borrow from the Bretton Woods Institutions.

17   Chagravati Raghavan, 'Doha SU Diminished, Not Dead, and Retrievable', *Third World News Network*, 23 December 2015, available at: www.twn.my.

18   *Financial Times,* 'Xi Jinping Delivers robust Defense of Globalization at Davos', 17 January 2017. The full speech is available at: america.cgtn.com.

19   Beijing's measures included arrest of nearly 200 people 'for spreading rumours online' – but these efforts in mid-2015 did not prevent an 8 per cent crash in two days in January 2016.

20   Philip Inman, 'Sky-High Carbon Tax Needed to Avoid Climate Catastrophe, Say Experts', *The Guardian,* 29 May 2017.

21   Ravi Kanth, 'Developing and LDCs to Pay Heavy Price for Hamburg Declaration', *South North Development Monitor* 8499, Penang, 11 July 2017.

22   Yash Tandon, 'G20: The Second Berlin War against Africa,' *Pambazuka News*, Nairobi, 20 July 2017, available at www.pambazuka.org.

23   Walden Bello, 'It's Not Only Necessary to Develop an Alternative to Globalization — It's Entirely Possible', 19 July 2017, available at: fpif.org.

24   Vijay Prashad, 'In the Ruins of the Present', *MROnline,* 26 March 2018, available at: mronline.org.

25   Simon Mevel, Siope Ofa, and Stephen Karingi, 'Quantifying Illicit Financial Flows from Africa Through Trade Mis-Pricing and Assessing Their Incidence on African Economies', United Nations Economic Commission for Africa presentation to the African Economic Conference, Johannesburg, 28–30 October 2013, available at: afdb. org.

26   Dev Kar and Joseph Spanjers, 'Illicit Financial Flows from Developing Countries, 2004-13', Global Financial Integrity, Washington, DC, available at: www.gfintegrity.org.

27   Harvey, 'Realities on the Ground.'

28   Fantu Cheru and Cyril Obi, 'Chinese and Indian Engagement in Africa', *Journal of International Affairs*, 64(2), 2011, p. 93.

29   Cheru and Obi, 'Chinese and Indian Engagement in Africa,' p. 99.

30   Mirette Magdy, 'It's End or Break for China's $20 billion Egyptian Capital Plan', *Bloomberg*, 21 March 2018.

31   The need for co-financing and the delays in these mega-projects in part reflect how much overinvestment Chinese firms made in prior rounds of infrastructure. Before 2015, project failures included China Railways in Nigeria ($7.5 billion) and Libya ($4.2 billion), Chinese petroleum in Angola ($3.4 billion) and Nigeria ($1.4 billion), and Chinese metal investors in the DRC and Ghana ($3 billion each). Subsequent to the 2015 commodity crash, many other mega-projects have been delayed. In East Africa, China desires a $2 billion coal-fired power plant on the Kenyan coast to supply electricity for the $15 billion Lamu Port-Southern Sudan-Ethiopia Transport project (one beseiged by local community and environmental critics), and in 2018 it requested that General Electric provide a 20 per cent 'clean coal' buy-in for support. In Tanzania, Beijing's China Merchants Holdings International reached out to Oman's State General Reserve Fund to finance the $12 billion Bagamoyo port, yet it is more likely that a (World Bank-funded) $500 million expansion of the Dar es Salaam port underway in 2018 will be a higher priority and will cripple Bagamoyo's viability. See Patrick Bond, *Africa Crashing, Burning but Resisting,* New York: Routledge, 2019.

32   CEPAL, *Explorando nuevos espacios de cooperación entre América Latina y el Caribe y China*, January 2018, p. 23, available at: repositorio.cepal.org.

33   CEPAL, *Explorando nuevos espacios de cooperación entre América Latina y el Caribe y China*, p. 41.

34   UNCTAD, 'International Investment Agreements Navigator,' Geneva, 2018, availabe at investmentpolicyhub.unctad.org.

35   Juan Hernandez Zubizarreta and Pedro Ramiro, 'Against the "New Lex Mercatoria," Observatory of Multinationals in Latin America', October 2016, available at: omal.info.

36   UNCTAD, *World Investment Report 2017,* p. 55.

37   CEPAL, *Fortaleciendo la relación entre India y America Latina y Caribe*, November 2016, p. 48, available at: repositorio.cepal.org.

38   India is currently reviewing its BITs with the aim of eliminating loopholes used by parties to file international arbitration claims against the country. See Prabash Ranjan,

'The White Industries Arbitration: Implications for India's Investment Treaty Program', *Investment Treaty News*, 13 April 2012, available at: www.iisd.org.

39   Rajiv Bhatia. 'India's Africa policy: Can we do better?', *The Hindu*, 15 July, 2010.

40   Export-Import Bank of India, 'Lines of Credit', available at: www.eximbankindia.in.

41   Cheru and Obi, 'Chinese and Indian Engagement in Africa,' pp. 99-100. A six-year (2014-2020) initiative called 'Supporting India Trade and Investment for Africa' was also launched for the purpose of promoting exports to five African countries (Ethiopia, Kenya, Rwanda, Tanzania, and Uganda).

42   The Tata Group concentrated 16 per cent of total Indian FDI between 2011 and 2015. CEPAL, *Fortaleciendo la relación entre India y America Latina y Caribe*, November 2016, p. 50.

43   CEPAL, *Fortaleciendo la relación entre India y America Latina y Caribe*, November 2016, pp. 56-57; Paul Anusree, 'Indian Foreign Direct Investment in Africa', *CUTS CCIER Working Paper*, No. 1/2012, available at: www.cuts-ccier.org.

44   Mohamed Amir Anwar, 'Indian Foreign Direct Investments in Africa: A Geographical Perspective', *Bulletin of Geography*, Socio-economic Series, 26(2014), pp. 35–49; CEPAL, *Fortaleciendo la relación entre India y America Latina y Caribe*, November 2016, pp. 40-41.

45   Cheru and Obi, 'Chinese and Indian engagement in Africa', p. 103.

46   Cheru and Obi, 'Chinese and Indian engagement in Africa', p. 103.

47   UNCTAD, 'International Investment Agreements Navigator,' Geneva, 2018.

48   Patrick Bond, 'South Africa: Talk Left, Walk Right', *Counterpunch*, 5 December 2014.

49   Patrick Bond, *Fanon's Warning*, Trenton: Africa World Press, 2005.

50   Baruti Amsi, Patrick Bond, Richard Kamidza, Farai Maguwu, and Bob Peek, 'BRICS Corporate Snapshots During African Extractivism,' in Bond and Garcia, eds *BRICS: An Anti-capitalist Critique*, Johannesburg: Jacana Media, 2015.

51   Padraig Carmody, 'The New Scramble for Africa', *Jabobin*, December 2015.

52   Darlene Miller, 'South African Multinational Corporations, NEPAD and Competing Regional Claims on Post-Apartheid Southern Africa', *African Sociological Review*, 8(1), 2004, pp. 176-202.

53   Carmody, 'The New Scramble for Africa.'

54   UNCTAD, *World Investment Report 2017*, pp. 66, 69.

55   UNCTAD, 'International Investment Agreements Navigator'.

56   UNCTAD, 'International Investment Agreements Navigator'.

57   Habiba Barka and Kupukile Mlambo 'Russia's Economic Engagement with Africa', *Africa Economic Brief*, 2(7), 11 May 2011. As it is the case for many of the BRICS, Russian investments are difficult to identify since they use subsidiaries in tax heavens to invest in third countries, as is the case of Renova Holding, registered in the Bahamas, Evraz plc in the UK and Gazprom International in the Netherlands. Alexandra Arkhangelskaya and Vladimir Shubin, 'Is Russia Back? Realities of Russian Engagement in Africa', *LSE Ideas*, 16, 2013, p. 31.

58   Arkhangelskaya and Shubin, 'Is Russia Back?'.

59   There is little research published on recent relations between Russia and Latin America. One can find information from a geopolitical US perspective in Evan Ellis, *The New Russian Engagement with Latin America: Strategic Position, Commerce and Dreams of the Past*. Carlisle, Pennsylvania: United States Army War College Press, 2015.

60   Baruti Amsi, Patrick Bond, Richard Kamidza, Farai Maguwu, and Bob Peek. 'BRICS corporate snapshots during African extractivism.'

61   Ellis, *The New Russian Engagement with Latin America*, p. 14

62   Baruti Amisi, Bobby Peek, Farai Maguwu, 'BRICS Corporate Snapshots During African Extractivism,' *Tensoes Mund*. Fortaleza, 10(18-19), 2014, pp. 413-452.

63   Brazil's cooperation budget for Africa was at its peak in 2010, the last year of the Lula da Silva government, with a volume of approximately R\$20 million. Under the Dilma Rousseff administration, resources for cooperation with Africa fell drastically to R\$5 million in 2014. See: www.abc.gov.br/Content/ABC/imagens/africa_financeiro.png

64   Brazil's new chancelor under Temer, Aluysio Nunes Ferreira, argues against 'populism' in the region and for pragmatic economic relations with traditional partners within MERCOSUR, a free trade agreement with the European Union, and expanded realtions with the US, China and Asian partner. 'Brazil's Foreign Policy is "Back in the Game"', *Americas Quarterly*, 17 April 2017.

65   According to the Brazilian Central Bank, the stock of Brazilian outward FDI between 2007 and 2016 reached around \$450 billion. Brazilian Central Bank, 'Ativos Brasileiros no Exterior', September 2017, available at www4.bcb.gov.br; and 'Investimento Brasileiro No Exterior Avança', *Diário de Comércio, Indústria e Serviços*, 6 April 2018.

66   For an overview of BRICS' investment treaties in Africa, 'BRICS in Africa: More of the Same? A Comparative Study of Investment Treaties Between the BRICS and African Countries', available at: www.pacs.org.br.

67   Fabio Morosini and Michele Ratton, 'The Brazilian Agreement on Cooperation and Facilitation of Investments (ACFI): A New Formula for International Investment Agreements?,' *Investment Treaty News*, 4 August 2015.

68   Ana Garcia. 'BRICS Investment Agreements in Africa: More of the Same?' *Studies in Political Economy*, 98(1), 2017, pp. 24-47.

69   UNCTAD, 'International Investment Agreements Navigator'.

70   Confederação Nacional da Indústria, 'Investimentos Brasileiros No Exterior 2015. A Governança Internacional dos Investimentos', Brasília 2016; Fundação Dom Cabral; 'Ranking FDC das Multinacionais Brasileiras 2017', available at: www.fdc.org.br.

71   Between 2007 and 2015, 542 projects received funds from BNDES Exim, which lent \$12 billion to construction firms for engineering services in Latin America and Africa. Odebrecht was alone awarded 414 projects, totalling \$7.5 billion. See: www.bndes. gov.br/SiteBNDES/bndes/bndes_pt/Institucional/BNDES_Transparente/consulta_ as_operacoes_exportacao/planilhas_exportacao_pos_embarque.html. For a discussion on the relation between capital and the state in Brazil during the PT goverments, see Virginia Fontes and Ana Garcia, 'Brazil's new Imperial Capitalism', in Leo Panitch, Greg Albo, and Vivek Chibber, eds, *Socialist Register 2014: Registering Class*, London: Merlin Press, 2013.

72   In Canada, the Steelworkers stood for eleven months on strike; in Mozambique, problems related to forced resettlement of over a thousand family farmers. Judith Marshall, 'Behind the Image of South-South Solidariy in Brazil's Vale,' in P. Bond and A. Garcia, eds, *BRICS: An Anti-Capitalist Critique*, Johannesburg: Jacana Media, 2015; 'International Movement of People Affected by Vale', *Vale Unsustainability Report 2012*; Human Rights Watch, 'What Is a House Without Food? Mozambique's Coal Mining Boom and Resettlements'. May 2013.

73 Ana Garcia and Karina Kato, 'A Road to Development? The Nacala Corridor at the Intersection Between Brazilian and Global Investments', unpublished paper, Rio de Janeiro, 2018; UNAC and GRAIN, 'The Land Grabbers of the Nacala Corridor,' Febrary 2015, available at: www.grain.org.

74 Ana Carolina Delgado, 'The TIPNIS Conflict in Bolivia', *Contexto Internacional*, 39(2), 2017; 'Bolivianos cobram da Petrobras posição sobre compra de gás', *Estado de Sao Paulo*, 5 December 2017.

75 Patrick Bond and Ana Garcia, 'Introduction,' in *BRICS, An Anti-Capitalist Critique*.

NEOLIBERAL CAPITALISM: THE AUTHORITARIAN TURN

MARCO BOFFO, ALFREDO SAAD-FILHO, AND BEN FINE

Inescapably we live in both interesting and disturbing political times. These are times, which, since the election of Donald Trump, yield daily experiences of new political extremities bordering between the unimaginable and the farcical. Nor is Trumpism an isolated example of a new political extremism, despite its specifically US features. His combination of media savvy and nationalist populism offers a salient reminder of the extent to which widespread dissent can drive electoral success elsewhere in our times, at least from the perspective of an erstwhile complacent belief in the secure position of liberal (even if not social) democracy. For, in the recent past, authoritarian governments have been installed in a wide variety of countries by different means, including more or less objectionable elections (Argentina, Hungary, India, Italy, Poland), judicial-parliamentary coups (Brazil, Honduras, Paraguay), the abuse of constitutional prerogatives (Turkey), and military coups (Egypt, Thailand).

While the concepts of neoliberal authoritarianism or authoritarian neoliberalism[1] are often used interchangeably to address these developments, the former suggests a neoliberal variety of a transhistorical political authoritarianism, while the latter – our preference – specifies an authoritarian turn within neoliberalism.[2] Yet, what careful analyses of these political forms share in common is attention, if not reduction, to economic factors and the political responses to them. This suggests that to understand the nature and causes of authoritarian neoliberalism, the (economic) nature of neoliberalism must be specified, and how it conditions both the political and the ideological and their contradictory relations. Indeed, the policies and practices associated with neoliberalism and financialization have been drawn into question in the wake of the global financial crisis of 2007-08.[3] In the domain of ideology, the mantra that unleashing free – especially financial – markets could sustain economic prosperity indefinitely, subject to a modicum of macroeconomic regulation through manipulation of interest rates by an independent central bank, was rudely shattered, revealing an extreme and naïve vanity. Tellingly, Alan Greenspan, erstwhile head of the US Federal Reserve when he was called no less than the 'Master of the Universe', confessed to being 'in a state of shocked disbelief', accepting that 'you found that your view of the world, your ideology, was not right, it was not working'.[4]

In aftermath of the crisis, state intervention was launched on an unprecedented scale to rescue finance through the provision of unlimited support to large financial institutions. The biggest of banks in the world were temporarily taken into public ownership and otherwise targeted for bail-outs and easy access to funds at minimal interest rates through emergency asset purchases and a policy of 'quantitative easing' (QE). After a decade of limited recovery, it is clear that these responses did not deliver a renewal of economic performance on the scale experienced during the 1990s, let alone over the post-war boom; recently, the global economy has entered a 'secular stagnation' with no end in sight.[5] Meanwhile, the economic tribulations of neoliberalism have been compounded by an escalating crisis of democracy and a drift towards authoritarian forms of rule in a growing number of countries. We show below that this shift cannot be reduced (as if these developments were epiphenomenal) to an easily reversible advance of untenable projects led by self-centred, thieving, or megalomaniac politicians.

So, what exactly is the nature of neoliberalism that it can simultaneously both rely upon state intervention and deny its efficacy by recourse to political and ideological populism, quite apart from appeals to other (conservative) collectivities – nationalism and racism, in particular – in the context of market individualism? Coherence is not the order of the day, but there is underlying order in the chaos as our argument here, summarized as follows, suggests.

First, what occurred in 2008-09 was a severe *crisis within neoliberalism*, exposing the limits of reliance on finance as the driver of global accumulation. Initially taken by many as a fatal crisis of neoliberalism, especially as the market failed spectacularly in its favoured arena of finance, the crisis proved nothing of the sort.[6] Indeed, despite such expectations, it never became a *crisis of neoliberalism*, since the reproduction of the system of accumulation was never threatened by a systemic alternative.[7] Consequently, despite the decline of GDP growth rates and the vast and continuing reverberations of the crisis, neoliberalism remains alive and well in the economic domain and beyond. Indeed, in most respects, neoliberalism has been *strengthened* during the last decade.

Second, the social and institutional changes brought about by neoliberalism, and furthered by the finance-first and fiscal 'austerity' policies imposed in the wake of the global crisis, have destabilized the political sphere formed under neoliberalism and steadily sapped the ideological legitimacy of the system of accumulation. Indeed, neoliberal policies had already hollowed out progressive forms of political participation partly through the weakening of labour as well as exclusionary forms of rule, facilitated by the capitulation of left-of-centre political parties as neoliberal prescriptions became both common sense and institutionalized in government. These developments have not quelled political activism entirely, but they have severely undermined its traditional forms of expression and created fertile conditions for more extreme politics as new vulnerabilities to livelihoods emerged.

Third, while neoliberalism was, previously, typically grounded in increasingly shallow and formal practices of liberal democracy,[8] its current political forms are transitioning towards unstable modalities of which authoritarianism is increasingly common, with 'spectacular' leaders driving right-wing exclusionary programmes and the emergence of mass movements of the right both supporting and pushing them forward. We argue that these political shifts are not transitory phenomena ensuing directly from poor economic performance, that will reverse once faster economic growth resumes. Instead, they are the outcome of the degeneration of liberal democracy under neoliberalism. Neoliberalism (in the long term) and the global crisis (in the short term) have fatally destabilized the political system built by neoliberalism from within, unmooring it from its former centre of gravity in the promotion of (global) capital and finance with minimal pressures and concessions.

Yet, to understand whether authoritarian neoliberalism is a transitory adjustment phase to the murky post-crisis world or becoming the 'best-fit' political arrangement for neoliberalism,[9] the tendencies and counter-tendencies characterizing the present phase of neoliberalism need to be identified and disentangled. For the fate of authoritarian neoliberalism inevitably hinges on how such tendencies will be resolved – a process which is chaotic, still in flux, and by no means predetermined.

CAPITALISM, NEOLIBERALISM, FINANCIALIZATION

Although we live in the age of neoliberalism, few would self-describe as neoliberals. The label marks a critique rather than acceptance for even the leading representatives of contemporary capitalism, just as authoritarians will describe themselves as democratic. The current (neoliberal) stage of capitalism emerged in the wake of the end of the post-war boom, first in the UK and the US, rapidly spreading to their core allies in Europe and the periphery through Atlanticism and the Washington Consensus, via a wide variety of paths in distinct countries and regions. The origins of neoliberalism are appropriately associated with Thatcherism and Reaganism, but these monikers can be misleading: even though neoliberalism has had a significant impact on many areas of social reproduction, it is not reducible to a mere shift in elected administrations, ideology, economic and social policies, class relations, or the otherwise undifferentiated relationships between state and market, workers and capital-in-general, or finance and society. Neoliberalism is each of these, but also more than them all. In short 'the originality of neoliberalism is precisely its creation of a new set of rules defining not only a *different* 'regime of accumulation', but, more broadly, a *different* society'.[10]

Neoliberalism's most salient feature is the financialization of production, exchange, and social reproduction, i.e. the subsumption of economic and social reproduction by the intensive and extensive accumulation of interest-bearing-capital.[11] Thus defined, financialization encapsulates the increasing role of (globalized) finance in ever more areas of economic and social life. In turn, financialization underpins the neoliberal system of accumulation, articulated through the power of the state to impose, drive, underwrite, and manage the internationalization of production and finance in each territory, often under the ideological veil of promoting non-interventionism.[12]

While financialization expresses the control of interest-bearing-capital over the main sources of capital, processes of resource allocation and levers of economic policy – including the exchange rate, the composition of employment, consumption, investment, international trade, and the financing of the state – the global reach of finance both incorporates and reflects the centralization of those levers in US-led financial institutions, and their regulation by US-controlled international organizations. Further, contemporary financialization derives from both the post-war boom and its collapse into the stagflation of the 1970s, and it has been one of the main drivers of the restructuring of the global economy since then – often under the guise of 'competitiveness' and 'inflation control'.[13] These mutually reinforcing processes have allowed financial institutions to appropriate an expanding share of the value produced in most neoliberal economies. For example, in the US the profits captured by financial companies jumped from a little over 10 per cent of total profits in the post-war period, to 41 per cent in 2002.[14] This share declined immediately after the crisis, but returned to over 30 per cent by 2009.[15] These transfers from the non-financial sector have contributed to the polarization of incomes under neoliberalism.

Neoliberalism and financialization have thus underpinned *both* the recovery of profitability after the crisis of Keynesianism, *and* rising inequality.

This approach to neoliberalism as a stage in capitalism supported by financialization informs a specific pattern of transformations in the processes of growth, investment, production, employment, finance, and consumption. As a result, some countries have been able to sustain impressive rates of growth, with northeast and southeast Asia to the fore; more recently, China has become the export assembly hub of the world. Yet, far from fostering an unproblematic 'global convergence', neoliberalism has created new patterns of uneven and combined development. Immense prosperity within and across countries and regions for specific social strata (popularly identified as financial or other elites or oligarchs, the top 1% or even the top 0.01%), coexists with new patterns of poverty, as well as the reproduction of mass poverty in areas where it already prevailed.

In short, financialization has become the main driver of economic and social restructuring both nationally and globally, creating a tendency to short-termism and speculation as opposed to long-term investment in pursuit of productivity increase at 'microeconomic', 'macroeconomic', and broader social levels, albeit unevenly and through a variety of mechanisms. Accordingly, accumulation under neoliberalism has generally taken the form of finance-driven bubbles, parasitical upon the enhanced exploitation of workers (through the restructuring of production at the global level and the expansion of precarious forms of labour, culminating in the 'gig economy'), exactions from the periphery (via unequal trade, financial extraction, rents, and so on), and relentless plunder of nature. These bubbles invariably collapse with destructive implications, and their containment and subsequent recovery require state-sponsored salvaging. Representative cycles include the international debt crisis of the early 1980s; the US savings and loan crisis of the 1980s; the stock market crashes of the 1980s and 1990s; the Japanese crisis and subsequent underperformance dragging on since the late 1980s; the crises in several middle-income countries at the end of the twentieth century; and the dotcom, financial, and housing bubbles of the 2000s, ultimately leading into the global financial crisis and its limited recovery. Thus, financialization has been attached to declining levels of investment and increased volatility within and across economic and social sectors, globally and nationally.

The economic contradictions of neoliberalism and financialization in the advanced economies have resulted in underperformance relative to the Keynesian 'golden age', despite unprecedentedly favourable conditions for capital accumulation wrought by the transition to neoliberalism. They include the West's victory in the Cold War; the collapse of most nationalist movements in the Global South; the liberalization of trade, finance and capital movements; unparalleled support to accumulation by competing states; the reduction of taxation, transfers and welfare provision in most countries; the decline of traditional sources of resistance within previous forms of capitalism (trade unions, peasant movements, left parties and social movements); and the ideological hegemony of a bogus but vociferous 'free market' capitalism. Finally, the availability of new technologies has served as a continuing source of productivity increases, to some extent offseting the effects of financialization, alongside significant increases in the global labour force, not least with China's integration into the capitalist world economy. Instead of thriving from these favourable conditions, global accumulation in core countries has been hampered by continuing instability and, since 2007, by the deepest and longest economic crisis and the weakest and most distributionally regressive recovery on record.[16]

In this light, we identify *the economic paradox of neoliberalism* as the staggering inability to capitalize upon extraordinarily favourable conditions for accumulation. This relationship between financialization and neoliberalism can be loosely divided into three phases separated first by the early 1990s, and later the global crisis of 2008.[17] These phases are more logical than chronological, as they can be sequenced, delayed, accelerated, or even overlain in specific ways depending on country, region and economic and political circumstances. The first is the transition or shock phase, going against the previous system of accumulation, with the aggressive promotion of private capital proceeding with limited regard to broader consequences. This transition generally requires forceful state intervention to contain labour, disorganize the left, promote the transnational integration of domestic capital and finance and put in place the new institutional framework. This can be illustrated by the military coups in Uruguay, Chile, and Argentina in the 1970s, which preceded global neoliberalism, followed by Thatcherism, Reaganism and their offspring in other advanced economies, 'structural adjustment' in Latin America and sub-Saharan Africa since the 1980s, and the transitions to capitalism in Eastern Europe, in the 1990s. This phase closes historically with the East Asian crisis in the late 1990s.[18]

The second phase emerged in the context of the reaction to the dysfunctions and adverse social consequences of the first. Associated especially with the social democratic 'third way' turn, it focused on the stabilization of the social relations imposed previously, the consolidation and expansion of the financial sector's interventions in economic and social reproduction, state management of the new modalities of international integration, and the 'rolling-out' of neoliberal social policies both to manage the deprivations and dysfunctions created by neoliberalism, and to (re)constitute neoliberal subjectivities. In this way, neoliberalism redefined the relationship between the economy, the state, society, and individuals, constraining the latter to give their lives an entrepreneurial form and subordinating social intercourse to narrow economic criteria.[19] The ideology of self-responsibility has been especially significant, since it is antagonistic to working-class culture and agency: it deprives citizens of their collective capacities, values consumption above all else, places the merit of success and the burden of failure on isolated individuals, and suggests that the resolution of every social problem requires further individualization and financialization of social intercourse.[20] None of this implies, it bears emphasizing, the retreat of the state (especially in its economic roles), as opposed to the emergence of increasingly centralized forms of control and subordination to financial imperatives.

After the shock of the financial crisis, a third phase emerged, characterized by the loss of legitimacy that followed the realization of the stunning – and exceptionally costly – flaws of financialization, the perception that neoliberalism had driven an accelerated concentration of income and wealth and imposed unpopular patterns of employment and social reproduction, and that, despite entirely favourable conditions, the neoliberal restructuring of the relationships between state, finance, and industry had failed to deliver a renewal of accumulation with macroeconomic stability. Yet the crisis eventually led to the reconstitution of the hegemony of finance and the reimposition of radicalized economic, social and political ambitions disguised by the neoliberal orthodoxies of 'free' markets and permanent austerity. These have all been part of the emerging forms of accommodation between large-scale finance and productive capital with, for example, states flirting with industrial policy and large-scale infrastructural provision as a means to shower money and contracts so that finance and industry will work together.[21]

Such developments have been enforced through increasingly repressive forms of rule, and validated – despite large cracks in their ideological hegemony – through the discourses and practices of (selective forms of) nationalism and (more or less disguised) racism. Their political form is authoritarian neoliberalism – a form of neoliberalism which, partially breaking out of its previous democratic shell, exacerbates the tendencies of neoliberalism to strengthen the coercive and security apparatuses of the state in order to sustain the system of accumulation despite its evident inability to realize any form of shared economic prosperity.

FROM GLOBAL FINANCIAL CRISIS
TO THE CRISIS OF NEOLIBERAL DEMOCRACY

Each capitalist crisis incorporates specific characteristics, whether by virtue of proximate causes, depth, breadth or incidence across the economy, ideology or political system, or through differential impact within and between economic sectors or upon segments of the working class in each country.[22] The global financial crisis was remarkable across a number of these dimensions. First, the crisis was not initiated by a speculative frenzy based on primary commodities (e.g. oil), luxury goods (tulips), or the expectation of profits from entirely new fields of investment (South Sea or dotcom). Instead, it was a new type of crisis, sparked by the issuing of mortgages to the poorest households in the US, subsequently re-packaged into new types of financial assets, traded through innovative channels that did not even exist a few years earlier.

Second, nobody could blame the poor for the speculative boom or the crash and its aftermath. Unlike other instances of economic malfunction, 'excessive' wages and benefits have nowhere been targeted as causal, along the lines of neoclassical, Keynesian, or even radical 'profit squeeze' views. In the past, these have helped to legitimize the shift of the burden of adjustment onto working people and the poor. This time, since the working class remains relatively disorganized and non-combative and thus blameless, mainstream explanations for the crisis had to be located in inter-capitalist relations in general, and financialization in particular. However, even if finance and its excesses were guilty, finance had to be rescued to prevent an even worse impact upon the rest of us, whose hardening times for years to come are thereby justified. While this still is presented as being essential to stabilize the public balance sheet in the wake of the extraordinary expenditures in the previous period, in reality 'fiscal austerity' has served to advance the neoliberal agenda on a wider front through higher taxes, lower transfers, and the expanded commodification of social reproduction. These policies might be dubbed 'socialism for the bankers and capitalism for everyone else', justified by ideological acrobatics claiming that heavy state intervention is essential to protect the free market, but must be paid for through austerity policies.[23]

Third, the sheer size and pervasiveness of the global crisis initially overwhelmed even the unprecedented levels and forms of (national and international) state intervention seeking to temper its worst effects. Those limitations of macroeconomic policy and international co-operation reflected the complexity of the asset structures and the intermingling of financial institutions built under financialization, creating significant difficulties in selecting what to target for rescue – by what criteria, to what end, how, for how long, and at what cost, and with what supplementary policies at the domestic and interstate levels.

Fourth, the locus of the crisis and its reverberations shifted over time. At first, the crisis was concentrated on advanced economies, with the US at the forefront, leading to home repossessions and rapidly climbing unemployment. Then its epicentre shifted to the eurozone periphery, with the Greek drama as its most powerful symbol. Finally, the crisis engulfed the middle-income countries, eroding fragile governments and economic strategies, with Argentina and Brazil as the clearest examples.

This interpretation of the crisis contrasts with other critical interpretations of neoliberalism focusing on its limitations and contradictions, especially the decline of real investment because of the comparatively easy returns promised by financial speculation, the erosion of effective demand due to low wages and the rising burden of household debt, or the adverse implications of deindustrialization because of the restructuring of global manufacturing capacity and its relocation to East Asia in general and China in particular. While undeniable, these processes neither directly *caused* the crisis and the social forms it took, nor did they directly imply that neoliberalism is weak, exhausted, or already being replaced by another system of accumulation. Quite the contrary: the crisis was symptomatic of the *strengths* of neoliberalism, especially the centrality of finance for economic and social reproduction, while the measures adopted in its wake were symptomatic of the hegemony of neoliberalism ideologically and policy-wise.

Even though the policies adopted after the crisis achieved the immediate goal of restoring the profitability of global finance, the causes of the cataclysm have remained unaddressed, and the policies deployed to contain it have created new and shifting vulnerabilities. For example, zero interest rates, the rescue policies, and QE were supposed to help reduce systemic (financial) risks. Instead, they are conducive to speculative bubbles that have become especially unstable in the Global South. Between the start of the crisis and 2015, the total debt of financial corporations increased by US$12 trillion, public sector debt increased by US$25 trillion (with more than US$20 trillion in eight OECD countries), and the liabilities of households rose by US$7 trillion.[24] Further, virtually all the gains achieved in the current recovery were captured by the top income strata. In the 2009–13 recovery in the US, *all* the income growth went to the top 10 per cent of families, while the income of the bottom 90 per cent fell.[25] Neoliberalism embodies strong tendencies towards the concentration of income when the economy grows, when it contracts, *and* when it recovers, given its tutelage by financial capital.

In contrast to those at the top who benefit through the policies associated with neoliberalism as well as those implemented in response to the global crisis, the fate of the majority has been subjected to volatile and variegated vulnerabilities[26] – as employment, wages, and economic and social reproduction more generally come under the direct and indirect sway of financialized neoliberalism. The politics of neoliberalism, and its unfolding crisis, are founded upon such vulnerabilities, and responses to them.

In addition to the economic processes outlined above, it is clear that, as both cause and effect, there is a wide variety of political paths of transition to neoliberalism. They range across its rollout by constitutional means (in most advanced economies), imposition by dictatorships (in several Latin American and sub-Saharan African countries), to coeval transitions to neoliberalism and bourgeois democracy (in Brazil, South Africa, South Korea and in Eastern Europe). Nonetheless, a 'typical' democratic political form of neoliberalism spread in the 1990s. Those neoliberal democracies were necessarily different from the political forms associated with the 'core' countries in the 'old' or 'classic' liberal period before World War I, or the social-democratic 'compromise' in place after World War II.

The limitations and contradictions of neoliberal democracy can be located at three levels. First, neoliberal democracies are heavily circumscribed, since they include an institutional apparatus designed to insulate decisions about economic policy from the 'interference' of the majority. In these regimes, the substantive choices about social provision, the composition of output, the structure of employment and the distribution of income are transferred to presumably 'technical' institutions, including ministries of finance dominated by neoliberal policymakers; so-called 'independent' central banks captured by finance and mandated to deliver legally-binding inflation targets (and rescue feckless financial institutions); Treasury departments constrained by maximum fiscal deficits (except when the provision of unlimited resources to finance becomes imperative); floating exchange rates that constrain governments to abide by the whims of market traders; privatized utility companies owned by transnationalized hedge funds; regulatory agencies captured by the conglomerates nominally under their authority, as well as business associations, international organizations, the European Commission, the US Treasury and State Departments, and their local enforcers. At a further remove, policy is both imposed and monitored by transnational financial institutions, the stock market, and the media, whose self-interested interventions can shift asset values in dramatic ways. Their authority is underpinned by a judicial system tasked with enforcing the laws imposed by neoliberalism itself. In this way, neoliberalism imposes discipline upon key social agents, with the workers at the forefront, but these institutional structures also discipline capital, the state, and even finance itself, with a growing intolerance of dissent. In reshaping the institutional structure of the economy, neoliberalism has also spawned specific forms of corruption and corresponding revolving doors between business, politics, civil service, the media, and unelected advisors.[27] These processes reinforce authoritarian tendencies and practices that recently have served to facilitate the accession of 'mavericks' to power, as well as spawned exceptional state structures that operate with limited checks and balances.[28]

These structures not only transferred to finance allocative functions previously performed by the Keynesian state, they also locked in neoliberalism institutionally. It became virtually impossible to shift the system of accumulation from within, following the political rules that neoliberalism had introduced. The outcome was the shrinkage of the policy space available to the institutions of nominally democratic states, in tandem with the contraction of space for legitimate opposition. Increasingly, the consolidation of neoliberalism reduced 'normal politics' to the competition between shades of orthodoxy in a circumscribed political market: New Labour versus moderate Tories in the UK; Clinton Democrats versus establishment Republicans in the US; centre-left versus centre-right in Canada, France, Germany and Italy, and so on, with the limits of their friendly duel being policed by an aggressive right-wing media.

These reforms were not simply imposed by narrow (financial) elites aiming to control the state for their own selfish interests. The growing impermeability and depoliticization of the economic domain, and the simultaneous concentration of economic and political power under neoliberalism, spring from the material structures of the system of accumulation and the imperative to secure international competitiveness according to the parameters set by global finance and the US-led 'international community'. The transnational integration of production and finance directly constrains policy space; globalized production and consumption require international legal and policy harmony through continual negotiations, policy conditionalities, and overlapping treaties, which drastically reduce the scope for variety in the modalities of social reproduction. And the reconstruction of US-led imperialism since the Vietnam War has been associated with a drive to impose neoliberal economic transitions alongside political transitions to 'democracy', leveraged by means of financial, commercial, and military pressures.

In neoliberal states, social forces as well as governments have, then, tended to lose the capacity to shape policy within their own borders, reducing the scope for the political system to find negotiated solutions to problems. The degradation of democracy undermines neoliberal claims to defend 'freedom of choice' and secure space for the 'realization of individual ambitions', and dents the legitimacy of neoliberal states and political systems. Their declining capacity to allow for, let alone address, conflicting demands constructively shows that, while they remain formally inclusionary, neoliberal democracies are exclusionary at the level of decision-making around neoliberalized daily lives – and even the illusion of participation has been eroded.

The second limitation of democracy derives from the fact that neoliberalism has been associated with economic restructuring, including of systems of production across labour processes, technologies, inputs and outputs, with implications for the modalities of international specialization, patterns of employment and consumption, and forms of social reproduction and community life. These processes have created a large array of economic 'losers', centred on the working class.

Under neoliberalism, the workers have tended to become increasingly divided, disorganized, disempowered, and deskilled, falling even further behind capital in political influence. Millions of skilled jobs have been eliminated, especially in the advanced capitalist economies (AEs), as entire professions have either vanished or were exported to cheaper shores. Employment opportunities in the public sector have languished because of privatization and 'retrenching', job stability has declined, and pay and conditions have tended to deteriorate. Severe losses have ensued for informal workers, whose prospects of stable employment have shrunk, and for skilled workers, who fear the export of their jobs while simultaneously bearing the stresses of overwork, as their employment has become increasingly precarious even in formal workplaces. Analogous pressures are felt by an indebted, impoverished, anxious, endangered, and increasingly vulnerable middle class. Across the wealthiest countries in the world, the remnants of this 'privileged' social strata previously characterized by rising real incomes, bewail their inability to bequeath similar improved material prospects to their offspring.

While the economic changes imposed by neoliberalism have created large numbers of 'losers', the transformation of social structures, institutions, and the law have tended to evacuate the political sphere, rendering the losers increasingly unable to resist against neoliberalism, or even to conceptualize alternatives. These processes help to explain the decline of left parties, their supporting organizations, trade unions, and most other forms of collective representation. While these outcomes can be advantageous for the consolidation of neoliberalism in the short term, they have also fostered mass disengagement from constitutional politics, created powerful tendencies towards apathy and anomie, and undermined the ideological hegemony and political legitimacy of neoliberalism.[29] With traditional parties, leaders, and organizations distrusted, avenues for effective dissent are minimal.

The third limitation of neoliberal democracy today is that the economic, political, ideological and institutional hegemony of neoliberalism has been accompanied by a dramatic narrowing of political ambition and scope for collective action to change society, because of two converging processes. One is the loss of sources of inspiration for policy alternatives after the collapse of national liberation movements and governments in the South, the end of the Soviet Union, the economic transformations in China, and the collapse of revolutionary left parties in most countries. The other is systematic escalation in the policing of dissent, across individual privacy, civil liberties, and collective action, which became especially prominent after 9/11. Consequently, although neoliberal ideology ostensibly promotes the values of 'democracy' and 'freedom' against its purported interventionist and repressive enemies, neoliberal political systems have enforced the logic of TINA (There Is No Alternative), regardless of its severely adverse impact upon the life prospects of the majority, whose concerns are thereby devalued.

The evacuation of neoliberal democracy tends to be perceived by the 'losers' through the lens of 'corruption' (of, and by, poorly specified 'elites') and 'undue privilege' (afforded to the 'undeserving poor', a multiplicity of self-identified minorities, aliens, and foreign countries). While these groups are falsely taken to be favoured by public policy, state institutions can be construed as being hostile to the 'morally upright' losers who, increasingly, find it hard to make ends meet. Today, everything seems to be upside down, in contrast with the misty olden days when people of good character, strong discipline, and sharing 'our' common values – typically males with the right ethnic background – could count on steady employment, rising incomes, promotion prospects, and secure pensions.

Because of the fragmentation of society and the ideological hegemony of neoliberalism, the demands of the 'losers' tend to be framed in general terms and grounded on simplistic discourses drawing upon 'common sense' and a universalist (classless) ethics founded on identity (that is, demanding acceptance within the system of accumulation), meritocracy, and revulsion at corruption (aiming to reform the system, since replacing it seems impossible). This approach to politics can lead to demands for the restoration of earlier privileges, veiled by a classless discourse centred on 'moral values', 'justice', a 'level-playing field', the assertion of 'traditional rights', demands for 'respect', and calls for 'honesty' in public life. *Nationalism* – grounded on presumably shared values – and *racism* – embedded in the notion of a shared background – offer readily available umbrellas to articulate these narratives.

The losers in contemporary neoliberalism are, then, driven to frame their disappointments, resentments, fears, and hopes through the prism of an ethical conflict between insiders and outsiders in a moral universe in which there is no generalized exploitation within the socio-economic system. Instead, members of 'our' group are surrounded by predatory non-members and, within the group, 'honest' individuals are besieged by dishonest characters: 'our' values of honesty and hard work are being undermined by politicians stealing 'our' money, immigrants crowding 'us' out of 'our' houses and hospitals, and distant countries stealing 'our' jobs – without this leading for a moment to the questioning of the processes and injuries of capitalism and imperialism.

These destructive tendencies have been intensified by the fiscal austerity imposed in the wake of the great financial crisis, the cumulative effects of low economic growth, and the growing awareness of the inequities of neoliberalism. The inability of neoliberal states to address those concerns has contributed to the perception of a loss of efficacy and legitimacy for policies, practices, parties, and leaderships that were previously unassailable. In the meantime, resentments old and new have fuelled mutually incompatible demands for 'change', destabilizing the neoliberal democracies built between the early 1980s and the mid-2000s. However, because of the social, institutional and political changes imposed by neoliberalism itself, the resumption of mass political engagement has fuelled a narrative that solutions must lie either outside conventional politics or based in intransigent campaigns (because it is necessary to push hard to elicit responses from a rigid system). Such a political scene also leads to the projection of social agency onto individual 'leaders', as the structures supporting collective action have been disabled. Political activity along these lines can have destabilizing – but not transformative – impacts on the system of accumulation. In this sense, the hegemony of neoliberalism (and the economic and political degradation of the working classes) has structurally destabilized neoliberal democracy, and severely limited the scope for alternatives.

The *political paradox of neoliberalism* concerns the disintegration of neoliberal democracy under the weight of its own internal contradictions. The political hegemony of neoliberalism is predicated on the discourse of the reduction of the economic role of the state while, in reality, it facilitates financialized modalities of social reproduction and an individualistic subjectivity, which are realized *through* the state. Neoliberalism reduces the spaces for political negotiation and collective initiative, so that self-serving agents are governed by neoliberal policy rules. The consolidation of this perverse political order simultaneously erodes its legitimacy, while the stresses of the global crisis undermines the ideological hegemony of neoliberalism.

These circumstances have fostered the rise of anti-systemic forces dominated by the far right, and polarized by authoritarian nationalist leaders vowing to confront the neoliberal state, finance, globalization, the elites, foreigners, and so on in order to garner the support of the losers, while simultaneously enforcing policies intensifying neoliberalism. The political crisis of neoliberalism is, then, about much more than Donald Trump (who received fewer votes than Hillary Clinton), Brexit (that won at the margin, and even though there was no possibility of an agreement about what the vote was *for*), or the myriad of authoritarian neoliberal leaders emerging elsewhere: this is a systemic crisis of great import for the system of accumulation.

THE RISE OF AUTHORITARIAN NEOLIBERALISM

The disintegration of neoliberal democracy became evident when elected governments were excluded from office and replaced by so-called non-party technocrats (in reality, experienced political operators committed to the status quo) in the Eurozone periphery (as in Greece and Italy).[30] Subsequently, the Syriza administration in Greece, elected for its advocacy of unconventional strategies, was forced to abandon them. The malaise eventually reached the 'core' NATO countries when Brexit won in the UK and Donald Trump was elected in the US. In France, Marine Le Pen of the Front National reached the second round of the Presidential elections, which were won by Emmanuel Macron, an unconventional politician leading a new party firmly aligned with neoliberalism. Nativist populism grows in Austria, Switzerland, and Scandinavia. Across the Eastern periphery of the EU, far-right politicians thrive on the basis of startlingly exclusionary and xenophobic programmes. Meanwhile, across the global periphery, authoritarian leaders and movements have won elections by fair means or foul (Argentina, Hungary, India, Russia, Turkey), while dissenting governments were more or less forcefully discarded (Brazil, Egypt, Honduras, Paraguay, and Thailand, with escalating pressures on Nicaragua and Venezuela). The policies pursued by these new administrations have converged around more overtly repressive and racist forms of neoliberalism, justified by unwieldy combinations of 'national' values and the imperatives of austerity.

In Europe, many traditional parties, especially the social democratic, have split, shrunk or even imploded – as exemplified by PASOK in Greece (with 'Pasokification' even becoming a new term of political discourse). Mainstream conservative parties have shown greater resilience, partly because they are more closely identified with the dominant ideology, and partly because the right is used to deploying misleading programmes and nationalist slogans to remain in power. However, even these parties have been compelled to navigate increasingly strident nationalist and exclusionary programmes as a new generation of nationalist parties and neo-fascist movements threatens their core vote. Given the electoral collapse of the radical left over the previous decades, there has been an unambiguous shift of the political spectrum towards the right.

The rise of a specifically authoritarian form of neoliberalism is neither a transitory political anomaly which, after inevitable failure, will soon lead to the restoration of centre-right 'normal' neoliberal politics, nor a marker of the 'end of neoliberalism'.[31] Instead, the rise of authoritarian neoliberal leaders is a symptom of the decomposition of neoliberal democracy, an indirect consequence of the crisis of 'restructured' economies, popular alienation from the political system and institutions of representation, and the mobilization of mass discontent by the far right. These are all signs of the emergence and potential consolidation of *new* hegemonic blocs under the leadership of the far right within global neoliberalism.

Such an emerging bloc is grounded on the vulnerability of the 'losers' to capture by the far right, because of the erosion of a sense of collectivity and potential agency based on shared material circumstances, and a degradation of working-class culture and organized political capacities.[32] Consequently, the very material feelings of social vulnerability of the 'losers', and their anger at the dysfunctionality of the political system, is mobilized by politicians, right-wing forces, and the media against social groups (immigrants, minorities) at the very bottom of society for the daily social anxieties inflicted. Crises of health care, education, or housing provision must be the fault of people even poorer than us, who are 'taking' what rightly is 'ours'. And larger crises of deindustrialization, unemployment, or deskilling, must be the fault of countries even poorer than 'us'.

These political views are necessarily destructive of progressive forms of collective identity. They are partly (if often perversely) tempered by the convergence of interests around the rejection of corruption (that offers the only legitimate form of political opposition within neoliberalism), and in support of nationalism (the only permissible form of collective identity under neoliberalism, although it all too easily slides into racism).

While corruption is perceived to undermine the economic system from above, the feckless poor and immigrants corrode it from below, and foreign countries attack it from outside. As neoliberalism's systemic shortcomings are displaced towards (individual and country-level) dishonesty, 'cheating', and the like, the failings of the system of accumulation are effectively concealed. Nationalism offers 'the people' a way to respond to these injuries, reaffirming their 'innate' virtues and spirit of cohesion. These binaries are being used to support reactionary programmes justified by appeals to common sense, and fronted by supposedly 'strong' leaders who can talk 'honestly', represent 'the people', and 'get things done' by force of will, often allegedly demonstrated by recourse to claims of business acumen, with seamless ideological shifts between machismo and the making of the new man or even woman. Personal strength of character is perceived to be both essential and sufficient to bulldoze the entrenched interests, corrupt politicians, selfish civil servants, and captured institutions that undermine 'our' nation and harm 'our' people.

The political autonomy and stature enjoyed by authoritarian neoliberal leaders has only superficial similarity with earlier political phenomena: their actions are not championing transformative economic, social, and political agendas aiming to break with the ancient order and stabilize a more advanced form of capitalism, nor do they derive their power from a temporary convergence of interests of antagonistic classes. Instead, they have made their way into political power by clever ploys, expensive advertising, planned agitation, and brute force, with the aim of enforcing a radical neoliberal programme grounded in a conservative politics willing to use a strong state to steamroll opposition. This is not mere 'populism', or Bonapartism under neoliberal conditions. It is, rather, the politics of demagogues, con men, and illusionists who have risen through the opportunistic exploitation of country-specific fractures in the neoliberal order. To their right stand even more dangerous movements claiming to represent the 'losers' in more belligerent and even violent ways. The transformation of authoritarian neoliberalism into a material force is the reflex of the increasingly desperate search by the losers for ways to short-circuit a political system that is unquestionably jammed, and to secure gains for people who have grown tired of feeling unfairly disadvantaged and losing out to undeserving 'others'.

The *paradox of authoritarian neoliberalism* is that it fosters the personalization of politics through the emergence of 'spectacular' leaders untethered by 'stabilizing' intermediary institutions (such as party structures, trade unions, social movements, and the law), who are strongly committed to both neoliberalism and the expansion of their own self-referential power, not least through the promotion of socio-economic agendas that harm their own political base. In government, these leaders invariably promote a radical version of neoliberalism while attacking all forms of opposition, promoting greater, and unchecked, globalization and financialization, even if indirectly, and rendering even more power to the fractions of the neoliberal elite who already support them. Society is further divided, wages decline, taxes become even more regressive, social protections are eroded, economies become more unbalanced, and poverty grows. Mass frustration intensifies, feeding further anxiety and discontent. It follows that authoritarian neoliberalism is intrinsically unstable and offers greater prominence and scope to the far right. In doing so, and as the economics and politics of neoliberalism are corroded from within, modern forms of fascism gain a fertile political terrain in which they can openly operate and prosper.[33]

CONCLUSION

Neoliberalism is trapped, we have argued, within its three paradoxes. The *economic paradox* is that the creation of favourable conditions for accumulation has been associated with a striking inability to capitalize on them. The *political paradox* is that the consolidation of neoliberal democracy undermines the hegemonic political order and the ideology that legitimated it, leading to the rise of anti-systemic forces dominated by 'spectacular' leaders, the rightward shift of the entire political spectrum and the emboldening of the far right. The *paradox of authoritarian neoliberalism* is that, since the emerging political leaders are equally – if uneasily – committed both to an extreme form of neoliberalism and the consolidation of their own power, their governments' radical version of neoliberalism enforces an economic programme that harms their own mass base of support.

Neoliberalism as a policy regime and form of social rule has been unable to create economic conditions for shared prosperity and has instead fostered new social instabilities and space for new administrative and explicitly political forms of authoritarianism to emerge. As these authoritarian political forms cannot deliver stability, they provide a potential conduit for the consolidation of new forms of fascism, which are bound to prosper as neoliberal economies face continuing volatility and mounting political instability. *In the absence of a strong political left*, neoliberalism is likely to enter a prolonged period of crisis politics: increasingly anti-trade in the epoch of globalization; pro-finance when the damages wrought by financialization are widely recognized; anti-immigrant in an age of unprecedented human movement; nationalist when international policy co-ordination is centrally important for capital accumulation, and so on. Yet, none of these conflicts and contradictions will spontaneously lead neoliberalism to be supplanted by a more progressive system of accumulation.

Authoritarian neoliberalism is, then, an original phenomenon. It has not emerged to shield capitalism against the insurgency of the left (as was the case amidst the initial emergence of neoliberalism in the 1970s) or in a period of much lower international integration of production (as was the case with fascism in the 1930s). The new form of authoritarianism is typically *neoliberal*: it expresses the (co-option of the) disorganized fury of the 'losers' under neoliberalism, in circumstances of an evacuated democracy, and is posited against a state apparatus that has lost legitimacy as the potential bearer of economic improvements and social cohesion. In the short term, the rise of authoritarian neoliberalism is due to the destabilization of economies, societies, and political systems – first by the global financial crisis and then by its strategy of containment through the intensification of financialization. In the longer term, it derives from the contradictions in the restructuring of production, social reproduction and structures of representation under neoliberalism. Instead of confronting strong systemic rivals both at home and abroad, neoliberal authoritarianism focuses on attacking the weak: immigrants, refugees, the 'undeserving poor', women, and so on, under the guise of addressing corruption or undue privilege.

In these circumstances, how best to address the regressive features, instabilities and limitations of neoliberalism? In certain sectors of the left, there remains the illusion that a return to Keynesianism can restore more favourable economic and social conditions today. Even though higher taxes, controls on trade, domestic finance, and capital flows, expanded social provision and the fine-tuning of aggregate demand can help to address competing macroeconomic goals and promote short-term improvements in economic performance and social welfare, these policies would have only limited bearing on the long-term performance and underlying dynamics of the global economy. They would also bypass completely the political limitations of neoliberalism. Consequently, even if social democratic policy aspirations were achievable today, they would remain hostages to the competitive imperatives conditioned by neoliberalism.

Any alternative programme must draw upon, first, traditional left concerns with equality, improved distributional outcomes, and the promotion of collectivity in the workplace and in society more generally. Second, it must involve the recognition that neoliberalism has repeatedly demonstrated its resilience both in practice and in the realm of ideas, and that overcoming it is an ambitious task that includes, but also transcends, conventional electoral strategies – at least to the end of securing changes in social, industrial, financial, or monetary policies. Third, and most important, in order to transcend neoliberalism it is necessary to recompose the working class politically. All three of these imperatives can be integrated, and widely different struggles can converge, around the *expansion and radicalization of political and economic democracy*. This can be rendered operational through an immediate programme of decommodification and definancialization of social reproduction (focusing on health, transport, housing, and so on), and advancing compelling economic, political and ideological cases for addressing environmental, industrial, and energy policies. Even neoliberal policymaking cannot avoid interventions into these sectors. The challenge will be to find cracks and contradictions within the state for alternative policies and forms of mobilization and policymaking that challenge the power of finance and the logic of enforcing corporate control over property and economic decision-making.

The political room for advancing such an anti-neoliberal programme was earlier glimpsed in Brazil and Greece, despite the stunning defeats suffered there. It was more recently rendered visible again through the Sanders campaign in the US and the gains made by the Labour Party in Britain under the leadership of Jeremy Corbyn. In fact, neoliberalism has never been so unstable, and its hegemony never so brittle. The mainstream economics that used to inspire neoliberal policymakers has been in turmoil for a decade, failing to anticipate the global financial crisis or deal with its long-term implications. The neoliberal orthodoxy is wholly unequipped, in practice even more than in theory, to address the political crisis of democracy. The economic and political crises in neoliberalism are, then, historically unique circumstances with grave implications for the left – but also a singular opportunity for organizational renewal, rekindling political ambition and the influence of socialist ideas.

NOTES

1   For neoliberal authoritarianism see: John Weeks, 'Free Markets & the Decline of Democracy', *Prime*, 4 February 2018, available at www.primeeconomics.org; for authoritarian neoliberalism see: Cemal Burak Tansel, ed., *States of Discipline: Authoritarian Neoliberalism and the Contested Reproduction of Capitalist Order*, London: Rowman & Littlefield, 2017.

2   This is not to suggest that authoritarianism is specific to the current phase of neoliberalism. Indeed, we have Stuart Hall to thank for the term authoritarian populism to characterize the rise of Thatcherism (and neoliberalism in its earliest of phases), and there is the example of fascism in the interwar period and beyond. Significantly, Stuart Hall reserved the term for Thatcherism as opposed to being of general applicability – see his 'Authoritarian Populism: A Reply to Jessop et al.', *New Left Review*, I/151(May-June), 1985. For the broad use of this term in the contemporary context, see Lizzie Dearden, "Authoritarian populism' Behind Donald Trump's Victory and Brexit

Becoming Driving Force in European Politics', *The Independent*, 21 November 2016; and Priya Chacko and Kanishka Jayasuriya, 'Trump, the Authoritarian Populist Revolt and the Future of the Rules-Based Order in Asia', *Australian Journal of International Affairs*, 71(2), 2017.

3   See, for example: Leo Panitch, Sam Gindin, and Greg Albo, *In and Out of Crisis: The Global Financial Meltdown and Left Alternatives*, Oakland: PM Press, 2010; Philip Mirowski, *Never Let a Serious Crisis Go to Waste: How Neoliberalism Survived the Financial Meltdown*, London: Verso, 2013; Trevor Evans, 'The Crisis of Finance-Led Capitalism in the United States of America', Working Paper No. 51, Institute for International Political Economy Berlin, 2015; Alfredo Saad-Filho, 'Marxian and Keynesian Critiques of Neoliberalism', in Leo Panitch and Colin Leys, eds, *Socialist Register 2008: Global Flashpoints*, London: Merlin, 2007; and Alfredo Saad-Filho, 'Crisis *in* Neoliberalism or Crisis *of* Neoliberalism?', in Leo Panitch and Greg Albo, eds, *Socialist Register 2011: The Crisis This Time*, London: Merlin, 2010.

4   Andrew Clark and Jill Treanor, 'Greenspan – I Was Wrong About the Economy. Sort Of', *The Guardian*, 24 October 2008.

5   Coen Teulings and Richard Baldwin, eds, *Secular Stagnation: Facts, Causes and Cures*, London: Centre for Economic Policy Research, 2014; Barry Eichengreen,'Secular Stagnation: The Long View', *American Economic Review*, 105(5), 2015; Robert J. Gordon, 'Secular Stagnation: A Supply-Side View', *American Economic Review*, 105(5), 2015; Lawrence H. Summers, 'Demand Side Secular Stagnation', *American Economic Review*, 105 (5), 2015; Lawrence H. Summers, 'The Age of Secular Stagnation: What It Is and What to Do About It', *Foreign Affairs*, 95(2), 2016. For an account of the origins of the concept in heterodox economics, compare with Roger Backhouse and Mauro Boianovsky, 'Secular Stagnation: The History of a Macroeconomic Heresy', *European Journal of the History of Economic Thought*, 23(6), 2016.

6   For policy responses that were initially mildly reflationary and welfarist, see: Isabel Ortiz and Matthew Cummins, 'The Age of Austerity: A Review of Public Expenditures and Adjustment Measures in 181 Countries', Initiative for Policy Dialogue and the South Centre, Working Paper, March 2013, available at: policydialogue.org,.

7   This argument was originally advanced in Saad-Filho, 'Crisis in Neoliberalism or Crisis of Neoliberalism?'.

8   Alison J. Ayers and Alfredo Saad-Filho, 'Democracy Against Neoliberalism: Paradoxes, Limitations, Transcendence', *Critical Sociology*, 41(4-5), 2015; Atilio Borón, 'The Truth About Capitalist Democracy', in Leo Panitch and Colin Leys, eds, *Socialist Register 2006: Telling the Truth*, London: Merlin, 2005; Colin Leys, *Total Capitalism: Market Politics, Market State*, London: Merlin Press, 2008; Peter Mair, *Ruling the Void: The Hollowing Out of Western Democracy*, London: Verso, 2009.

9   This is to be contrasted with political democracy as the 'best fit' for the pre-crisis phase of neoliberalism, see Ayers and Saad-Filho, 'Democracy Against Neoliberalism'.

10 Pierre Dardot and Christian Laval, *The New Way of the World: On Neoliberal Society*, London: Verso, 2013, p.14.

11 See, for example: Sam Ashman and Ben Fine, 'Neo-Liberalism, Varieties of Capitalism, and the Shifting Contours of South Africa's Financial System', *Transformation,* 81/82, 2013; Ben Fine, 'Financialisation From a Marxist Perspective', *International Journal of Political Economy*, 42(4), 2013-14; Ben Fine and Alfredo Saad-Filho, 'Thirteen Things You Need to Know About Neoliberalism', *Critical Sociology*, 43(4-5), 2016; Ben Fine

and Alfredo Saad-Filho, 'Marx 200: The Abiding Relevance of the Labour Theory of Value', *Review of Political Economy*, 2018; Saad-Filho, 'Crisis *in* Neoliberalism or Crisis *of* Neoliberalism?'; and Alfredo Saad-Filho and Deborah Johnston, eds, *Neoliberalism: A Critical Reader*, London: Pluto Press, 2005.

12   Ashman and Fine, 'Neo-Liberalism, Varieties of Capitalism', pp.156-57; see also Brett Christophers and Ben Fine, 'The Value of Financialization and the Financialization of Value', in P. Mader, D. Mertens and N. van der Zwan, eds, *International Handbook of Financialization*, London: Routledge, 2019 (forthcoming).

13   For a historical overview see: Peter Gowan, *The Global Gamble: Washington's Faustian Bid for World Dominance*, London: Verso, 1999; Leo Panitch and Sam Gindin, *The Making of Global Capitalism: The Political Economy of American Empire*, London: Verso, 2012; Chris Rude, 'The Role of Financial Discipline in Imperial Strategy', in Leo Panitch and Colin Leys, eds, *Socialist Register 2005: The Empire Reloaded*, London: Merlin, 2004; and Alfredo Saad-Filho, 'Monetary Policy in the Neoliberal Transition: A Political Economy Review of Keynesianism, Monetarism and Inflation Targeting', in R. Albritton, R. Jessop, and R. Westra, eds, *Political Economy and Global Capitalism*, London: Anthem Press, 2007.

14   Martin Wolf, 'Cutting Back Financial Capitalism Is America's Big Test', *Financial Times*, 15 April 2009.

15   Matthew C. Klein, 'Crush the Financial Sector, End the Great Stagnation?', *Financial Times*, 16 February 2015.

16   See, for example, Pavlina R. Tcherneva, 'When a Rising Tide Sinks Most Boats: Trends in U.S. Income Inequality', Policy Note 2015/4, Levy Economics Institute, 2015.

17   Ben Fine and Alfredo Saad Filho, 'Politics of Neoliberal Development: Washington Consensus and Post-Washington Consensus', in H. Webber, ed., *The Politics of Development: A Survey*, London, Routledge, 2014.

18   Drawing upon the experience of Labour Governments from the 1980s in Australia (and that in the UK in the 1970s), it can be observed that the first phase of neoliberalism does not necessarily involve right-wing assaults; it can be promoted by presumably left-of-centre administrations, even incorporating the complicity of the labour movement (see: Elizabeth Humphrys and Damien Cahill, 'How Labour Made Neoliberalism', *Critical Sociology*, 43(4-5), 2017; Damien Cahill and Martijn Konings, *Neoliberalism*, Oxford: Polity Press, 2017. For similar analyses of the French Socialist Government in the early 1980s, see also: Rawi Abdelal, *Capital Rules: The Construction of Global Finance*, Cambridge: Harvard University Press, 2007; and Serge Halimi, *Quand la gauche essayait. Les leçons du pouvoir (1924, 1936, 1944, 1981)*, Marseille: Agone, 2018).

19   Philip Mirowski, *Never Let a Serious Crisis Go to Waste: How Neoliberalism Survived the Financial Meltdown*, London: Verso, 2013. Martijn Konings, 'From Hayek to Trump: The Logic of Neoliberal Democracy', in Leo Panitch and Greg Albo, eds, *Socialist Register 2018: Rethinking Democracy*, London: Merlin Press, 2017.

20   Jo Littler, *Against Meritocracy: Culture, Power and Myths of Mobility*, London: Routledge, 2017.

21   By way of illustration, consider the travails of British Rail which, following privatization, has failed continually under private hands, only to be selectively renationalized and reprivatized like a merry-go-round. The two enduring features that underpin this sorry tale, apart from deficiencies in passenger service and safety, have been downward

pressure on the workforce and a grim determination to ensure the profitability of private contractors underpinned by dependence on private finance. In short, the role of the state is not removed, but it shifts from public to private provision and, simultaneously, to public provision of financialized profits. See Andrew Bowman, et al., *The Great Train Robbery: Rail Privatisation And After,* Manchester: CRESC Public Interest Report, 2013, and Tom Haines-Doran, 'Derailing Neoliberalism', *Jacobin,* 19 October 2016. A little more caution has been exercised in relation to British banks nationalized in the wake of the GFC; they cannot be allowed to fail as opposed to trains running on time. For the other key services, see Kate Bayliss, Ben Fine, Mary Robertson, and Alfredo Saad-Filho, *Financialised Neoliberalism and the Political Economy of Social Provision in the UK,* Aldershot: Edward Elgar (forthcoming).

22 See Alfredo Saad-Filho and Ben Fine, *Marx's 'Capital',* 6th edition, London: Pluto Press, ch. 15.

23 'In the short term defending capitalism means, paradoxically, state intervention. There is a justifiable sense of outrage among voters and business people (and indeed economic liberals) that $2.5 trillion of taxpayers' money now has to be spent on a highly rewarded industry. But the global bail-out is pragmatic, not ideological. When François Mitterrand nationalised France's banks in 1981 he did so because he thought the state would run them better. This time governments are buying banks (or shares in them) because they believe, rightly, that public capital is needed to keep credit flowing', 'Capitalism at Bay', *The Economist,* 16 October 2008.

24 Richard Dobbs, Susan Lund, Jonathan Woetzel, and Mina Mutafchieva, *Debt and (Not Much) Deleveraging,* McKinsey Global Institute Report, February 2015, available at: www.mckinsey.com.

25 Tcherneva, 'When a Rising Tide Sinks Most Boats', p. 3, figure 4.

26 Ben Fine, 'A Note Towards an Approach Towards Social Reproduction', available at: http://iippe.org/wp-content/uploads/2017/01/sroverviewben.pdf.

27 David Whyte, ed., *How Corrupt is Britain?*, London: Pluto Press, 2015; Colin Crouch, *The Knowledge Corrupters: Hidden Consequences of the Financial Takeover of Public Life,* Cambridge: Polity Press, 2016.

28 With the transition from Mbeki to Zuma in South Africa a telling example, see Robert van Niekerk and and Ben Fine, 'Conclusion: Harold Wolpe, Towards the Politics of Liberation in a Democratic South Africa', in J. Reynolds, R. van Niekerk, and B. Fine, eds, *Race, Class and the Post-Apartheid Democratic State,* Durban: UKZN Press, 2019.

29 Ayers and Saad-Filho, 'Democracy against Neoliberalism'.

30 Peter Nedergaard and Holly Snaith, ''As I Drifted on a River I Could Not Control': The Unintended Ordoliberal Consequences of the Eurozone Crisis', *Journal of Common Market Studies,* 53(5), 2015; Magnus Ryner, 'Europe's Ordoliberal Iron Cage: Critical Political Economy, the Euro Area Crisis and its Management', *Journal of European Public Policy,* 22(2), 2015; Werner Bonefeld, *The Strong State and the Free Economy,* London: Rowman & Littlefield International, 2017.

31 See, for example, Cornel West, 'Goodbye, American Neoliberalism: A New Era Is Here', *The Guardian,* 17 November 2016.

32 A parallel process is described by Karl Marx in the *Eighteenth Brumaire of Louis Bonaparte,* 1852.

33 'Neoliberalism ... has helped create the conditions for the re-emergence of the far-right whilst, at the same time, the far-right has focused on attacking what it sees as the

symptoms of neoliberalism through racializing its social, political and economic effects … It is not then that neoliberalism *causes* racism … in the sense that racism is an organic dimension of it, but rather that neoliberalism is grounded on a *collective socio-economic insecurity* that helps facilitate a revival of pre-existing racialized imaginaries of solidarity', Neil Davidson and Richard Saull, 'Neoliberalism and the Far-Right: A Contradictory Embrace', *Critical Sociology*, 43(4-5), 2017, pp. 715-16. See also Leo Panitch and Greg Albo, eds, *Socialist Register 2016: The Politics of the Right*, London: Merlin, 2015.

HUMANITARIAN INTERVENTION TODAY

UMUT ÖZSU

In the 2004 *Socialist Register*, which appeared less than a year after the Second Gulf War commenced, Amy Bartholomew and Jennifer Breakspear published an essay on the prevalence of human rights rhetoric in what they and many others were then inclined to characterize as the 'new imperialism'.[1] They put pen to paper in the wake of a flurry of troubling developments in the United States: the Bush administration's withdrawal from the Kyoto Protocol in March 2001; the attacks of September 11, 2001; the invasion and occupation of Afghanistan; the administration's 'unsigning' of the Rome Statute of the International Criminal Court in May 2002; the invasion and occupation of Iraq; the normalization and programmatic consolidation of a variety of neoconservative proposals to realize a 'new American century'; and the concomitant elaboration of the 'Bush Doctrine' of pre-emptive or anticipatory self-defence, according to which powerful self-styled 'liberal democracies', chief among them the United States, are entitled to intervene in other states for the purpose of neutralizing imminent or prospective threats.

Taking stock of these developments, Bartholomew and Breakspear trained their lens on Michael Ignatieff, whose writings provided a foil for their argument on behalf of a 'critical cosmopolitanism' that would avoid utopian idealism while encouraging trenchant critique of state power.[2] In their view, socialist strategy necessitated commitment to international legality and international morality alike. And this, in turn, called for a cosmopolitanism that would take human rights seriously enough to countenance the temporary suspension of post-1945 norms of non-intervention and sovereign equality under exceptional circumstances. 'A critical cosmopolitanism', wrote Bartholomew and Breakspear, 'should develop a position that links a commitment to nonintervention to a commitment to human rights and makes an exception to the nonintervention principle to the extent that systematic human rights abusers would forfeit the right to sovereign equality'.[3] Sovereignty was to be respected and safeguarded, but not at the expense of losing sight of the importance of protecting human rights or fetishizing the 'defined territory' that international lawyers continue to regard as constitutive of statehood.[4]

The world today is substantially different in many ways from the one in which Bartholomew and Breakspear wrote, and the international legal landscape to which they felt compelled to respond has also undergone significant change. This essay revisits the questions with which they were concerned, but it adopts a different posture and offers a different set of responses. It does so with an eye to the current conjuncture, highlighting continuities between the Trump administration and its predecessors in regard to questions of humanitarian intervention. I argue that the modalities of such intervention have evolved since 2004, with the most prominent contemporary form being the 'responsibility to protect', an 'emerging doctrine' of sorts whose conceptual imprecision renders it all the more useful politically. I argue further that recent actions in Syria and elsewhere have demonstrated that the animating logic of humanitarian intervention – that military action may be 'legitimate', indeed necessary, even when in violation of relevant law – remains operational to a very significant degree. The willingness of Trump and others to mobilize the moralistic rhetoric of 'humanity' in support of bombing campaigns works hand-in-glove with their disdain for many forms of international law (including, importantly and not without irony, human rights). Indeed, such interventionism builds upon efforts to de-formalize international law governing the use of force that have been underway since the conclusion of the Cold War, particularly since NATO's bombing of Yugoslavia in 1999. In the context of questions of intervention, Trump's is not a world 'turned upside down' so much as a particularly crass expression of a world that many have sought to craft for the better part of three decades by recourse to more 'flexible' forms of (military and non-military) intervention.

LAW'S STRUGGLE

Pashukanis famously argued that law is immanent in and fundamentally inseparable from commodity exchange – that 'as the wealth of capitalist society assumes the form of an enormous accumulation of commodities, society presents itself as an endless chain of legal relationships'.[5] Just as the exchange of commodities of abstract equivalence is underwritten by real inequalities in politico-economic power, so too, he maintained, is law's claim to formal equality vitiated by immense factual inequality.[6] Interpreted uncharitably, this 'commodity-form theory' effectively converts a central tenet of historical materialism – that the economic is ultimately determinative of social relations – into the significantly broader and more ambitious proposition that it is 'the *only* determining factor', which, as Engels observed long ago, is 'a meaningless, abstract, ridiculous piece of jargon'.[7] Such a stark interpretation also struggles to do justice to the fact that even 'classical Marxism' generally advanced the critique of formal legal equality in order to underscore the limits of exclusively rights-based strategies, not in order to do away with all reliance upon law during the course of social struggles – a fact evidenced famously and with particular acuity by Marx's analysis of the struggle around factory legislation in nineteenth-century Britain.[8]

In this spirit, Poulantzas argued that the state, and the legal field embedded in it, is the material crystallization of the struggle between different classes and class fractions – the set of material apparatuses that refract and give expression to the relation between the dominant and dominated classes, and also between different factions of the dominant class within a given power bloc. Neither a self-standing subject nor a passive 'thing' amenable to seizure and manipulation from without, the state is a 'strategic field', a 'relatively autonomous' matrix of institutions that embodies the capital-relation, its constituent structures inscribing the class compromises and contradictions by which it is traversed.[9] A structurally similar argument may be made about international law. While anchored in capitalist production and exchange, international law nevertheless commands a degree of normative and institutional autonomy. Possessed of considerable constitutive power, it feeds the contradictions and transformations of the capitalist mode of production and cannot therefore be relegated to the 'superstructural' sphere pure and simple.[10] Further, international law's rules and institutions register the settlements of past struggles, some of which are capable of being deployed as part of anti-capitalist and anti-imperialist programmes (at least when accompanied with a high degree of awareness and selectivity).[11] Poulantzas cautioned against ultra-leftist strategies that insisted upon nothing less than frontal confrontation with state power, observing that the 'revolutionary break' could 'pass through the state' and that it was therefore necessary to wage a struggle on its strategic terrain.[12] Similarly, leveraging principles of non-intervention and self-determination need not necessarily entail liberal legalism, or a hyper-formalist fetishization of the law; it may simply signal a willingness to marshal political gains, however limited, that have been sedimented in law in furtherance of broader transformative projects.[13]

International law is the material and ideological product of a series of real struggles, and by no means only between states. It is, to be sure, structurally hardwired so as to favour the North over the South, the exploiter over the exploited – in much the same way that state policies and institutions tend to reflect the material interests and ideological self-understandings of the capitalist class (or one or another fraction of it). But it has also proven useful at times to anti-capitalist and anti-imperialist movements of various stripes, which is precisely why socialist and non-aligned states, not to mention stateless peoples, social movements, and national liberation movements, pressed as hard as they did to harness it during the waves of decolonization that swept Asia, Africa, Oceania, and the Caribbean in the decades after the Second World War. Reinforcing the principle of permanent sovereignty over natural resources, revising rules about state succession to treaties and other legal instruments, bolstering the power of capital-importing states to nationalize foreign-held assets, developing and pressing for the realization of a 'new international economic order' that would redistribute capital, resources, and technology on a global scale – these and other modifications to classical international law were widely regarded as central to the project of economic and political decolonization.[14] In order to come to grips with the systemic logic of international law, it is necessary to recognize that such law crystallizes the capital-relation and therefore contains the residue of wide-ranging social contests. It would be fundamentally misguided to exaggerate the 'achievements' of the 'rule of law', but it would also be erroneous and self-defeating to cast law aside on account of a puritanically romantic attachment to non-legal forms of resistance. The eight-hour working day – a quintessentially legal protection if ever there was one – was achieved through legal no less than extra-legal struggle.

INTERVENTIONS

The question of how international law governs military intervention by one state (or group of states) in another state is notoriously thorny. There is, of course, little inherently 'progressive' about the idea of non-intervention. While its history reaches back centuries, the idea of a general principle of non-intervention acquired considerable durability during the course of nineteenth-century debates about the management of conflict within Europe, in no small part through the suppression of revolutionary movements and the displacement of inter-imperial rivalry to the extra-European world.[15] It was not for nothing, after all, that Mazzini claimed that non-intervention was in a significant measure 'intervention on the wrong side; intervention by all who choose, and are strong enough, to put down free movements of peoples against corrupt governments' – the extension of something dangerously akin to a blank cheque to tyrants determined to crush popular and working-class insurrections.[16] Nor was it accidental that

Marx recognized in his writings on the 'Eastern Question' that the Concert of Europe's prioritization of the European balance of power was generally predicated upon the permissibility of intervention in 'semi-civilized' states like China, Japan, and the Ottoman Empire, not to mention unfettered access to a large number of 'uncivilized' peoples and markets.[17] Thus, not only has formal recognition of the juridical equality of (at least some) states been belied by massive substantive inequalities between (and within) states, but the very idea of non-intervention is also rooted to no small degree in the history of imperialist conquest and colonial capitalism.

The tradition of socialist internationalism is a complex one in this regard. On the one hand, this tradition has done much to secure legal recognition for self-determination and state sovereignty, as exemplified by Lenin's writings on the topic in the 1910s,[18] the 1920 Baku Congress of the Peoples of the East,[19] and the early Soviet state's rapid conclusion of treaties of friendship on terms of equality with a variety of 'eastern' states.[20] On the other hand, it has also made room for intervention in support of proletarian uprisings and socialist movements that have threatened to destabilize existing distributions of sovereign authority. This was the case during Cuba's long-running intervention in Angola.[21] It was also, of course, the justificatory rationale employed by the Soviet Union when it entered Hungary in 1956 and the Warsaw Pact when it rolled into Czechoslovakia in 1968, the latter leading to the articulation of the highly controversial 'Brezhnev Doctrine' of collective action on the part of socialist states in response to efforts to reverse developments toward socialism.[22]

Unsurprisingly, questions pertaining to 'humanitarian intervention' figure prominently in debates about the international law of the use of force. Attempts to curb military (and, to some degree, non-military) intervention through legal means did not arise *ex nihilo* after 1945, as is often believed. In response to the brutality of trench warfare and aerial bombardment, the 'peacemakers' of 1919 did not outlaw war or intervention as such, but the League of Nations Covenant did encourage disarmament and peaceful settlement of international disputes. The 1928 Kellogg-Briand Pact subsequently sought to outlaw war, and while it famously proved ineffective, many jurists have argued that it contributed to the development of customary international law, the body of legal rules that international lawyers regard as generated from practices of states that are recognized to be legally binding.[23] The drive to reconstruct and stabilize international legal order after the Second World War brought with it a renewed commitment to prohibit forceful intervention. International peace and security, as re-conceptualized in the wake of the Second World War, placed legitimate violence in the hands of a consortium of latter-day great powers endowed with the authority to grant or withhold legal sanction to prospective applications of military might.

According to the UN Charter and related customary international law, the conditions under which military intervention may be undertaken in the interests of 'humanity' are tightly circumscribed. Absent authorization from the Security Council or an express invitation by the government of the state that is subject to intervention, the use of force by one state against another is unlawful save for circumstances in which the former may plausibly be said to act in self-defence. This is the case even when unilateral or multilateral deployment of force is claimed to be necessary on moral or humanitarian grounds. Article 2(4) of the Charter prohibits the threat or use of force against any state's territorial integrity and political independence, Article 2(7) precludes intervention by the United Nations in matters that are essentially within the domestic jurisdiction of states, and Article 51 allows for an important exception to 2(4)'s otherwise comprehensive prohibition in cases of individual or collective self-defence: if a UN member state finds itself subject to an 'armed attack' (the meaning of this term naturally being the subject of considerable disagreement), it may exercise its right to defend itself, within certain parameters, even before the Security Council has taken actions to maintain international peace and security.

Of crucial significance here is the fact that the Charter underscores the foundational status of sovereign equality – the principle that all states are juridically equal, and that, as a corollary, no state commands a general right to intervene in or use force against another. This commitment to the nominal equality of states found expression in a battery of treaties and other instruments in the decades following the Charter's adoption in 1945. The two 1966 human rights treaties – concluded after the disintegration of most European empires and the emergence of a world of formally sovereign (though generally politically weak and economically dependent) states – commenced with sweeping, if ambiguously worded, commitments to self-determination that carried strong implications for questions of intervention.[24] A raft of General Assembly resolutions lent further weight to such pronouncements, with the 1970 'Friendly Relations Declaration' denouncing 'armed intervention and all other forms of interference or attempted threats against the personality of the State or against its political, economic and cultural element'.[25]

The demise of the Soviet regimes brought about a certain loosening of these constraints, de-formalizing much of the international law associated with the post-Second World War settlement. The Security Council first authorized use of force against a state pursuant to its powers to maintain international peace and security in 1990, when it approved multilateral action against Iraq. Not until NATO's bombing of Yugoslavia in 1999, though, did the expression 'unlawful but legitimate' begin to gain widespread popularity as a means of conceptualizing uninvited military intervention in the context of large-scale violence – the kind of violence that, at its worst, the 'international community' had done precious little to stop during the Rwandan genocide. In addition to receiving support from a number of governments, this moralistic formula was quickly approved in the Independent International Commission on Kosovo's ex post assessment of the bombing campaign, which threw its weight behind the view that intervention without consent or Security Council authorization may be justifiable on moral and humanitarian grounds.[26] Influential in policy and academic circles alike, the report remains best known for its controversial claim that uninvited and unauthorized intervention may be illegal but nevertheless acceptable, in the sense of enjoying a significant measure of moral authority (and perhaps even moral necessity).

This 'unlawful but legitimate' approach – and the 'flexible' and purportedly more 'modern' understanding of the use of force it exemplifies – violates the basic principles of the UN Charter just as much as the unilateral humanitarian intervention of old. Yet it gained adherents, particularly among Western jurists and policymakers, soon after its initial articulation. The 'responsibility to protect' – often touted as a successor to traditional humanitarian intervention, a way of repackaging such intervention while jettisoning its discursive baggage – has proven to be its most influential variant. Supporters of the 'responsibility to protect', known colloquially as 'R2P', seek to replace the conventional model of sovereignty as effective control over a distinct territory and distinct population with a new model that is grounded in the state's duty to protect its own population, principally from genocide, war crimes, ethnic cleansing, and crimes against humanity.[27]

For the boldest partisans of R2P, a state that fails to discharge this duty of protection loses its claim to legitimate sovereignty, and other states are thereby endowed with the authority to use force to protect civilians without obtaining advance approval from the Security Council and without a compelling argument about invitation or self-defence. As with the Kosovo commission, Ignatieff was a key member of the International Commission on Intervention and State Sovereignty, a body sponsored by the Canadian government and tasked with examining the conditions under which military intervention in the name of human rights and humanitarianism may be justified. The commission's final report, published in 2001 and prepared as the first major programmatic effort to lay the conceptual groundwork for R2P, served as the basis upon which the idea's proponents later pled their case before the General Assembly, the Security Council, and countless international conferences.[28]

Notwithstanding its conceptual indebtedness to early modern theories of the sovereign as the quintessential guarantor of protection,[29] the legal credentials of R2P are questionable. For one thing, there is no multilateral treaty governing R2P. For another, it does not find strong expression in customary international law. Most of the relatively meagre support that has been lent to R2P over the years has come in the form of non-binding policy documents and vague references in UN resolutions,[30] and a large number of states in the 'global south' explicitly oppose it, at least when it is understood as a right to intervene without invitation, without a strong argument about self-defence, and without obtaining approval in advance from the Security Council.[31] While it is undeniable that such arguments have the effect of strengthening ruling elites and national bourgeoisies, the legal point is a sound one. A number of other states, including Australia, Canada, France, the United Kingdom, and the United States, have situated themselves, periodically if not in every instance, on the other side of this debate. At root, the basic argument on this front is that there is a growing consensus that the UN Charter's prohibition of non-defensive uses of force which have not received Security Council authorization is out-dated and insufficient in an age of terror, 'state failure', and generalized 'security crises'. State sovereignty should not serve as a shield for systemic human rights violations, and intervention under conditions in which the protective mechanisms of sovereignty have 'failed' should not be denounced as a form of imperialism or unjustified interference in domestic affairs. The plausibility of such views varies from one context to another, and they are certainly not accepted widely enough to yield a new, legally binding norm of customary international law. Nevertheless, R2P's proponents continue to point to them when seeking to reinforce their position, sometimes in tandem with claims that uninvited intervention unauthorized by the Security Council ought to be permitted on defensive grounds when a given state proves 'unwilling or unable' to suppress terrorist organizations or other non-state groups operating within its territory.[32]

CONTINUITY AND CONJUNCTURE

The pattern of justification that underlies post-Kosovo humanitarian intervention – a rationale that owes much to political science scholarship on state building and the indexes of 'state fragility' compiled by Western governments and international organizations[33] – underwrote much of the multilateral military intervention in Libya in 2011. Of particular relevance in this regard were Security Council resolutions 1970, 1973, 2016, and 2040, which formalized UN approval for different facets of the enterprise and referred broadly and somewhat vaguely to the Libyan authorities' responsibility to protect the country's population. Pointing to Tripoli's unwillingness to accede to opposition demands and its central role in the internecine violence that began to engulf the country in February 2011, the Obama administration and its NATO allies undertook countless strikes, engaged in large-scale drone warfare, provided arms and logistical support to rebel forces, and orchestrated diplomatic recognition of a new rebel-controlled provisional government by international organizations and a large number of states. Far from shielding civilians from violence, NATO's intervention weakened state institutions, stifled provision of social services, encouraged human trafficking, strengthened the hand of ISIS, facilitated the operation of innumerable militias, and furthered social alienation and dislocation throughout the country. Language similar to the kind found in the Security Council resolutions about Libya also found its way into resolutions concerning multilateral responses to events in Côte d'Ivoire, Mali, Sudan, Yemen, and elsewhere, though for different purposes and with different outcomes. In some of these cases, as in Yemen, no effective multilateral humanitarian effort has been mounted. In still other cases, as with the Myanmar government's massacre and displacement of the Rohingya, the Security Council has offered no resolutions with R2P-style language of any kind.

Of course, the rhetoric of humanitarian intervention has found a degree of expression not simply in UN resolutions, but also in arguments advanced by particular states acting without formal UN approval and without being able to point to official invitations to intervene on the part of relevant local authorities. Some Russian diplomats and international lawyers, for instance, have drawn upon R2P-style arguments when attempting to justify Moscow's unlawful occupation and annexation of Crimea in early 2014, as well as its ongoing support for self-declared 'people's republics' in the Donbass.[34] Similarly, while the Obama administration ultimately decided not to conduct airstrikes in response to Assad's alleged use of chemical weapons in mid-2013 (due partly to its inability to secure approval from Russia and China in the Security Council), notions of humanitarian intervention figured prominently in the arguments that were floated in favour of such a move in the United States and elsewhere.[35] Harold Koh, a Yale law professor who spent nearly four years as the State Department's legal adviser under Obama, and who repeatedly defended the administration's penchant for targeted killings,[36] articulated the underlying approach crisply: '[i]f modern international law cannot be read to permit such a limited use of force to enforce international law, international lawyers should seize on Syria as a moment to reframe international law'.[37] More pointedly still, various ideas about humanitarian intervention circulated widely in the midst of Western airstrikes on Syrian government installations in 2017 and 2018 – which occurred without the consent of Damascus, without authorization from the Security Council, and without a plausible argument about the need to act defensively in the face of an 'armed attack'. Tellingly, the Trump administration did not bother to offer a legal defence of its unilateral strike on the Damascus-controlled Shayrat airbase in April 2017. Inasmuch as international legal arguments *were* offered in the case of the joint Anglo-French-American strike on multiple government sites in April 2018, they were characterized by nebulous invocations of the need to intervene in the interests of 'humanity', marshalling R2P-inflected claims about the overriding urgency to protect civilians.[38]

The current conjuncture is, of course, reducible neither to 1991 nor to 1999 nor to 2003. Doubts about the future prospects of neoliberal globalism, significant centrifugal forces within the European Union, rapidly changing networks of production and distribution, the rise of ultra-nationalist authoritarian governments and well-resourced xenophobic movements, often in former centres of 'liberal democracy' – the world today is not the world of twenty or thirty years ago. The political salience of most international human rights movements, and the sort of 'democracy promotion' whereby they rose to prominence in the 1970s and 1980s,[39] appears to have experienced something of a downturn, at least in human rights' role as a set of weaponized 'norms' harnessed for *realpolitik* purposes by foreign-policy establishments.

As is so often the case, the United States provides the leading example here. The first US National Security Strategy document appeared in 1987, and it specified as one of its 'major objectives in support of U.S. interests' the advancement of 'the cause of democracy, freedom, and human rights throughout the world'.[40] Such sentiments only gained traction over time, with the 2001 National Security Strategy, published in December 2000, elevating the project of 'promoting democracy and human rights' to a 'guiding principle of engagement'.[41] Even the 2002 document, prepared in the early stages of the 'war on terror' and as part of the build-up to the Second Gulf War, contains the occasional injunction to protect human rights.[42] The 2017 document marks a sharp break in this respect. In contrast to those released during Obama's presidency,[43] the term 'human rights' appears only once in this report, and even then only in the context of a rather unequivocal assertion of nationalist power: 'We are under no obligation to offer the benefits of our free and prosperous community to repressive regimes and human rights abusers.'[44]

Yet, in spite of this decline in human rights talk (and Trump's recent move to withdraw from the UN Human Rights Council), the US practice of intervening militarily in the name of 'humanity' – a mode of humanitarianism with complex historical and conceptual links to human rights – shows no signs of diminishing. Indeed, if anything, the relative insignificance of human rights as an element of the foreign policies of the United States (and some other countries today) appears only to have encouraged more capacious forms of military intervention, sometimes without so much as bothering with minimally passable legal justifications. There is ultimately more continuity than discontinuity between Trump's references to the suffering of Syrian children – references that conveniently elide his administration's refusal to accept significant numbers of refugees from Syria and elsewhere – and Obama's statement (in his Nobel Peace Prize acceptance speech) that 'force can be justified on humanitarian grounds, as it was in the Balkans, or in other places that have been scarred by war'.[45] The willingness to deploy military force in the face of violence – and to do so inconsistently, hypocritically, and with an eye to larger geopolitical or geo-economic considerations (Libya boasts extensive hydrocarbon resources, for instance, while many other countries do not) – is rooted in a broader post-Cold War shift toward 'just wars'.

The de-formalization of the international law on the use of force over the past thirty odd years is key to understanding the enduring – and possibly growing – appeal of this sort of 'flexible', morally charged intervention. This process of de-formalization, which bears more than a passing resemblance to the 'flexibilization' of social relations under financial capitalism, has manifested itself in several key tendencies:

- a tendency to conceptualize civil wars and similar conflicts in terms of systemic human rights violations, rather than, say, as struggles between competing self-determination claims, each with its own politico-economic causes and consequences;
- a tendency to downgrade the antecedent economic, political, and legal involvement of the 'international community' in creating the conditions that subsequently make intervention appear necessary (think of the Bretton Woods institutions' promotion of austerity and structural adjustment programmes in Yugoslavia, which accelerated

the growth of nationalist chauvinism, and of Assad's pro-market reforms in the years leading up to 2011, which benefited particular groups and exacerbated socio-economic inequalities);[46]

- a tendency to mystify the degree to which intervention and post-conflict reconstruction are undertaken in accordance with broader commitments to privatization, state restructuring, and foreign ownership of key enterprises;
- a tendency to condition full-throated recognition of the sovereignty of weaker states upon adherence to specific political 'values', economic arrangements, and administrative practices;
- and, more generally, a tendency to denigrate 'roguish' or otherwise unpalatable conduct while celebrating 'the international' as the singular guarantor of security, prosperity, accountability, and morally defensible order.

Each of these tendencies has been developed significantly in the context of R2P and analogous modes of humanitarian intervention, whose supporters press to reconfigure the post-1945 international order with a view to juridifying ever more ambitious forms of interference. The struggle between those who seek to preserve and those who seek to upend those elements of the post-1945 settlement that relate to the use of force is a struggle over both the form and content of contemporary international law, one with wide-ranging politico-economic implications. Contemporary humanitarian intervention is not simply an outgrowth of a particular mode of great-power politics reflective of post-Cold War dynamics. It is also a juridical complement to the transformation of territories and populations that were formerly suspicious of unfettered privatization. This has proven to be the case from Kosovo to Iraq, where state building following military intervention has proceeded alongside the institution of new social property regimes and the introduction of new trade and investment policies.[47] There is little reason to think that it will not continue to prove the case in the future.

When all is said and done, the modes of humanitarian intervention with which we are currently confronted are remarkably similar, both formally and substantively, to earlier incarnations. Even when government officials do not explicitly offer a particular legal rationale, as with Trump's 2017 Shayrat strike, much of the political, diplomatic, and journalistic work that is done to arm the operation with ideological authority trades upon the essential logic of such intervention. In this respect, the interventions of the past few years, though responsive to shifts in the international balance of forces, have not deviated significantly from the path staked out by those who resuscitated 'just war' claims of various kinds after the Cold War.

For obvious reasons, humanitarian interventions have traditionally been undertaken by advanced capitalist countries against weaker states, near and far. But there is no reason, in principle or in practice, why that must always and necessarily remain the case, particularly given the rampant de-formalization of the relevant law and the inherent imprecision of the concept of humanitarianism. After all, the moralistic mantle of 'justice' is capable of being claimed by all and sundry, for any number of different ends.

Inasmuch as international law's constituent structures are distinguished by a degree of autonomy from the politico-economic forces by which they are ultimately fuelled, formal sovereignty is capable, at least on occasion, of providing a bulwark against aggression – however facilitative it may undeniably be of unequal class relations within and across states. To deny it even that limited capacity – or to refuse to harness it owing to what Poulantzas termed 'the simplistic illusions of anti-institutional purity' – is to succumb to juridical nihilism, trading cautious investment in legal arguments that may prove effective for an 'infantile disorder' that is all but certain to be wholly ineffective.[48]

One need not lionize sovereignty, turn a blind eye to suffering, admire the machinations of the Security Council, or ignore the sordid reality of many apologies for non-intervention in order to recognize that international law may under certain circumstances offer a modicum of protection from at least the most direct and visible forms of imperialism. To eviscerate this law in the name of 'humanity' – a concept as general as it is malleable – eliminates even the possibility of such protection, thereby encouraging a free-for-all of violence.

NOTES

I want to thank Ntina Tzouvala for conversations on issues relating to the topic of this essay.

1   See Amy Bartholomew and Jennifer Breakspear, 'Human Rights as Swords of Empire?', in Leo Panitch and Colin Leys, eds, *Socialist Register 2004: The New Imperial Challenge*, London: Merlin Press, 2004.

2   Bartholomew and Breakspear devoted particular attention to Ignatieff's writings in the *New York Times Magazine*. See especially 'The Burden', *New York Times Magazine*, 5 January 2003; and 'I Am Iraq', *New York Times Magazine*, 23 March 2003.

3   Bartholomew and Breakspear, 'Human Rights', p. 137.

4   For the conventional definition of statehood in international law, see Convention on Rights and Duties of States Adopted by the Seventh International Conference of American States, signed 26 December 1933, art. 1, *League of Nations Treaty Series*, 165, 1936, p. 25.

5   Evgeny Pashukanis, 'The General Theory of Law and Marxism', translated by Peter B. Maggs, in Piers Beirne and Robert Sharlet, eds, Evgeny Pashukanis, *Pashukanis: Selected Writings on Marxism and Law*, London: Academic Press, 1980, p. 62.

6   China Miéville and others have attempted to extend this theory to international law. Miéville anchors international law in the very imperialism it is ostensibly designed to counter, arguing that '[t]he chaotic and bloody world around us *is the rule of law*'s and that it is therefore delusional or hypocritical to invest in international law as a 'progressive' force. China Miéville, *Between Equal Rights: A Marxist Theory of International Law*, Leiden: Brill, 2005, p. 319 (original emphasis). Others have offered a more generous reading of Pashukanis, one that emphasizes politically conscious reliance upon particular facets of international law's substantive content without falling prey to dogmatic legal formalism. See, e.g., Robert Knox, 'Marxism, International Law, and Political Strategy', *Leiden Journal of International Law*, 22(3), 2009.

7   Frederick Engels to Joseph Bloch, 21[-22] September 1890, in *Karl Marx and Frederick Engels Collected Works*, vol. 49, London: Lawrence & Wishart, 2010, p. 34 (original emphasis).

8   Karl Marx, *Capital: A Critique of Political Economy*, vol. 1, translated by Ben Fowkes, Harmondsworth: Penguin, 1990, ch.10.

9   Nicos Poulantzas, *State, Power, Socialism*, translated by Patrick Camiller, London: Verso, 2000, especially pp. 127–36.

10   See B. S. Chimni, *International Law and World Order: A Critique of Contemporary Approaches*, 2nd edition, Cambridge: Cambridge University Press, 2017, pp. 449–62. For a classic Soviet rendering of a similar point, albeit one that owes more to legal positivism than to any 'Marxism', see G. I. Tunkin, *Theory of International Law*, translated by William E. Butler, Cambridge: Harvard University Press, 1974, pp. 234ff. Interestingly, in addition to boasting strong roots in the work of Karl Renner and E. P. Thompson, this claim also found a home in the (preponderantly anti-Marxist) 'critical legal studies' movement of the 1970s and 1980s. See especially Duncan Kennedy, 'The Role of Law in Economic Thought: Essays on the Fetishism of Commodities', *American University Law Review*, 34(4), 1985. For commentary see: Jairus Banaji, *Theory as History: Essays on Modes of Production and Exploitation*, Leiden: Brill, 2011, pp. 15, 42.

11   See especially Chimni, *International Law and World Order*, ch. 7. See further Bill Bowring, 'Positivism versus Self-Determination: The Contradictions of Soviet International Law', in Susan Marks, ed., *International Law on the Left: Re-examining Marxist Legacies*, Cambridge: Cambridge University Press, 2008; Paul O'Connell, 'On the Human Rights Question', *Human Rights Quarterly*, 40, 2018, forthcoming.

12   Nicos Poulantzas, 'The State and the Transition to Socialism', in James Martin, ed., *The Poulantzas Reader: Marxism, Law, and the State*, London: Verso, 2008, pp. 340–41. See further Poulantzas, *State, Power, Socialism*, pp. 153, 158.

13   Of course, not every Marxist scholar of international law can be categorized on the basis of this abbreviated and somewhat ideal-typical contrast between Pashukanis and Poulantzas. For positions that do not fall neatly within one or the other category, see Susan Marks, 'False Contingency', *Current Legal Problems*, 62(1), 2009; Akbar Rasulov, '"The Nameless Rapture of the Struggle": Towards a Marxist Class-Theoretic Approach to International Law', *Finnish Yearbook of International Law*, 19, 2008; Mark Neocleous, 'International Law as Primitive Accumulation; Or, the Secret of Systematic Colonization', *European Journal of International Law*, 23(4), 2012.

14 From a growing body of literature see especially Nico J. Schrijver, *Sovereignty Over Natural Resources: Balancing Rights and Duties*, Cambridge: Cambridge University Press, 1997; Antony Anghie, *Imperialism, Sovereignty, and the Making of International Law*, Cambridge: Cambridge University Press, 2005, pp. 211–20; Matthew Craven, *The Decolonization of International Law: State Succession and the Law of Treaties*, Cambridge: Cambridge University Press, 2007; Sundhya Pahuja, *Decolonising International Law: Development, Economic Growth and the Politics of Universality*, Cambridge: Cambridge University Press, 2011; *Humanity*, 6(1), 2015 (special issue titled 'Toward a History of the New International Economic Order').

15 In 1859 John Stuart Mill wrote that '[t]o suppose that the same international customs, and the same rules of international morality, can obtain between one civilized nation and another, and between civilized nations and barbarians, is a grave error, and one which no statesman can fall into'. John Stuart Mill, 'A Few Words on Non-Intervention', in John M. Robson, ed., *The Collected Works of John Stuart Mill*, vol. 21, Toronto: University of Toronto Press, 1984, p. 118.

16 Giuseppe Mazzini, 'On Nonintervention', in Stefano Recchia and Nadia Urbinati, eds, *A Cosmopolitanism of Nations: Giuseppe Mazzini's Writings on Democracy, Nation Building, and International Relations*, Princeton: Princeton University Press, 2009, p. 217.

17 Karl Marx, *The Eastern Question: A Reprint of Letters Written 1853–1856 Dealing With the Events of the Crimean War*, Eleanor Marx Aveling and Edward Aveling, eds, London: Swan Sonnenschein & Co., 1897, pp. 270, 405. For the international legal implications, see especially Georg Schwarzenberger, 'The Standard of Civilisation in International Law', *Current Legal Problems*, 8(1), 1955; Gerrit W. Gong, *The Standard of 'Civilization' in International Society*, Oxford: Clarendon, 1984; Martti Koskenniemi, *The Gentle Civilizer of Nations: The Rise and Fall of International Law 1870–1960*, Cambridge: Cambridge University Press, 2001, ch. 2; Gerry Simpson, *Great Powers and Outlaw States: Unequal Sovereigns in the International Legal Order*, Cambridge: Cambridge University Press, 2004; Anghie, *Imperialism*, ch. 2.

18 See especially V. I. Lenin, 'The Right of Nations to Self-Determination', in *Lenin: Collected Works*, vol. 20, Moscow: Progress Publishers, 1964; V. I. Lenin, 'The Revolutionary Proletariat and the Right of Nations to Self-Determination', in *Lenin: Collected Works*, vol. 21, Moscow: Progress Publishers, 1964. See further Bowring, 'Positivism versus Self-Determination'; John Quigley, *Soviet Legal Innovation and the Law of the Western World*, Cambridge: Cambridge University Press, 2007, pp. 133–71; Scott Newton, *Law and the Making of the Soviet World: The Red Demiurge*, London: Routledge, 2015, pp. 216–40.

19 John Riddell, *To See The Dawn: Baku, 1920—First Congress of the Peoples of the East*, New York: Pathfinder Books, 1993. See also Alexandre A. Bennigsen and S. Enders Wimbush, eds, *Muslim National Communism in the Soviet Union: A Revolutionary Strategy for the Colonial World*, Chicago: University of Chicago Press, 1979.

20 See especially Treaty of Friendship between Persia and the Russian Socialist Federal Soviet Republic, signed 26 February 1921, *League of Nations Treaty Series*, 9, 1922; Treaty of Friendship between Russia and Turkey, signed 16 March 1921, *British and Foreign State Papers*, 118, 1923.

21 See especially Edward George, *The Cuban Intervention in Angola, 1965–1991: From Che Guevara to Cuito Cuanavale*, London: Frank Cass, 2005; Candace Sobers, 'Investigating Cuban Internationalism: The First Angolan Intervention, 1975', in Alessandra Lorini

and Duccio Basosi, eds, *Cuba in the World, the World in Cuba: Essays on Cuban History, Politics and Culture*, Florence: Firenze University Press, 2009. See also Piero Gleijeses, *Conflicting Missions: Havana, Washington, and Africa, 1959-1976*, Chapel Hill: University of North Carolina Press, 2002.

22   For a standard Soviet account of the doctrine's international legal dimensions, see Tunkin, *Theory of International Law*, chs. 19–20. For an American assessment see John Norton Moore and Robert F. Turner, *International Law and the Brezhnev Doctrine*, Lanham: University Press of America, 1987.

23   For the most recent argument to this effect see Oona A. Hathaway and Scott J. Shapiro, *The Internationalists: How a Radical Plan to Outlaw War Remade the World*, New York: Simon & Schuster, 2017. For the text of the pact see General Treaty for Renunciation of War as an Instrument of National Policy, signed 27 August 1928, *League of Nations Treaty Series*, 94, 1929.

24   International Covenant on Economic, Social, and Cultural Rights, signed 16 December 1966, art. 1, *United Nations Treaty Series*, 993, 1976, p. 5; International Covenant on Civil and Political Rights, signed 16 December 1966, art. 1, *United Nations Treaty Series*, 999, 1976, p. 173.

25   Declaration on Principles of International Law Concerning Friendly Relations and Co-operation Among States in Accordance with the Charter of the United Nations, princ. 3, GA Res. 2625 (XXV), UN Doc. S/RES/25/2625 (24 October 1970).

26   Independent International Commission on Kosovo, *The Kosovo Report: Conflict, International Response, Lessons Learned*, Oxford: Oxford University Press, 2000, pp. 163–98. Sponsored by the Swedish government, this commission was headed by Richard Goldstone, the South African jurist who had struggled against apartheid and would later come to be known for his association with the UN fact-finding mission into the 2008–9 Gaza War, and Carl Tham, a Swedish politician and development advocate of broadly liberal-democratic persuasion. As is so often the case with international commissions of this sort (think, for instance, of Olof Palme's commission on disarmament and security issues or Willy Brandt's commission on 'North-South dialogue' in regard to developmental questions), the Goldstone/Tham commission's other members hailed from a variety of regions and ideological traditions, ranging from Ignatieff through Martha Minow, a leading authority on mass violence and transitional justice, to Richard Falk, a longtime advocate of Third World causes and best known for his staunch opposition to the Vietnam War.

27   The first three categories received their most authoritative formal expression in the immediate aftermath of the Second World War, at Nuremberg and in a variety of international treaties. The fourth and final category was popularized during the 1990s, principally in response to the dissolution of Yugoslavia and the Rwandan genocide.

28   International Commission on Intervention and State Sovereignty, *The Responsibility to Protect: Report of the International Commission on Intervention and State Sovereignty*, Ottawa: International Development Research Centre, 2001, pp. 1–18.

29   See Anne Orford, *International Authority and the Responsibility to Protect*, Cambridge: Cambridge University Press, 2011, especially pp. 112–24.

30   See especially GA Res. 60/1, paras. 138–39, UN Doc. A/RES/60/1 (24 October 2005); SC Res. 1674, para. 4, UN Doc. S/RES/1674 (28 April 2006); UN Secretary-General Ban Ki-moon, 'Address at Event on "Responsible Sovereignty: International Cooperation for a Changed World"', 15 July 2008; UN Secretary-General,

'Implementing the Responsibility to Protect – Report of the Secretary-General', UN Doc. A/63/677 (12 January 2009).

31   Such sentiments have consistently found a home in official reports of the Non-Aligned Movement. See, e.g., Non-Aligned Movement, Final Document of the Sixteenth Summit of Heads of State or Government of the Non-Aligned Movement, 31 August 2012, paras. 25(2), 28–31, available at: namiran.org. For earlier sentiments along the same lines, see also Group of 77, Declaration of the South Summit, 10–14 April 2000, paras. 4, 54, available at: www.g77.org. For discussion see further Olivier Corten, *The Law Against War: The Prohibition on the Use of Force in Contemporary International Law*, translated by Christopher Sutcliffe, Oxford: Hart, 2010, pp. 432–35.

32   See especially Ashley S. Deeks, '"Unwilling or Unable": Toward a Normative Framework for Extraterritorial Self-Defense', *Virginia Journal of International Law*, 52(3), 2012; Daniel Bethlehem, 'Principles Relevant to the Scope of a State's Right of Self-Defense Against an Imminent or Actual Armed Attack by Non-State Actors', *American Journal of International Law*, 106(4), 2012. Proponents of a 'flexible' approach to the application of extraterritorial force against non-state actors often point to examples of state endorsement or acquiescence. Such efforts typically focus on the practices of Western states. See, e.g., Elena Chachko and Ashley Deeks, 'Who Is on Board with "Unwilling or Unable"?', *Lawfare*, 10 October 2016, available at: www.lawfareblog. com.

33   See especially Sally Engle Merry, 'Measuring the World: Indicators, Human Rights, and Global Governance', *Current Anthropology*, 52(3), 2011. See also Nehal Bhuta, 'Governmentalizing Sovereignty: Indexes of State Fragility and the Calculability of Political Order', in Kevin Davis, Angelina Fisher, Benedict Kingsbury, and Sally Engle Merry, eds, *Governance by Indicators: Global Power through Quantification and Rankings*, Oxford: Oxford University Press, 2012.

34   For extensive discussion see *German Law Journal*, 16(3), 2015 (special issue titled 'The Crisis in Ukraine Between the Law, Power, and Principle').

35   The British government, for example, explicitly based its support for any such strike on the 'doctrine of humanitarian intervention'. See UK Prime Minister's Office Policy Paper, 'Chemical Weapon Use by Syrian Regime: UK Government Legal Position', 29 August 2013, available at www.gov.uk.

36   See especially Harold Hongju Koh, 'Keynote Address: The Obama Administration and International Law', *American Society of International Law Proceedings*, 104, 2010, p. 218.

37   Harold Hongju Koh, 'Syria and the Law of Humanitarian Intervention (Part II: International Law and the Way Forward)', *Just Security*, 2 October 2013, available at: www.justsecurity.org.

38   See especially UK Prime Minister's Office Policy Paper, 'Syria Action – UK Government Legal Position', 14 April 2018, available at: www.gov.uk. Notably, neither France nor the United States attempted to offer a detailed international legal justification of this strike. However, see Deutscher Bundestag Sachstand, 'Völkerrechtliche Implikationen des amerikanisch-britisch-französischen Militärschlags vom 14. April 2018 gegen Chemiewaffeneinrichtungen in Syrien', 18 April 2018. For a legal opinion from the US Office of Legal Counsel that focuses on the president's constitutional powers and essentially ignores international law, see US Office of Legal Counsel, 'April 2018 Airstrikes Against Syrian Chemical-Weapons Facilities', 31 May 2018, available at: www.justice.gov.

39   From a voluminous literature see especially Nicolas Guilhot, *The Democracy Makers: Human Rights and the Politics of Global Order*, New York: Columbia University Press, 2005; Samuel Moyn, *The Last Utopia: Human Rights in History*, Cambridge: Harvard University Press, 2009; Samuel Moyn, *Not Enough: Human Rights in an Unequal World*, Cambridge: Harvard University Press, 2018.

40   *National Security Strategy of the United States*, January 1987, p. 5, available at: nssarchive.us.

41   *A National Security Strategy for the Global Age*, December 2000, p. 12, available at: nssarchive.us.

42   *The National Security Strategy of the United States of America*, September 2002, pp. 4, 22, 28, available at: nssarchive.us.

43   The 2015 report, for instance, stressed that '[d]efending democracy and human rights is related to every enduring national interest'. *National Security Strategy*, February 2015, p. 19, available at: nssarchive.us.

44   *National Security Strategy of the United States*, December 2017, p. 42, available at: nssarchive.us.

45   'Transcript and Video: Trump Speaks About Strikes in Syria', *New York Times*, 6 April 2017; 'Nobel Lecture by Barack H. Obama, Oslo', 10 December 2009, available at: www.nobelprize.org.

46   The Yugoslavian case is well-documented. Michel Chossudovsky, 'Dismantling Former Yugoslavia, Recolonizing Bosnia', *Capital & Class*, 21(2), 1997; Anne Orford, *Reading Humanitarian Intervention: Human Rights and the Use of Force in International Law*, Cambridge: Cambridge University Press, 2003, pp. 13, 87–96; Susan L. Woodward, 'The Political Economy of Ethno-Nationalism in Yugoslavia', in Leo Panitch and Colin Leys, eds, *Socialist Register 2003: Fighting Identities*, London: Merlin Press, 2003; Edward S. Herman and David Peterson, 'The Dismantling of Yugoslavia', *Monthly Review*, 59(5), 2007. See further Johanna Bockman, *Markets in the Name of Socialism: The Left-Wing Origins of Neoliberalism*, Stanford: Stanford University Press, 2011.

47   See, e.g., Filiz Zabci, 'Neoliberalism and the Politics of War: The Case of Iraq', in Alfredo Saad-Filho and Galip L. Yalman, eds, *Economic Transitions to Neoliberalism in Middle-Income Countries: Policy Dilemmas, Economic Crises, Forms of Resistance*, London: Routledge, 2010; Maj Grasten and Luca J. Uberti, 'The Politics of Law in a Post-Conflict UN Protectorate: Privatisation and Property Rights in Kosovo (1999–2008)', *Journal of International Relations and Development*, 20(1), 2017; Maj Grasten and Ntina Tzouvala, 'The Political Economy of International Transitional Administration: Regulating Food and Farming in Kosovo and Iraq', *Contemporary Politics*, 2018, forthcoming.

48   Poulantzas, *State, Power, Socialism*, p. 153; Vladimir I. Lenin, '"Left-Wing Communism": An Infantile Disorder', in *Lenin: Collected Works*, vol. 31, Moscow: Progress Publishers, 1966.

'DEATH TO THE CORPORATION':
A MODEST PROPOSAL

DAVID WHYTE

One of the things that is most often repeated about the US and UK response to the 2007-08 financial crisis is that nobody went to jail for the frauds and financial crises associated with the crash. Whilst there have been some limited prosecutions of middle ranking managers and individual traders, the people who knowingly developed and sold new forms of worthless derivatives – those bankers and traders that actively created the huge toxic debt – have been largely exonerated. President Obama and his officials argued that although 'greed and other moral lapses were evident in the run-up to the crisis, their conduct was not necessarily illegal'.[1] This is not quite true. As a number of commentators have argued, there was more than enough evidence of illegal practice to ensure that at least some at the top went down.[2] After all, critics of this apparent paralysis in US and European criminal justice systems point out, Iceland managed to set an example by jailing twenty-six of its top banking executives.[3]

Some banks have been forced to pay large-scale settlements with the US Department of Justice for their sales of financial products in the run-up to the financial crisis. In May 2018, the total imposed on the Royal Bank of Scotland (RBS) for those offences rose to over $10 billion. This came on the back of similarly large fines levied on US and European banks.[4] Despite the burden of the fines, each of the major banks has 'been aggressively returning money to shareholders through stock buybacks and dividends'. The fines are effectively dwarfed by the value of the bailout to those banks. Those North American, British and mainland European banks were, as the cliché goes, 'too big to fail'.[5]

Although we tend to argue for 'more punishment' in response to white collar and corporate offending, the form that regulation takes in capitalist societies almost always guarantees impunity to the property owning class. As this essay will argue, the impunity guaranteed to the most powerful executives following the 2008 crash, when considered alongside the fines levied against the banks and financial institutions, reveals a set of tensions and contradictions in regulation that are normal in capitalist societies: they do not merely apply to the biggest banks, and they do not merely apply in times of acute crisis.

The purpose of all forms of regulation in capitalist states is to maintain the steady rate and function of the machinery of industry and commerce. As such, its purpose is to seek a stable and uninterrupted system of production, distribution and consumption. Its primary purpose is not to punish or to seek justice for wrongs that have been done. Of course, occasionally some powerful individuals and institutions may be punished, but the extent to which this occurs can never be allowed to seriously disrupt regimes of profit accumulation. Iceland is a good example. The response of the Icelandic state to the 2008 crash has enabled the economy to stabilize and grow at a rate that is not matched anywhere else.[6]

Therein lies a core contradiction: when regulation (and punishment) is effective, it has the effect of stabilizing the system. When regulation is most effective, it enhances the longevity of capitalism as a system. Yet as socialists, we know that this is not in the interests of everyone. When we demand effective regulation, and when we demand justice for a criminal ruling class in such moments, we are also demanding that capitalism corrects itself. This is why demanding punishment of corporations, or of their executives, as a panacea to such crises or to the problems caused by capitalism can only ever be a strategy of limited or modest reform.

This essay will explore how we can demand justice in ways that both seek to ameliorate the deadly harms produced by capitalism in the short term, but at the same time weaken capitalism as a system in the long run. The purpose of this essay, therefore, is to think how our demands for the punishment of corporate crime are targeted in ways that might usefully contribute to a transformative strategy.

THE DOUBLE MOVEMENT OF REGULATION

Marxist scholars have always been clear that the purpose of regulation is to ensure the reproduction of value.[7] In the most basic sense, regulation prevents capitalism from destroying itself. As Marx put it in the context of the nineteenth century Factory Acts, which imposed limits on the working hours of factory operatives:

These Acts curb the passion of capital for a limitless draining of labour power, by forcibly limiting the working day by state regulations, made by a state that is ruled by capitalist and landlord. Apart from the working class movement which daily grew more threatening, the limiting of factory labour was dictated by the same necessity which spread guano over the English fields. The same blind eagerness for plunder that had in one case exhausted the soil, had, in the other, torn up by the roots the living force of the nation.[8]

The factory owning class, Marx argued, was precipitating 'the slow sacrifice of humanity' in its 'were-wolf hunger for surplus labour'.[9] This passage of *Capital* captures the double movement that arises in struggles for regulatory standards. The first arises from class struggle from below. When we demand and campaign for 'more' regulation we do it because we know this can have real, material effects that mitigate the human costs of capitalism. We know that whether we campaign as trade unionists demanding higher safety standards in our workplace, or as communities demanding tighter limits on emissions from industrial sites in our neighbourhoods, that regulatory standards can save lives. Yet the paradox is that regulation also makes capitalism more durable. The outcome of a more carefully regulated system is that workers will continue to be injured and killed (albeit at a lower rate) and communities will still be polluted (albeit not quite so badly).

The second movement can be characterized as *system preserving*: as class struggle from above. Marx notes in the *Grundrisse* (in a passage dealing with the development of commodity markets) that capital cannot and does not recognize limits to expansion in the spheres of production and circulation. In the context of the expansion of global markets, he notes that for capital, '[e]very limit appears as a barrier to be overcome'.[10] He was not talking about the dynamic of regulatory law here, but nonetheless this is precisely the same dynamic that regulation confronts. Capital must be controlled because in its 'blind eagerness' it perceives no limits to its own insatiable urge to accumulate. States must impose limits on the conditions of accumulation, since capital has a dominant instinct in relation to law: to see regulatory limits merely as barriers to be overcome. Having said this, the representatives of capital themselves often recognize that regulation is in their long-term interest, even where the immediate impulse is to reject state intervention. The managers of large firms in particular are generally unwilling to subordinate themselves to the vagaries of the market.[11]

Demands for 'more regulation' by the trade union movement and other social movements rarely contemplate the full implications of this double movement of class struggle. We rarely contemplate how our struggle for 'more regulation' or 'more punishment' from below might, in an unintended sense, complement struggles for regulation from above. This means we rarely consider the struggle for regulation in more long term, strategic ways: how our struggles for regulation can enhance the prospect for social transformation.

THE RISE OF THE CORPORATE CRIMINAL

The legal and administrative structures that emerge to regulate capital, whether in the financial market or the factory, can be understood as 'unequal structures of representation' that absorb and dissipate conflicts between opposing interests. Paraphrasing Antonio Gramsci, regulatory agencies are not simply 'policemen' – that is, their relation to capital is not merely one of opposition and externality – but they play a much more general role in reproducing the social conditions necessary to sustain unequal class relations.[12]

The end of the nineteenth century saw the proliferation of forms of regulation aimed at social protection (food standards, pollution controls and so on) and rules to prevent the concentration of power in the economy across capitalist societies (anti-trust, banking regulation and so on). The first Factory Acts, for example, carried a sliding scale of fines to be imposed on factory masters. However, as Carson's history of the emergence of factory legislation shows, both the factories inspectors and the courts very quickly developed ways of ensuring those crimes went unpunished: the social power of the factory owners ensured that those crimes became 'conventionalized' and 'routinized' as normal business practice.[13] The legal device that was developed (a different form of criminal liability known as 'strict liability') was ideally suited to the prosecution of the *company*, not merely the factory owner. Because for a strict liability offence the court does not need to establish individual fault, *corporations* rather than individuals could be found guilty of those factory crimes.[14]

In the United Kingdom, the proportion of 'companies' (as opposed to real persons) prosecuted for breaches of the Factory Acts in the mid-nineteenth century varied between 30 and 40 per cent.[15] By the end of the nineteenth century, 50 per cent of prosecutions for such breaches were laid against corporate persons, rather than the factory masters themselves. Through the twentieth century although there has been an ongoing debate about the enforcement of the law against criminal individuals, illegal practices have generally been dealt with by imposing large fines against corporations in procedures that circumnavigate the courts. Indeed, towards the end of the twentieth century jurisdictions in Europe and in North America developed more explicit forms of corporate criminal liability. Fines of several billion dollars levied on financial institutions for illegal practices are now commonplace in the US. And this practice is now spreading to

European regulatory systems. In cases of environmental disasters and the killing of workers, it is generally the corporation that is prosecuted. In the case of breaches of safety law by employers against workers in the UK, for example, only around 3 per cent of prosecutions are laid against directors or senior managers; and it is normally only in the smallest companies that those individuals face punishment.[16]

In the rare moments the state actively campaigns to prevent corporate crime, the object is the *corporation*. The punishment of the *corporation* is the principal mechanism through which the double movement of regulation is achieved. By punishing the corporation, the system can claim it is intervening to protect the workers, the community, and so on, whilst at the same time maintaining the steady rate of production, consumption, and financial transactions. We can call this a principle of regulatory tolerance, whereby the system upholds regulatory standards whilst at the same time tolerating corporate offending. It is not an effective mode of regulation. A recent in-depth study of a wood particleboard manufacturing plant operated by Sonae in Kirkby in the northwest of England illustrates how this principle of regulatory tolerance can play out.[17] Over a twelve-year period, the plant was prosecuted six times for offences against workers and the environment. The company was also the subject of constant safety inspections and formal notices issued by the two state regulators, the Health and Safety Executive and the Environment Agency. This did not appear to make any difference, as a litany of corporate offending culminated in the deaths of three workers in two separate incidents towards the end of this period, in 2010 and 2011. The remarkable feature of this case was that the corporation, Sonae, withstood an unprecedented level of prosecution and state intervention, and it did so without any interruption to or disruption of its accumulation of profit. It was effectively tolerated as a killer firm by the local and national states. Indeed, when the factory closed down in 2012, it was due to the global restructuring of the firm and declining global revenues, rather than anything the British criminal justice system had accomplished.

The key issue that the principle of punishing the *corporation* raises is: why would punishing an abstract entity produce results? We are often told that the threat of reputational damage is the mechanism that can force corporations to comply. But this assumption fundamentally misjudges the balance of class forces at work here. Even if the corporation does suffer reputational damage, it still acts as a shield behind which the reputations of real people are masked. If executives occasionally appear in court, owners and shareholders are rarely even identified in such cases. We are beginning to reveal how the system of punishment applied to corporate and white-collar offending has an intrinsically class character. To grasp the precise nature of the class character of regulation in this sphere, we need to explore a little more deeply how the corporation acts as a proxy for accumulation strategies.

THE CORPORATE PERSON

The corporation was in many ways an ingenious invention for the property owning class. One of the earliest recognized advantages of incorporation was that the entity would not die – it remained immortal – so did not pay death duties that would otherwise have been owed by an individual owner or investor's estate.[18] Similarly, if a 'partner' or 'shareholder' became bankrupt, the entity's assets could not be used to pay the debts as the assets belonged to the entity rather than the individual shareholder. Thus, by creating a formally autonomous organization – a corporation – individuals could be protected from liability for any particular losses.

Since at least the end of the nineteenth century, the corporation has been the key institutional mechanism in capitalist social orders through which surplus value is accrued and then re-distributed and re-invested. The 'corporation' is always talked about as something that is abstracted from the real people and the real social relationships that make up the corporation: its managers, its owners, its workers, and so on. The corporation is thus abstracted from its core social purpose: the reproduction of class power through the accumulation of surplus value in the form of profits on behalf of its 'owners' or 'shareholders'. By virtue of its creation as an autonomous entity in law and in accounting practice, the corporation is able to claim that 'it', as a 'corporate person', is responsible and therefore liable for the consequences of 'its' actions.[19] Thus executives and directors are almost always guaranteed immunity. For individual shareholders, the abstract edifice of the corporation offers much grander advantages. When the corporation formally becomes the owner of the *corporation's* assets and the party responsible for the *corporation's* liabilities, investors/shareholders in the corporation are thus able to 'limit' their liabilities to the value of the sum invested; the value of their 'share'. Shareholders are generally not held responsible for the debts or other liabilities of the company, or for the costs of any legal proceedings that may arise from its activities.[20] Corporate lawyers use the term 'corporate veil' to describe the protective shield that exists to protect the shareholders of the corporation from liability for the harms caused by the corporations.[21]

Other advantages enjoyed by investors are granted by proxy 'through' the corporation. Not least of these advantages is that the *corporate* person is for legal purposes regarded as the employer, rather than any flesh and blood person. Thus, the owners of the company are not held directly responsible for any liabilities that arise from the labour relationship. Nor do they have any obligation to know about, far less do anything about, the labour conditions faced by workers in the companies that they own. In complex chains of ownership, the autonomy granted to each unit in the chain as a separate and autonomous employer makes it easy for both individual shareholders and executives to avoid responsibility for their subsidiaries' unfair labour practices or acts of employment discrimination. Supply chains and chains of ownership insulate primary owners and buyers from liability for violations of rights at the labour intensive end of the supply chain. The corporate veil in tort cases involving multinationals has, with a few scattered exceptions, prevented workers from seeking compensation.[22] Corporate subsidies and corporate welfare constitute other key privileges that are granted to investors by proxy through the corporation.[23]

We are often told that the corporation is given a central role in capitalist economies because it is an *efficient* producer of goods, employer of workers or provider of services. Yet when we consider that value accumulation is immeasurably enhanced by the series of privileges set out above, the corporation appears to be a wholly inefficient form of organization. All of the privileges and commercial advantages appear to accrue to the corporation itself (rather than its owners or shareholders). This is a deception largely because the corporation claims to benefit a range of stakeholders (workers, communities, customers) vicariously through the corporation. Yet if we consider the real social relationships encapsulated by the corporation, this is revealed as a sleight of hand. Those stakeholders (workers, communities, customers) actually generate value for the corporation, and therefore generate value for owners and shareholders. Stakeholders do not extract value from the corporation (in the form of share dividends of the rising value of shares) as owners and shareholders are able to do.

Very simply, then, the corporation is a device that simultaneously allows exceptional privileges to be accrued by the property owning class and at the same time masks those privileges in a process of abstraction.[24] The key point to grasp is that this process of abstraction is itself a *process of regulation*.

THE FAILURE OF 'EXTERNAL REGULATION'

If we return to the example of the 2008 financial crisis, the regulatory issues at stake are not merely that the state *failed* to regulate new speculative derivative products, or that it *failed* to bring the biggest institutions into line. Much more than this, at every single turn, the state creates the conditions that permit particular forms of organization to accumulate profit in particular ways. From this perspective, regulation enabled the 2008 crash; it did not merely fail to prevent it.

Demands for regulation fail to recognize the *productive* capacity the state uses to give life to the corporation: the complex of rules and infrastructure, and the laws and practices that give corporations the permission to act in particular ways. In other words, when we demand 'more regulation' is used to control corporations, we fail to recognize that the state is *constantly* regulating, and the corporation depends upon the minutiae of those rules and practices for its very existence.

The productive capacities of states are in and of themselves regulatory mechanisms in which the roles and the interests of state and capital are closely inter-woven. Corporations are given life in order to employ workers, to 'trade' in various forms of 'market' and to accumulate and distribute the profits that arise from its activities. Corporations are given life by the rules that govern labour and commodity markets, as well as by the laws that establish the social and economic obligations of corporations. In a *productive* sense, this regulatory framework in its entirety depends on the ongoing and ever-present integration of corporations into the economic and social fabric of the social order. The main legislative response in the UK to the 2008 crash was to ring fence 'retail banking' and 'investment banking'. Without entering into a debate about the merits or failings of the measures that were introduced, this form of regulation can be said to be *productive*, because it sets the rules of entry into and the conditions of participation, in markets.[25]

Yet public discussions about the regulation of corporations tends to view regulation only in a narrow controlling sense, whereby the relationship between the state and corporations or 'business' is one of *externality* – that is, the state stands as an institution or ensemble of institutions that are always seen in *oppositional* terms to capital. This logical turn allows the regulatory relationship to be represented as part of a heroic effort on the part of the state to control the excesses of capital. Even for the most progressive thinkers, adopting this *external* logic impulsively leads to a naïve demand for 'more regulation'. Yet, no matter how hard the heroic state has sought to regulate in an *external* sense, it has not solved the problem of capital's destructive tendencies. This is because the productive capacities of state regulation empower corporations to engage in socially destructive and harmful activities.[26]

Corporations kill people, steal, defraud, and engage in deception on a scale that quite simply dwarfs the toll of the same crimes and harms committed by individuals. If such a claim might appear to be rather extreme to those who have not reflected on or studied the problem of 'corporate crime', it is a claim that is convincingly supported by a wealth of empirical studies that reveal the ubiquity of corporate law breaking.[27] In criminology today, the discipline that limits itself to studying 'crime', one would be hard-pushed to find any credible expert who would deny that corporate crime is an endemic and systematic feature of contemporary capitalist societies. Cases such as the Volkswagen emissions scandal revealed routine law breaking in the company going back to the 1980s – not only on the part of one German manufacturer, but also on the part of a very large number of household name automobile companies.[28] The routine nature of law breaking is revealed in detailed case studies across jurisdictions and across industrial sectors.[29] The point is that the toll of this offending is beyond the capacity of any criminal justice system. We simply do not have the resources to control a problem that is as endemic and everyday as corporate offending.

Surveillance and prosecution aimed at controlling the crimes committed by corporations is dealt with by specialist agencies that are not given the same political priority as police forces. Different categories of law have been developed to ensure such crimes are regarded in the courts, and a wider cultural sense, as being less serious than other forms of theft or violence. In the neoliberal period, even token levels of inspection and enforcement in relation to corporate crime have been sharply eroded. British workers, for example, can expect a workplace safety inspector to call less than once every 50 years. Even when serious offences are investigated, the chance of a prosecution is negligible.[30]

When serious offences are punished, they are generally dealt with by fining corporations; and fines are rarely effective. The oil major BP presents a particularly stark example of how little even the largest fines can matter to refocusing executive decision-making. BP's Deepwater Horizon catastrophe in 2010 came after a series of very serious offences, including an explosion that killed 15 workers in their Texas refinery in 2005 (which led to a record $50.6 million fine), and a series of oil spills in Alaska in 2006 (which led to a $25 million fine). At a grand total of $65 billion, the compensation ordered by the courts for Deepwater Horizon dwarfed those earlier fines. Yet those fines failed to make any difference to BP's profit-over-safety approach to management. The earlier fines represented a very small fraction of BP's annual revenue. The Texas refinery fine represented 0.017 per cent of the BP Group's revenue for 2010, the year the fine was levied, and the Alaska fine amounted to around 0.007 per cent of the group's revenue for 2011, the year that the fine was levied. The bill for Deepwater Horizon has, as the financial press have enthusiastically noted, been absorbed largely by the recent sharp rise in oil prices.[31]

The fines imposed on corporations for breaching financial rules are generally much higher relative to those for offences related to worker safety or environmental offending. Yet, the huge fines imposed on corporations for designing the financial products that precipitated the crisis has not even dented their ability to accumulate.[32] When the largest part of the fine against RBS noted in the introduction to this essay was confirmed, Chief Executive Ross McEwan announced '[o]ur current shareholders will be very pleased this deal is done'. Indeed, on the day the fine was announced, RBS shares rose 5.5 per cent in early trading, and later traded nearly 3 per cent higher for the day.[33]

Of course, large fines may have an impact upon the reputation of the company, and the fines may dent profits. Yet because fines are generally levied on the 'corporation', rather than targeted at a particular group within it, the cost burden of even the largest fine can be absorbed and redistributed; those costs might be offset against a particular budget heading (they might result in cuts to wages or other operational costs), or they may be passed onto customers and clients in the form of price rises, or onto suppliers by reducing the market value of a product. Fines for violating safety laws and causing fatalities in the workplace may be absorbed by workers in the form of wage cuts and downsizing.[34]

Fines imposed on companies, for all of the reasons outlined here, have little more effect than perpetuating a structure of power that is ultimately designed to shield class interests. Little wonder then that studies on the impact of pecuniary penalties on the corporation generally find little correlation between the imposition of fines and a deterrent effect.[35] *External* regulation thus fails on its own terms; it does not solve the problem it sets out to solve, precisely because it cannot meaningfully challenge the immense social power of corporations. By focusing predominantly on the corporation, external regulation simply reproduces the reification of the *corporation* as the problem, rather than problematizing the class that stands behind it.[36] In such contexts, the state does not look particularly punitive. Thus, when we limit our demands for regulation to the representatives of capital (*executives*) and to the *corporation* itself, we are unlikely to achieve accountability, or to provide a basis for progressive social change. This raises a fundamental question: can this seemingly endless cycle of corporate crime be broken if we could target regulatory intervention more effectively? Are there ways to punish corporate and white-collar crime that can limit capital's 'werewolf' hunger?

A MODEST PROPOSAL

When we contemplate the full force of capital's capacity for social destruction, external forms of regulation as a panacea quickly appear redundant. This is obvious when we consider the role regulation has played in a wider sense, in enabling the most harmful consequences of industrial development. When we regulate corporations, even in the moment that the state appears to be punitive, class interests are ultimately protected in ways that are often counterintuitive.   Therefore, if we are to demand 'more regulation' and 'more prosecution' in the aftermath of capitalism's crises, then we need to be sure that we are not merely strengthening the institutional forms of power that created the crisis in the first place.

What, then, are the forms of regulatory response that we might propose in the aftermath of a crisis such as the 2008 crash (i.e. beyond a few prosecutions)? A significant radical demand has been that we should simply nationalize the banks. Indeed, in some jurisdictions this is effectively what happened. Yet the model of nationalization in most places where there was a bailout, was structured to protect the largest investors. As part of the bailout deal, the British government wholly acquired RBS, for example. This ownership has not altered the management of the bank substantially, and indeed the government has been ensuring its liquidity until the point it will be handed back to private investors at a net loss to taxpayers estimated at £26 billion.[37]   The general principle of the bailout was to reinforce the controlling class interests in banking and finance.

Our argument as socialists should be that regulatory intervention that is aimed at finding a lasting solution to the crisis must ensure that the power structure that produced the crisis is not protected or strengthened. Otherwise, we will simply be reproducing the conditions that created the crisis in the first place. The punishment following the 2008 crash should therefore have been focused on weakening the class interests that stand behind the banking corporations.

One of the more radical strands of argument in the research dealing with corporate crime is a resurgence of the idea of the 'corporate death penalty'. It may seem like an extreme measure, and one that is a utopian aim, but this option is actually currently available to courts in a large number of jurisdictions that carry unlimited fines for serious corporate offences. A large enough fine can immediately divest a corporation of all of its assets, thus effectively putting it into liquidation.[38] A second scenario in which the corporate death penalty can be applied, though also rare, is when civil damages are imposed at a level which has the same effect. Ramirez and Ramirez propose that a version of 'three strikes and you're out', notoriously used by the US and other states from the 1980s onwards to deal with relatively low-level offending, could apply to corporations.[39] Instead of going to jail, the 'out' would be that the corporation would be 'put to death', or put into liquidation by the courts.

Yet in Ramirez and Ramirez's version of the corporate death penalty, justice is class-blind. When a company is forced into liquidation by the courts, of course the outcome is not class-neutral. Shareholders are likely to lose their investment. However, because of limited liability, the fall out for them stops at this point. Other creditors risk losing much more. This counts especially for workers who generally not only lose their livelihoods, but risk losing their pension, health care plans, and in some cases may suffer a series of knock-on effects (they may lose their home, in private education systems be unable to contribute to their children's education, and so on). Moreover, the wider community loses out if there are a large number of job losses. The corporate death penalty, therefore, may have exactly the same effect as large fines: they may make victims of the most vulnerable. We therefore need to think about how to respond to such crises so as not to punish the most vulnerable by proxy through the corporation; punishments that do not simply shore up the class interests standing behind the corporation.

If the corporate death penalty is targeted not merely at 'killing' the abstract corporation, but is targeted at ending all existing class privileges and rights, senior executives, managers, *and* shareholders[40] could be forced to forfeit the rights and privileges that are granted to them by proxy through the corporation. If we are saving jobs, or maintaining a particular service in the community, we need a corporate death penalty to trigger forms of ownership that are both equitable and sustainable, such as democratic public ownership, or worker-led cooperatives. Of course, the ownership model would need to depend on the scale and nature of the enterprise. It is more feasible for example to envisage a chipboard factory to be solely worker-owned rather than a major bank. The bank might be forced into a democratic form of public ownership.

The point is that persistent criminal and anti-social behaviour on the part of the corporation can be taken as reason to forfeit the right to ownership and profit. After all, this is the logic that the criminal justice system applies to other forms of commercial criminals in the illicit markets. Drug dealers and fraudsters have their funds and assets sequestrated by the courts routinely. All we are doing here is applying the same logic.

We already have a developed methodology that, in theory at least, could be applied for this purpose. There is an important but little-known body of research that develops the concept of equity fines.[41] The basic idea of equity fines is that shareholders are forced to absorb punitive costs when the corporate activities they profit from break the law through the re-socialisation of part of the corporation. Equity fines reclaim value directly from shareholders through a process of share dilution.[42] The courts, or the administrative authority in this proposal, order the issue of a new batch of shares worth a proportion of the corporation's existing equity. The shares could then be controlled by a defined set of fund-holders. The fund could be controlled by a state-appointed body, a collective of workers, or the local community. In cases where this is warranted, full ownership of the corporation could be transferred. Thus, we can envisage a form of the corporate death penalty where 'death' really means the forfeiture of class entitlements. After this 'death', the corporation can be reborn under new democratic forms of ownership.

CHALLENGING THE CLASS POWER BEHIND THE CORPORATION

Thinking through proposals such as this is a utopian exercise. I am certainly not claiming in this essay that the refined approaches to the punishment of corporate and white collar crime outlined above alone can transform the system. Moreover, there are a series of broader problems involved in conceptualizing a new ownership structure: should a new form of organization also enjoy corporate personhood, limited liability, and all the other attendant privileges; what use is a new form of common ownership if it is still conditioned by capitalist market forces? Having said this, the logical development of this argument for a corporate death penalty raises important questions about how, ultimately, a transformative strategy needs to involve a wholesale removal of the rights and privileges of corporate owners and shareholders. Such proposals need to be worked through in a strategic, rather than a merely tactical, approach[43] precisely because they address the material conditions of the social relationships that are abstracted by the corporation. These strategies can therefore only be a starting point in thinking through how regulatory demands and struggles can attack the source of corporate power in meaningful ways. Once we recognize the class character of how regulation works through the corporation, then we can be more clearly focused on struggles that meaningfully challenge the class power that stands behind the corporation.

Of course, we cannot abandon struggles that reinforce and restore social protections. After all, workers and other social groups had, and still have, a more immediate set of concerns about regulation: how can the law protect us from being killed at work? How can the law ensure our food doesn't poison us, or ensure that our communities are not exposed to toxic emissions? We cannot ignore the huge advances in the living conditions of ordinary people in the nations that have been forced to develop systems of social regulation. Neither can we fail to recognize that social regulation has been so easily dismantled in the neoliberal period.

Let us put it this way: if the corporation did not exist, and we were asked to create a form of institution that would accelerate inequality, hasten the global dominance of neoliberal capitalism, embed the financialization of social relations in everyday life, and produce climate change and other critical ecological crises, then we would be hard pressed to find a better design. It is time to turn our attention to how we can accelerate the end of the corporation and the class privileges that stand behind it.

NOTES

1   Editorial, 'No Crime, No Punishment', *The New York Times Sunday Review*, 25 August 2012.

2   William D. Cohan, 'How Wall Street's Bankers Stayed Out of Jail', *The Atlantic*, September 2015; Charles Ferguson, *Inside Job: The Financiers Who Pulled Off The Heist Of The Century*, Oxford: Oneworld, 2012.

3   Ian Birrell, 'Iceland Has Jailed 26 Bankers, Why Won't We?', *Independent*, 15 November 2015.

4   The 10 largest total penalties imposed by the US Government on financial institutions are as follows (figures in $US billions): Bank of America ($76.1); JPMorgan Chase ($43.7); Citigroup ($19); Deutsche Bank ($14); Wells Fargo ($11.8); RBS ($10.1); BNP Paribas ($9.3); Credit Suisse ($9.1); Morgan Stanley ($8.6); Goldman Sachs ($7.7); and UBS ($6.5); Steve Goldstein, 'Here's The Staggering Amount Banks Have Been Fined Since the Financial Crisis', *Marketwatch*, 24 February 2018, available at: https://www.marketwatch.com.

5   Patrick Jenkins and Ian Bott, 'What Happened to the 'Too Big to Fail' Banks?', *Financial Times*, 24 August 2017.

6   Alan Shipman, 'Iceland Pulled Off a Miracle Economic Escape', *Business Insider*, 29 May 2016, available at: http://uk.businessinsider.com.

7   Michael Aglietta, *A Theory of Capitalist Regulation: The US Experience*, London: Verso, 2000.

8   Karl Marx, *Capital*, London: Lawrence and Wishart, 1954/1887, p. 229.

9   Marx, *Capital*, pp. 33-4.

10   Karl Marx, *Grundrisse: Foundations of the Critique of Political Economy*, Harmondsworth: Penguin, 1973, p. 408. Or, as David Harvey put it: 'Capital can't abide a limit.' ('The Crisis of Capitalism', address to the RSA, London, 26th April 2010, available online at: https://www.thersa.org).

11   Frank Pearce, Crimes of the Powerful: Marxism, *Crime* and *Deviance*, London: Pluto, 1976, p. 82-4.

12   Rianne Mahon, 'Regulatory Agencies: captive agents or hegemonic apparatuses?', *Studies in Political Economy*, 1, 1979, pp. 162-200; Steven Bittle, and Lori Stinson, 'Corporate Killing Law Reform: A Spatio-Temporal Fix to a Crisis of Capitalism?' *Capital and Class* (forthcoming); Fiona Haines, *The Paradox of Regulation: What Regulation Can Achieve and What It Cannot*, Cheltenham: Edward Elgar, 2011; Antonio Gramsci, *Selections from the Prison Notebooks, Vol. 1.*, London: Lawrence and Wishart, 1996, p. 261.

13   W.G. Carson, 'The Conventionalization of Early Factory Crime', *International Journal for the Sociology of Law*, 7, 1979, pp. 37-60.

14 David Whyte, 'The Criminal at the heart of the State', in Grietje Baars and Andre Spicer, eds, *The Corporation: A Critical, Interdisciplinary Handbook*, Cambridge: Cambridge University Press, 2017.

15 Those estimates are derived from the author's as yet unpublished analysis of the prosecution tables produced in the annual reports of the HM Factories Inspectorate between 1854 and 1904.

16 Steve Tombs and David Whyte, *Safety Crimes*, Cullompton: Willan, 2007.

17 S. Tombs and D. Whyte, 'Toxic Capital Everywhere: Mapping the Coordinates of Regulatory Tolerance', *Social Justice*, 41, 2014, pp. 28-48.

18 Rebecca Spencer, *Corporate Law and Structures: Exposing the Roots of the Problem*, Corporate Watch, 2004.

19 Harry Glasbeek, *Wealth by Stealth*, Toronto: Between the Lines, 2017.

20 Harry Glasbeek, *Class Privilege: How Law Shelters Shareholders and Coddles Capitalism*, Toronto: Between the Lines, 2017.

21 This principle is by no means universal, and there are a series of significant cases in which the courts have been prepared to pierce the corporate veil. John Matheson, 'The Modern Law of Corporate Groups: An Empirical Study of Piercing the Corporate Veil in the Parent-Subsidiary Context', *N.C. L. Rev.* 87, 2009, pp. 1091-1155; Stephen M. Bainbridge, 'Abolishing Veil Piercing', *J. Corp. L.*, 26, 2001, pp. 479-535; David Milton, 'Piercing the Corporate Veil, Financial Responsibility, and the Limits of Limited Liability', *Emory L.J.*, 56, 2007, 1305-1382; Stéfanie Khoury, 'Corporate (Non) Accountability and Human Rights: Approaches From the Regional Human Rights Systems and Prospects for the ASEAN', *Asian Journal of Social Science* (forthcoming).

22 M. Anderson, 'Transnational Corporations and Environmental Damage: Is Tort Law the Answer?' *Washburn Lj*, 41, 2001, pp. 399-426; Stephanie Khoury and David Whyte, *Corporate Human Rights Violations: Global Prospects for Legal Action,* London: Routledge, 2017, pp. 77-8.

23 Steve Tombs and David Whyte, *The Corporate Criminal: Why Corporations Must Be Abolished*, London: Routledge, 2017.

24 On this process, see also Glasbeek, *Wealth by Stealth*.

25 Tim Wallace, 'Britain's Biggest Banks to be Forced to Separate Retail Banks From Investment Arms', *Daily Telegraph*, 15 October 2015.

26 Ignasi Bernat and David Whyte, 'State-Corporate Crime and the Process of Capital Accumulation: Mapping a Global Regime of Permission from Galicia to Morecambe Bay', *Critical Criminology*, 25, 2017, pp. 71-86.

27 Edwin Sutherland, *White-Collar Crime: The Uncut Version*, New Haven, Connecticut: Yale University Press, 1983; M. Clinard, M. and P. Yeager, *Corporate Crime*, New York: The Free Press, 1980; Gary Slapper and Steve Tombs, *Corporate Crime*, Harlow, UK: Longman, 1999.

28 David Whyte, 'It's Common Sense, Stupid! Corporate Crime and Denial in the Automobile Industry', *Crime, Law and Social Change*, 66, 2016, pp. 165-81.

29 David Friedrichs, *Trusted Criminals: White Collar Crime in Contemporary Society*, Wadsworth, 2010; and Greg Barak, *Unchecked Corporate Power*, London: Routledge, 2017.

30 Steve Tombs, *Social Protection After the Crisis: Regulation Without Enforcement,* Bristol: Policy Press, 2016.

31   Adam Vaughan, 'BP's Deepwater Horizon Bill Tops $65bn', *Guardian*, 16 January 2018.

32   One bank, Citigroup, calculated that in the first quarter of 2009, a fall by 0.25 per cent in the LIBOR rate would earn the bank $936 million in a quarter (see C. Snider and T. Youle, 'Does the LIBOR Reflect Banks' Borrowing Costs?' *SSRN*, 2010, available at: http://ssrn.com). This equates to around double the total fine the bank was made to pay for rate fixing.

33   Julia Kollewe, 'RBS settles US Department of Justice Investigation With $4.9bn Fine', *Guardian*, 10 May 2018.

34   Tombs and Whyte, *Safety Crimes*.

35   Jennifer Arlen, 'The Potentially Perverse Effects of Corporate Criminal Liability,' *The Journal of Legal Studies*, 23, 1994, pp. 833-67; Wallace Davidson III and Dan L. Worrell, 'The Impact of Announcements of Corporate Illegalities on Shareholder Returns', *Academy of Management Journal,* 31, 1988, pp. 195-200; John Coffee Jr., 'Corporate Crime and Punishment: A Non-Chicago View of the Economics of Criminal Sanctions', *Am. Crim. L. Rev.*, 17, 1980, pp. 419-78.

36   Glasbeek, *Class Privilege*; Grietja Baars, 'Its Not Me, It's the Corporation: the value of corporate accountability in the global political economy,' *London Review of International Law*, 2016 (4), pp. 127-63

37   Kollewe, 'RBS settles US Department of Justice investigation'.

38   Michael Jefferson, 'Corporate Criminal Liability: The Problem of Sanctions', *Journal of Criminal Law*, 65, 2001, pp. 235-61.

39   Mary Kreiner Ramirez and Steven A. Ramirez, *The Case for the Corporate Death Penalty: Restoring Law and Order on Wall Street*, New York: NYU Press, 2017.

40   The composition of the ruling class makes it often difficult to distinguish between the two groups. See Maurice Zeitlin, 'Corporate Ownership and Control: The Large Corporation and the Capitalist Class', *American Journal of Sociology*, 79, 1974, pp. 1073-1119.

41   For example, support for the principle of equity fines features in the following works: John Coffee, "No Soul to Damn: No Body to Kick': An Unscandalized Inquiry into the Problem of Corporate Punishment', *Michigan Law Review*, 79, 1981, p. 386; John Braithwaite, 'Penalties for White Collar Crime', AIC *Conference Proceedings*, 20-23 August 1991, Australian Government; Brent Fisse, 'Sentencing Options Against Corporations', *Criminal Law Forum*, 2, 1990; Harry J. Glasbeek, 'Why Corporate Deviance is Not Treated as a Crime: The Need to Make 'Profits' a Dirty Word', *Osgoode Hall Law Journal*, 22, 1984, pp. 393-439; James Gobert and Maurice Punch, *Rethinking Corporate Crime*, London: Butterworths, 2003; Neil Gunningham and Richard Johnstone, *Regulating Workplace Safety: Systems and Sanctions*, Oxford: Oxford University Press, 1999.

42   The New South Wales Law Reform Commission floated the process of share dilution in the 1980s, as did the Australian Law Reform Commission more recently. The idea was supported by the Scottish Executive Expert Group on Corporate Homicide in 2005 and debated – though rejected – by the Scottish Parliament in 2010 as the Criminal Sentencing (Equity Fines) (Scotland) Bill (SB 10-54).

43   Robert Knox, 'Strategy and Tactics', *Finnish Yearbook of International Law*, 2010 (21), pp. 195-229.

AMERICA'S TIPPING POINT?
BETWEEN TRUMPISM AND A NEW LEFT

NICOLE ASCHOFF

'Liberal democracy is crumbling.' A Harvard Law Professor opened a recent talk with this matter-of-fact statement, and the audience readily murmured its assent – as if the existence of a deep political crisis in the United States were a foregone conclusion. While this sentiment has become increasingly commonplace since the 2016 presidential election, it has not come entirely out of the blue. Talk of systemic crisis has lingered in the air since the 2008 financial meltdown sparked predictions of the end of financialization, globalization, and even capitalism. Yet, following the US and European bank bailouts and quantitative easing programmes, corporate profits resumed and unemployment declined. For a time the establishment's fears seemed to have been put to bed. Then came Donald Trump – on the heels of Britain's surprise referendum vote to leave the European Union. Just as the respective 1979 and 1980 victories of Margaret Thatcher and Ronald Reagan came to be regarded as a political-economic turning point, in 2016 it appeared that once again developments in Britain and the United States marked the beginning of a global shift.

Francis Fukuyama, in a post-election op-ed, declared Trump's victory 'a watershed not just for American politics, but for the entire world order'. Gideon Rachman, chief foreign affairs columnist at the *Financial Times*, saw the 'period of optimism and expansion for liberal and democratic ideas' that followed the end of the Cold War as having 'been definitively ended by Mr. Trump's victory'. In the *Washington Post* even the conservative political columnist Charles Krauthammer wrote of the death of the 'liberal democratic idea'. A more recent *Financial Times* op-ed spoke of a 'descent into disorder': 'The end of the cold war produce[d] a big idea. Now, as we are daily reminded by Mr. Trump's Twitter feed, it is being swapped for a very bad idea.'[1]

Emotions ran high in the United States after the election. But even after the liberal majority learned to choke down the words 'President Trump', the widespread sense of unease has not faded. Voices declaring the country to be in the throes of a system-wide political crisis have only grown louder since Trump sauntered into the Oval Office. Granted, some see a path to salvaging the status quo of the past three decades. The Democratic Party and its media minions have focused on the shadowy forces that derailed Hillary's campaign – Russians, internet mischief, and treachery in the Executive Branch. The underlying message in the Democrat's approach is that Hillary won the majority, and would have won the presidency if not for these machinations and a few strategic errors made along the way. With some minor tweaks, a Hillary-like figure could win the 2020 election and the party would be back on its merry way. The Republicans for their part seem to have adopted a grin-and-bear it stance, waiting for Trump to go away so they can rebuild the coalition that has dominated the party in recent decades.

But many observers are less sanguine about the possibility of resurrecting the post-Cold War neoliberal consensus. Titles like Edward Luce's *The Retreat of Western Liberalism* and Patrick J. Deneen's *Why Liberalism Failed* are straining bookstore shelves. In a working paper examining the 2016 presidential election, Thomas Ferguson, Paul Jorgensen, and Jie Chen bluntly declare that 'American politics has strayed into some strange new Twilight Zone'.[2] They show that after a precipitous decline in voter participation in the 2014 mid-term elections – numbers not seen since the pre-Jacksonian era – something even weirder happened in the 2016 election: Americans came out in droves for political figures who actively contravened the reigning political consensus and, against all odds, elected one of them. Ferguson et al. locate growing mistrust of existing institutions in the power of corporations and moneyed interests to shape public discourse. They argue that the stranglehold of business on both mainstream parties and the media-hamstrung politicians, preventing them from speaking in a clear way about issues that matter to people. By 2016 Orwellian political discourse had pushed Americans to the brink; fed up with doublespeak and corporate shills, voters rebelled at the polls, ticking the boxes of candidates willing to speak plainly about jobs, trade, debt, and insecurity. Both the Trump and the Sanders candidacies reflected a sharp de-alignment between centrist elites and ordinary Americans. In 2016, a candidate was elected who was far beyond the pale, vis-à-vis the elite consensus of the past three decades – a result that was, as Ferguson and his co-authors' careful analysis shows, 'perhaps the greatest upset in American political history'.[3]

In an article for *American Affairs*, Nancy Fraser argues that Trump and Trumpism are the result of a breakdown of the previous hegemonic model

– progressive neoliberalism – with its signature blend of 'an expropriative plutocratic economic programme with a liberal-meritocratic politics of recognition'. She contends that we are witnessing,

> a dramatic weakening, if not a simple breakdown, of the authority of the established political classes and political parties. It is as if masses of people throughout the world had stopped believing in the reigning common sense that underpinned political domination for the last several decades. It is as if they had lost confidence in the bona fides of the elites and were searching for new ideologies, organizations, and leadership.[4]

Are we, as Fraser contends, in the midst of a 'broader, multifaceted crisis, which also has other strands – economic, ecological, and social – all of which, taken together, add up to a general crisis'? The daily headlines certainly seem to confirm this assessment.

Yet, the nature of the crisis remains murky. While it is clear that in 2016 we witnessed an unprecedented display of shifting political sentiments, it is far less clear what the implications of this shift are. Nor are the contours of the 'multifaceted crisis' so obvious. One could piece together stylized facts to support either contention – that we're in a crisis, or that crisis talk is overblown. On the one hand, a recent Federal Reserve study found that four in ten Americans would be unable to cover an unexpected $400 expense.[5] The United States is riven by skyrocketing inequality, surveys report record levels of distrust of both politicians and mainstream media, and to top it all off the country is wrestling with a rampant opioid crisis. On the other hand, stock and bond markets are robust, official unemployment is at a seventeen-year low, and corporate profits are high. The International Monetary Fund reported the 'broadest synchronized global growth upsurge since 2010' at its 2018 annual meeting in Davos.[6] What's going on? More specifically, has America reached a tipping point in which the contradictions built up over the past three decades have become an insurmountable barrier to the continuation of the post-Cold War neoliberal consensus?

In what follows, a schema for interpreting the present crisis is provided by revisiting another crisis. The 1970s was a decade fraught with simultaneous and intersecting economic, social, and political crises.[7] It was a multidimensional crisis that catalyzed a new phase of capitalism, both in the US and globally. Returning to that earlier crisis helps us parse the present landscape. Today's crisis of neoliberalism is global and tied to the contradictions of US-led global capitalism; mapping its contours is beyond the scope of this brief inquiry. Here the analysis is situated within the borders of the United States so as to get our bearings, and locate potential points of intervention for the American Left moving forward.

I

The 1970s was a decade of crisis and uncertainty worldwide. The United States was a hotspot of turmoil, experiencing an economic crisis the depths of which hadn't been seen since the 1930s. Expenditures regularly overran revenues, and the state struggled with ways to increase the latter as growth and productivity stalled amidst strong social movement demands for spending, and the surging costs associated with playing global policeman during the Vietnam War. Inflation and erratic financial flows were a major cause of concern. Meanwhile, business leaders saw profits fall and productivity stagnate, yet found themselves unable to recoup losses through more investment, raising prices, or cutting wages.

The economic crisis of the seventies had its roots in the post-Second World War Bretton Woods system. For two decades after the Second World War, the Bretton Woods framework provided a stable, nurturing environment for capital and states to rebuild. The US-led global system of fixed exchange rates, gold-dollar convertibility, semi-protected domestic markets, and restricted finance – combined with the political wiggle room provided by the Soviet Union – enabled Europe to rebuild. At the same time, countries in what was then referred to as the Third World were able to make long-term development plans and enjoy a degree of economic sovereignty. While the world economy was rebuilding, and US capital was ascendant, this global system was relatively stable. Declining poverty and high growth rates prevailed, and the American state was able to pay for its Cold War activities/atrocities and domestic spending responsibilities through growing tax revenues and the seigniorage earned from the dollar's status as the international means of payment.

However, as countries and companies recovered (with some surpassing the US technologically in some sectors) competition increased, driving down profit rates and investment in the United States and across the core capitalist countries. Third World countries grew frustrated with the limits of US-led development and financial instability increased. Firms sought better returns in the Eurodollar market, oil prices spiked in 1973 and 1979, growing inflation caused swings in the value of the dollar, and the US state continually overspent in its pursuit of its global 'guns and butter' strategy.[8] As Sam Gindin and Leo Panitch argue, by the early 1970s the contradictions that the successes of the 1960s had produced came to a head. In the midst of a crisis of corporate profitability and financial instability, the simultaneous rise of both inflation and unemployment ('stagflation') confounded any consistent application of fiscal and monetary policy not only in the US, but in all the advanced capitalist states.[9]

The economic crisis intersected with a growing social crisis in the United States (as well as in Europe and the Global South). Profit squeezes and declining productivity pushed companies to recoup losses through speed-ups, price hikes, and wage freezes while inflation ate into workers' take-home pay and raised the cost of living. But workers, empowered by Keynesian full employment objectives, weren't having it. Powerful, militant unions demanded their share of the pie in the 1970s. Massive strikes, involving hundreds of thousands of railroad workers, autoworkers, teachers, taxi drivers, construction workers, longshoremen, and coal miners, won substantial wage increases to offset inflation.

There was more to the social crisis than maintaining a standard of living, however. In the United States there was a broader sense of revolt against the old ways. Industrial workers experienced widespread malaise and dissatisfaction with the drudgery of factory life and protested being trapped in 'gold-plated sweatshops'. The revolt on the assembly lines was connected to a bigger revolt outside the factory gates. In Detroit for example, black autoworkers fed up with exploitative companies and a racist union formed the League of Revolutionary Black Workers in 1969. The League was connected to the nationwide movement for civil rights that worked in parallel to other nationwide movements fighting for women's rights and consumer rights, and against war, nuclear weapons, colonialism, and corporate polluters.

To many, America felt like a country on the verge of revolution. Political leaders bemoaned an 'excess of democracy' as city-level movements for change proliferated. In Boston, a group of black, lesbian, anti-capitalist radicals formed the Combahee River Collective, fighting against forced sterilization and sexual assault, and for the rights of low-wage workers, many of whom were women and people of colour.[10] Across the river in Cambridge, nearly a hundred countercultural schools, businesses, and organizations flourished during this time period. Cell 16, a militant feminist group, ran a magazine and a martial arts studio, while groups such as Citizens League Against the Sonic Boom and the Assassination Information Bureau drew in local residents.[11] There was a genuine sense that people were building a different society.

The economic and social crises put intense pressure on the US state; it seemed plagued with uncertainty about how to resolve the situation. Spiraling inflation, decreased investment, and a growing public clamour for redistribution and recognition created a severe political crisis by the end of the 1970s, encapsulated in Carter's 1979 'crisis of confidence' speech. Business had lost confidence in the capacity of US institutions to foster a stable environment for profit making, both developed and developing countries began to question the American state's ability to superintend the global economy, and the wider American public became convinced that the US government was incompetent.

It took a decade, but the US government restored confidence. It did so through a set of ad hoc processes that have been lumped together and labelled neoliberalism, financialization, and globalization. Neoliberalism was a process of reversal − both ideologically and in practice − of the central principles of Keynesianism, in particular a strong social welfare state and ambitions toward full employment. To get through the crisis, the US government and capital worked in concert to break the back of organized labour, most visibly by crushing the 1981 PATCO strike and forcing deep concessions from unionized Chrysler workers during the company's government-led overhaul early in the decade.[12] Broadly speaking, the 1980s were a time of massive restructuring of whole economic sectors to promote competition between workers and between countries.[13]

The architecture of the financial system was reorganized through trial and error at the same time. What we describe today as financialization was a direct result of steps that began during the 1970s (the abandonment of the fixed exchange rate in 1973 and the removal of interest rate ceilings on consumer loans) and early 1980s (the Volcker shock and the creation of new derivative and financial instruments) and culminating in the 1999 repeal of Glass-Steagall. Capital flows from around the world were redirected into US financial markets, and finance moved to the centre of the economy.

The globalization of production that accompanied financialization was both a political project and a concrete process of restructuring global value chains. The US government spearheaded new inter-state trade and financial agreements, while companies outsourced low value-added production to low-wage zones. However, globalization brought much more than a debt crisis for poor countries and a race-to-the bottom in production: companies also moved production to wealthy countries with big domestic markets while the market for business and financial services exploded.

The 1970s crisis highlights two key points relevant for examining the present crisis. The first is that the crisis of the seventies was a deep, intersecting crisis; the simultaneous economic, social, and political crisis created a chaotic environment that demanded resolution from above. Both elites and ordinary people believed the government and perhaps even capitalism were in danger of collapsing from economic disorder and democratic dissent. A bipartisan consensus emerged that dramatic moves were needed to restore business confidence and create the political space for the massive restructuring of capital and class relations. Alan Greenspan remarked at the time how Republicans and Democrats demonstrated 'a convergence of attitudes' that agreed upon the need to 'restrain inflation, cut deficit spending, reduce regulation, and encourage investment'.[14] In short, the crisis was impossible to ignore, resolve, or displace through minor policy adjustments and rhetorical flourish.

The second main take-away from the crisis of the seventies is the broad restructuring it catalyzed – a decade-long process of experimentation, resolve, and luck by ruling elites to restore confidence and establish a new status quo. Changing course – abandoning Keynesianism and the principles of stability and sovereignty that underlay the Bretton Woods model – rejuvenated American capital and the state. Yet, the resolution was fraught with contradictions. Recovery on the backs of workers and households alongside finance-driven growth created a volatile environment prone to economic crisis and characterized by increasing polarization and anomie.

II

What about today? Insofar as revisiting the decade-long crisis of the seventies provides some useful points of comparison to assess the present crisis, this is not because history repeats itself. On the contrary, one could argue that the present crisis is a result of the unresolved contradictions of the seventies crisis. Instead, the comparison is useful because it provides a schema for parsing the crisis in the United States and also for locating potential points of intervention for the American left.

From the perspective of capital an economic crisis is no longer apparent. Corporate profits are strong; 2017 marked a five-year high for S&P 500 firms. Firms recovered from the 2008 financial crisis within a few years, and today many are sitting on mountains of cash. The stock market is strong, if not always steady. The two factors that have traditionally acted as a constraint on capital – labour and finance – are for many firms a minor concern. Borrowing costs are low, making it easy for firms to finance production and buy back shares. Meanwhile, real wages have barely budged since the 1970s, and firms have wide leeway to organize workers and work processes as they see fit. Expectations about work have completely shifted in the past few decades. As Allison Pugh argues, workers today expect nothing more than a paycheck and a modicum of respect from their employers.[15] The potentially negative impact of stagnant wages on consumer spending has been mitigated by dual-earning households and increased hours spent working.

An economic crisis is also no longer apparent from the perspective of the state, even if specific worries over debt loads remain. The bailout following the 2008 crisis coupled with several years of quantitative easing created a soft landing for capital, and in the years since the Fed has maintained a low-interest rate environment. If anything, persistently low inflation and a predictable, docile labour market have left policy makers scratching their heads about the validity of core macroeconomic principles. Robust financial markets keep foreign capital flowing into the US and, thus far, Trump's erratic policy objectives have engendered fury and puzzlement from world leaders but little discernible economic blowback.

It remains to be seen whether or not this situation is sustainable. Trump's tariff war, for instance, seems to be gathering steam. A range of radical commentators were recently asked, 'Are we headed for another economic crash?' and most asserted that we are. Wolfgang Streeck answered, 'Yes ... and it's not going to be pleasant', while Cédric Durand declared the impending mortality of financial hegemony. Susan Newman foresees a crash coming because 'the underlying conditions that brought about the financial crisis of 2007-08 remain'. Meanwhile Heikki Patomäki sees an erosion of 'the basis of genuine growth' amid a growing 'underlying super bubble'. Both David Kotz and Minqi Li agree that even if a crash is not around the corner, a deep recession is most certainly on the near horizon.[16] Such prognoses are not confined to the left.

From the perspective of state and local governments one could certainly argue that times remain very tough. Puerto Rico is being strangled by debt; Detroit declared Chapter 9 bankruptcy in 2013; and Chicago seems to be perpetually wrestling with a pension crisis. According to the National Conference of State Legislatures, 22 states have school districts operating a four-day school week to save money on transportation, heating and staffing.[17] In 2017, 33 states saw budget shortfalls (the highest number since 2010), while 23 states made mid-year budget cuts totaling $5 billion.[18] Declining tax revenues and increased health-care cost projections are set against collapsing infrastructure. The American Society of Civil Engineers recently gave America's infrastructure (bridges, dams, ports, levees, schools, roads, etc.) a D+ and projected a $4.6 trillion price tag to make necessary improvements, up from $1.3 trillion in 2001.

The situation for individuals and households is mixed. The most recent

Federal Reserve report on the economic well-being of American households argues for a story of 'overall improvement' in people's financial lives, based on the fact that 'a large majority of individuals report that financially they are doing okay or living comfortably'. The researchers find, moreover, that 'most workers are satisfied with the wages and benefits from their current job, and are optimistic about their future job opportunities'. Yet, the Federal Reserve's survey also indicates the persistence of deep and long-standing divides in well-being between urban and rural dwellers, between those with at least a bachelor's degree and those with only a high school education or 'some college', and between whites and non-whites.[19]

Peter Temin characterizes these divides as America's 'dual economy' (a term coined by W. Arthur Lewis in the 1950s to describe developing economies) – a track for subsistence workers and another for upwardly mobile, skilled workers.[20] The wealth divide, which has widened since the 2008 crisis, certainly supports this conclusion.[21] Americans are also highly indebted; the New York Fed recently reported that total household debt increased to $13.15 trillion in the last quarter of 2017, the fifth consecutive year that mortgage, student, auto, and credit card debt increased for US households.[22] Meanwhile, new job growth is primarily part-time or temporary work and concentrated in low-wage sectors. Economic Policy Institute data shows a widening gap between top earners and everyone else:

> The bottom seven deciles have seen annual growth of hourly wages of 0.5 percent or less since 2000. The way rising inequality has directly affected most Americans is through sluggish hourly wage growth in recent decades, despite an expanding and increasingly productive economy. For example, had all workers' wages risen in line with productivity, as they did in the three decades following World War II, an American earning around $40,000 today would instead be making close to $61,000.[23]

These facts paint a dire picture for local governments and working families. Yet neither the economic crisis of state and local governments, nor the crisis for working people, are recent phenomena. Cuts in social support and the degradation of work have been a decades-long process tied to neoliberalism, financialization, and globalization. Charles Post dates the beginning of the end to the post-Second World War period, when the ouster of the 'militant minority' from the labour movement destroyed earlier organs of working-class struggle – a fact that goes far in explaining why massive cuts in services and the proliferation of lousy jobs have proceeded without significant resistance over the past few decades.[24]

This economic picture raises the possibility that what we are now witnessing may be more a social crisis than an economic crisis. The accumulated effects of the destruction of working-class livelihoods have certainly created a crisis of social well-being. Research by Anne Case and Angus Deaton reveals the American white working class to be prematurely dying at an alarming rate.[25] Mass incarceration and a hopelessly broken parole system have destroyed millions of lives, particularly those of poor people of colour. One in five children live in families eking out an existence below the poverty line, and the escape route of education is increasingly blocked by the re-segregation of public schooling and skyrocketing college tuition. To top it off, the country is fighting an opioid epidemic (care of the pharmaceutical industry) amidst a growing wave of working-class alienation and despair. Sixty-four thousand Americans died from drug overdoses in 2016 in states ill equipped to handle the crisis after years of service and budget cuts.

This, however, is a social crisis of a different nature than how we characterize the social crisis of the 1970s. The 1970s was also a decade that saw poverty, inequality, and addiction, but when we talk about social crisis in the context of the seventies we are primarily referring to the disruptive, sustained, and radical actions of large, powerful social movements. Mass strikes and a huge anti-war movement existed alongside effective, large-scale organizations demanding women's rights, civil rights, consumer rights, and environmental rights.

Are we seeing a social crisis of a similar nature today? We have certainly seen embryonic social movement formations develop in the US (as well as globally) in the decade since the 2008 financial meltdown. Occupy encampments appeared in 2011, growing quickly and visibly, but also fizzling rapidly as a result of both design and police repression. The Movement for Black Lives coalesced following the killing of Trayvon Martin in 2012 and then Michael Brown in 2014. This movement, unlike Occupy, has persisted with a strong social media presence and concrete steps to move forward in the form of the Black Lives Matter platform. On the heels of the Women's March in January 2017, the largest march in the history of the US, a consciousness-raising women's movement has emerged under the hashtag #MeToo. This movement has led to the ouster of numerous high-profile abusers and has fuelled an international conversation about sexism. In terms of nationally visible protest actions, we could add the Dakota Access Pipeline encampment, immigrant rights protests in response to Trump's xenophobic policies, the nascent youth-led movement for gun control (#NeverAgain), and the membership surge in the Democratic Socialists of America (DSA).

Yet, the contrast between recent social movement crystallizations and those of the seventies is clear. In the seventies, economic and social crises created a political crisis for the ruling class. It was a crisis that demanded action from above. Today we are not witnessing an economic or social crisis that demands a militant response from capital – or at least we're not seeing it yet. Jane McAlevey's distinction between mobilizing and organizing is useful here: We've seen some exciting and heartening mobilizations in the past few years, but these haven't yet evolved into effective movements organizing for change that force a response from elites.

Perhaps a major reason why is the missing US labour movement, which has been completely de-fanged over the past three decades. Private sector density has declined to less than 7 per cent – numbers not seen since before the 1935 Wagner Act was passed at the high point of the New Deal. Labour unions have seen their place as junior partner in the Democratic Party taken over by Silicon Valley. According to the *Financial Times*, 'in the 2016 election, the internet industry gave 74 per cent of its $12.3m in congressional campaign contributions to Democrats'.[26] It's also unclear who speaks for organized labour, and it rarely advocates for itself. Several high profile unions, including the Communication Workers of America, the International Longshore and Warehouse Union, and the United Electrical, Radio, and Machine Workers of America as well as the Amalgamated Transit Union, the American Postal Workers Union, and National Nurses United, came out in support of Bernie Sanders in the 2016 election. But on the whole organized labour – despite its once-fabled history as America's most successful progressive social movement – has shown little inclination to engage in, let alone lead, anything resembling what used to be called a 'class war' on behalf of working families. This partly explains why millions of union rank-and-filers voted for Trump, particularly in rust-belt towns who've seen manufacturing jobs decline under the rule of Democrats in the past decade.

III

Yet, despite the absence of an economic crisis or an upsurge of mass social movement organizing demanding elite resolution, observers across the spectrum are convinced that we're in the midst of a deep political crisis. So what is the nature of the political crisis? What do people mean when they say 'liberal democracy is crumbling'? There seem to be (at least) two broad interpretations floating around. The first is that the US government has taken an authoritarian turn and that Trump, through doltishness, design, or both, is sabotaging the functionality of the state, rendering it incapable of carrying out the basic duties of democratic governance.

Harvard professors Steven Levitsky and Daniel Ziblatt argue that, unlike any previous US presidents, Trump meets the markers for authoritarianism.[27] Meanwhile, a new book by political scientists Christopher Federico, Stanley Feldman, and Christopher Weber situates Trump's rise within a broader shift in political and cultural attitudes, whereby authoritarianism 'has become part and parcel of Republican identity among non-Hispanic white Americans'.[28] Lt. Col. Ralph Peters, an Army veteran and longtime Fox News contributor, made headlines in March 2018 when, pointing to the administration's 'profoundly dishonest assaults on the FBI, the Justice Department, the courts, the intelligence community', he withdrew from the network, saying that it had begun to act as a 'propaganda machine for a destructive and ethically ruinous administration'.[29] From the left, David Kotz warns in an article for *Jacobin* that Trump is trying to establish a right-wing nationalist regime. Certainly, the President's recent policy of separating children from their parents at the US-Mexico border drives home the seriousness of this threat.

The view of Trump as authoritarian and/or psychologically unfit (60,000 mental health professionals signed a petition declaring Trump mentally unfit for office) dovetails with arguments that the President is sabotaging the bureaucratic functioning of the US government, to the point of 'appointing people to run federal agencies who are opposed to the work and, sometimes, to the very existence of those agencies'.[30] Rick Perry – US Secretary of Energy – once vowed to dismantle the department he now heads. Scott Pruitt – made responsible for the Environmental Protection Agency – has described himself as a 'leading advocate against the EPA's activist agenda'. And the Secretary of Education, Betsy DeVos, is a vociferous proponent of privatizing public education who memorably declared in a *60 Minutes* interview (perhaps channeling Thatcher): 'What's an education "system"? There's no such thing!'

Jeff Hauser, who runs the Center for Economic Policy and Research (CEPR) 'Revolving Door Project' – an effort to 'increase scrutiny on executive branch appointments and ensure that political appointees are focused on serving the public interest' – argues that the Trump administration is purposely trying to disempower Congressional scrutiny by leaving key posts, such as the commissioner of the Internal Revenue Service, open.[31] According to an ongoing study by the *Washington Post* and the Partnership for Public Service, as of April 2018, Trump had failed to nominate 208 out of 656 keep positions that required Senate confirmation.[32] With the ouster of Rex Tillerson, the State Department finds itself with eight of ten top jobs vacant, including 'positions overseeing the agency's role in U.S. trade policy, stopping the spread of nuclear weapons, refugee issues and efforts to counter human trafficking'.[33] Asked about all the vacant positions in an interview with Fox News the President replied:

'We don't need all the people they want. I'm a businessman, and I tell my people, "When you don't need to fill slots, don't fill them." But we have some people that I'm not happy with there. Let me tell you, the one that matters is me. I'm the only one that matters, because when it comes to it, that's what the policy is going to be.'[34]

The sense that liberal democracy is crumbling is further sustained by the growing sense that people have lost faith in the government – both in its ability to act in their interests and in the belief that they have a meaningful voice or a place in the demos. On a basic level this loss of faith can be seen in polls showing a steady drop in trust in the government. According to Pew, as of December 2017 'Public trust in the government remains near historic lows. Only 18 per cent of Americans today say they can trust the government in Washington to do what is right "just about always" (3 per cent) or "most of the time" (15 per cent)'.[35] The loss of faith is partly a disavowal of the Third Way project of the past three decades – a rejection of globalism and neoliberalism. As Mark Shields has argued, this reflects the extent to which 'the forces and the advocates of globalization have been primarily obsessed with the well-being of the investor class and the stockholders and the shareholders, and been indifferent, oftentimes callous to the dislocation and suffering of people in countries affected by this trade'.[36]

Robert Reich echoed this sentiment shortly after Trump's victory: 'Recent economic indicators may be up, but those indicators don't reflect the insecurity most Americans continue to feel, nor the seeming arbitrariness and unfairness they experience'.[37] Despite low unemployment, workforce participation remains down significantly since 2008, and also 2000 when it peaked. Many people have simply stopped looking for work, particularly older people, as good jobs have become scarce. Wisconsin, Michigan, and Pennsylvania saw a fresh round of good jobs wiped out as anti-union drives ripped through those states between 2008 and 2016.

The loss of faith also extends to a rejection of the mainstream parties. In a recent report by the Rand Corporation entitled 'Truth Decay', the authors argue that we're not just seeing a loss of faith in politicians, but also an 'erosion of trust in and reliance on objective facts in political debate and civil discourse about public policy' demonstrated by 'declining trust in formerly respected sources of factual information'. This phenomenon of 'truth decay' does not just erode Americans' ability to 'have meaningful political debates about important topics; it also contributes to political polarization and paralysis, undermines civic engagement, perpetuates the proliferation of misinformation and disinformation, and leads to widespread uncertainty and anxiety throughout the U.S. electorate.'[38]

Such assessments of the political crisis – that we're witnessing growing authoritarianism and sabotage of democratic institutions, on the one hand, and that people have lost faith in the government, on the other – in fact fit together. At the very least they signal a deep crisis of legitimacy for neoliberalism, reflecting a deep level of dissatisfaction with the legitimating framework of contemporary American capitalism.

IV

Returning to the question we posed at the beginning of this essay of whether we've reached a tipping point: If reaching a tipping point means a loss of legitimacy for the status quo and a loss of faith in the reigning elite consensus, then we have certainly reached it. But if the tipping point means the emergence of a powerful force that compels a response from elites in the form of a new legitimating framework, or a new way of organizing capitalism, then we haven't yet reached a tipping point.[39]

At this point, the greatest factor pushing politicians to respond to public demands is bad social media coverage. People are deeply unsatisfied but there are no material factors (such as an economic crisis) or organizational factors (such as a set of powerful social movements) to catalyze a deep change, let alone channel the political crisis into a progressive movement for change. People are, as Fraser argues, looking around for 'new ideologies, organizations, and leadership' but which ones will take us from dissatisfaction to disruption remains an open question.

Disruption is of course the calling card of Silicon Valley. Fuelled by endless streams of free money care of the Fed, pension funds, venture capital, and others, Silicon Valley has captured the public imagination in an unprecedented way since the 2008 crisis eroded the prestige of Wall Street rainmakers. With stories about smart cities, self-driving cars, and rockets to the moon, Silicon Valley 'wonder boys' have become the new masters of the universe, spreading an ideology rooted in fantasies of freewheeling entrepreneurs summoning the future with their algorithms and apps. Promising high-paying jobs (for the highly educated) and life-changing consumer products, Google, Facebook, Amazon, and Apple have become the purveyors of the New American Dream. As a result, the Silicon Valley ethos of 'move fast and break things' and 'ask for forgiveness, not permission' has permeated business as well as interactions between start-ups and community institutions.

The Silicon Valley vision is an elite vision. Its politics – of a future fuelled by technological fixes, brilliant entrepreneurs, and new frontiers of digital commodification – is transparently pro-capitalist and anti-state, despite the long history of state funding for nearly every modern technological innovation. Moreover, the libertarian bent of Silicon Valley's leading lights sits comfortably alongside opinion makers far to the right. So while most valley dwellers vote Democrat, and were horrified by PayPal founder Peter Thiel's enthusiastic support for Donald Trump, Thiel's general worldview is not incongruous with the deeply held beliefs of tech elites regarding capitalism, markets, and state regulation.

Thiel's public support for Trump was unusual, however, in that few conservative elites supported the real estate mogul's candidacy. Instead, his base (until the very last weeks of the campaign) consisted largely of ordinary voters, many of whom were attracted to his right-wing nationalist political sensibilities – a phenomenon being repeated in a growing number of countries around the globe.[40] Trump's rhetoric is rooted in racist nostalgia, fear, and nationalism. He took the baton from Steve Bannon, who took it from the Tea Party – a group that emerged after the 2008 financial meltdown with a message of fiscal prudence and nationalist resurgence, supported by a base of (primarily) white 'patriots'.

Both of these emergent political sensibilities – Silicon Valley's techno-utopia and Trumpism – reveal deep concerns, and thus points of intervention, for the American left. In the most basic sense they highlight a growing need for a left, anti-capitalist vision rooted in the tradition of labour internationalism. The left should be at the head of the line in demanding respect for democracy, civil liberties, and protection from corporations. This is already happening to some degree, but liberal voices dominate public discourse, particularly around issues of war and US military interventions.

Unpacking the popular appeal of a Silicon Valley future or a Trumpian future also highlights other issues the left needs to take on. In the case of tech, scandals over data privacy and a growing public recognition of the vast power that Facebook, Google, Amazon, and Apple have accumulated over daily life highlights the need to exert social control over technology. It also creates an opening to demand a commanding role in our collective technological future: control over the data we generate, stronger state regulation of these modern-day monopolies, and also recognition that the internet, social media, and e-commerce are essential to daily life and should be treated as utilities – accessible and regulated to benefit everyone.

Trumpism's appeal is rooted in a deep racism and xenophobia central to the development of American capitalism. But it is also rooted in the contradictions of Third Way liberalism and the profound sense of exclusion and alienation felt by the white working class. The refusal of liberal elites to acknowledge that the political-economic direction of the past three decades was less about abstract goals of efficiency, personal responsibility, connectedness, etc., than it was about enriching elites has been deeply alienating for working people. As history has shown, the right is incapable of providing a project for justice and security for the working class, so it is up to the left to develop a mass political movement that creates a genuine voice and vehicle for the working class.

V

What is the potential for the left to accomplish this? Assessing the response of the US left to the 2008 financial crisis, Adolph Reed and Mark Dudzic bluntly declared: 'There is no left worth talking about in the United States and there has not been one for quite a while.'[41] Certainly any comparison between the strength of progressive social movements – particularly the labour movement – of the 1970s and those of today drives this point home. But at the same time, developing new capacities is not off the table; building a strong left rooted in a strong labour movement today is difficult, but not impossible. Working classes are continuously being reshaped and remade and new working classes are always emerging.

Kim Moody, in a recent book, argues that after decades of capitalist restructuring and change in the composition of the working class we have arrived at a moment of newfound potential.

> We fight now on new terrain. The trends that created barriers, pitfalls, divisions, and minefields for working-class organization and power, while not disappearing, have been altered through capitalism's own inherent dynamics of competition and expansion, which has led to the consolidation, integration, and relocation of capital in ways that are potentially more advantageous for working-class resistance, organization, and power.[42]

Moody suggests that the conditions workers face in their everyday (still mostly full-time and long-term) work lives – 'lean production, electronic and biometric forms of work measurement and monitoring, the new contours of just-in-time supply chains, and the "logistics revolution' – have generated powder-keg conditions ready to explode in an upsurge of strike activity and union growth.[43]

We haven't seen this explosion yet, but there are promising new developments in the labour movement. Most people just don't hear about them because, as McAlevey notes, the mainstream press doesn't cover them.[44] The disparate coverage of the 2014 United Auto Workers' election loss in Chattanooga compared to the Verizon workers' 2016 collective bargaining win is a clear example: dozens of think pieces dissected the autoworkers' loss while mainstream discussions of the Verizon win were cursory at best.

McAlevey and others on the left have been filling the coverage gap, writing about striking nurses in Massachusetts and Philadelphia, and more recently about striking teachers in West Virginia.[45] Teacher discontent is spreading rapidly – Arizona, Oklahoma, Los Angeles. An upsurge of teacher strikes suddenly seems possible. Not only do these actions demonstrate the continued relevance of the strike as a powerful tactic, they also show communities actively resisting the prevailing 'common sense' that there are no resources to fund good jobs. Teachers and nurses are demanding that the money be found, and they're winning, with the support of their communities.

These strikes also show the potential for building a labour movement that transcends political 'constituencies'. The teachers, staff, and supporting families of the West Virginia strike included both Trump and Clinton voters yet they managed to work together as a collective to achieve a concrete aim. Talking to McAlevey, the president of the United Teachers of Los Angeles Alex Caputo-Pearl remarked, 'This isn't a red state issue, it's a blue state issue too'. Gearing up for a possible strike at the start of the fall term, Caputo-Pearl declared, 'The rank and file are going to take the fight to the Democrats who have been complicit in the attack on public education and teachers unions'.[46]

It does seem the case that, in the years since the 2012 Chicago teachers' strike, the radical potential of rank-and-file workers is on the upswing. To say this is not mere cheerleading of the type Sam Gindin rightfully warns against.[47] Taken alongside the persistence of the Movement for Black Lives, the recent #MeToo eruptions, and growing fights around issues of climate change and immigrant rights, it is clear that political sentiments are shifting. Perhaps nothing demonstrates this shift more than the 2016 Bernie Sanders presidential run. Ferguson and his co-authors argue that the Sanders campaign demonstrates,

something we are confident is without precedent in American politics not just since the New Deal, but across virtually the whole of American history: a major presidential candidate waging a strong, highly competitive campaign whose support from big business is essentially zero.[48]

The groundswell of support for Sanders confirmed that the left is slowly emerging from its 'deep-rooted economic fatalism'.[49] There is growing demand to share the fruits of technological advance and economic resources hoarded by the few. Sanders' platform threw into vivid relief the widespread support for 'non-reformist reforms' such as healthcare and education for all.

Yet, in its present incarnation this emergent left impulse is also confused and conflicted. Sanders did not emerge from a social movement, and while he remains extremely popular, his base hasn't moved concertedly toward solidifying a mass political movement. At the same time, raging social media wars over how race, class, and gender divide America, and the obsession that Trump is a Demon King requiring our singular attention, present significant hurdles. Our limited success in coming together in a way that both recognizes and affirms clashing progressive viewpoints and then moves forward in a common struggle toward a collective goal reveals a left uncertain of the horizon it seeks. Shifting sentiments have not yet translated into gains on a broad scale.

That said, the passion we've witnessed over the past few years in mobilizations against police brutality and racism, gun control, immigrant rights, and violence against women is promising. There's no reason the left can't build strong social movements outside the labour movement. Indeed we must, because, as Beverly Silver has observed, trade unions occupy an 'ambiguous structural position' in capitalism: ultimately they are 'part of the solution but not the full solution'.[50] Concrete gains in the 1970s regarding women's rights, civil rights, environmental rights, and consumer rights were made by groups operating outside the workplace – groups who were able to move beyond consciousness-raising to organizing rooted in community-based institutions, some of which developed the capacity to leverage that power on a state and national level. Even more important today is the need to bridge the workplace and the community – to 'figure out how to combine workplace bargaining power and the power of the street' as Silver says, or to engage in what McAlevey calls 'whole worker organizing'.[51]

At the same time we shouldn't romanticize social movements of the past. After all, those movements suffered painful and lasting defeats. Some of those defeats were a result of counter-revolution from above, but as Keeanga Yamahtta-Taylor shows so clearly in her interviews with founding members of the Combahee River Collective, many such defeats also resulted from dysfunctions rooted in the racist, sexist, homophobic norms and practices that permeated social movement organizing at the time.[52] Increased awareness and appreciation of the importance of tackling racism, sexism, and homophobia within social movement organizing over the past thirty years, although uneven and unfinished, has been a positive development that in many respects makes the nascent social movements of today potentially more resilient and dynamic than those of the past.

To realize this resilience and dynamism, our politics needs to move from the cloud to the community. The recent successes of political candidates aligned with the DSA suggest one way this might be starting to happen. The organization has focused heavily on fostering a new anti-racist, anti-sexist, anti-capitalist political culture for 'very online' millennials. But recent electoral victories – particularly Alexandria Ocasio-Cortez's surprising win over New York City Democratic stalwart Joseph Crowley[53] – demonstrate both the appeal of a democratic socialist platform in working-class communities and a potential path for translating consciousness-raising into concrete political gains.

Socialism is not yet on the horizon. But at the same time, a genuine political opening has emerged for the first time in decades. The challenge for the left in this moment is, in many respects, the same as it has always been: to translate political discontent into a constellation of radical, democratic, anti-capitalist social movements that represent working people and have the capacity to challenge capital and win. But this challenge is also more urgent than it has ever been.

NOTES

1   Francis Fukuyama, 'US Against the World? Trump's America and the New Global Order,' *Financial Times*, 11 November 2016; Gideon Rachman, 'Donald Trump and the Dangers of America First', *Financial Times*, 9 November 2016; Philip Stephens, 'How the World Swapped a Big Idea for a Bad One', *Financial Times*, 5 April 2018; Charles Krauthammer, 'After a Mere 25 years, the Triumph of the West is Over', *The Washington Post*, 1 December 2016.

2   Thomas Ferguson, Paul Jorgensen, and Jie Chen, 'Industrial Structure and Party Competition in an Age of Hunger Games: Donald Trump and the 2016 Presidential Election', Working Paper No. 66, *Institute for New Economic Thinking*, January 2018.

3   Ferguson et al., 'Industrial Structure and Party Competition', p. 4.

4   Nancy Fraser, 'From Progressive Neoliberalism to Trump and Beyond', *American Affairs*, 1(4), Winter 2017.

5   'Report on the Economic Well-Being of US Households in 2017', Board of Governors of the Federal Reserve System, May 2018. Note however, that this number has declined from 2013, when half of American adults reported being unable to meet the same expense.

6   Chris Giles, 'IMF Hails "Broadest" Upsurge in Global Growth Since 2010', *Financial Times*, 22 January 2018.

7   Greta Krippner identifies the crisis of the 1970s as an intersecting fiscal, social, and legitimacy crisis. In this paper, the decade's triple crisis is defined more broadly, as an economic, social, and political crisis. See Greta Krippner, *Capitalizing on Crisis: The Political Origins of the Rise of Finance*, Cambridge: Harvard University Press, 2011.

8   Giovanni Arrighi, *The Long Twentieth Century: Money, Power, and the Origins of Our Times*, London: Verso, 1994.

9   Leo Panitch and Sam Gindin, *The Making of Global Capitalism: The Political Economy of American Empire*, London: Verso, 2012, p. 133.

10   Keeanga Yamahtta-Taylor, *How We Get Free: Black Feminism and the Combahee River Collective*, Chicago: Haymarket Books, 2017.

11   Cara Giaimo, 'Mapping the Lost Countercultural Hotspots of Cambridge, Massachusetts', *Atlas Obscura*, 24, April 2018.

12   See Kim Moody, *An Injury To All: The Decline of American Unionism*, London: Verso, 1988.

13   Panitch and Gindin, *The Making of Global Capitalism*, pp. 183-93.

14   Panitch and Gindin, *The Making of Global Capitalism*, p. 165.

15   Allison Pugh, *The Tumbleweed Society: Working and Caring in an Insecure Age*, New York: Oxford University Press, 2015.

16   Cihan Aksan and Jon Bailes, 'One Question Economic Crash', *State of Nature Blog*, 15 January 2018, available at: stateofnatureblog.com.

17   National Conference of State Legislatures, available at www.ncsl.org.

18   John W. Schoen, 'States in crisis: Embroiled in the Worst Budget Battles Since the Great Recession', *CNBC*, 11 July 2017.

19   'Report on the Economic Well-Being of US Households in 2017'.

20   Peter Temin, *The Vanishing Middle Class: Prejudice and Power in a Dual Economy*, Cambridge: MIT Press, 2017.

21   'Changes in US Family Finances from 2013 to 2016: Evidence from the Survey of Consumer Finances', *Federal Reserve Bulletin*, 103(3), September 2017.

22   Press Release: 'Household Debt Jumps as 2017 Marks the Fifth Consecutive Year of Positive Annual Growth Since Post-Recession Deleveraging,' Federal Reserve Bank of New York, 13 February 2018.

23   Elise Gould, 'The State of American Wages 2017', *Economic Policy Institute*, 1 March 2018.

24   Charles Post, 'The Forgotten Militants', *Jacobin*, 22, Summer 2016.

25   Anne Case and Sir Angus Deaton, 'Mortality and Morbidity in the 21st Century', Brookings Papers on Economic Activity, 23 March 2017.

26   David J. Lynch, 'Big Tech and Amazon: Too power to break up?' *Financial Times*, 30 October 2017.

27   Steven Levitsky and Daniel Ziblatt, *How Democracies Die*, New York: Crown, 2018.

28   Thomas B. Edsall, 'The Contract with Authoritarianism', *New York Times*, 5 April 2018.

29   Michael M. Grynbaum, 'Fox News Analyst Quits, Calling Network a "Propaganda Machine"', *New York Times*, 20 March 2018.

30   Masha Gessen, 'What the Ronny Jackson Debacle Reveals About Donald Trump and the "Swamp"', *The New Yorker*, 26 April 2018.

31   James Hohmann, 'The Daily 202: Trump has no nominees for 245 important jobs, including an ambassador to South Korea', *The Washington Post*, 12 January 2018.

32   'Tracking How Many Key Positions Trump Has Filled So Far', *The Washington Post* and Partnership for Public Service.

33   Bill Faries and Mira Rojanasakul, 'At Trump's State Department, Eight of Ten Top Jobs Are Empty', *Bloomberg*, 2 February 2018.

34   Hohmann, 'The Daily 202', *The Washington Post*, 12 January 2018.

35   'Public Trust in Government: 1958-2017', Pew Research Center, *US Politics and Policy*, 14 December 2017.

36   'Shields and Brooks on Voter Disenchantment Across the Globe', *PBS News Hour*, 24 January 2016.

37   Robert Reich, 'Why We Need a New Democratic Party', *Alternet*, 13 November 2016.

38   Jennifer Kavanagh and Michael D. Rich, 'Truth Decay: An Initial Exploration of the Diminishing Role of Facts and Analysis in American Public Life', Santa Monica: Rand Corporation, 2018.

39   A systematic analysis of Trump's behavior and its repercussions – the impact of his sabotage, whether we are becoming an authoritarian state, etc., are important questions but fall beyond the scope of this piece.

40   See Leo Panitch and Greg Albo, eds, *Socialist Register 2016: The Politics of the Right*, London: Merlin Press, 2015.

41   Adolph Reed and Mark Dudzic 'The Crisis of Labour and the Left in the United States', in Leo Panitch and Greg Albo, eds, *Socialist Register 2015: Transforming Classes*, London: Merlin Press, 2014.

42   Kim Moody, *On New Terrain: How Capital Is Reshaping the Battleground of Class War*, Chicago: Haymarket Books, 2017, p. 171

43   Moody, *On New Terrain*, p. 75

44   Sarah Jaffe, 'Jane McAlevey Talks About the Power of the Strike', *The Progressive*, 28 March 2018.

45   See for example, Jane McAlevey, 'This Massachusetts Nurses' Union is Reviving the Strike', *The Nation*, 19 July 2017; and 'The West Virginia Teachers Strike Shows that Winning Big Requires Creating a Crisis', *The Nation*, 12 March 2018.

46   Jane McAlevey, 'Teachers Are Leading the Revolt Against Austerity', *The Nation*, 9 May 2018.

47   Sam Gindin, 'Chasing Utopia', *Jacobin*, 10 March 2016.

48   Ferguson, et al., 'Industrial Structure and Party Competition', p. 25.

49   Pierre Bourdieu, 'A Reasoned Utopia and Economic Fatalism', *New Left Review*, 1(227), 1998.

50   Beverly Silver, 'Workers of the World', *Jacobin*, 22, Summer 2016.

51   Silver, 'Workers of the World'; Jane McAlevey, *No Shortcuts: Organizing for Power in the New Gilded Age*, New York: Oxford University Press, 2016.

52   Yamahtta-Taylor, *How We Get Free*.

53   See Michelle Goldberg, 'The Millennial Socialists Are Coming', *New York Times*, 30 June 2018.

THE EUROPEAN CRISIS AND THE LEFT

ALAN CAFRUNY

Less than two decades ago the prospects for an 'ever closer' European Union (EU) seemed virtually limitless. Agreement on a Stability and Growth Pact in 1997, followed by the successful launch of the third stage of the Economic and Monetary Union (EMU) in 1999, suggested that the establishment of the euro could underwrite dynamic economic growth and preserve Europe's distinctive social model while extending the zone of democracy into central and eastern Europe. Closer political integration was certain to follow ineluctably, while the new international reserve currency would lay the basis for a broader European challenge to the American superpower.

If the decision to adopt EMU was thus a result of many proximate factors operating in both the geopolitical and economic spheres – not least the attempt to contain a reunified Germany – it also served to consolidate Europe's turn to finance-led growth and neoliberalism. Neoliberal policies that had been introduced in an Anglo-American context that was more susceptible to the calls for 'freedom' from Margaret Thatcher and Ronald Reagan were justified on the continent in terms of 'Europeanization'. The onset of the 2009 sovereign debt crisis posed an enormous challenge for European leaders. As Chancellor Merkel proclaimed in 2011, 'The euro is much, much more than a currency. The euro is the guarantee of a united Europe. If the euro fails, Europe fails.'[1] Membership in the EMU had temporarily insulated chronic debtor countries from currency crises even as it kept their borrowing costs artificially low. At the same time, of course, it precluded devaluation as a means of regaining competitiveness in favour of domestic austerity or 'internal devaluation.' Household debt in the southern periphery skyrocketed to offset the structural current account deficit arising from the expanding German trade surplus while German and other core-nation banks became massively over-exposed. Harsh austerity plans – effectively socializing the debt and channelling public funds to the banks – were imposed as the price of emergency injections of capital at punitive rates. As the crisis spread to the north and east, the EU's policies in response to the crisis ironically transformed the region that had once been the heartland of the post-World War II class compromise into the epicentre of global neoliberalism. Widespread disillusionment and popular opposition gathered momentum, culminating in the vote for Brexit in June 2016. The architects of 'ever closer union' now warned of an 'existential' crisis.

THE CRISIS IS PERMANENT

Since 1945 Europe has passed through two distinctive regulatory projects of integration. The first such project, arising out of Europe's post-World War II economic and geopolitical predicament, sought to prevent another European war – and consolidate the US-led hegemonic order – through the establishment of modest forms of economic cooperation. While giving rise to the concept of supranational integration, this project in fact served to buttress the European nation-states and promote national economic development and political stability.[2] The modest supranational initiatives corresponded to the broad contours of the 'embedded liberal' social- and Christian-democratic welfare settlements that became institutionalized within the context of an organic US hegemony.[3] The anti-democratic features of the Union were inherent in the Treaty of Rome, but of relatively little import when the main levers of economic and social policy remained with the member states.

A second, neoliberal, project arose out of the crisis of the post-war Bretton Woods system and was constitutionalized[4] through three formative treaties: the Single European Act of 1987, the EMU of 1993, and the Lisbon Treaty of 2009. The project was based on the assumption uniting parties of the centre-right and centre-left that a decade of stagflation and failed attempts at regional monetary coordination after the collapse of the Bretton Woods system meant there was 'no alternative' to national and regional neoliberalism. The neoliberal 'relaunching' greatly reduced national prerogatives without giving rise to the pan-European democratic polity necessary to lend stability and cohesion to these radical developments. The exit from the post-war settlement and entry into a monetary union predicated on 'competitive austerity'[5] was facilitated by the gradual erosion of working-class power as a result of growing unemployment, financialization, and the opening up of the former Soviet bloc economies (and later China) with the resultant abundant pools of cheap and unprotected labour. Already in 1985 the highly influential European Round Table (ERT), representing the common interests of Europe's national capitalist classes, had called for a single currency but rejected the Keynesian and fiscal stabilizers inherent in previous plans for monetary union.[6]

The EU responded to the crisis by introducing a set of radical neoliberal policies, in essence reprising the structural adjustment policies that were imposed by the International Monetary Fund (IMF) on much of the global south during the global debt crisis of the 1980s. The rescue packages for Portugal, Ireland, Italy, Greece, and Spain (the so-called 'PIIGs'), were directed to protecting French and German banks.[7] An authoritarian 'fiscal compact' ('Treaty on Stability, Coordination and Governance in the Economic and Monetary Union') in 2012 limited the structural budget deficit to 0.5 per cent, enforced by fines levied by the European Court of Justice. The resultant harsh austerity elicited condemnation even by the US Treasury and International Monetary Fund (IMF). In 2011 – no less than three years into the global financial crisis – the European Central Bank (ECB) raised interest rates twice even as Europe experienced deepening stagnation and mass unemployment. ECB President Mario Draghi's declaration in July 2012 that he was 'ready to do whatever it takes to preserve the euro' brought the most acute phase of the crisis (for the EU although not for Greece) to an end. In 2017 the member states of the EU collectively returned to growth. The recovery has been especially pronounced in the northern countries of the EU. In 2017 Germany experienced its lowest level of unemployment (3.5 per cent) since 1980.

Notwithstanding these developments, the eurozone crisis has not ended. Positive growth indicators need to be set against a long period of stagnation and even negative growth rates experienced by many member states after the crisis broke out in 2009. The region's recovery has been both shallow and uneven, and the return to modest growth was achieved in the context of a decade-long global boom that appears to be coming to an end. Since 2008 global debt levels have risen to a record high of 237 per cent of GDP, exceeding the level of 2009.[8] US debt levels are expected to increase dramatically as a result of the massive decrease in corporate taxes signed into law in 2017, even as the Trump administration pursues an aggressive strategy of financial deregulation.[9] The IMF has concluded that the surge in risky asset prices is reminiscent of the pre-2008 period. By April 2018 growth in the eurozone slowed to 1.2 per cent amid signs that the effects of quantitative easing were waning.[10] Italy has experienced almost no productivity growth since adopting the euro. With a debt-to-GDP ratio of 132 per cent, 'The EU has no instruments to cope with an Italian sovereign debt crisis. Italy is too big to fail and too big to save.'[11] The structural problems of the eurozone have not been resolved.

Levels of inequality and poverty have increased dramatically during the past decade and the crisis has brought about, in John Grahl's words, 'the slow death of social Europe'.[12] Since 2007 labour market insecurity has increased and welfare state retrenchment has led to an overall decrease in security and protection.[13] The European Commission (EC) estimates that 39 per cent of Europeans are now engaged in non-standard and self-employed work, with a significantly greater risk of poverty.[14] 55,000 private companies control massive supply chains, and hire, transport, and house workers throughout the EU.[15] In 2015, after having shrunk by 26 per cent since 2009, the Greek economy finally registered a primary budget surplus. But since that time, it has managed a total growth rate of only 2.8 per cent, and continues to stagger under 248 billion euros of debt (equal to 176 per cent of GDP).[16] The Central and Eastern European countries (CEE) have outpaced the southern tier member states that have been subjected to the most draconian structural reform programmes imposed by the 'Troika' (the ECB, EC and IMF). Yet even in this region, trade unions have been gravely weakened and wages have failed to keep pace with productivity increases. The experience of Romania is emblematic of Europe's east. Heavily penetrated by Western banks and German production chains, Romania in 2011 deregulated its labour market in return for a 20 billion euro bailout package from the IMF and EU. The new labour code, introduced under strong pressure from the European Commission and US Chamber of Commerce, has been 'catastrophic' for Romanian society as it has reduced union membership, workers' rights, and driven down wages.[17]

As the trend towards regional convergence has been thrown into reverse, conflicts among Europe's ruling classes have intensified. Divisions along the east-west, and north-south axes are deepening, and the prospect of a 'multi-speed' Europe, effectively relegating the CEE and southern member states to semi-colonial status, has been broached by the Commission and most powerful states. At the same time, a growing 'democratic deficit' separates the administrative elites from the European people. In this increasingly toxic atmosphere, right-wing populist movements and parties with clear fascist tendencies have strengthened in many countries, and have consolidated power in Hungary and Poland. Skillfully exploiting the surge in migration following Angela Merkel's decision to open Germany's borders in 2015, and resentment of centre-left and centre-right complicity with neoliberal policies, they are strengthening in much of Europe's core. In Austria and the Netherlands, social democratic parties have suffered catastrophic defeats. In Germany, the Social Democratic Party (SPD) returned to the Grand Coalition in January 2018 after having received just 20.5 per cent in the parliamentary elections of September 2017. The party fully recognized that a return to the grand coalition might condemn it to further decline, but also feared that a new election would see it lose second place to the neo-fascist Alternatives for Germany (AfD), which entered the Bundestag for the first time on the strength of 12.6 per cent, and surpassed the SPD in popularity in February 2018. In the French Presidential Elections of April 2017, Socialist candidate Benoit Hamon received just 6 per cent of the vote, while in the subsequent May parliamentary elections the Parti Socialiste received just 29 seats, down from 280 in 2012. The Italian elections of March 2018 represented a massive defeat for the Italian left and centre-left at the hands of the populist Five Star Movement (M5S) and far-right Northern League.

In November 2011 Greece experienced the full force of what has aptly been called 'eurozone fiscal colonialism'.[18] Having announced plans to conduct a national referendum on the Troika's bailout proposal, Prime Minister George Papandreou was replaced by a 'national unity government' of 'technocrats' led by the unelected former Vice-President of the ECB, Lucas Papademos when France and Germany threatened to withhold financial support. The result was the wholesale restructuring of Greek society and economy under the diktat of the Troika. By 2014, as a result of a series of bailout agreements, the official level of unemployment had risen to 27 per cent, and remained at 20 per cent in 2018. Youth unemployment exceeded 50 per cent amid large cutbacks in social services and social provision, including a reduction of the budget for health care by one-half, the dispossession of Greek public assets, and the emigration of 400,000 Greeks, mostly educated youth, since 2010.[19] The rise of Syriza reflected widespread disillusionment with the two main establishment parties of the center-left and center-right, Pasok and New Democracy, and the inability of the Greek Communist Party (KKE) to elicit support for a radical socialist strategy. In national elections of January 2015, Syriza came to power, in coalition with a small nationalist party, with 36.3 per cent of the popular vote. Neither during the campaign nor after forming a government did the party's leadership advocate withdrawal from the eurozone. Rather, it sought to achieve an 'honorable compromise' with the European institutions including decreased austerity and debt write-offs through mass mobilization and appeals to the European left for solidarity.

The Troika threatened to cut off liquidity to Greek banks if the government did not submit to all elements of the bailout program. Syriza's bargaining power was very limited and there was very little evidence of European solidarity. In July 2015, *hundreds* demonstrated in Berlin against austerity for Greece; by contrast three months later *150,000* protested in Berlin against the Transatlantic Trade and Investment Pact. In a referendum called by Syriza in July 2015, 62 per cent of Greek voters rejected a new, harsher bailout package. However, Prime Minister Alexis Tsipras and the Syriza leadership remained unwilling to exit the eurozone, a strategy that would almost certainly have had massive destabilizing economic as well as political consequences. Faced with the ECB's threat to cut off liquidity, the government capitulated to a new round of savage budget cuts, tax increases, and privatizations of infrastructure in return for an additional 86 billion euros. After expelling its radical wing, which had called for exit from the eurozone, Syriza returned to power in September elections with 35.5 per cent of the vote, condemned to preside over continuing austerity.

The Troika's *diktat* applies not only to Greece but also to Italy, founding member and third largest economy in the EU. In 2011 Prime Minister Silvio Berlusconi was compelled to resign under pressure from Brussels and the financial markets in favor of the 'technocrat' and former European Commissioner for Competition, Mario Monti. A similar situation arose in May 2018, when in the throes of a new financial crisis resulting from the establishment of the M5S-Northern League coalition government, Italy's president Sergio Mattarella vetoed the appointment of an avowed euroskeptic, Paolo Savona, and sought to appoint a former IMF official and advocate of austerity, Carlo Cottarelli, rather than the coalition's choice, Giuseppe Conte, as prime minister. This was despite the fact that the leaders of both the Northern League and M5S had moderated their criticisms of the EU and euro. Although Conte was eventually named prime minister, the statement of EU Budget Commissioner Gunther Oettinger once again clearly indicated the limits of national sovereignty and democracy: 'My expectation is that the coming weeks will show that developments in Italy's markets, bonds and economy will become so far-reaching that it might become a signal to voters after all to not vote for populists on the right and left.'[20]

IS THERE A PROGRESSIVE WAY OUT?

Can the condition of permanent crisis be resolved through the transition to a progressive European fiscal and monetary federalism within the framework of existing European institutions? Given the widespread disparities within the eurozone, there is general agreement that, at minimum, three fundamental reforms would need to be adopted: first, the establishment of an EU budget with the power of supranational taxation could allow for counter-cyclical policy as well as an industrial policy. At the present time the EU budget is 1 per cent of EU GDP, and national budgets are subject to strict fiscal controls. Such a budget would need to be substantially larger, perhaps within the range of 5-7 per cent, as called for in the McDougall Report of 1977. A second reform is the transformation of the existing European Stability Mechanism, based in Luxembourg, into a fully-fledged European Monetary Fund under supranational authority that would allow for the issuance of Eurobonds and the mutualization of debt. A third reform is a genuine banking union along the lines of the US federal deposit insurance corporation. These reforms would lay the basis for a set of additional measures including corporate tax harmonization, a financial transactions tax, and a social chapter. The end result of these reforms would be a break with policies of internal devaluation and austerity in favour of a progressive fiscal federalism along more or less left-Keynesian lines. Arising from within heterodox and Keynesian circles, these measures have been advocated ever since the Maastricht Treaty, most notably in *EuroMemorandum*, the annual report of the EuroMemo Group. [21]

As the case of Greece showed, reforms of this scale inevitably lead to confrontation with European institutions and a northern bloc of member states led by Germany. Their realization would require either a substantially greater degree of progressive federalist solidarity than was achieved during the Greek crisis, or else a dramatic transformation of the very nature of German hegemony in Europe. The former would entail at the very least a highly mobilized and pan-European labour movement while the latter would require a transition from German 'ordoliberalism', resulting either from enlightened self-interest or pressure from other states, most obviously France. Yet, at the present time, none of these scenarios appears realistic.

Franco-German Restoration?

The leading contemporary approach to eurozone reform centres around a reassertion of Franco-German leadership, a strategy premised on the ability of France to secure the conversion of German geo-economic power into a more or less benevolent and at least bilaterally shared systemic leadership position. Following his victory in the French Presidential elections of April 2017 and the success of his political party En Marche in the National Assembly in May, Emmanuel Macron has sought to reassert France's traditional shared leadership status over the EU that has been surrendered as a result of years of slow growth and mounting indebtedness. His self-proclaimed 'Revolution' is essentially disciplinary and neoliberal. Having achieved two decisive electoral victories over the Parti Socialiste, from which he resigned in 2016, Macron has sought first to complete the domestic exit from the post-war social settlement started by Francois Mitterrand in 1981: 'I want to get out of the status quo that was established between 1945 and 1970.'[22] Sweeping reforms are designed to appease the German Finance Ministry and, more broadly, German ordoliberal sensitivities and resistance to a 'transfer union'. Under Macron the budget deficit was reduced to 2.6 per cent, leading to the cancellation of the Commission's 'excessive budget procedure' even as budget minister Gerald Darmanin insisted that 'the right deficit is zero'.[23]

Macron has launched a frontal assault on the French welfare state and an increasingly divided and demoralized labour movement. In November 2017, he used a 'fast track process' to diminish the authority of the National Assembly and pass a set of anti-union labor laws that are more far-reaching than the El Khomri labour decrees of 2016, deemed insufficiently transformative by Macron. Macron then challenged the French National Railway Company (SNCF) unions, demanding reforms in all dimensions of rail services, including working rules and pensions that have been described by *Le Monde* as 'the biggest change for the SNCF since its founding in 1937'.[24] Victory over the railway unions, and especially the militant CGT (Confédération générale du travail), would reprise in France Margaret Thatcher's decisive defeat of the UK coal miners in 1984, the subsequent defeat of the remains of the post-war settlement, and the consolidation of neoliberalism.

Macron has appealed to a resurgent spirit of 'Europeanism' which, as noted above, has historically served as the rhetorical justification for neoliberal policies, while simultaneously appeasing German ordoliberal sensitivities and consolidating his domestic standing vis a vis the Rassemblement Nationale (formerly Front National). Thus he proposed transnational lists in the European Parliament. By pursuing a more militarist and Atlanticist foreign policy, including joint US-French operations in Africa and culminating in French participation in US-led missile strikes against Syria of April 2018, he has sought to demonstrate French political-military leadership of Europe.

The confrontation with the rail unions represents a trial of strength that will determine the future of France's welfare state. Macron's attempts to stoke resentment against the rail unions by referring to 'rail worker privilege' has been aided by the trend towards a two-tiered labor market that has been gathering over the past decades, with precarity now already the fate of large numbers of French workers, especially youth. Regardless of the fate of Macron's grand project, Germany has indicated that it will not make significant concessions with respect to the eurozone. Following inconclusive national parliamentary elections of September 2017, which led to months of negotiations and the departure of hardline ordoliberal German finance minister Wolfgang Schäuble, there was speculation that the new government would respond favourably to Macron's overtures. However, the new Grand Coalition has moved significantly to the right, in no small part in reaction to the performance of the AfD. The September elections demonstrated the weakness of the German centre-left resulting in large part from their association with two decades of neoliberal reforms, first under the Schroeder government and then as junior partners in Merkel's Grand Coalition. It appears likely that Germany will only agree to an EMF that is primarily dedicated to strengthening budget discipline and a relatively modest investment fund that falls well short of Macron's more ambitious plans. At the same time, the significantly watered down financial transaction tax proposed by Macron has been abandoned alongside plans for a digital tax. Adding insult to injury, Germany exerted considerable political muscle to ensure that the European People's Party (EPP), the centre-right grouping in the European Parliament (EP), led the decisive movement against the Macron proposal for a transnational list. Germany also conspicuously refused to join Anglo-U.S.-French strikes on Syria. German support for 'Europeanization' is essentially rhetorical, and predicated on concrete guarantees of ordoliberal policies and continuing German authority.

In November 2017, EU heads of state convened for the first time in two decades to discuss social questions. As a result, in March 2018 the Commission published proposals for a Social Fairness Package that boldly declared: 'Regardless of the type and duration of their employment relationship, workers, and, under comparable conditions, the self-employed, have the right to adequate social protection.'[25] Yet in ignoring the European Trade Unions Council's call for a Directive, the proposals were entirely in the form of recommendations, reliant on national governments for implementation. As a result, the Commission thereby only confirmed ECB President Mario Draghi's admission in February 2012 that 'the European social model is dead'.[26]

German Hegemonic Transformation?

A second approach to progressive reform proceeds not from the logics of progressive federalism or intergovernmental bargaining, but rather from the possibility of benevolent German leadership. Can the structural interests of German capital accommodate the developmental and political needs of the eurozone as a whole? Could Germany as a matter of 'enlightened self-interest' reprise in the eurozone a form of hegemonic leadership analogous to that played by the United States in the Bretton Woods system? After all, the absence of eurozone reform has potentially massive costs for Germany. Elite circles in Germany are well aware that eurozone crisis is a 'latent but chronic condition'[27] and that a break-up would be catastrophic. Not only would the failure of structural reform deprive German industry of an undervalued currency, it also leaves the eurozone vulnerable to future crises, imperiling the euro itself. By gravely weakening Macron, it would lay the basis for a resurgence of the French far-right.

There is plenty of support for this scenario.[28] Indeed, the strategy has been advocated in some form almost everywhere but Brussels and Berlin, including in the US Treasury and the IMF, which have strongly opposed German-led ordoliberal policies. An underlying assumption among proponents of this scenario is that the resistance to reform in Berlin is essentially intellectual and cultural, a reflection of more or less intractable ordoliberal orthodoxy. Yet there are reasons to doubt that Germany policy towards the eurozone is primarily a matter of ideology, and not power and interest. After all, in 2003 Germany had no qualms about violating the Stability and Growth Pact.

Does the German state have the power and resources to carry out essentially left-Keynesian macro-economic policies necessary to stabilize the eurozone? Germany's incremental strategy of crisis management through bailouts and austerity has itself been costly.[29] The Bundesbank remains liable for massive contributions to the Target2 credit system. The ECB has already bought large quantities of sovereign bonds and is now carrying out significant asset purchases through its quantitative easing. The mutualization of debt via the introduction of Eurobonds would represent a significant new liability for Germany. The establishment of a debt redemption fund – pooling debt over 60 per cent of GDP – would require significant new spending, which explains why Germany has categorically rejected joint liability in the form of a genuine banking union. Germany's financial liability could also increase substantially if it were to accept a European deposit guarantee scheme, rejected in 2013 as an act of 'brutal power politics'[30] and perhaps even less likely under the new Grand Coalition. Significant fiscal expansion – now prohibited under Germany's own balanced budget law – would increase debt and reduce the ability to recapitalize Germany's weakened banks. The moral hazard implicit in Eurobonds would be likely to expand significantly the cost of these programmes.

The growing strength of the right in Germany as reflected in the September 2017 elections greatly strengthens political resistance to a 'transfer union'. Reacting to the formation of a Five Star Movement/Northern League coalition government that will preside over a budget deficit equal to 130 per cent of GDP, the German weekly *Der Spiegel* complained of 'Moochers in Rome'. Matteo Salvini, leader of the Northern League, responded that 'Italy is not a colony, we are not slaves of the Germans or the French, the spread, or finance'. In addition, Germany faces a host of longer-term structural challenges including projected low growth rates far into the future, population decline, years of low public investment and productivity,[31] and migration. Germany's vulnerability is perhaps illustrated most vividly in its core automobile sector, challenged not only by Donald Trump's threatened trade wars but also by technological changes in automobile production that are reducing Germany's advantages and working to the benefit of China.[32]

These macro-economic and other realities indicate the tremendous difficulties that Germany would encounter in seeking to implement a project of genuine hegemonic leadership. The German commitment to austerity – even at the expense of potential eurozone instability – does not ultimately derive from 'vindictive madness',[33] 'abysmal ignorance',[34] or 'prevailing addiction'.[35] Rather, it is grounded in the export mercantilist model that has served as the central organizing principle of German foreign policy since World War II, as the German economy has become 'structurally reliant on foreign demand for its growth'.[36] Since the late 1990s, German capital has pursued a strategy of relentless cost cutting and austerity in support of this model. A succession of reform programmes and 'employers' offensives'[37] undertaken by both the centre-right Christian Democratic Union (CDU)/ Christian Social Union (CSU) and centre-left Social Democratic Party (SPD) dramatically decreased unit labour costs, especially after 2002 in conjunction with fiscal austerity and ensuing Hartz IV labour reforms. Agenda 2010 resulted in sweeping changes in unemployment protection and social assistance.

To this end, crucial stages of German manufacturing and commodity supply chains have been relocated throughout central and Eastern Europe, thereby enabling the German export model to maintain international competitiveness.[38] These supply chains illustrate an 'astonishing continuity in the basic structure of German capitalism'.[39] Their size and significance indicate the vast scope of German control over the European economy, and that the time for dual Franco-German leadership has passed. Germany accounts for approximately 25 per cent of EU exports and 30 per cent of European GDP. However, if the supply chains (which are closely dependent on the continuation of the Schengen Agreement, allowing the free flow of commodities across borders) are taken into account, the figures are considerably higher.[40] And this is further reinforced by Germany's position as the central hub linking Russian natural gas to Europe, a position it has thus far maintained despite massive opposition from many EU member states, the Commission, and the United States. The 'export mercantilist' orientation that has governed Germany since 1945 has only become more pronounced and qualitatively more significant in the context of the eurozone. In 2017 Germany's trade surplus was 234bn euros (compared to China's 390bn euros and Japan's 140bn).

The traditional link between export-led growth and expansion of the domestic market based on increasing wages has been weakened, but it has not been completely severed. In contrast to most other advanced capitalist states, the German strategy of outsourcing has served to strengthen the domestic manufacturing base, as primarily low-skill and labour-intensive production is located outside of Germany. In his path-breaking analysis, Julian Germain has identified a 'distinctive complementarity between German foreign investment and domestic production that sets Germany apart from its neoliberal peers and illuminates its austerity course'.[41] The euro has of course underwritten the extraordinary increase in its export ratio from 26 per cent of GDP in 1998 to 46 per cent in 2016, facilitating an overall export surplus of approximately 8 per cent.

By 2015 the United States surpassed France as Germany's largest export market, a position it had held since 1960. But Germany's ordoliberal export strategy has also generated increasing dependence on emerging markets, most notably China (15 per cent of the revenue of the top 30 German companies is derived from their sales in China), but also in the European periphery.[42] In the latter case, this involves a tendential transformation of the significance of the eurozone from 'sales market' to 'supply zone' that 'relegates the eurozone to a subsidiary role as a regional production center for German manufacturers'.[43] At the same time, German capital is deepening its ties with the Western Balkans, and especially Serbia. The 'Berlin Process' and 'Berlin Plus Process' launched by Chancellor Merkel in 2016 are designed ultimately to incorporate the entire region within the EU framework.[44] Serbia and Montenegro have begun what will undoubtedly be lengthy accession negotiations. All six have obtained visa-free travel and Stabilisation and Association Agreements. Heavily dependent on the German economy, the Visegrad countries, notwithstanding their populism and Euroscepticism, have strongly adhered to German economic policy.[45] For its part, Germany has sought to reduce EU pressure on Hungary and Poland for violating EU policies on migration, refugees, and the rule of law.

All this provides the lie to the assertions repeated ad nauseam in mainstream media that Germany under Chancellor Angela Merkel is becoming the new saviour of the multilateral global trading order. Germany's current account surplus with most of the rest of the eurozone drains net savings from trading partners while imposing a logic of austerity, slow growth, and internal devaluation. For the past two decades the EU has grown at only 1 per cent per year; Italy has essentially stagnated as its economy is 5 per cent smaller per capita that it was in 2001. In the first decade of its membership in EMU, Italy lost 20 per cent of its export competitiveness; Greece and Spain experienced worse.[46] Although no saviour, at the same time German FDI is a crucial source of capital for much of the rest of the EU; 50 per cent of German FDI is undertaken in the eurozone itself. This is especially the case for the CEE member states. The rise of German economic power and the resultant conflicts of interests demonstrate that although there is clearly a European 'business elite', there is strictly speaking no European 'transnational capitalist class'.[47] Yet, given the absence of an alternative strategy and their continuing reliance on the German market and (limited) financial support, there is little likelihood that subaltern capitalist classes would prefer to exit the eurozone in favour of a resumption of regional monetary rivalry. In the context of the weakness of the European left, they are condemned to remain in what Magnus Ryner has aptly called the 'ordoliberal iron cage'.[48]

THE AMERICAN EMPIRE FRACTURED?

Germany's export mercantilist strategy has provoked conflict with the United States, most notably over energy policy and trade policy. In 2016 the US Treasury added Germany to a list of countries engaging in 'unfair currency practices' even though Germany does not have its own currency.[49] In June 2018, the United States made good on its threat to impose tariffs on EU exports of steel and aluminum even as Donald Trump threatened additional protectionist measures against German automobile exports. Yet this does not amount to anything like inter-imperial rivalry. Precisely because it is so deeply inserted within the broader American global imperium, German power is entirely 'geo-economic' and neither Germany nor the EU have reduced their dependence on NATO as the continent experiences growing militarism even in the context of a new cold war.[50] Germany might in these terms at most be designated as 'sub-imperial', as the regional power located within the constellation of American hegemony.

That Germany is simultaneously powerful enough to pursue a regional strategy, and yet lacks the capacity to underwrite a genuinely progressive alternative to austerity, has ominous implications for Europe's future. This is especially so given the crosswinds blowing from across the Atlantic. The United States remains for Europe – and especially for Germany – a crucially important export market. At the present time, however, the Federal Reserve has begun to tighten monetary policy and, as noted above, the Trump administration has placed Germany in the crosshairs of its trade offensive. In December 2017, it passed a tax bill that is designed to increase the profits and market shares of corporate America at the expense of American workers, but also of European, and especially German, firms. [51]

Thus Europe is caught between an uncertain 'America First' offensive and an ambitious 'Made in China 2025' project. When the Treaty of Rome was signed in 1957, the present member states accounted for 12 per cent of the world's population; the figure is set to decline to 4 per cent by 2060. The EU's share of global GDP is projected to decline to less than 20 per cent by 2030, and this will greatly accelerate with the exit of the UK, the world's fifth largest economy and second largest contributor to the EU budget, in 2019. Nevertheless, for the time being the transatlantic space continues to represent by far the most important region in the world economy. It accounts for one-third of global GDP and one-half of global personal consumption. US foreign affiliate sales in Europe in 2016 of $3 trillion were greater than total US exports. 60 per cent of US imports from the EU comprised intra-firm trade, a much higher figure than that for the Asia-Pacific nations. In 2017, 64 per cent of US FDI outflows went to Europe, with just 16 per cent to the Asia Pacific region. Europe accounted for 70 per cent of the $3.7 trillion invested in the US in 2016; its total stock of investment in the US is more than four times that in Asia. The transatlantic economy accounts for 80 per cent of weapons-related spending and 90 per cent of research. [52]

Is the EU destined to remain subordinated to an increasingly vulnerable but still-powerful and unpredictable American hegemon? During the 1960s there was considerable debate concerning the nature of the US-led transatlantic imperium. Ernest Mandel concluded that European capitalism was gradually amalgamating under the umbrella of the EU and therefore becoming a co-equal.[53] Mandel's thesis was consistent with the assumption of a nascent transnational European capitalist class that was thought to have re-emerged in the 1990s in the context of the relaunching of the EU.[54] The contemporary crisis of US hegemony has given rise to similar assumptions.[55] By contrast, Nicos Poulantzas was more sceptical of the prospects for an autonomous European centre of accumulation. Focusing on the implications of massive US FDI in Europe, the continuing dependence of European export capital on the US market, US technological leadership, and the growing significance of money-capital, he proposed the term 'interior bourgeoisie'[56] to describe the continuing subordination – and fragmentation – of European capitalist classes.

From the perspective of 2018 there can be little doubt that Poulantzas offered the more prescient analysis, and one that remains relevant today. Europe's second, neoliberal, project of integration was carried out within the framework of Wall Street and Washington and closely tethered to the NATO imperium.[57] Despite the considerable institutional and constitutional development of the EU, the neoliberal project greatly reduced national prerogatives without giving rise to a pan-European polity. Ironically,

Europe's greatest degree of geopolitical and economic autonomy – albeit still sharply constrained by Washington – was achieved not in the post-Maastricht era as so many had predicted, but rather in the post-1965 'empty chair' era, which saw the expulsion of NATO from French territory, the development of ostpolitik, and France's momentary resistance to US monetary hegemony. Germany's political-military subordination to the American superpower finds its complement in its reliance on the Euro-Atlantic economy. Notwithstanding conflicts within the transatlantic space, the linkages binding it together remain deep and comprehensive. Yet, Germany's strategic dependence on exports into a world market that is subject to growing financial instability and protectionism places both Europe and Germany itself in a precarious position.

THE LEFT AND EUROPE

The misplaced confidence of official Europe in an 'ever closer union' was based on an idealized and teleological narrative, reinforced by an academic establishment that has been funded lavishly by the European Commission.[58] This narrative has ignored the substantive conflicts and contradictions among and within capitalist classes and states that have shaped the EU since its inception. The institutions of the EU are not politically neutral, but rather designed to further the collective interests of the European capitalist classes, under the leadership of German capital. The most common scenarios for reform within the context of existing treaties and institutions do not correspond to the realities of Germany's 'sub-imperial' strategy, let alone the present balance of power among classes and states or the existing level of pan-European solidarity.

What should be the left strategy for Europe? The left has not been able to take advantage of the eurozone crisis. It has been unable to mobilize effectively against austerity and has suffered a string of electoral defeats during the past year alongside the ominous rise of far-right populist parties and movements. There are, to be sure, also some positive trends and achievements to be set against this record. Austerity has sparked the rise of numerous resistance movements throughout Europe, including in France where Macron's assault on the French welfare state has not gone unchallenged.[59] At the same time, the programmes of right-wing populists are incoherent and ineffective; in most cases, notwithstanding campaign rhetoric, they represent not a challenge to neoliberalism but rather its intensification in more authoritarian form. The further growth of these parties is certainly not inevitable. The performance of Jeremy Corbyn's Labour Party in the general elections of 2017, marked by dramatic surge in party membership, indicates considerable energy and commitment, especially among British youth and draws obvious comparisons with Podemos in Spain, Syriza in Greece, and even the 2016 presidential campaign of Bernie Sanders in the United States. In France, Jean-Luc Melanchon's France Insoumise received 20 per cent of the vote in the first round of the April presidential elections of 2017.

A radical-Keynesian (not to mention socialist) programme would certainly encounter massive and undying resistance from the EU. The 2017 British Labour Party election manifesto advocates a return to Keynesian policies of public investment along with income redistribution, nationalization, and greater social spending. These policies would certainly propel the UK into confrontation with European and global capital, and certainly the EU institutions as well.[60] However, the Leave campaign was not waged on the basis of an alternative socialist or even left-Keynesian strategy. It prevailed in large part as a result of racism and xenophobia, greatly overshadowing a campaign for a progressive 'Lexit' that was very weak. Brexit has empowered the most reactionary and recalcitrant fractions of the ruling class and it is likely to facilitate even harsher neoliberal measures.

As Thomas Fazi and William Mitchell write: 'Abandoning the EU provides the British left – and the European left more generally – with a once-in-a-lifetime opportunity to show that a radical break with neoliberalism, and with the institutions that support it, is possible.'[61] However, the experience of Greece illustrates the great challenges that a victorious left party would face in implementing a strategy of 'socialism in one (European) country' when European capitalism is more tightly organized than ever within complex global production chains and financial circuits. Syriza explicitly adopted a parliamentary path to power based on remaining within the EMU, and clearly sought to obtain the support of the Greek electorate on the basis of this strategy. Exit from the eurozone had potentially ominous implications for Greek democracy for which the majority of Greek people were unprepared. The economic consequences of exit from the EMU, moreover, would likely have been devastating no matter how radical the government, how careful the preparation, and how extensive the degree of popular mobilization. In any case, it is not clear that a real threat of exit would have increased Syriza's bargaining power. German Finance Minister Schäuble is widely reported to have favoured Greece leaving the eurozone.[62]

The case of Greece cruelly exposes the realities of hierarchy and power that lie beneath the EU's façade of equality and democracy. Member states cede crucial aspects of sovereignty to the EU; the weaker the country, the more this is the case. Moreover, EU treaty obligations greatly reduce the legal as well as political authority of member states to carry out an independent industrial strategy. Public ownership is not explicitly ruled out, but much harder in practice to establish. At the same time, state aid and public procurement are subject to strict competition rules.

As Costas Lapavitsas asserts, 'The internationalism of the left is unrelated to the internationalism of the EU.'[63] Yet, a strategy towards the EU should not divert attention from the constraints posed by national power relations. Overemphasis on technical mechanisms in relation to a strategy of Lexit reinforces illusions concerning the possibilities of reforms in a single member state. The same can be said of the reverse strategy of federal reform within existing EU institutions. The Democracy in Europe Movement 2025 (DIEM2025), founded by Yanis Varoufakis, Syriza's former finance minister from 2012-15, illustrates the strengths, but also the significant limitations, of federalism at the present time. Launched in 2015, DIEM25 seeks to establish 'full-fledged democracy with a sovereign Parliament respecting national self-determination and sharing power with national Parliaments, regional assemblies and municipal council'.[64] In 2018, it constituted itself as a transnational political party led by a Coordinating Collective and Advisory Board, with local chapters of Spontaneous Collectives. The party plans to contest the 2019 European Parliamentary elections on the basis of transnational European solidarity. It self-consciously sets itself against left movements that have advocated exit from the EMU or EU, explicitly seeking to work within the framework of existing institutions in order to bring about a 'European New Deal' comprising the aforementioned left-Keynesian reforms. However, DIEM25 provides no compelling account of how the balance of social forces at the present time could overcome the massive resistance to such a program that would be mounted by all sectors of European capital and European institutions. It overestimates – at least at the present time – the transnational capacities and commitments of social movements.

Marc Boteng aptly characterizes the potential problems with both Lexit and EU reform: 'On the one hand, both lack ambition by offering de facto a better management of capitalism. On the other, both downplay the importance of extra-parliamentary action.'[65] Membership within the EU or EMU is not the principal impediment to a socialist strategy. This is obvious from the many experiences across time and space since the 1970s of progressive governments whose Keynesian macro-economic programs coupled with industrial policies brought them into serious conflict, and ultimately defeat, at the hands of global financial markets. A socialist island in a sea of European and Atlantic hostility would face massive resistance at both the economic and geopolitical levels, quite possibly in the context of a global financial crisis that is deeper than that of 2008. As the experience of Brexit shows, 'sovereignty' in the contemporary world economy is largely mythical. This underlines the importance of transnational solidarity. But it is absolutely clear that any serious strategy for Lexit will need to arise from within an already advanced process of socialist transformation, and not largely independently of it.

NOTES

1   'Merkel Says EU Must Be Bound Closer Together', *Spiegel International*, 7 September 2011.

2   Alan Millward, *The European Rescue of the Nation State,* Berkeley, California: University of California Press, 1992; Alan Cafruny and Magnus Ryner, *Europe at Bay: In the Shadow of U.S. Hegemony*, Boulder, Colorado: Lynne Rienner Publishers, 2007.

3   Leo Panitch and Sam Gindin, *The Making of Global Capitalism: The Political Economy of the American Empire*, London: Verso, 2012; Magnus Ryner and Alan Cafruny, *The European Union and Global Capitalism: Origins, Development, Crisis*, London: Palgrave, 2017.

4   Stephen Gill, 'European Governance and New Constitutionalism: Economic and Monetary Union and Alternatives to Disciplinary Neo-Liberalism in Europe', *New Political Economy,* 3(1), 1998.

5   Greg Albo, '"Competitive Austerity' and the Impasse of Capitalist Employment Policy', in Ralph Miliband and Leo Panitch, eds, *Socialist Register 1994: Between Globalism and Nationalism*, London: Merlin Press, 1993.

6   Bastiaan van Apeldoorn, *Transnational Capitalism and the Struggle over European Integration*, London: Routledge, 2002.

7   Former Bundesbank head Karl Otto Pohl characterized the rescue package for Greece in the following terms: 'It was about protecting German banks, but especially the French banks, from debt write-offs. On the day the rescue package was agreed on, shares of French banks rose by up to 24 per cent. 'Bailout Plan Is All About 'Rescuing Banks and Rich Greeks', *Der Spiegel*, 18 May 2010.

8   Bloomberg, 'Global Debt at Record Level', *Business Week*, 10 April 2018.

9   Federal Reserve Bank of New York, 'Household Debt Jumps as 2017 Marks the Fifth Consecutive Year of Positive Annual Growth Since Post-Recession Deleveraging', Press Release, 18 February 2018.

10   Gavyn Davies, 'The Mystery of the eurozone Slowdown', *Financial Times*, 15 April 2018.

11   Wolfgang Munchau, 'Eurozone Downturn and Lack of Reform Presage Existential Crisis', *Financial Times,* 22 April 2018.

12   John Grahl, 'Social Europe and the Crisis of the European Union' in Johannes Jäger and Elisabeth Springler, eds, *Asymmetric Crisis in Europe and Possible Futures: Critical Political Economy and Post-Keynesian Perspectives*, New York: Routledge, 2015, p.168.

13   Sotiria Theodoropoulou, 'Drifting into Labour Market Insecurity? Labour Market Reforms in Europe after 2010', Brussels, European Trade Union Institute, March 2018.

14   Employment, Social Affairs, and Inclusion, *Access to Social Protection*, Brussels: European Commission, 13 March 2018.

15   Liz Alderman, 'Europe's Thirst for Cheap Labor Fuels a Boom in Disposable Workers', *New York Times*, 11 December 2017.

16   IMF, *World Economic Outlook*, Washington, D.C., April 2018.

17   Aurora Trif, 'Surviving Frontal Assault on Collective Bargaining Institutions in Romania: The Case of Manufacturing Companies', *European Journal of Industrial Relations,* 22(3), 2016.

18   Philippe Legraine, 'Euro-Zone Fiscal Colonialism', *New York Times*, 21 April 2014.

19   Stathis Kouvalikis, 'Borderland: Greece and the EU's Southern Question', *New Left Review,* 110(March-April), 2018.

20   Anne-Sylvaine Chassany, Tobias Buck, and Mehreen Khan, 'EU Leaders Spar as Italy's Crisis Deepens', *Financial Times*, 31 May 2018.

21   See, inter alia, EuroMemo Group, *Euromemorandum 2018: Can Europe Still Be Saved? The Implications of a Multi-Speed Europe*, 2018; Joseph Stiglitz, *The Euro: How a Common Currency Threatens the Future of Europe*, New York: W.W. Norton, 2016; Costas Lapavitsas et al., *Crisis in the Eurozone*, London: Verso, 2012; Heiner Flassbeck and Costas Lapavitsas, *Against the Troika*, London: Verso, 2015; Yanis Varoufakis, *Adults in the Room: My Battle with the European and American Deep Establishment*, New York: Farrar, Strauss, and Giroux, 2017. Prescient early critiques include Wynne Godley, 'Maastricht And All That', *London Review of Books,* 14(8), October 1992; Paul De Grauwe , 'The euro and financial crises', *Financial Times*, 20 February 1998.

22   Anne Sylvaine-Chassany, 'Emmanuel Macron Seizes Moment to Take on French Unions', *Financial Times*, 15 March 2018.

23   Anne-Sylvain Chassany, 'Budget Chief Aims to Restore France's Credibility in Europe', *Financial Times*, 18 May 2018.

24   Dick Nichols, 'France: Unions, Left Confront Macron's Attacks on Rail Services, Jobs', *The Bullet,* 29 March 2018, available at https://socialistproject.ca.

25   Liina Carr, 'Widening the Social Protection Safety Net', *Social Europe,* 1 May 2018.

26   Brian Blackstone, Matthew Karnitschnig, and Robert Thomson, 'Europe's Banker Talks Tough', *Wall Street Journal*, February 24, 2012.

27   Andreas Kluth, 'When 'More Europe' Is and Is Not the Answer', *Handelsblatt*, 26 April 2018.

28   See, inter alia, Mark Blyth and Mattias Matthijs, 'The World Waits for Germany', *Foreign Affairs* June 2012; Simon Bulmer and William Patterson, 'Germany as the EU's Reluctant Hegemon? Of Economic Strength and Political Constraints', *West European Politics,* 20(10), 2013; Simon Bulmer 'Germany and the eurozone Crisis: Between Hegemony and Domestic Politics', *West European Politics* 37(6), 2014; 'Europe's Reluctant Hegemon,' *The Economist*, 15 June 2013; Yanis Varoufakis, 'Europe Needs a Hegemonic Germany', London: Zed Books Blog, 2013; Mark Blyth and Simon Tilford, 'How the eurozone Might Split: Could Germany Become a Reluctant Hegemon?' *Foreign Affairs*, 11 January 2018.

29   Federico Steinberg and and Mattias Vermeiren, 'Germany's Institutional Power and the EMU Regime after the Crisis: Towards a Germanized Euro Area?', *Journal of Common Market Studies,* 54(2), 2016.

30   Spiegel International Edition, "Brutal power politics": Merkel's Banking Union Under Fire', 16 December 2013.

31   Marcel Fratzscher, *The Germany Illusion: Between Economic Euphoria and Despair*, Oxford: Oxford University Press, 2018.

32   'China's Car Revolution is Going Global', *Bloomberg Businessweek*, 23 April 2018.

33   Costas Lapavitsas, 'To Beat Austerity Greece Must Break Free from the Euro', *The Guardian*, 2 March 2015.

34   Heiner Flassbeck, 'Das Arrogante Europa der Machtigen', *Makroskop*, 15 July 2016.

35   Camilla Hodgson, 'Soros on Europe: Everything that Could Go Wrong Has Gone Wrong', *Financial Times*, 29 May 2018.

36   Simon Tilford, *How to Save the Euro*, Brussels: Centre for European Reform, September, 2010, p. 6.

37   Daniel Kinderman, 'Pressure From Without, Subversion From Within: The Two-Pronged German Employer Offensive', *Comparative European Politics* 3, 2005.

38   International Monetary Fund, *German-Central Europe Supply Chain – Cluster Report*. IMF Multi Country Report No. 13/263, Washington DC, August, 2013; Sam Gross, *The German Economy Today: Exports, Foreign Investment, and East-Central Europe*. New York: Center for European and Mediterranean Studies, New York University, 2013.

39   Julian Germain, 'Beyond Geo-economics: Advanced Unevenness and the Anatomy of German Austerity', *European Journal of International Relations*, 31 July 2017.

40   France Strategie, 'The Economic Cost of Rolling Back Schengen', Paris, 5 February 2016.

41   Germain, 'Beyond Geo-Economics', pp. 13-14.

42   Ulf Sonmer, 'A Great Wall of Against German Investment', *Handelsblatt*, 24 May 2018.

43   Germain, 'Beyond Geo-Economics', pp. 3,18.

44   Antonia Colibasanu, 'Germany Keeping an Eye on the Balkans', *Geopolitical Futures*, 29 November 2017.

45   Beata Farkas, 'Economic and Political Relations between Germany and Visegrad Countries in Turbulent Times', paper presented at ECPR General Conference, Prague, September 2016.

46   Leila Simona Talani, *The Political Economy of Italy in the Euro: Between Credibility and Competitiveness*, London: Palgrave, 2017, p. 96.

47   Alan Cafruny and Magnus Ryner, 'Alternative Perspectives on European Integration', in Henk Overbeek and Bob Jessop, eds, *Transnational Capital and Class Fractions: The Amsterdam School Perspective Revisited*, London: Routledge, 2019.

48   Magnus Ryner, 'Europe's Ordoliberal Iron Cage: Critical Political Economy, the Euro Area Crisis, and Its Management', *Journal of European Public Policy*, 22(2), 2015.

49   U.S. Treasury, *Foreign Exchange Policies of Major Trading Partners of the United States: Report to Congress,* Washington, Office of International Affairs, 29 April 2016.

50   Alan Cafruny, 'The European Crisis and the Rise of German Power', in Jäger and Springler, eds, *Asymmetric Crisis in Europe and Possible Futures*.

51   Charles Wallace, Katharina Kort, and Donata Riedel, 'Germans Fear Huge Loss of Jobs from U.S. Tax Reforms', *Handelsblatt*, 14 December 2017.

52   These data are compiled in Daniel Hamilton and Joseph Quinlan, *The Transatlantic Economy 2018: Annual Survey of Jobs, Trade, and Investment between the United States and Europe*, Washington, D.C.: Center for Transatlantic Relations, Paul H. Nitze School of Advanced International Studies, Johns Hopkins University, 2018.

53   Ernest Mandel, *Europe Vs. America: Contradictions of Imperialism,* London: New Left Books, 1969.

54   See, *inter alia*, van Apeldoorn, *Transnational Capitalism*; Overbeek and Jessop, eds, *Transnational Capital and Class Fractions*.

55   Hans Kundnani, 'Leaving the West Behind: Germany Looks East', *Foreign Affairs*, January/February 2015.

56   Nicos Poulantzas, *Classes in Contemporary Capitalism*, London: New Left Books, 1975, p. 164.

57   Panitch and Gindin, *The Making of Global Capitalism*; Cafruny and Ryner, *Europe at Bay*.

58   Magnus Ryner, 'Financial Crisis, Orthodoxy, Heterodoxy and the Production of Knowledge about the EU', *Millennium: Journal of International Studies* 40(3), 2012; Alan Cafruny, 'European Integration Studies, EMU, and the Resilience of Austerity in Europe: Post-Mortem on a Crisis Foretold', *Competition and Change,* 19(2), 2015.

59   Nikolai Huke, David Bailey, Monica Clua-Losada, Julia Lux, and Olatz Ribera Almandoz, 'Disrupting European Authoritarianism: Grassroots Organizing, Collective Action, and Participatory Democracy During the eurozone Crisis', Brussels: Transnational Institute, April 2018.

60   Costas Lapavitsas, 'Jeremy Corbyn's Labour vs. the Single Market', *Jacobin*, 30 May, 2018.

61   Thomas Fazi and William Mitchell, 'Why the Left Should Embrace Lexit', *Jacobin*, 29 April 2018; see also Alex Callinicos, 'The Internationalist Case Against the EU', *International Socialism*, 148, 5 October 2015; Cedric Durand, 'The Workers Have No Europe', *Catalyst,* 1(4), Winter 2018.

62   'Schäuble's Push for Grexit Puts Merkel on the Defensive', *Der Spiegel*, 17 July 2015.

63   Costas Lapavitsas, 'A Socialist Strategy for Europe', *Catalyst,* 1(3), Fall 2017, p. 61.

64   DIEM25 Manifesto, available at https://diem25.org/manifesto-short-version, 2018.

65   Marc Botenga, 'Building a Different Europe', *Catalyst,* 1(4) Winter 2018, p. 19.

CORBYN AND BREXIT BRITAIN: IS THERE A WAY FORWARD FOR THE LEFT?

COLIN LEYS

In Britain, the political reaction to globalization has followed two separate and perversely interlinked paths. One was a reaction against the impoverishment of former industrial regions of the country, exacerbated by the financial crash of 2007-8, and against the right-wing response to this in the form of drastic cuts to public spending and public services. The other was a reaction against the undemocratic character of the European Union.

Of the two, it was anti-EU sentiment that was first tapped into and exploited. As early as 1993 Nigel Farage, a wealthy commodities trader of uncompromising neoliberal views, grasped the fact that the undemocratic elite character of the EU offered a perfect focus for popular disenchantment. He left the Conservative Party, helped to found the UK Independence Party (UKIP), and led it from 2006 onwards, laying the blame not on globalization, but on the EU and on the large-scale immigration from Europe (especially Eastern Europe) that membership of the EU had made possible. In 2014 UKIP won the largest share (26 per cent) of the votes cast in the UK elections for the European Parliament; and in 2016 a UKIP-inspired campaign, with the potent slogans of 'taking back control' and 'taking our country back', went on to win, narrowly but decisively, a referendum on EU membership, committing the UK to leave the EU.[1] The 'Leave' and 'Remain' votes did not follow party lines: both the Conservatives and the Labour Party were split on the issue, in different ways. With the referendum won, UKIP virtually disappeared, but both parties – Labour as much as the Conservatives – felt it politically impossible not to respect the result, confronting them equally with the prospect of losing support when it came to implementing it.

The Conservatives, who had called the referendum and were in office, had to face the problem first. After calling an ill-judged election in 2017 they lost their parliamentary majority; from then on their survival in office depended on a small group of hard-line 'leavers' in the cabinet and on

Northern Ireland's anti-EU Democratic Unionist Party, while a majority of Conservative MPs were remainers. This led to paralysis over their negotiating position with the EU and frantic efforts to find compromise formulae, all of which the EU-27 negotiators had already made it clear they would not accept. By March 2019, when Britain is due to exit the EU, it seemed increasingly possible that no agreement would be reached, and that the UK would lose its existing access to the EU single market and customs union, with endlessly complex consequences for trade, production, jobs, labour markets, legal rights and more. During the referendum these implications had not seriously figured in the debates, but by 2018 they were all too clearly in view. The realization gradually dawned that almost every aspect of life in Britain had become intricately intertwined with the EU: the practical effects of leaving were going to prove so far-reaching and costly that little else could be seriously attended to for years to come after 2019, whichever party was in government.

The reason why a left-wing political reaction to globalization, and to austerity, came so much later was that until 2015 the Labour Party was complicit with both. Tony Blair and Gordon Brown, its leaders from 1997 to 2010, had emptied it of progressive purpose and democratic energy. They had ruthlessly converted it into a party of business, run from the top in conformity with 'the new reality' of global corporate power and American imperial rule.[2] Membership fell and working-class voters stayed at home. But unlike other European socialist parties, Labour was, paradoxically, saved from electoral meltdown by the UK's archaic first-past-the-post electoral system, which makes it virtually impossible for new alternative parties to win seats unless they are nationalists based in a distinctive region of the country. Thus the Scottish Nationalist Party, and to a lesser extent the Welsh nationalist party, Plaid Cymru, were able to take votes from Labour – in the case of Scotland, reducing Labour to a single Scottish MP in the 2015 general election – by combining broadly social-democratic socio-economic policies with a call for national independence; but successive attempts to form a new left-wing party in England (which comprises 84 per cent of the UK population) invariably come to nothing.[3] In 2015, seven years on from the financial crash, and after five years of Conservative-imposed austerity, with mounting inequality and drastic cuts to social services, Labour's policies, dubbed 'austerity lite', were still broadly close to those of the Conservatives; and in the general election in June that year the party barely increased its share of the vote, at 31 per cent. Yet it still had a third of the seats in the House of Commons. No left alternative could break its grip.

But at this point chance, and hubris, entered in. Under a rule change in 2014, the Labour leader was in future to be elected by the party's membership and any Labour Party 'supporter' who had paid a fee of £3, although candidates for the leadership still needed to be nominated by at least 15 per cent of the party's sitting MPs. The thinking was that these arrangements would ensure that only a 'moderate' candidate could win.[4] When Ed Miliband resigned the leadership immediately after failing to win the 2015 election, the new rules came into operation. The handful of socialist Labour MPs who had survived the Blair-Brown years urged their colleagues to nominate one of their number, Jeremy Corbyn, on the grounds that the party's left wing should at least be represented on the ballot. Just enough MPs, including several who considered Corbyn to be an irrelevant idealist, agreed.[5] But to everyone's astonishment he went on to win, with nearly 60 per cent of the 423,000 votes cast, three times as many as his nearest rival. Most Labour MPs were dumbfounded and outraged, and a year later, in June 2016, three-quarters of them signed a vote of no confidence in him and called on him to resign.[6] When he declined to do so they called for a new leadership contest and supported a challenger. The members, however, re-elected Corbyn with an increased majority.

The MPs had radically misread the views and feelings of the party's rank-and-file, and those of the great majority of the paid-up 'supporters' who also voted, but they continued to believe that the wider electorate would reject Corbyn's politics. And when in 2017 the Conservative Prime Minister, Teresa May – convinced, like them, that under Corbyn Labour would be decimated at the poll – called a snap general election, observers and pollsters almost unanimously agreed that Labour would be trounced. Then, one week into the campaign, Labour's election manifesto, *For the Many, Not the Few*, promising a complete break with austerity and wide-ranging social-democratic reforms, was leaked to the press. And instead of the leak damaging Labour, as the leaker presumably expected, the manifesto proved an instant success.[7] Labour's campaign took off. In the course of the six-week campaign the party increased its share of the vote from 31 per cent to 40 per cent, an unprecedented jump.

It was not quite enough to win. But the Conservatives, with just 42 per cent, lost their overall majority of seats and became dependent on the conditional support of ten MPs from Northern Ireland's far-right Democratic Unionist Party. They were also wracked with divisions over Brexit, which they had brought about and which promised further damage to the economy. A Labour government under socialist leadership suddenly seemed a realistic possibility.

How had this come about? Was it a flash in the pan? The impact of the financial crisis of 2007-8 had clearly altered the electoral calculus, but the predictably relentless demonization of Corbyn by the mainstream media seemed likely to gradually erode his popularity; and the opposition of most Labour MPs to Corbyn's politics seemed likely to mean that even if Labour were to win the next election, Corbyn's small team of like-minded MPs would find it difficult, if not impossible, to pass any radical measures. The tasks of government would entangle them in the established institutions of the state, bogging them down in struggles with reluctant civil servants, cutting them off from the party membership and leading to compromises – including those likely to be called for by trade union leaders worried by any policy that might jeopardise members' jobs – that would empty the project of its radical potential; while the disinclination of investors to either invest or lend would lead to a fall in living standards and drain away popular support. In a word, was there any reason to believe that the idea of a 'parliamentary road to socialism' in the UK was any less illusory in 2018 than it had proved to be in the heyday of the 'new left' from the 1960s to the 1980s?[8]

THE REACTION AGAINST GLOBALIZATION

The main reason to think that a parliamentary route to socialism might have a better chance in the twenty-first century than the in the second half of the twentieth was that public dissatisfaction with the effects of globalization had finally begun to crystallise into disenchantment with neoliberalism, if not with capitalism itself. But until now there had been no left-wing outlet for this feeling equivalent to the right-wing outlet offered by UKIP. Under Blair and Brown the Labour Party had been committed without reservation to globalization. Labour's de-industrialised working-class 'heartlands' were seen as safe seats for New Labour MPs, not as a massive challenge of economic and social regeneration. As Calderbank and O'Connell noted,

New Labour's strategists could barely conceal their disinterest in traditionally Labour-voting, mostly working class electorates concentrated in the party's safe seats ... Far from articulating the anger of communities ripped apart by Thatcher's de-industrialisation of Britain, high unemployment, rising drug addiction, and the transformation of the labour market into a low-skilled, low-paid and often casualised festival of exploitation, New Labour was welcoming the 'benefits of globalisation', further deregulating the financial sector, levering private capital further into the public sector ... and welcoming Thatcher's anti-trade union laws. What did it matter what the 'core vote' did? They'd likely vote Labour anyway, since the Tories were even worse.[9]

In 2010, two years after the financial crisis had struck, Labour lost office to a new coalition government of Conservatives and Liberal Democrats who embarked on a programme of massive public spending cuts. The response of most Labour MPs to the party's defeat was to want to shift policy still further to the right. Ed Miliband, who succeeded Gordon Brown as leader in 2010, opposed this, but was persuaded by advisors to rely on the unpopularity of the Coalition's austerity policies to win the next election without risking an internal party battle to shift it to the left. And as spending cuts led to the disappearance of tens of thousands of public sector jobs and the social services they had provided, from social care to libraries, the pain was felt everywhere, not just in the ex-industrial areas. Yet Labour's vote barely increased, and the Conservatives returned to power. Corbyn's nomination thus finally provided the first left-wing outlet for public disaffection. The result was his successive leadership election victories; a massive influx of new members into the party (up from just under 200,000 in 2010 to over 550,000 by the end of 2017);[10] the emergence of Momentum, a potent new organisation of left-wing Labour activists; and the dramatic 2017 election advance.

Corbyn and his small group of left-wing MPs were as surprised as everyone else.[11] No one had tested the potential of the shift in public opinion that the response to his nomination revealed. Perhaps the huge crowds that gathered to hear and cheer him everywhere he went would lose interest. Perhaps public support would fall short of what was needed to enable Labour to win the next election, not required to be held until 2022. And if Labour did win the next election, would public support be strong enough to allow the government to face down, in addition to resistance from many of its own MPs, the predictably ferocious opposition of capital and its media allies to even the mild social-democratic measures promised in the party's 2017 manifesto – let alone anything that could lead beyond social democracy, to a real challenge to capitalism? These were the questions the left now had to answer.

The idea of going 'beyond social democracy via social democratic reforms' – as one member of Corbyn's team succinctly summarised the project – is clearly in the tradition of Eduard Bernstein's 'evolutionary socialism', and is open to the objections raised against it by a long line of critics, from Luxemburg and Kautsky to Ralph Miliband and Leo Panitch.[12] But although leading members of the team were well aware of these debates, they were notably indifferent to them. Perhaps there was no such route to socialism, but this could not be known in advance. The dire state of British society and economy, the incompetence and opportunism of the ruling class, the threats to peace and the biosphere, all presented an acute need for action, and the public seemed readier for radical change than at any time since 1945. There was an obligation to act, to make use of all the experience accumulated in the previous hundred years, and to push the possibilities of socialist advance to their limits.

THE PROJECT

The project was described by one leading activist as follows:

> The long run aim is to achieve a radical shift in the balance of power and the balance of income and wealth, a political, economic and social shift. You then work back to the steps to that end. A basic one is winning elections so as to be able to make major changes that improve the lives of ordinary people. With power, you have to make changes politically (democratising the state), economically (de-privatising, democratising work and economic life), and socially – a shift in the balance of social forces.
>
> From this it follows that you must pass several major measures in the first term of office. The measures must also contribute to shifting the hegemony – they must be radical, and attract opposition – not reforms by stealth like Brown's tax credits, which are being undone, but like the minimum wage, which can't be.[13] The essence is for reforms to be radical but at the same time common sense.

The sophistication of this formulation is striking, with its blend of strategic and tactical considerations, its integration of the struggle for hegemony – Gramsci's 'war of position' – with planning for the short term (the 'war of movement'), and its strong emphasis on democracy, both in the organization of the state and in the struggle itself. All these elements are crucially important, and combining them in this way has no parallel in the thinking of previous Labour governments; but what is most distinctive to the Corbyn project, and most critical for the future, is the commitment to democratization. From his initial decision to consider standing for the leadership, through his refusal to step down when told to do so by the great majority of Labour MPs, to the unprecedented success of his election campaign, it was the support of thousands of people in the streets that was the key to Corbyn's success. This was partly due to his personality and style – calm, unassuming, honest, likeable – but also to his conception of politics. Unlike some left-wing leaders in other European countries, his appeal was 'not centred on himself as a charismatic leader'.[14] He was always most at home among social activists and when speaking with ordinary people, inviting them to contribute to party policy and to become active participants in helping to get it enacted and implemented. He was 'one of a tiny handful of MPs who commanded near-universal respect among grassroots campaigners … [He] had addressed so many rallies and meetings over the years on such a range of causes that he could count on a bedrock of support from the off'.[15] And this marked his leadership as much after the 2017 election as before. A slightly envious complaint by a senior colleague needing decisions on urgent strategic issues was that 'Jeremy is touring four days a week'.

Yet it was more than a personal preference: it was a point of principle, adopted by the new left in the 1970s and 1980s and reinforced in reaction to the way top-down party management of the Blair-Brown years had led the party to become unrepresentative of its base, and eventually hard to distinguish, in important respects, from the Conservatives. The big question for the next phase of the struggle was how far this democratic commitment could be made normal and generalized, both inside the party and in the party's relations with the electorate, so that genuine power continued to be exercised by Labour members and voters.

MOMENTUM

A key element in answering this question will be what happens to Momentum, a new organisation of Labour activists that emerged from among the thousands of people who flocked to campaign for Corbyn in his first 2015 leadership bid. The Labour Party already had left-wing groupings, most notably the Campaign for Labour Party Democracy, inherited from the Benn years; and it was the leading activist of the CLPD, Jon Lansman, who now, more than 30 years later, played a key role in capitalizing on the sudden availability of thousands of enthusiasts to create Momentum.[16] What began as a swiftly assembled election campaign organization, using clever new online apps that allowed a local group of any size to start canvassing, expanded with each successive electoral challenge. By spring 2018 Momentum had 41,000 paid-up members, a budget of about £500,000, and a paid staff of twenty. According to Lansman, who became chair of Momentum's National Coordinating Group, Momentum members accounted for only some 2-3,000 of the roughly 40,000 Labour members who made political activism a major commitment; but the coordination provided by Momentum's national office gave these members a confidence and weight beyond their numbers, and the digital skills of the younger members, especially, gave the organization a formidable social media impact.

As with other new left organisations in Europe, such as Syriza and

Podemos, Momentum comprised many different currents, from peace and tenants' rights activists to former members of the Communist Party, and it had some initial difficulty in combining them. One tendency saw Momentum primarily as an internal force to break the grip of the right-wing majority of Labour MPs and the party's 400-plus professional staff, many if not most of who had been appointed under Blair and were also hostile to Corbyn; and to fight parliamentary election campaigns for socialist candidates. Another tendency was focused on seeking to drive a cultural change by integrating party membership with social activism. After some conflict a constitution was adopted in early 2017 which went far to resolving these tensions. Broad policies are laid down by the National Coordinating Group, consisting of a large minority of representatives elected online by local members, plus a small majority of nominated representatives of affiliated trade unions and other national bodies (including the CLPD, for example). But within these broad policies, members can choose their local priorities and organize as they see fit.

Much is unclear about Momentum's long term potential, which its enemies are inclined to exaggerate, and with good reason: for example, Momentum's main inner-party rival, the Blairite group 'Progress', had just 2,382 members in 2016, and 50 in its youth section.[17] The Labour right's absurd denigration of Momentum as a gang of Marxist fanatics and their idealist dupes intent on a 'power grab', and its constant vilification in the mainstream media, attributed more influence to Momentum than it really had, but it was a force to be reckoned with. Its mobilizing capacity and the digital skills of its organisers had been crucially important to the left's electoral success in both the leadership elections and the 2017 general election. Momentum's organising techniques were gradually adopted by party headquarters, and when in early 2018 a Community Campaigns Unit was established in the Leader's Office with a remit to organize in a key range of formerly Labour seats and a paid staff of field workers, several of them were drawn from Momentum staff.

Momentum has also played a significant role in changing the party's internal balance of power by actively engaging in elections to party posts, as well as in constituency elections. By late 2017 the National Executive finally had a pro-Corbyn majority; the General Secretary and several senior staff officers had been replaced by Corbyn supporters; while the Director of Communications, located in the Leader's office, had been a close supporter of Corbyn from the start.

Getting left-wing candidates adopted for winnable parliamentary seats was much harder. Under Blair, the party's National Parliamentary Panel had ruthlessly excluded left-leaning potential candidates from being considered, bequeathing a Blairite majority of MPs as the biggest immediate obstacle to the Corbyn project.[18] After the 2017 election new candidates needed to be selected in some 75 constituencies. About half of those selected were left-wing candidates backed by local Momentum activists. All of these were in winnable seats; but even if all won at the next election, the balance of forces inside the parliamentary party would not be greatly changed. Securing support for socialist measures would depend on whether public opinion moved more decisively in a socialist direction.

That is where Momentum's outward-looking work, as summarised by its national coordinator, Laura Parker, could be important:

Momentum is not an alternative policy-making organisation from the party. It was born as a sort of praetorian guard for Jeremy – to get him elected and keep him there. It shouldn't be seen as rent-a-rally, but as an innovator, developing new ways of campaigning. For example, promoting the discussion of current issues like universal basic income and universal basic services, our job should be to 'stretch' it – to go further, challenging the leadership, but in a sophisticated way which is not provocative.

We should be working out the role of a party in the twenty-first century in which so many people live precarious lives – on short-term contracts, struggling with money and housing – but also much more fluid lives. People no longer grow up reading just one newspaper, watching just two or three TV channels. How does the party relate to this? People don't have time to go to party branch meetings – where is the return for doing that? They need to feel they can actually shape politics – whether doing it from home on their laptop, or out on the street.

We have to be strong and focused so as to keep going after Jeremy goes – the transformational agenda he has set out isn't the work of just one parliamentary term.

In practice this meant Labour activists engaging in local struggles of all kinds, joining trade unions and social movement organizations, and making available additional resources, such as videos, which Momentum's central staff could provide. The aim was not to try to make local struggles and initiatives into Labour-led struggles and initiatives, but to make Labour as a party feel, and be seen to be, behind them; and to link together struggles in different domains, from tenants' rights to union rights to immigrants' rights, and set them in the context of a broader socialist vision of society.

In the long run this work would clearly be crucial to the democratization of everyday life that the socialist project calls for, and would also be crucial for maintaining morale and activity between elections. After Corbyn's successful re-election as leader in 2016 there was a distinct loss of excitement and sense of direction among Labour activists which was only reversed the following year by Theresa May's decision to call a general election.

Momentum's value to the party was acknowledged, but whether its independence would survive remained to be seen. It was not hard to imagine that at some point in the future the party leadership's interest in keeping control of policy and priorities would lead it to want to curb the decentralized democratic culture to which Momentum was committed.

WINNING ELECTIONS

For the left to move forward, it needs to show that Labour can win elections on a left programme. If Labour had not dramatically improved its position in the 2017 election, Corbyn's position as leader would have come under renewed threat, not least from the trade unions, which had preferred even the unrewarding Blair and Brown Labour governments to a Conservative one.[19] Instead, the electoral gain in 2017 seemed to portend an election victory under Corbyn's leadership next time.

But under the UK's electoral system winning a parliamentary majority will be extremely difficult. If Labour was able to raise its share of the vote from 40 per cent to even 43 per cent it would not necessarily secure a majority of seats. Thanks to the collapse of the Liberal Democrats' vote after 2015, and the collapse of the UKIP vote after the Brexit referendum in 2016, for the time being the electorate is highly polarised between Labour and the Conservatives. Thus in 2017 Labour under Corbyn won 40 per cent of the vote but secured only 266 seats; whereas back in 2001 Blair's very similar share of the vote (40.7 per cent) had yielded 412 seats, giving him a massive overall majority. That was because 27 per cent of the votes cast in 2001 had gone to the Liberal Democrats, UKIP, and the nationalist parties, without yielding them a corresponding number of seats, thanks to the first-past-the-post voting system. Winning a parliamentary majority is also difficult because Labour voters tend to be concentrated in big cities, piling up large majorities which under a proportional electoral system would yield more seats. On top of this a revision of constituency boundaries – necessitated by a planned reduction of the number of MPs from 650 to 600, and due to come into effect at the next general election – is expected, and was probably intended, to aggravate Labour's problem.[20]

The Labour right argue that all this makes it necessary to revert to a 'centrist' programme capable of appealing to 'swing' voters in marginal constituencies.[21] Momentum's activists believe that these seats can be won if more young working-class voters, who in the past have tended not to vote, can be mobilised to go to the polls,[22] and if older voters can be won back. That in turn depends on whether the policies that had such appeal in 2017 can be developed and made convincing over the years before the next election, and on the mobilizing efforts of Labour activists.

It also depends on whether the leadership proves able to neutralise the cynical drum-beat of denigration by the party's own right wing, amplified by the mainstream media. Within the first few months of 2018 Corbyn was accused, first, of having been a spy for Czechoslovakia, and then of being an ally of Putin (for refusing to fall in line with the government's insistence, without evidence, that Putin had ordered the poisoning of a former Russian spy living in England), and finally of condoning antisemitism. The press and the BBC unanimously gave top coverage to this canard, alleging that the Labour Party was a hotbed of antisemitism and that Corbyn condoned it. The (Conservative-linked, and nominated not elected) Jewish Board of Deputies denounced Corbyn, and were joined in a public demonstration against him outside Parliament by some prominent right-wing Labour MPs.[23] Only some online sources pointed to the lack of evidence for these claims, to the deliberate equation of support for Palestine with antisemitism, and to evidence of Israeli government efforts to encourage, and even finance, elements in the Labour Party to reduce the chances of Corbyn becoming Prime Minister.[24] The timing was clearly aimed at influencing the impending local government elections in May, and was credited with having prevented Labour from gaining control of at least one of the two remaining Conservative-controlled councils in London.[25]

The charge that Corbyn had spied for Czechoslovakia was quickly disproved and some observers thought it had backfired in his favour, but over time the cumulative effect of such constant media smears could prove electorally damaging. Corbyn's transparent honesty was the left's biggest electoral asset. If the right succeeds in making him look less scrupulous, or naïve, or weak, it could seriously affect the left's prospects – already far from assured – of winning the all-important next election.

A final problem is Brexit. In opposition Corbyn was able to avoid taking a very clear position, but Labour was no less divided on the issue than the Conservatives. Any eventual agreement with the EU that permitted continued unlimited immigration of EU workers to the UK would likely cost seats in Labour's old heartlands, which had voted massively 'leave', while the young voters whose support had been so important in 2017, and educated middle-class Labour voters in general, were predominantly 'remainers'. Fashioning a policy on Brexit, above all on immigration, that would not cost votes with both groups of supporters looked extremely difficult. The prospects for socialist advance through the post-EU thicket were, to say the least, hard to envisage.[26]

PROGRAMME AND OBSTACLES

Two days after Labour's 2017 election manifesto, *For the Many, Not the Few,* was leaked to the press, the *Daily Mirror* published an opinion poll which showed that

> Renationalising the railways, the Royal Mail and the energy industry ... each had the support of roughly half the public, with only about a quarter opposed. Seventy-one percent wanted zero hours contracts banned. Sixty-three percent supported the radical idea of requiring any company bidding for public contracts to adopt a maximum pay ratio of 20:1 between their highest and lowest paid staff. Taxing the rich, for so long taboo in British politics, turned out to be a big hit. Sixty-five per cent liked the idea of raising the income tax of those earning over £80,000, including a majority of Tory voters.[27]

Ending tuition fees for students, lifting the austerity-driven pay cap for public sector workers, protecting the state pension from erosion, and closing the gender and racial pay gaps also found wide support. But as Alex Nunns noted, 'the whole was more than the sum of its parts. Taken together it painted a picture of how society could be organised on fundamentally different lines. Its distinctive themes were collectivism and universalism, after years of individualism and means-tested entitlements.'[28]

Whether or not a majority of the electorate would come to see it this way depends on how far the Labour leadership and Labour activists succeed in joining the dots between the different elements in the programme and making them seem no more than plain common sense. And if Labour won, how far the programme would prove feasible would depend on whether the radical break with austerity it represented, and the radical programme of social democratic measures it contained, could be carried through in face of predictably intense resistance – from shareholders and investors, the Conservative Party, the media, the City of London, the Treasury and the civil service, the 'deep state', the US state, and NATO – in the context of a corporate sector highly integrated with global markets.

Yet, given the ferocity of the assault on Labour that began to be mounted in early 2018, once the right had begun to reckon with the consolidation of Corbyn's leadership, it is disconcerting to read the 2017 manifesto and see just how moderately social-democratic it was.[29] Among its leading commitments were:

- to renationalize (de-privatize) water supplies, rail services, and the Royal Mail and gradually renationalize energy supplies;
- to establish a national transformation fund to invest £250bn over ten years in the national infrastructure, and a national investment bank to lend another £250bn over ten years to regenerate and rebalance the economy;
- to restore workers' legal rights and end super-exploitative employment practices such as zero hours contracts and bogus forms of self-employment;
- to end university fees, restore maintenance grants for students, reduce school class sizes, and extend free child care;
- to repeal the legislation which had broken up the national health service and was increasingly privatising clinical services;
- to build 100,000 publicly-owned housing units a year and to control rent increases in the private rental sector;
- to cover the cost of the promised investments and reforms by attacking tax avoidance and raising taxes on corporations and higher paid taxpayers.

COMMON SENSE?

This was clearly a programme that could be made to seem 'plain common sense'. It offered to improve the lives of ordinary people in important ways that people cared about, and included 'landmark' measures whose radical nature was clear and aroused opposition (they were instantly denounced as Stalinist, economically illiterate, incoherent and unaffordable). When implemented, they would symbolise a new order. The tax increases to pay for them were to fall on corporations whose tax avoidance had become notorious, and on the rich who had done well out of both the boom and the crisis. And the long list of measures to restore workers' rights implied a significant shift in the social balance of power, potentially beginning to restore working class confidence shattered by years of unemployment and trade union decline.

There were plenty of omissions and weaknesses, some due to the speed with which it had to be composed in conditions of a snap election. Sympathetic critics pointed to whole areas of policy that needed far more radical measures, while others noted the failure to follow through on Corbyn's longstanding opposition to nuclear power and nuclear weapons.

This was due in large part to the determination of the country's largest trade union, Unite, to keep its members' jobs in the nuclear industry.[30] Also missing was serious attention to the narrowing ecological space for human life on the planet, which within at most two generations is liable to supersede most other concerns. As Jeremy Gilbert has pointed out, the manifesto shows no recognition that 'what is required to avoid ecological catastrophe is a radical reorientation of economic priorities away from the industrial capitalist obsession with economic growth'.[31]

One crucial element in the socialist project that was also largely missing from the manifesto was any significant move towards democratizing the state. There was a promise to establish a Constitutional Convention 'to examine and advise on reforming the way Britain works at a fundamental level', and a commitment to an elected upper house of Parliament and to reducing the voting age to 16, but nothing more concrete. There was no suggestion that there should be a written constitution, to make the electoral system more democratic, or to end the exercise of unaccountable executive power through the 'royal prerogative' and other archaic institutions. There was nothing on ending the corporate capture of the state – the downsizing of the civil service, the rampant influence of unregulated corporate lobbying,[32] the 'revolving door' between the senior civil service and private corporations, or the corporate-style 'executive boards' that had been set up for each government department, largely filled with private sector personnel.[33] There was no proposal to end government reliance on management consultancies whose main clients are corporations, or on the undemocratic nature of the BBC, nominally a politically neutral public service but in practice a key component of the capitalist state system.[34] There was no suggestion of ending subsidies to private schools through which the rich constantly renew their dominant positions in the state and corporate elites.

Still further from the agenda of the 2017 manifesto was any thought about new forms of public ownership which could draw directly on the expertise and insights of ordinary people, on the lines pioneered by the Lucas Aerospace shop stewards in the 1970s and the London County Council in the 1980s, as urged by Hilary Wainwright.[35] Nor were there any proposals for the new forms of accountability at all levels of the state and public services that are needed for a 'public realm' that has been corrupted by spin and disinformation. But some important signs of more radical thinking were provided in a speech by John McDonnell in February 2018 in which he stated that when public infrastructure and services were returned to public control, workers and service users would be put in charge:

We should not try to recreate the nationalised industries of the past. ... we cannot be nostalgic for a model whose management was often too distant, too bureaucratic and too removed from the reality of those at the forefront of delivering services. Taking essential industries away from the whims of the market is an opportunity to move away from profit as the driver of investment and hiring decisions. But just as importantly it's an opportunity for us to put those industries in the hands of those who run and use them.[36]

The capacity of the civil service to manage re-nationalized services was also being reviewed, and the practicalities were being explored of not only establishing a universal basic income but also of making other basic services, in addition to education and health care, universal (i.e. free) too.

How far these ideas would be endorsed within the shadow cabinet, let alone the parliamentary party, remained to be seen, but the will to go beyond the 2017 manifesto was clear. And even liberal commentators recognize that the degraded version of a representative state that currently exists in Britain is responsible for a catalogue of policy failures by successive governments, on a scale that the next Labour government cannot afford.[37]

FEASIBILITY

In considering the overall feasibility of the manifesto programme, there would be four main kinds of obstacle to overcome: the right wing of the parliamentary party; the state; the mainstream media; and capital.

The most obvious and immediate obstacle was the hostility of a majority of Labour MPs. If they stayed in the party and fought the next election on a manifesto like that of 2017 they would have a formal obligation to support it in office, but they would be tempted to sabotage its implementation if they could do so without losing their seats through deselection by their local party members. Given the gap in attitudes between so many MPs and the party's membership, there is a strong case for reintroducing mandatory reselection of all MPs, which had been secured by the new left in 1979 but abandoned after the left's defeat in the 1980s.[38] The notion that MPs are professional representatives with a lifetime right to their seats is clearly incompatible with the concept of a democratised party. Corbyn, however, has ruled out re-adopting reselection, evidently fearing that a direct confrontation with Blairite MPs would consume energies in an intra-party struggle when extra-party tasks had higher priority.[39] Yet without it the leadership have few levers at their disposal, and the active opposition of so many MPs remains the Corbyn project's most acute immediate − and indeed longer-run − weakness.[40]

Resistance from the state would take many forms. A general problem would be the unconscious absorption by most existing public servants of a professional mind-set geared to neoliberal values and processes.[41] Moreover, the 'New Public Management' and austerity have reduced the British civil service by a fifth between 2008 and 2017;[42] and the senior (policy-making and implementing) civil service has been has been hollowed out to the point where it lacks both planning and implementation capacity.[43] To implement the programme of de-privatization and re-regulation envisaged in the 2017 manifesto, new kinds of civil servants and managers would need to be recruited and trained. In short the state would need to be rebuilt as an agency for implementing social democratic policies.

There are things that a well-prepared government could do before these obstacles had to be confronted in office. Not all the manifesto's economic measures would need primary legislation, or even new spending. The railways, for example, would revert automatically to public ownership as the private rail companies' limited-term franchises ended. Ending university fees for students – a high-profile promise, affecting half of the student age group – would also not necessarily cost much more than the state-backed loans currently made to students to cover the fees, since some 45 per cent of the loan total is not expected to be repaid. And one effect of austerity – which was supposed to eliminate the structural deficit and has signally failed to do so, while impoverishing millions of people – was to make ordinary people aware that no official pronouncements on public finances could be trusted. As a result the argument that spending on public infrastructure, regional redevelopment, health and education services is 'unaffordable' can no longer be relied upon to work.

The shift of readers from print to online news and comment, and from major broadcasters and newspapers to social media, could sometimes work to the advantage of the left – the 2017 election has been described as the first 'post-tabloid' election, in which hysterical attacks on Corbyn by the *Daily Mail* and other right-wing papers made no detectable impact. But over time heavily-funded social media may also give an advantage to the right, so that the gross bias shown by the BBC as well as the right-wing press remains a serious long-term handicap that needed to be tackled. At some point the political cost of not confronting it could come to seem greater than the cost of taking it on.

The fourth kind of obstacle – resistance from capital, both from the owners of productive companies and from the purchasers of government bonds – is predictable and impossible to deflect. The real economy is already weak from decades of low investment, running an unsustainable balance of payments deficit (now equal to 6 per cent of GDP), and consequently dependent on the foreign exchange earnings of a global financial services sector ('the City'), which has no interest in the real economy.[44] All these problems are likely to be made worse by Brexit, which is widely predicted to reduce economic growth under even the most optimistic scenario.[45] Whether a Corbyn government would be able to borrow at an affordable rate of interest, and whether corporations would resume investment in the context of a determined social-democratic economic policy, were known unknowns.

A Labour government could thus be faced, as a result of business hostility, with recession, job losses, and an inability to deliver on any policies that entailed significant costs. John McDonnell, the shadow chancellor of the exchequer (minister of finance), stated in autumn 2017 that plans were in hand to deal with this eventuality (understandably he did not indicate what they were).[46] The logical response to a refusal by companies to invest for long-term productivity growth would be to impose capital controls and shift the direction of investment from banks to the state, though this would have such severe consequences for the global role of the City of London that it is hard to envisage.

Once again, a necessary condition of success would be understanding and support from the public, which in 2018 was far from ready for that kind of challenge. In a wide-ranging speech in June 2018 McDonnell outlined a coherent plan for state-led economic transformation which he claimed had support from many people in the financial sector. It included, besides state-funded regional investment banks and a Strategic Investment Board, the possibility of making the Bank of England responsible for helping to boost productivity (and not just controlling inflation), and inducing the country's 'high street' banks to shift their lending from real estate to productive investment – in themselves hardly radical ideas, but nonetheless signalling a decisive shift from neoliberal to social democratic thinking.[47] But in spite of its reasonable tone and feasible-sounding agenda the speech was not extensively reported and most people still had no clear picture of what would be involved in Labour's plans for restoring the state's capacity to manage the economy, or to insulate some aspects and sectors from exposure to market forces and embark on rebuilding the country's capacity to export – a precondition of socialist transformation. A further risk was that the trade unions – and not least Unite, which occupied a strategic position in the party, besides having members in key sectors of the economy – could withdraw their support if implementing a Labour government's policies appeared to threaten their members' jobs in the short term, even if the long term results looked to be beneficial for jobs in general.[48]

PREPARING FOR GOVERNMENT

In thinking about the challenges awaiting the Labour leadership if it does win the next election, it is instructive to look at the experience of Syriza, which was carried into office in Greece on a similar wave of anti-neoliberal sentiment in 2015 – only to succumb, eventually, to the demands of the neoliberal 'troika' (the EU Central Bank, the European Commission and the IMF) and accept an extreme version of austerity.

A leading Syriza activist, Andreas Karitzis, has argued that Syriza's failure was not due just to Greek voters' unwillingness to give up the Euro, but also to failings of Syriza's own.[49] At bottom, he argues, Syriza failed because it sought to create an egalitarian social-democratic order by means of the existing system of representation, and the existing state. Instead, he argues, the left everywhere needs to focus on empowering ordinary people to opt out of the global economy, and create a new kind of networked local economy relying on the know-how and practical experience they already possess: otherwise they cannot avoid being trapped in the constraints and norms of global economic forces.

This line of thinking is echoed by some leading activists on the Labour left, such as Hilary Wainwright. But Karitzis also draws lessons of a more proximate kind. Whatever vision of socialist advance a left-wing party may have, he argues, Syriza's experience shows that it needs to have a collective strategy for government, and not leave it to individual prospective ministers to work out plans for particular sectors in isolation. It needs to use the official resources made available to it as the leading opposition party – amounting in the UK case to £6.4 m. in 2016[50] – to support this collective work, rather than give it to individual shadow ministers. Ministries should also be assigned to people with relevant skills or knowledge, and who have connections to the social forces whose support will be needed to get things done. The party needs to think through the problems involved in implementing policies, with timelines for legislative and executive action and clear ideas about which organs of the state or other bodies have the capacity to do what is needed: for this, task forces with the needed mix of expertise and policy skills need to be set up. And there needs to be an agreed policy for channelling state resources to social movements to enable them to strengthen their capacity to both support new state policies and undertake innovatory work of their own. And so on.

In 2018 the Labour Party was far from being able to meet these requirements or develop such ideas. Preparing Labour for government was the remit of Jon Trickett MP, shadow minister for the cabinet office. In early 2018, he did call on every member of the shadow cabinet to produce their five priorities for government, with a view to focusing minds on detail and implementation. There was also a strategy group, consisting of Corbyn, MacDonnell, Trickett, and Diane Abbott, the shadow Home Secretary, plus Seamus Milne, the party's director of strategic communications, and Andrew Murray, the chief of staff of the largest trade union, Unite, who had been seconded to assist in the leader's office during the 2017 election campaign. But it did not seem to meet regularly and had no secretariat. These arrangements perhaps represented the limits of the possible, though it was hard to avoid the impression that more could have been done if the leadership had seen it as a priority.

WAR OF POSITION – HEGEMONY

The point has already been made that to get to socialism via social democracy calls for a major hegemonic shift, but it is not clear that Labour's new leaders have yet addressed the problem of securing it. It is said that when Margaret Thatcher's close lieutenant, Sir Keith Joseph, first took office as Secretary of State for Industry in 1979, he gave his senior civil servants a list of key neoliberal texts, such as Hayek's *Road to Serfdom,* and told them to read them so they would understand the radical shift in policy they were going to be expected to implement after 35 years of social democracy. It is not obvious what would be on an equivalent reading list that Corbyn's team might give senior civil servants following an election victory. There are no equivalent founding texts of Corbynism, and there has been no recent equivalent of the long evolution of socialist thinking and planning that preceded the election of a Labour government in 1945 (or of the 30-plus years of work by the neoliberal think tanks and conferences built up by the followers of Hayek and Friedman that preceded Thatcher's election in 1979).[51] There is not yet a widely shared coherent 'story' that defines what is wrong and who and what is responsible for it, which makes sense of people's current experience and their remembered (i.e. recent) past, and which implies a set of 'obvious' reforms.[52]

This means that the most urgent hegemonic task, necessary to make a socialist agenda seem common sense, will initially have to emerge from practice. A Labour government's first measures would have to exemplify the common sense by being popular and practicable *and* attracting ideological opposition – so that their successful implementation would signal a decisive ideological shift, which the leadership would have to reiterate and develop in every speech. The socialist intelligentsia would have to flesh it out and argue for it in the widest possible range of settings. Party members would have to articulate it in their daily interactions and their work with local organisations, and trade unions would have to articulate it in the way they framed their demands and in the way they supported other causes. In early 2018, however, little of this was happening. The mismatch between the scale of the task and the number of people so far mobilised to tackle it was undeniably big. The most obvious and urgent need was for the leadership to find time to enlist the active support of the much larger network of people with expertise and talent that was potentially available to join in the task.

CONCLUSION: IS THERE A WAY FORWARD FOR THE LEFT?

The failure of most Labour MPs to notice that disillusionment with neoliberalism had shifted public opinion radically to the left allowed a small group of socialist MPs to take control of the party through the very mechanism – letting the members choose the leader – that was meant to ensure that this could never happen. The left now controlled not just the party's policy but also its financial resources, swollen by the addition of more than 350,000 new dues-paying members. It would take longer to secure full control of the party's professional machine, but that process had begun too. Corbyn had a mandate from two-thirds of the party's members, and the party led by him had received a vote of confidence from 40 per cent of the electorate.

But the obstacles in the way of success were so great, and the team around Corbyn was so small, that it was hard to be confident that they could win an election, form a convincing government, and set in motion significant steps towards socialism. In addition to the opposition of global capital and the steadily rising costs of adapting the country's infrastructure to global warming, changed economic conditions resulting from Brexit could derail the most carefully planned advance towards social democracy, let alone towards socialism.

Yet the circumstances were so volatile that it was not possible even to be pessimistic with any degree of confidence. The quality and commitment of many of those most actively involved in the Corbyn project was impressive. The Conservatives might prove unable to change course and respond convincingly to the public's disenchantment with neoliberalism, and Labour MPs might finally stop wishing they could elect another people (as Brecht famously put it) and start trying to relate to the one that actually existed.[53] The party might manage to resolve its policy dilemmas, mobilize a wider cadre of socialists (or at least social democrats), win an election, and take some decisive first steps into the post-neoliberal era. Or 2017 could prove to have been the project's high point: not the beginning of a transition to socialism but rather an early moment – if a historic one – in what is, after all, likely to be a much more protracted transition than most of Corbyn's supporters ardently hope for.

NOTES

1   Technically the referendum was purely advisory, but after a majority had voted 'leave' no party dared suggest it was not binding. An outstanding analytical overview is Anthony Barnett, *The Lure of Greatness: England's Brexit and America's Trump – Why 2016 Blew Away the World Order*, London: Unbound, 2017; although Barnett's conclusion as to what should follow politically is unconvincing. For a succinct account of the insoluble constitutional dilemmas which leaving the EU presents for the UK, see: Sionaidh Douglas-Scott, 'Brexit vs. the Constitution', *London Review of Books* 24 May 2018, pp. 40-41.

2   In place of the original Clause IV in the party's constitution calling for public ownership of the means of production and exchange, Blair's Clause IV called for 'a dynamic economy, serving the public interest, in which the enterprise of the market and the rigour of competition are joined with the forces of partnership and co-operation to produce the wealth the nation needs.'

3   The left-wing anti-imperialist party 'Respect', founded in 2004, secured a handful of local council seats, and one of its founders, George Galloway, successively won parliamentary seats in two different constituencies in 2005 and 2012 respectively. But by 2016 its remaining leadership had joined Corbyn's Labour Party, and Respect had folded. Left Unity, founded by the filmmaker Ken Loach in 2013 with the aim of uniting 'all those who seek to authentically voice and represent the interests of ordinary working people', lost most of its small membership to Labour following Corbyn's election as Labour leader in 2015. On Left Unity and all attempts to form left-wing parties in opposition to Labour, see: Andrew Murray, 'Left Unity or Class Unity? Working Class Politics in Britain', in Leo Panitch, Greg Albo and Vivek Chibber, eds, *Socialist Register 2014: Registering Class,* London: Merlin Press, 2013, pp. 266-304.

4   The aim was to reduce the influence of both the trade unions and Labour activists, generally seen as being on the left, by diluting it with the votes of the membership at large, who were considered loyal centrists, and supporters, seen as even more so. When large numbers of new members joined (or in many cases re-joined) the party to support Corbyn, the National Executive adopted a new rule excluding from voting anyone who had not been a member for at least six months at the time of the vote. When this was challenged the NEC spent a large sum defending its action in the courts, and eventually succeeded. Support for Corbyn in the second leadership election would obviously have been still higher but for the disenfranchisement of these members. Supporters, however, who were not covered by the new exclusion rule, also voted for Corbyn by a significant majority.

5   This account of Corbyn's two leadership elections, and subsequent success in the 2017 general election, is drawn from Alex Nunns, *The Candidate: Jeremy Corbyn's Improbable Path to Power*, London: OR Books, 2018, a brilliantly written and well researched

account. See also Richard Seymour's shrewd assessment in *Corbyn: The Strange Rebirth of Radical Politics*, Second Edition, London: Verso, 2017.

6   246,000 of the votes cast were cast by party members, of whom 49.6 per cent voted for Corbyn. The balance of the votes cast were by paid-up 'supporters', a large majority of whom also voted for him.

6   The no confidence vote followed a failed 'coup' in which a large number of Corbyn's shadow cabinet resigned en masse, wrongly assuming that he would feel unable to continue. What lay behind both moves was the fact that under the fixed-term-elections law passed by the coalition government in 2011, the next election was not due till 2020. Labour MPs opposed to Corbyn therefore reckoned they had four years in which to get rid of him. But after David Cameron lost the 2016 referendum on whether to remain in the EU, he resigned. It was then immediately assumed that his successor, Theresa May, would call a much earlier election to consolidate her position, and that with Corbyn as leader Labour would lose badly, putting many Labour MPs out of a job. Getting rid of him suddenly became urgent.

7   The leak was traced to the office of the leader of the Labour Party in Scotland, Kezia Dugdale, an opponent of Corbyn, and was judged to be a deliberate and notably extreme attempt to injure him (Nunns, *The Candidate*, p. 312). Dugdale resigned as Scottish leader in August 2017. Her successor, Richard Leonard, elected in November, supported Corbyn.

8   For the case against the parliamentary road to socialism after the defeat of the new left in the party in the 1980s, see: Leo Panitch and Colin Leys, *The End of Parliamentary Socialism*, London: Verso, 1997 (second edition, with David Coates, 2001).

9   Michael Calderbank and Paul O'Connell, 'Confronting Brexit', *Red Pepper*, 20 March 2017, available at: https://www.redpepper.org.uk/confronting-brexit.

10   *Membership of UK Political Parties*, House of Commons Library briefing paper Number SN05125, 1 May 2018, available at: researchbriefings.files.parliament.uk/documents/SN05125/SN05125.pdf

11   Nunns, *The Candidate*, pp. 62-63, 71.

12   See: Ralph Miliband, *Parliamentary Socialism: A Study of the Politics of Labour*, London: Allen and Unwin, 1961; and Panitch and Leys, *The End of Parliamentary Socialism*.

13   As Chancellor of the Exchequer in 2002, Gordon Brown introduced a new form of income support for all families with children of school age, including those with annual incomes up to £58,000, and for families with breadwinners on low pay. The support took the form of a reduction in tax liability. One of the first austerity measures taken by the Coalition government in 2010 was to start cutting these tax credits.

14   Hilary Wainwright, *A New Politics From the Left*, Cambridge: Polity Press, 2018, pp. 34-5.

15   Nunns, *The Candidate*, p.128.

16   A key move was to ensure that the contact details of party members that were made available to Corbyn for his leadership campaign remained in his hands after it, and could be used by Momentum as an organisation 'inspired' by him.

17   Electoral Reform Services, Final Report of Voting, 17 November 2016, available at: http://www.progressonline.org.uk/content/uploads/2012/08/Final-Report-of-Voting-171116.pdf. For a list of inner party groups or factions in 2015, see Anoush Chakelian, 'Labour's Warring Factions: Who Do They Include and What Are They Fighting Over?', *New Statesman* 23 October 2015, available at: https://www.

newstatesman.com. The other significant right-wing party group in 2018 was Labour First, a pre-Blair group, mainly of MPs, dedicated especially to the Atlantic alliance and NATO; see https://labourfirst.wordpress.com/about/2018: 'Labour First is a network which exists to ensure that the voices of moderate party members are heard while the party is kept safe from the organised hard left'.

18   Lewis Minkin, *The Blair Supremacy: A Study in the Politics of Labour Party Management*, Manchester, UK: Manchester University Press, 2014, chapter 12.

19   Union support for Corbyn was mixed. Len McCluskey, the leader of the largest union, Unite, originally backed the former shadow health secretary Andy Burnham for the leadership, but came out strongly for Corbyn after Burnham threw away his chances. The strongest support came from a group of smaller unions known as the Awkward Squad, with which John McDonnell had longstanding ties: the Public and Commercial Services Union (chiefly professional civil servants), the Fire Brigade Union and the Bakers' Union. Their general secretaries meet regularly with a further seven mainly smaller unions in a Trade Union Coordinating Group. A different group called TULO/Trade Unions Together coordinates the twelve unions that are affiliated to the Labour Party. Differences between unions and the Labour leadership include Unite's commitment to Trident, the country's submarine nuclear weapons system, which Corbyn has always opposed but has accepted as Labour policy as a necessary condition of Unite's support.

20   See Boundary Commission for England, '2018 Review,' https://boundarycommissionforengland.independent.gov.uk/2018-review.

21   See e.g. Luke Akehurst, the main spokesperson for Labour First: 'We have nothing to lose – this is how we can beat Momentum', *Labour List,* 28 November 2017, available at: https://labourlist.org.

22   See Liam Young, *Rise: How Jeremy Corbyn Inspired the Young to Create a New Socialism*, London: Simon and Schuster, 2018, especially pp. 57-64.

23   Ashley Cowburn and Benjamin Kentish, 'Hundreds of People Protest Outside Parliament Against Antisemitism in the Labour Party', *Independent*, 26 March 2018. For a review of the issue by the BBC, see: 'Jeremy Corbyn and Labour's Anti-Semitism Row Explained', 27 April 2018, available at: http://www.bbc.co.uk.

24   On the distinction between anti-Zionism and antisemitism, see the former Appeal Court judge Stephen Sedley, 'Defining Anti-Semitism', *London Review of Books* 39(9), 4 May 2017; on Israeli state involvement recorded by Al-Jazeera, see: Alex MacDonald and Stephen Sedley, 'Israeli Diplomat Worked Inside Labour to Discredit 'Crazy' Corbyn', *Middle East Eye*, 8 January 2017 (and on Middle East Eye's affiliations see https://en.wikipedia.org/wiki/Middle_East_Eye).

25   This was Barnet in north London, which has a large community of Jews. But in general the results of the May 2018 council elections were not encouraging for Labour: Labour gained 65 council seats (half of them in London) but lost 40. The Conservatives gained 62 and lost 54, and the Liberal Democrats marginally increased their position at the local level, gaining 39 seats and losing 30, although half of the gains were in just four councils – i.e. the gains did not signal a nation-wide Lib-Dem revival.

26   A strong left-wing case for leaving the EU is that its rules would make much of Labour's 2017 Manifesto programme impossible: see Costas Lapavitsas, 'Jeremy Corbyn's Labour vs. the Single Market', *Jacobin*, 30 May 2018. Corbyn's personal position was to support

remaining in the EU and reforming it, as advocated by Yanis Varoufakis, Syriza's former minister of finance and leader of DiEM25 ((Democracy in Europe Movement 2025).

27   Nunns, *The Candidate*, p. 313.

28   Nunns, *The Candidate*, p. 314. Given how far the Manifesto was from the thinking of most Labour MPs, it is interesting that it was adopted with so little opposition. Part of the reason was that the election was called at short notice, so there was no time for debate. Part was MPs thinking that, as the party was bound to lose under Corbyn, his programme might as well be discredited too. Part was due to the final meeting to approve the document being held the day after it had been leaked and proved popular. But more was perhaps due to the fact that it drew on documents already prepared for the party's National Policy Forum in 2016, after Corbyn's re-election as leader, and had been discussed in prior consultations with shadow ministers; see: Mike Phipps, ed., *For the Many: Preparing Labour for Power*, London: OR Books, 2017, pp.11-13; and Nunns, *The Candidate*, pp. 311-14.

29   The Labour Manifesto, *For the Many, Not the Few*, is available at: https://labour.org.uk/manifesto.

30   For proposals to strengthen the manifesto see Phipps, *For the Many*.

31   Jeremy Gilbert, 'Leading Richer Lives', in Phipps, ed., *For the Many*, p. 175.

32   Tamasin Cave and Andy Rowell, *A Quiet Word: Lobbying, Crony Capitalism and Broken Politics in Britain*, London: The Bodley Head, 2014.

33   Aeron Davis, *Reckless Opportunists: Elites at the End of the Establishment*, Manchester, UK: Manchester University Press, 2018, p. 126.

34   On the BBC, see Tom Mills, *The BBC: Myth of a Public Service*, London: Verso, 2016; and 'Democracy and Public Broadcasting', in Leo Panitch and Greg Albo, eds, *Socialist Register 2018: Rethinking Democracy*, London: Merlin Press, 2017, pp. 150-171.

35   Wainwright, *A New Politics from the Left*.

36   John McDonnell, plenary speech at the 'Alternative Models of Ownership' conference, De Vere Grand Connaught Rooms, 61-65 Great Queen Street, London, 10 February 2018, available at: https://www.john-mcdonnell.net/john_s_speech. The way this important speech was reported in the mainstream media illustrates the extreme difficulty faced by the Labour leadership in getting heard. The only 'broadsheet' to give it reasonable coverage was the online-only *Independent*. The BBC's news coverage was limited and negative; see: 'John McDonnell: Labour Public Ownership Plan Will Cost Nothing', 10 February 2018.

37   Anthony King and Ivor Crewe, *The Blunders of Our Governments*, London: Oneworld, 2014.

38   See Panitch and Leys, *The End of Parliamentary Socialism*, pp. 139-45. In the 1970s the aim of mandatory reselection had been to make MPs more accountable to left-wing local party members and more likely to resist pressure to toe the leadership's right-wing line. Now the need was the opposite – to make right-wing MPs more likely support a left-wing leadership. A tempting opportunity briefly suggested itself in April 2018 when it was reported that a group of 'centrist' MPs were planning to create a new party with £50m from a rich donor (Michael Savage, 'New Centrist Party Gets 50m Backing To 'Break Mould' of UK Politics', *The Guardian* 8 April 2018). Any Labour MP joining it would automatically be deselected, and the political eclipse of the 28 Labour MPs and their leaders who defected to form the Social Democratic Party in 1981 seemed likely to deter most of them from joining in another such initiative.

39 Jon Lansman, as chair of Momentum's national coordinating group, declared that Momentum would not seek to deselect any MPs, but would not discourage local party members from trying to deselect their MP under existing party rules (see Ashley Cowburn, 'Momentum Chair: 'Enthusiasm For an Alternative Government Will Grow Stronger, Not Weaker', *Independent*, 23 January 2018.)

40 Steps to ensure that at least right-wing MPs will not be able to prevent a left-wing candidate being elected to succeed Corbyn were foreshadowed in proposals contained in a review of the party's internal democracy by Katy Clark, a former senior staffer in Corbyn's office, details of which were leaked to the press in June 2018 (see Jessica Elgot and Heather Stewart, 'Labour Proposals "all-but guarantee leftwing Corbyn successor"', *The Guardian*, 26 June 2018). The proportion of Labour MPs needed to nominate a candidate would fall from 10 to 5 per cent. Another proposal was to have the leaders of Labour-controlled local councils elected by party members. Under the Blair governments local councils were reorganized on business lines with large powers vested in the leader, creating strong local fiefdoms which are often in right-wing hands.

41 On this general point see Yanis Varoufakis' insightful analysis in his account of the Syriza government's negotiations with the Troika, *Adults in the Room: My Battle With Europe's Deep Establishment*, London: Vintage, 2017, chapter 1.

42 Office for National Statistics, Statistical Bulletin: 'Civil Service Statistics, UK: 2018', available at: https://www.ons.gov.uk/employmentandlabourmarket/peopleinwork/publicsectorpersonnel/bulletins/civilservicestatistics/2017.

43 In 2017 the National Audit Office recognised that the civil service can no longer do all that is needed for the effective planning and administration of current policies (see National Audit Office, 'Capability in the Civil Service', Report by the Comptroller and Auditor General, 24 March 2017, available at: https://www.nao.org.uk/wp-content/uploads/2017/03/Capability-in-the-civil-service.pdf). The Auditor General told MPs that 'in many parts of government the capability of even acting as a prime contractor is not necessarily there. That is not a fault, it is decision that a number of departments have made over time' (Richard Johnstone, 'NAO Chief on How Civil Servants Should Write Submissions on Outsourcing After Carillion', *Civil Service World*, 25 April 2018). A short NAO blog is at https://www.nao.org.uk/naoblog/stretching-civil-servants-capability.

44 Although the foreign exchange earnings of the City of London's global financial and investment banking services are a crucial offset against the UK's huge trade deficit on goods, its activities have very little to do with financing UK's non-financial sector, and fund managers who do invest in the shares of UK-based firms are focussed exclusively on their share price and rarely have any interest in their long-term productivity plans. 'The best way to think about the City … is essentially [as] an off-shore phenomenon, half-way between a Caicos Island and an oil rig' (Martin Taylor, the former chief executive of Barclays bank, cited in Tony Golding, *The City: Inside The Great Expectation Machine*, second edition, London: Prentice Hall, 2003, p. 5).

45 This judgment is disputed by advocates of leaving the EU, including the government ministers responsible for negotiating it, but it is hard to find any convincing estimates that support their view. For others, see a government analysis leaked in February 2018 by Paul Dallison, 'UK Analysis Shows Big Economic Hit From Brexit', *Politico*, 7 February 2018; and a roundup of analyses: Shafi.Musaddique, 'Cost of Brexit: The

impact on Business and the Economy in 2017 and Beyond', *Independent*, 26 December 2017.

46   'Labour Plans For Capital Flight or Run On Pound If Elected', *Financial Times* 26 September 2017.

47   The social-democratic nature of the proposals was underlined by McDonnell's pitch to the business audience he was addressing: 'when we go into government, we want you to come with us, alongside representatives from our manufacturers, our trade unions and wider civil society. There will be a seat at the policy making and policy delivering table for you.' His proposals were, he claimed, supported by many people in the financial sector, and were not inconsistent with the thinking of the Bank of England's Governor, Mark Carney (see 'A "new start" for Labour and the finance sector – McDonnell's full speech in the City', *LabourList,* 19 April 2018).

48   Both Corbyn's chief of staff and the party's General Secretary came from Unite and were close to Unite's General Secretary, Len McCluskey.

49   Andreas Karitzis, *The European Left in Times of Crises: Lessons From Greece*, Amsterdam: Transnational Institute, 2017.

50   'Short Money', House of Commons Library briefing paper, 19 December 2016, http:// researchbriefings.parliament.uk/ResearchBriefing/Summary/SN01663.

51   The Mont Pelerin Society was founded in 1947. On the history of the neoliberal hegemonic campaign in the UK see Richard Crockett, *Thinking the Unthinkable*, Fontana Press, 1995. Thatcher inherited a cadre of capable young MPs, and some civil servants, with a shared neoliberal formation.

52   For a recent relevant discussion of the need to displace a dominant narrative with another one, see George Monbiot, *Out of the Wreckage: A New Politics For An Age of Crisis*, London: Verso, 2017, chapter 1.

53   'After the uprising of the 17th June/ the Secretary of the Writers Union/ had leaflets distributed in the Stalinallee/ stating that the people/ had forfeited the confidence of the government/ and could win it back only/ by redoubled efforts./ Would it not be easier/ in that case for the government/ to dissolve the people/ and elect another?' (Bertolt Brecht, 'The Solution').